S0-BBU-923

PIEGAN

RICHARD LANCASTER

PIEGAN

A LOOK FROM WITHIN AT THE LIFE, TIMES,
AND LEGACY OF AN AMERICAN INDIAN TRIBE

Illustrated by Nancy McLaughlin

CARL A. RUDISILL LIBRARY
LENOIR RHYNE COLLEGE

DOUBLEDAY & COMPANY, INC.   GARDEN CITY, NEW YORK

"Why the White Man Will Never Reach the Sun" by Richard Lancaster, from *And Horns on the Toads* edited by Mody Boatright. Copyright © 1959, Texas Folklore Society, Austin. Reprinted by permission of the Texas Folklore Society and the publisher, Southern Methodist University Press.

970.3
L22 p
60660
Jb. 1968

LIBRARY OF CONGRESS CATALOG CARD NUMBER 66–17071
COPYRIGHT © 1966 BY RICHARD LANCASTER
ALL RIGHTS RESERVED
PRINTED IN THE UNITED STATES OF AMERICA

Author's Note

With *Piegan* scheduled to burst like a poppy pod upon the field of American letters, urgent communications inform me that I must hasten to trumpet its advance with some sort of preface or author's note. Personally, I regard such an introduction as quite unnecessary —comparatively few professors of English would in its absence attempt to establish *Piegan* as a lost Shakespearean drama—but with our electricity here on the ranch knocked out by the wind last night, the events in *Piegan* have run pretty much full-circle, and possibly this is a good time, after all, to set down just exactly how it all came about.

Piegan is actually the title given to a journal which I kept in 1962 during a visit with my adoptive Indian father, Chief of the Piegan Blackfoots of Montana. (The Chief, who can on occasion be surprisingly academic, has insisted from the very first that I refer to his people as the Black*foots,* not the Black*feet,* in order to distinguish them from small bands of other Indian nations which called themselves Blackfeet; namely, the Blackfeet Sioux, the Blackfeet Crow, and the Blackfeet Shoshoni.) My reason for keeping this journal was simply that during my previous and first lengthy visit with the Chief and my Indian brother, Jim, in 1958, I had *not* kept a journal; time passed, and the days and the details of this first visit gradually lost their separateness and blended into memories at once indistinct and sufficiently compelling to induce me, four years later, to chuck graduate school and to return to the Blackfoots with an eye and an ear toward keeping an intimate day-to-day record of my experiences.

I did keep such a record, but even in the keeping I felt that something more was being achieved than the compilation of cold experience and data. Day by day, the journal was filled with surprises, even for myself. There was humor here—when an Indian chief more than one hundred years old attempts to say coffee and enunciates instead a clear and unmistakable "cowpee," who but the most dyspeptic Mephisto could suppress a smile! There was tragedy, too. But most of all there was truth. The lives of these people were touching my own life, and not the least of the discoveries I was making were discoveries which bore upon my own culture, and upon my personal self.

My original journal was very detailed and very long, but not all portions of this volume appeared therein. Some of the Chief's stories were on tape and had to be transcribed in their entirety and inserted in a manner duplicating the time and the place of their original telling. Also, my subsequent visits with the Chief—and I have been spending more and more time among the Piegans—have produced additional information which has been added in the form of footnotes. Otherwise, nothing has been changed—and absolutely nothing has been contrived: these are the words and the actions; these are the feelings and the thoughts; these are the people.

Most important, of course, are the people, and foremost among the people is the Chief. At this writing, the Old Fellow is well—and as dynamic as ever. His birthday was on May 10, but I gave him his birthday party on Sunday, May 8, in conjunction with a meeting of the Crazy Dog Society. (I have been elected a member of the Crazy Dogs.) No record of the precise date of the Chief's birth has been found, but since everything else he has ever told me has eventually checked out 100%, I accede to the Chief's belief that he was born on May 10, 1857, and consequently has just celebrated his 109th anniversary—assuredly he is well past the century mark.

Some time ago, the Chief told me that both his birth and his baptism had been recorded by a Roman Catholic priest whom he knew only by his Indian name, "Marten Cap," and it was in pursuit of my belief that "Marten Cap" was in reality a Jesuit missionary named Fr. Imoda that I came closest to establishing (verifying) the Chief's true age. In the records of old St. Peter's Mission, dated Dec. 31, 1875, entered in the hand of Fr. Imoda himself, I came upon the following: *"Ego C. Imoda S.J. prope flumen Natokiokas bapt. seq.* [I, C. Imoda, of the Society of Jesus, near Two Medicine River, baptised the following]." Listed then, in both English and Latin, were the baptismal names of seven of the children of Onistáipokah, the Chief's father. The Chief's Christian name ("James *Jacobum*") was among those listed, but since the Chief was by this time a well grown youth, and since Fr. Imoda was able to give only an approximation of his age at the time of baptism, the mystery lingers.

This journal, *Piegan,* was written less than four years ago, but those four years have seen many changes, both great and small, here on the Reservation. In Browning, in "Moccasin Flat," there is scarcely a dwelling that does not now have inside water, electricity and a television set (but precious few of them have an inside toilet).

6

Here on the ranch, in addition to the fact that the Chief has developed a passion for Juicy Fruit gum and chews five sticks at a time, I would list as our major changes: the refrigerator which has replaced the pantry, and the electric percolator which has put the old granite coffee pot out of business excepting on days such as today when the power lines are down. (Brother Jim being brother Jim, we do not have an ordinary percolator but a huge thing that makes 35 cups at a throw and stands so high on the cupboard that you can't get the doors open.) Brother Jim, like the Montana weather, is one of those things that will never change because they are completely unpredictable to begin with. It is June, but since last night a mountain blizzard has been whistling snow against the west side of the house, and as Jim came in this morning with an armload of fuel for the woodstove (which is still our source of heat around here) he said, "Goddam, I had enough of this goddam windy!"

Both Jim and the Chief have gone into town to prepare for the Crazy Dog dance which will begin at Mrs. Big Spring's house at about 1:00. I will take my Crazy Dog rattle and drive in to join them, and I know that at the dance I will be impressed by the one change among the Blackfoots that really touches me. So many of the old people are gone now: Chewing Black Bones, Dan Bull Plume, Juniper Old Person, Jim White Grass, Cecile Last Star, Fish Wolf-robe—so very many others. I miss them, and it is to their memory, as well as to the Chief, that this book is dedicated.

RICHARD LANCASTER

White Calf Ranch
Blackfoot Indian Reservation,
Montana
June 4, 1966

History and Lore of the Blackfoot Nation

Told by Running Wolf, Chief White Calf of the Piegan Blackfeet

9

No house is quite so empty as a house recently lived in.

When finally I arrived at the ranch—feeling very much the voyageur, and quite strenuously put-upon by motels, gas stations, and all manner of tourist trap—it was just before dusk, and nobody was there. The whole place was locked up tight, all the stock had been turned out onto the range, there was no fresh manure in the horse corral, and although I could see by way of the uncurtained windows that the house was full of furniture and stuff, I hadn't the foggiest whether Jim and the Chief still lived there. As a fact, I didn't even know for certain that the Chief had not taken that last lonely journey to the Sand Hills. It has been four years since I was up here in Montana (has it been *that* long?), and brother Jim and I have not exchanged letters in more than a year. The Chief would be 105 years old, now.

After an unsuccessful go at all doors and windows, I drove rather disheartedly back to the road and thence westward to seek information at the nearest dwelling place—two small houses, actually, a couple of miles away, on the very edge of the creek which casually parallels the unpaved roadway. I was very tired, and as I pulled into a debris-littered yard in which numerous yapping dogs and children were engaged in after-supper play, the dull brilliance of twilight loaned an aspect of fantasy to the scene.

The eldest of the children, a boy of perhaps twelve—very tall, very thin, and obviously very retarded—was marching about in delighted obedience to the commands of the other youngsters, a tiny popgun over one frail shoulder. His oddly shaped (pointed, really) head was close-cropped, and a black patch—apparently a birthmark —covered one side of his forehead, and he smiled perpetually the depressing but somehow covetable contentment of those who will never know. Ordinarily, I should have passed such an encounter without undue personal involvement, but fatigue, uncertainty with regard to the whereabouts of Jim and the Chief, and the distressing emotional iotacism which at times plagues even the best of us, conspired to evoke within my personal self an almost articulate resentment that my unannounced return to the Reservation had not been rewarded with a panorama somewhat more inspiring.

By the time I had turned off the ignition and gotten out of the station wagon, I found myself being converged upon by two Indian men, each from his separate abode—and neither, I soon learned, destined to elevate my currently subterranean morale. One man was quite young and effusively, almost obsequiously, eager to please, and from him I learned that the Chief is very much alive indeed and that he and Jim are over in Canada, at Gleichen, attending a Blackfoot Sun Dance (Medicine Lodge). Damn, but I wish I were with them! The Sun Dance is the very focus of Blackfoot religious ritual, and it is becoming an increasingly rare episode in Indian life. Only the very old Indians know how properly to sponsor and conduct the ceremony, and since the Holy Woman (an Indian lady, always above any moral reproach, who makes the formal vow to the Sun) and all the other principals must undergo a fast of four days, those persons who are both qualified and physically able to participate in the Sun Dance are very few indeed.

There has not been a Blackfoot Sun Dance here in the States for several years, and I doubt seriously that there will ever again be one. The so-called Sun Dances held by Plains Tribes other than the Blackfoots are ersatz gestures at best and are significantly performed during the height of the tourist season. These ceremonies are in the same category as the "adoption" ceremonies—innumerable Whites believe that they have been "adopted" by one Indian tribe or another—which are not adoption ceremonies at all but merely name-giving ceremonies (one of which, thanks to the publicity-conscious Great Northern Railway, can be purchased from even the Blackfoots for fifty bucks). A true Blackfoot adoption ceremony involves a ritual of four days duration, and it is a very serious and a rather strenuous procedure for all parties involved. One does not properly become adopted into the Blackfoot *tribe;* one becomes an adopted member of a Blackfoot *family,* with all the privileges and responsibilities attaining to true family membership. Very, very few persons of White blood have ever been awarded this honor.

The Blackfoots were the last of the Western tribes to have intercourse with the White Man, and they never had any more to do with him than they had to, and so the Blackfoots are the last American Indians to retain anything resembling their pre-White culture. But I saw very little today which could have served to sustain this reality. Neither of the men with whom I was conversing was by any means a vision of the Noble Amerind: the younger man, who was generally reminiscent of pool halls, exuded all the masculinity of a used Kleenex, while the older chap was small and skinny and had on a corduroy cap with the ear-loppers tied at the top and was wearing what appeared to be the Buster Brown-type of shoes that I wore in grade school. What might have been Buster's saving grace was a ready smile, but unfortunately his was ready for a dentosurgeon because those few teeth that had not already waved bye-bye sported a lush overgrowth of moss and lichen along the gums, from which they depended precariously. To an eye less wearied than mine, his verdant incisors might have appeared as a selfless contribution to the "Keep Montana Green" campaign, but I saw them only as one more affront to my already moribund sensibilities. These people were not the Blackfoots as I remembered them, and as darkness came I drove back to Browning—a distance of about twenty miles—in brave expectation of more reassuring social encounters.

Browning is the agency town of the Blackfoot Indian Reservation, and it would be difficult to imagine a hamlet more isolated from the conventional grind of civilization. Browning tickles the toes of the Rocky Mountains; it is thirty-five miles from the nearest village of consequence and about one hundred and thirty miles from anything that might be considered a city of any size. But as I drove into the town this evening I saw that the insidious same-making of the neon sign had robbed even poor little Browning of those few villatic charms which the place had possessed. (Damn neon signs anyway! I think that the southern approach to Austin, Texas would be one of the most inspiring sights in the world—the ladder of lights on Congress Avenue paving a dignified and beautiful approach to the magnificent pink granite Capitol Building—if it were not for the huge neon hotel signs that overreach the capitol itself and greet the traveler or the home-comer with a nice fat commercial smack between the eyes.)

But you can't hold back "progress," and nothing less than a neon sign informed me that Browning has a shiny new gin-mill right in the middle of town. But even gin-mills have their function (where else can a stranger find somebody to talk to!), and after five days of steady driving, plus three days of being trapped in a Bozeman motel while the old Ford underwent surgery, I was not above seeking companionship in an opium den. The trouble is, in a gin-mill you don't exactly meet the intellectually elite—and I certainly didn't.

I ordered a beer—the first in weeks—and immediately a hugely tall Indian skidded alcoholically onto the next stool and asked me to buy him one. He was about six-six, had on dirty denims and a black-and white-striped straw hat, and was drunk as the proverbial skunk (other similarities to that same fragrant quadruped were equally apparent, and more literal). He had deep-set, protruding eyes—if such a thing be possible, and with this cat anything was—and until seeing him I had always regarded Faulkner's description of the eyes of "Popeye" in *Sanctuary* (". . . two knobs of soft black rubber") in the light of pure symbolism. This Indian version of Popeye had eyes exactly like small black rubber balls.

The bartender—a modern businessman-type Indian, stocky, large-headed and efficient—drew Popeye his brew from a special tap (ten-cent beer). And for the next half hour or so, as I dismally watched my fellow patrons—the joint was jumping, even at this early hour—drinking and arguing and playing the juke box and dancing and occasionally (including the women) shoving one an-other around, Popeye proceeded to agitate the hell out of me by pulling me around by the shoulder and asking, time after I-had-already-told-him time, where I was from. Few things are more an-noying than to have a drunk paw at you, especially when you are tired, and Popeye (who slathered that his name was something-or-other "Gun") failed to endear himself to me even further by claiming to be related to the Chief. (I sure as hell hope not!) He also claimed to be a great boxer, but, in view of the facts that his upper front teeth are home on the shelf and his nose has been fisted flat and off-center, I don't think he is too sharp on the defensive side.

I had purposely sequestered myself at the end of the bar nearest the escape hatch, but it was inevitable, I suppose, that the empyreal torch of my manhood should shine through the gloom and that the moths, poor helpless creatures, should come wheeling mesmerically to the flame. A more thoroughly anaphrodisiac straggle of females defies imagination, and to a wench they entertained the same prac-ticed overture: "Say, how about giving me a cigarette, huh?" But I do not smoke, and with the aid of the bartender—whose shrewd eye had discerned the aristocracy of my purse, and who wielded a mighty (albeit ulterior) truncheon in its defense—my virtue was spared for yet another hour. Besides, if the truth be known, the girls were saturninely disappointed with my professional status. My Texican clothes—from run-over boots to battered sombrero—had falsely informed them that I was either a cowboy or a sheepherder, and upon the confidence that I was actually making my way through life as an Emotional Funambulist (a phrase which would have been orphaned in most college classrooms, let alone an Indian booze-barn) they retreated in hasty if somewhat overawed disillusionment. (Only Tonto, my faithful Indian valet, knows that I am in reality a Professional Masochist, or Graduate Student.)

The evening did manage to provide one comforting experience, though. Eventually a young chap named Dog-Taking-Gun entered and seated himself on the other side of me, away from Popeye, and he possessed those qualities of courtesy and generosity which I recall as characteristic of my Blackfoot friends. Instead of asking me to buy *him* a beer, Dog-Taking-Gun insisted upon buying *me* one ("For friendship"). Out of deference to his pocketbook, I ordered the dime kind. Dog-Taking-Gun was a veteran of Korea, he said, and he was definitely at odds with Popeye, who continued to paw at my shoulder as I turned my back on him to chat with D-T-G.

D-T-G and I have many friends in common on the Reservation, including Jim and the Chief, and I was enjoying my talk with D-T-G, and the air was filled with muted sounds and all that jazz. But I was fatigued and generally disenchanted with my homecoming—you are apt to become disenchanted with any environment if you restrict your social research to gin-mills—and the straw that slipped the camel's disc arrived in the person of a madame of unrecent vintage who sidled up behind me, gyrated her vendible portions against my wallet pocket, and with a venereal smile gave tender song to her infatuation: "Say, you pretty good-looking, you know it! I like a had you in my bed." Whereupon some man, presumably the lucky bridegroom, and as drunk as she, dragged her away. This was a far war whoop from the old days, when an unfaithful Blackfoot wife was apt to have her nose cut off—or even, if she were childless, to be hung. And it was at this point that I, in trepidation equally of vengeful husbands and bacterial consequences, purchased Dog-Taking-Gun a beer in return and then bowed a courtly leave.

Popeye, who had never ceased to be an annoyance, followed me outside, and he had by this time bummed enough beer (but not from me) to become wildly and pugnaciously plastered. For a minute I thought I might have to cool him, but gentler measures soon prevailed—I ushered him to an unexpected seat on the pavement, got quickly into my car, and drove off with him shaking fearful threats at the rear-view mirror. Thanks awfully, but no more bars for a while, please. I will wait until the Chief and my Indian brother, Jim, get home.

Three days of mouldering in a Bozeman motel, where "air-conditioning" turned out to be a window fan which enticed into my lungs all the insalubrious vapors of a neatly concealed backyard swamp, had cured me of any desire to seek commercial lodgings, so I drove back to the ranch to pitch camp. While conducting a Polly-anna re-check of the doors and windows of the ranch house, I discovered that the pantry window had a small piece broken out, and when I stuck my arm in to fish around for a latch, the whole pane gave way. So I crawled through. No electricity, but there was a kerosene lamp with juice in it. Opened the back door and brought in my sleeping bag and rolled in with my clothes on. Conked out immediately, totally bushed.

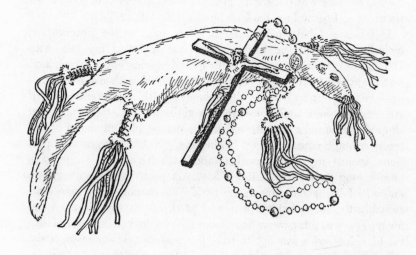

Thursday, August 30

Last night was cold as a landlord's heart, and I slept like a (rolling) log. Strange that sleeping in an unheated house should be colder than sleeping out-of-doors. When I camped in Rabbit Ears Pass, in Colorado, a week ago, I awoke to find the water in my water bag frozen into a solid block. It was much colder in Rabbit Ears than it was here last night, and yet down there I slept comfortably. Maybe it is that you *expect* a house to be warmer. I could have slept in Jimmy's sack, but I hate to take such a liberty, and of course I would not consider even opening the door to the Chief's room—his medicine bundles are in there, and entry is strictly *verboten*. This does not imply any lack of acceptance of me by the Chief; the Chief has never actually forbidden me to enter his room, but if I were to go in there I might inadvertently perform some gesture improper to the sanctity of his medicine, and so we have an unspoken understanding that I will not so dishonor my Indian dad. I would really like to examine the Chief's room, though, and of course he would never know that I had been in there. But I would know.

I was awakened finally at 4:30 A.M. by what I thought was the whining of a dog but which turned out to be the creaking of the outhouse door, blown back and forth by the wind. Strangely enough, two dogs really did appear, about an hour later. Both of them are very thin, and apparently they belong here because they have accumulated in the back yard a collection of deer bones, horses' hooves, and other chewables. Indians generally are not unkind to animals. A Blackfoot legend tells of a young man who was so cruel as to partially skin a female prairie dog alive, and who was haunted by a vision of the poor tormented creature until he became insane. But Indians do not believe in interfering with nature any more than is necessary, and they feel that a horse or a dog that cannot take care of itself is not worth having. The Blackfoots, by the way, never ate dogs, whom they regarded as guardians of the camp, and the Blackfoots looked down their regal noses at those several tribes—Sioux, Assiniboine, Cree, etc.—that habitually consumed dog flesh.

One of the dogs that showed up this morning, a female, looks exactly like a coyote, and she spends most of her time hunting field mice. The other dog apparently is Coyote's pup for he keeps trying to nurse on her although the lazy bum is at least four months old. In lieu of hunting mice for a living, he has chosen the profession of archaeology and has pock-marked the yard with small, inutile excavations. I named him Rascal, because that's what he is.

The old woodstove in the ranch house kitchen now has a small butane burner on top of it, and on this I fried eggs and warmed some tinned beef. The rest of the house appears pretty much as I remember it, but in the living-room I noted two additions: on the table by the Chief's chair is a model of an F-86 jet fighter plane, poised in an attitude of strafing the tabletop, and on the wall is a framed portrait of Jesus with an accompanying pronouncement signed by a Roman Catholic priest that the family of J. White Calf has been consecrated to the Sacred Heart.

With no disrespect intended toward anyone, I could not help smiling at this formal proclamation of the Chief's conversion. In the first place, this is at least the second time that the Chief has been officially accepted as a Roman Catholic; in the second place, the Chief is a Methodist in good standing and is an honorary steward of the Browning Methodist Church; and in the third place, the Chief is at this very minute participating in a Sun Dance, the most important of all *Blackfoot* religious ceremonies. So I am afraid that I shall have to view this documentary evidence of the Chief's new religious status in a common light with the figure-painted chunk of animal hide which is given (sold, rather, unless you happen to be a big-shot politician) to Whites as official documentation of their "adoption" by the Blackfoot Indian Tribe.

The Chief believes (as do I) that worship of the Almighty should bring people closer together, not drive them further apart. The Chief will participate in Christian religious services in the same spirit of syncretism with which a tolerant Christian will attend an Indian Medicine Lodge, and it is important to be aware that this does not imply that there is anything in his religious attitude which suggests either hypocrisy or indulgence. The Chief does genuinely accept the Christian concept, but he does not feel it necessary to abandon his own traditional beliefs in order to do so. Membership in one religious body does not dissuade him from accepting membership amongst yet another denominational group—not any more than the fact of my already having a White father had any effect upon the Chief's adopting me as his own son. The Chief accepts the *New* as a complement to the *Old*, not as a replacement of it, and his religious philosophy thus derives from a blending—a concrescence, so to speak, and hence an enrichment—of the many separate ways in which man searches for a closer relationship both to God and to his fellowman.

Interestingly enough, the precursor of Christian missionary enterprise amongst the Blackfoots was himself an American Indian. Ignace Lamoose, an Iroquois who had attended the Jesuit Mission of Caughnawaga, near Montreal, Canada, was attempting to introduce the elements of Christianity among the Salish (Flatheads) as early as 1830. Old Ignace eventually was killed by the Sioux, but not before his efforts had paved the way for the founding among the Flatheads of the first Roman Catholic mission in the Great Northwest. The mission was inaugurated by the famous Father Jean Pierre DeSmet and two assistants, and according to Jesuit records it was at this mission, on Christmas Day, 1841, that the first Blackfoot converts—an old chief and his family—were accepted in Christian baptism by Father DeSmet.

The Roman Catholic missionaries, whom the Blackfoots called "Black Robe Medicine Men," were followed shortly by the Protestants ("Short Coat Medicine Men"): a Methodist, the Rev. Robert T. Rundel, ministered to the Blackfoots at Ft. Edmonton, Canada, in 1840, and a Presbyterian, the Rev. Elkanah Mackey, whose wife was the first White woman to be seen in Blackfoot country, spent a *whole month* at Ft. Benton in 1856.

Actually, no permanent Protestant mission was established among the Indians of Montana until the 1890's, and this mission was a delayed result of the well-known "Peace Policy" of President Grant. After an attempt to place the Indian Bureau under the jurisdiction of the Army (which probably would have meant the extinction of the Indian) had been defeated in Congress in 1870, Grant's administration decided, incredibly, to allot the several Indian reservations to the influence of various organized church groups. Despite the fact that no Methodist missionary had ever been among the Blackfoots in the United States, the Blackfoot Reservation fell to the Methodist Episcopal Church. The Jesuits, who with the active encouragement of Blackfoot Agent Major Alfred J. Vaughan, himself a Protestant, had already established a mission among the South Piegans, were literally forced to withdraw from the Reservation and to confine their missionary efforts to the wandering Blackfoot bands.

From the very first, Christian missionaries among the Blackfoot Indians found themselves hoeing a very rocky row. The desire of the Blackfoots to be converted to Christianity did not exactly create a Coney Island crush around the baptismal fount, and there were several very obvious reasons for this. (1) The Blackfoots could not understand the rivalry and dissention among various factions of the same religion (the Black Robes vs. the Short Coats). (2) The Blackfoots could not quite dig a religious attitude which simultaneously venerated motherhood and condemned sex. The shortage of men caused by hunting accidents and constant intertribal warfare made polygamous marriage among the Plains Tribes a social and economic necessity, and those Indians that took one wife in Christian marriage invariably kept a few spares around the teepee (frequently the younger sisters of wife No. 1) in accordance with the Indian concept of matrimony. (3) The Indians were understandably unenthusiastic about religious tenets which condemned two of the primary virtues of traditional Plains Indian culture—the stealing of horses and the eradication, whenever possible, of one's enemies.

At one point, though, there was no dearth of Blackfoots who earnestly desired to become accepted for baptism into the Roman Catholic Church. In the summer of 1846, Chief Victor and his Flatheads, aided by a dozen lodges of Small Robes (the Small Robes were a rather independent band of Piegans who were friendly toward the Flatheads) achieved a smashing victory over a superior force of Absaroka (Crow) Indians. And when the Flatheads attributed their remarkable success to the power and protection of the "Black Robes' God", this was all the Blackfoots needed to hear. Baptism by the Black Robes was obviously a guarantee of victory over your enemies, and the more bloodthirsty the Blackfoot warrior, the more ardent became his petition for baptism. But since this attitude did not reflect the concept of Christian thought which the good priests of the Church had been attempting to convey, Father Point (the Blackfoots called him "Tusks"), who headquartered on the Missouri River at the American Fur Company's post of Ft. Lewis, recorded that of the 651 Blackfoot Indians he was able in all good conscience to accept for baptism, 625 were children, 22 were women, and only four were grown men.

The foregoing notwithstanding, Roman Catholicism was always more successful than Protestantism amongst the Blackfoots, and it is not difficult to suggest several reasons why this should have been so. Although the old-time Indians could in some measure reconcile the more abstractive philosophy of the Protestants with certain sciotheistic elements of their own religious inheritance, the more tangible paraphernalia associated with Roman Catholic ritual was much more impressive to them, and much more easily identified with aspects of their existing beliefs. During a Blackfoot Sun Dance or Medicine Lodge, buffalo tongue is cut into small pieces and distributed among certain participants; this gesture is in all respects strikingly similar to the Christian sacrament of the Eucharist. Also during the Medicine Lodge ceremony, Indian women will step forth and openly confess their sins, and this, of course, suggests the confessional both of the Roman Catholic Church and of the high order of the Episcopal Church. (It is important to realize that these Medicine Lodge ceremonies were not derived from the Christian religion but had their existence before the coming of the White Man.)

From the point of view of the Blackfoot fighting man, two aspects of religious tradition possessed by the Roman Catholics were especially easy to accept. A crucifix constituted a nifty recruit to the warrior's collection of protective amulets and charms, and when a priest endowed the converted Blackfoot with the name of a Catholic saint, this was to the Indian very much like his own custom of taking a new name (very often the name of a former chief or hero of his tribe) upon the occasion of achieving a significant coup against the enemy. To this day, a substantial number of Blackfoots have as a given name the name of a saint. Offhand I can think of Evangeline Big Beaver, Theresa Bull Child, Dennis Bad-Old-Man, Michael Scabby Robe, Bernard Red Head, Ursula Running Crane, Theola Cut Finger, Bernadette Red Head, Clement Big Springs, Serena Little Dog, Paul Calf Looking, Calvin Kicking Woman, Jason Dusty Bull, Rufus Good Striker, Terrence Little Bull, Angeline Old Person, Maurice Red Horn, Frederick Takes Gun, Francis Bull Shoe, Agnes Comes-At-Night, Woodrow Calf Robe, Anthony Mountain Chief, Tyrone White Grass, Hiram Daniel Calf Looking, Aaron Skunk Cap . . . There are many others.

The names Joseph and Mary are especially popular here on the Reservation, and the Chief once mentioned that he used to have an aunt named John—which is not at all funny if you know anything about the Blackfoots and their language. Blackfoot names have no sexual connotation, and a female is distinguished from a male by having the suffix *áki* (woman) added to her name. Incidentally, although popular fiction would have us believe that all Indian maidens are called "Shining Water" or "Morning Star," the truth is that Blackfoot girls, who were (and usually still are) named by a male relative or by some prominent male member of the tribe, were *not* named in imitation of some aesthetic object or experience. They were named in honor of a particularly notable war achievement by the name-giver, and instead of being named "Sweet Prairie Flower," a girl was more apt to go through life as "Kills Instead," "Found A Gun," or "Two Cutter" (the actual Indian names of some very fine Blackfoot ladies of my acquaintance).

Whatever the reason for the success or failure of the early Catholic missionaries, the strength of the Roman Church on the Reservation today (take it from a Protestant who knows) is in the presence here of such men as Father Mallman, the marvelous old Jesuit priest who has been ministering to the Catholic faithful down at Heart Butte for God-knows-how-many years. Father Mallman loves and understands the Blackfoots, and the Blackfoots love and respect the Father in turn. The Catholic congregation at Heart Butte is large and faithful in attendance, and if some members celebrate Mass and Blackfoot religious ceremonies back to back, and if a Blackfoot religious article slips into the grave at a good Catholic funeral, and if the grave is decorated not with flowers but with yard goods, blankets, tobacco or children's toys, the good Father does not see these things. His concern is with lives and with souls, not with gestures, and perhaps this is one of the reasons that all the Blackfoots, of whatever religious belief, hold him in such high regard.

Volumes could be written about Father Mallman, but I think that a single anecdote of recent occurrence will suffice. It is no secret that when an elderly "long-hair," a member of the Father's congregation, was laid to rest with Catholic rites a few years ago, a horse was killed in the man's honor (an ancient Indian gesture of respect for the deceased). And when some sanctimonious grimalkin came tattling to Father Mallman about the horse, the Father's only comment was that he hoped it had been a very good horse because the deceased had been a very good Catholic.

I think that the basically syncretistical attitude of the Blackfoot toward Christianity—an attitude which *must* be understood if one is to achieve any real understanding of the Indian himself—is well expressed in a story which the Chief told to me four years ago, after he had adopted me as his son. This was the traditional Blackfoot story of the Creation, and although it became apparent as the story unfolded that much of the traditional Christian belief had by now become incorporated into the Blackfoot tradition, it became apparent too that here was not only a classic of American Indian legendry but a classic statement of philosophical and religious tolerance from which our overly sophisticated modern world might well derive a meaningful lesson.

The occasion of the Chief's telling this story also hosted my first attempt to transcribe Blackfoot into English, and a rereading of this virginal effort never fails to paint my downy cheek with the rubescence of embarrassment. There was nothing wrong with my translation—that was fine—but when it came to preparing the story for publication I apparently felt compelled to imitate the asininities of certain of my predecessors in the field of Indian study because I loaded the phrasing with such conventional Indian corn as, "Hear me!" and "I have spoken!" Granted that a word-for-word translation of Blackfoot into English would not be possible, and granted also that these lofty phrases represent a perfectly valid interpretation of the meanings implicit in the Blackfoot phrases from which they were taken, the fact remains that the very same Blackfoot phrases could with equal validity have been rendered as, "Get this straight, Buster!" and, "You heard what I said, so don't give me any jazz about it!" I hate a phony. Especially when he is me.

My first writings about the American Indian admittedly were lacking in maturity, but there is considerable satisfaction for me in knowing that I at least managed to avoid the crudity so often perpetrated by anthropologists, ethnologists and just plain pain-in-the-ologists: at least I did not refer to the Indians as "bucks" and "squaws." Webster defines the word "squaw" as follows: "An American Indian woman; among Indians, any woman; a female." This is pure manure! I am familiar with a word of Eastern Algonkin origin which is vaguely similar to "squaw," but the word "squaw" in itself is a White Man's word and it does *not* mean "woman" in any Plains Indian language. Furthermore, I have never heard any American Indian employ the word "squaw" in respectful reference to any female. Further-furthermore, Indians enjoy being referred to as "bucks" and "squaws" just about as much as non-Indians would enjoy being referred to as "studs" and "bitches." My Indian brother, Jim, feels so strongly on this point that he invariably translates the Blackfoot word for "man" as "gentleman" and the Blackfoot word for "woman" as "lady." It does sound rather odd to hear Jim say something like, "Then the Blackfoot gentleman scalped the Crow gentleman and gave the scalp to a Blackfoot lady," but I don't blame Jim a darn bit—as a matter of fact, Jim's attitude toward this subject has served only to increase my already monumental respect for him.

Despite the quantity of corn transplanted therein by guess-who, the Blackfoot story of the Creation is a fascinating tale. Blackfoot stories have no titles as such, but for reasons of publication, and because of the contemporary incident—the early attempts to orbit a satellite—which induced the Chief to relate this tale, I titled it, "Why the White Man Will Never Reach the Sun."

I am Running Wolf, the same who is Chief White Calf, Chief of the Piegan Blackfeet, given to be chief in the year 1897 by my father, Last Gun, who was Chief White Calf of the Blackfoot Nation before me, and who gave me to be chief because he was getting pretty old. I tell you who I am so you will know that what is spoken here is spoken by me, and you know that I am Chief White Calf of the Piegans and I speak with one tongue. What I say here is the truth, and if anybody says to you that it is not the truth then you ask them how they know, for they were not there at the beginning.

Hear me, I am Chief White Calf of the Blackfeet, and you

are my son, Last Gun, for I have given to you the name of my father who was Chief White Calf before me and who was called among the Piegans as Last Gun. I have given you the beaded gloves to show that I am glad to have you for my son and I love you as my son, and your brother, Jimmy Eagle Plume, has given you the beaded moccasins to show he is glad to have you for a brother and he loves you for his brother, and now I give you this story, for this is the way it was in the beginning.

I am Chief White Calf of the Blackfeet, and I am one hundred and one years old, and I give you this story that I got from my father, Last Gun, who got it from the old men of the tribe. I am one hundred and one years but I am not old, for when I was a young man and hunted the buffalo and made war on the Crees and Assiniboines and Crows and counted coup on them and stole their horses I was never afraid because Nah-tóh-sey came to me in a dream and told me that I would live a long time but I would never be old. But he gave me just so long to live and I don't know when I will die, so I give you this story so it will not be lost. No other of the Blackfeet know this story because I have not told them, because it is the true story of how things were in the beginning and it is given by the Chief to his son so it will not be forgotten. You are my son, and I am White Calf, Chief of the Piegan Blackfeet and I give it to you.

Only once before I tried to give this story. There was a missionary and I called him son and gave him a name and tried to give him this story but he would not take it because he said that this is not the way things were in the beginning. But I was not proud to have him for my son because he says there is only one path through the forest and he knows the right path, but I say there are many paths and how can you know the best path unless you have walked them all. He walked too long on one path and he does not know there are other paths. And I am one hundred and one, and I know that sometimes many paths go to the same place.

Hear me, you are my son, Last Gun, and I know you will tell this story the way I tell it to you and not change it the way White men do, and so I give this story to be yours, for this is the way it was in the beginning.

In the beginning there were just two of them, a Man and a Woman, and they made the whole world. There were no oceans at the beginning of the world, and there were no mountains and no trees and no rivers that flow into the oceans.

So before they began to build the world, the Woman said to the Man, "We have a lot of work to do to build the world, so let us have two children right away so they can help us with the work."

And the Man answered her: "No, we are not ready for children yet. We will have them later on."

But the Woman said that they should have children right away and the Man said no, they were not ready yet. Three times the Woman asked to have children to help build the world, and three times the Man said no, they were not ready for children yet. But the fourth time the Woman said they should have children, the Man finally said all right and he asked her if she wanted boys.

And the Woman said, "I want two boy children, so they can help us build the world, for girls could not help us as well as boys could."

So two boys were born, and they grew to be eight years old. One of the boys was very wise and clever and he has no Indian name but is known as Mo-ká-ki, which means "very smart" in the Blackfoot tongue. But the other boy, whose name is Náh-pi, was pretty stupid and the Blackfeet call him Mut-tsáhp-tsi, which means "crazy" or "old man."

Then one day Mo-ká-ki, who was the wise boy, found that his mother was running around with another man. So he told his brother, Náh-pi, who was not so smart, and Náh-pi asked him what they should do about it. And Mo-ká-ki said, "We will tell our father that our mother is running around with another man." And so they told him.

"When our mother goes out to build the world," they said, "she works for only a little while and then she goes down by the big tree and plays with another man."

But the Father said, "This cannot be, for there are only the four of us in the world. We are not yet ready for other people until we finish building the world."

So Mo-ká-ki, who was the smart boy, said to his brother that they would go down and hide by the big tree and spy on their mother. So they hid down there, and pretty soon the Mother came down and began to hit all around the tree. The tree was really just a big stump, and after the Mother had beat all around the big stump for a while, a big snake with a horn on his head came out of the top of the stump and started to crawl down. And when he was halfway down the stump, he jumped, and when he landed on the ground he was a handsome White Man. And the White Man and the woman began playing together by the big stump. And the boys ran back and told their father that the Mother was playing with the White Man down by the big stump, but the Father would not believe them. "There are only the four of us," he said. "We are not ready for other people yet until we finish building the world."

So two more times the boys hid down by the stump and watched the Mother playing with the White Man, and each time they ran back and told the Father that when the Mother went out to make the world she would work for just a little while and then go down by the big stump and play with the White Man. But the Father would not believe them.

So for the fourth time the boys went down to watch their mother, and this time when they came back to tell their father he believed them. So the Father sent his wife out to work again but pretty soon she came back, and he said to her, "You should keep working. We have a lot of work to do to build this world."

So the Woman went back to work, and while she was busy working, the Man put on a woman's dress and combed his hair like a woman and went down to the big stump and beat on it like a woman. And pretty soon a big snake with a horn on his head came out of the stump and started to crawl down, and when he was halfway down he jumped and when he landed on the ground he turned into a White Man. So then they fought, and pretty soon Man killed the big snake.

And then Mo-ká-ki, who was the smart boy, said to his father, "Our mother will be after us now for sure, because we have killed the White Man she was playing around with. She will try to kill you, Father, but you should try to kill her first. We are your sons, and we will help you fight."

And sure enough, the Woman chased after her husband and caught him and then they fought for a long time. Finally the Woman got her husband down and was going to kill him, but the boys helped their father fight and together they killed the Mother and cut off her head.

But pretty soon the Mother's head began to chase after them and the Father said, "Boys, we are going to leave here and go some other place."

So they started to travel, and the Mother's head chased after them, so the Father started to build up the timber behind him and the boys so the head could not get through. But the head got through anyway.

So after he built the timber, the Father built up the mountains so the Mother's head could not follow. But the Mother's head followed anyway.

So then Mo-ká-ki, who was a pretty smart boy, said to his father, "Father, Mother's head must be back together again with the body, otherwise she couldn't follow us so fast. Now that the timber and the mountains are finished, we have no place to go. How are we going to get away from our mother?"

But the Father said, "Boys, we have one more thing to do to get away from your mother." So then he made the oceans all around the place where he was so the Mother couldn't follow, and he stayed on the islands where he was and that was the Indian country. Nowadays they call it United States.

So then the Father started to make the rivers and the streams, and his son Mo-ká-ki, who was pretty smart, said, "Father, you keep this up and pretty soon you'll have this land all covered with water."

But the Father, who was pretty smart too, said, "No, this land will never be covered with water, because I make the streams to run into the rivers and the rivers to run into the ocean."

You can see this is the true story, because even today the rivers all run into the ocean and the land is not covered with water.

But then when the streams and rivers were finished, Mo-ká-ki, the wise son, went to his father and said, "Father, Mother is here. She came across the ocean."

So the Father said, "Now I don't have any more place on this world to go, so now I'm going to another world. But first I'm going to send your mother to another place so she won't see me go. She will disappear for thirty days, and four days after the thirty days she will be back, but I will be gone. When your mother leaves it will be dark, so she can't see, but when I leave it will be bright daylight so you will all be able to see. No matter how hard they try, nobody will ever be able to get to the world where I am going."

So Woman went up to the moon in the dark of night, and Man went up to the sun in bright daylight, and even today there is a woman in the moon and a man in the sun.

But before he left for his new world, Man spoke to his two

sons: "Boys, I've got to leave for my new world, but my work here is not finished because I haven't made the people yet. So you two boys will have to finish my work for me. Mo-ká-ki, who is the cleverest one, will go back across the ocean and make the people there, and Náh-pi, who is not so clever and who will be called Mut-tsáhp-tsi, will stay here and make the people here. Mo-ká-ki, who is clever, will go back across the ocean and make people, and for them he will make machines and big weapons. He will do this because he is clever. But Náh-pi is pretty stupid, so he will stay here and just make the people.

"The people of Mo-ká-ki will have white skins, and in the beginning they will all speak the same tongue. The people of Náh-pi will have red skins and in the beginning they will have their own language that they will all speak. The people of Mo-ká-ki will be clever and have many tools, and one day they will try to build a big tower and reach the new world of Man, but one day when the tower is only just so high, one of the men will say to another, 'Hand me that tool there,' and at that time the man will not understand him because the language will change and everybody will speak a different tongue. And from then they will be enemies and fight amongst themselves because they cannot understand one another, and they will be so busy fighting that they will forget all about the tower.

"And at the same time that the languages change amongst the whites, they will change among the red men, and each tribe will speak a different tongue and they will fight amongst themselves because they do not understand one another."

And all that Man said came to pass. Even then there were dogs and they spoke like men, so when the Woman in the Moon played around with other men, the dogs could spy on her and tell Man in the Sun. But at the same time as the language changed, Woman in the Moon put filth in the mouth of Dog and said, "From this time on, no dog can talk to any man; dogs will understand what men say, but when Dog tries to tell Man about Woman, Man will not understand." And so now when it is four days past the thirtieth day, Dog howls at Woman in the Moon to come and give him his voice back. So when you hear the dog howl at the moon, you know that this is the true story of how it was long ago in the beginning.

I do not know how Mo-ká-ki worked when he made the people over the ocean, for I do not understand the ways of the

White men. But the Indian people were made by Náh-pi, and he made them like little dolls from clay. When he had finished he put them into little groups, so that each one knew what group he belonged in, and then after four days they began to walk around.

Pretty soon Náh-pi married one of his people and then pretty soon they had a boy child. Then Náh-pi said to his wife, "When we die we will die for four days, and then we will come back."

But his wife said, "No, that way there will soon be too many people. Why don't we die for good!" And pretty soon Náh-pi said O.K.

But then their little boy who was their only child died, and Náh-pi's wife said to him, "Why don't you say it again—to die for four days and come back!" But Náh-pi said, "No! It's too late now. We die for good!"

And then Jesus was born across the ocean. When he was born, the Jews tried to find him and kill him as a baby because they were afraid he would become chief of all the tribes. But then he grew up, and finally they found him and crucified him on a cross. He stayed on the cross four days and then came back to the village and said, "Good-bye, I'm going to the other world."

So the Catholics knew there would be a big flood at that time and they built a big boat and almost everybody got on it. And while they were on the boat a pigeon brought a leaf to them, and then the priest made magic and all the water turned to land again. So that is why you find the bones of the buffalo in the banks alongside the streams.

So over there they call him Jesus whom they saw going up. So over there they believe in him as God. But here they believe in the Sun and the Moon, and they pray to Sun, the Man, and Moon, the Woman. For Náh-pi said to his people to pray in the nighttime to Mother Moon, and in the daytime to pray to Father Sun. And that is the true story of how things were in the beginning, and you know that it is I who tell you this and that what I tell you is true, for I am Running Wolf, Warrior of the Crazy Dog Clan of the Piegans, known as Chief White Calf, Chief of the Blackfoot Nation.

And now I hear that White men are trying once again to reach the New World, Sun, home of Man. But they will never get there. Their towers will get just so high and no higher, but they will never reach the New World, Sun, where Man and

Jesus went up, because their tongues are different and they do not understand one another, and they fight amongst themselves and do not work together.

And the same is true for the Indians. Their tongues are different and they do not understand one another and they fight amongst themselves. So they can never reach the New World.

Only when all men are of one tongue and one heart and work together and stop fighting amongst themselves will Man and Jesus return. In the meantime the only way to get to the New World where Man and Jesus live is to be dead for good.

Hear me, I am Chief White Calf, Chief of the Piegans and all the Blackfeet, and I have spoken.

Shortly after breakfast, an Indian came prancing up to the house on a frisky bay, wearing denim pants, cowboy boots, a wide-brimmed felt hat, and a western jacket. He said that he was looking for stray horses, so naturally I invited him in for something to eat; whereupon he drank several cups of heavily sugared coffee and ate the remains of my breakfast plus numerous molasses cookies thickly spread with strawberry jam. He is quite handsome, and with his crew-cut he closely resembles Perry Como; however, he has the usual bad Indian teeth. His name is Stanley White Man (*Náhpi-quon*), and he, too, claims to be related to the Chief.

Stanley neglected to tie his horse, and while we were talking the bay strayed about half-a-mile. We foolishly chased him on foot for about an hour, until finally I asked Stanley if we couldn't borrow a couple of horses somewhere and rope his mount. He said, "Yah, sure," and we drove in my station wagon to a neighboring ranch, high up in the aspens, owned by an unfriendly character whose name, according to Stanley, is "Hommagunna." This is a new word to me, but Stanley says that he doesn't know the English equivalent.

Stanley borrowed a very fine sorrel cutting-horse and caught his bay in short order; he rides magnificently. Stanley asked me to carry a saddle up to the corral and I thought that it was for the horse I was going to ride, but Stanley threw it on the sorrel and took off. This burned me. Horse manners may vary between Texas and Montana, but you never carry another man's saddle, and I had a few words to say to Stanley when he got back.

After lunch I drove to town and bought some chow and picked up two letters at General Delivery. Came back and brought a couple of buckets of water from the spring—really a small spring-fed pond down by the road. The spring is extremely low, and I noted cow and horse tracks in the mud. The water is full of small specks, but most of them settle out in the bucket. Brought in some wood for the woodstove, and ate, and fed the starving hounds and lit the kerosene lamp (I wonder why there is no electricity) and brought the journal up to date and sacked out on the floor again. Still tired.

Friday, August 31

Slept pretty well, thanks to the cozy old woodstove, and got up at five and ate an uninspiring breakfast of fried eggs and canned chili and biscuits and coffee. Went into town and looked for old friends but didn't see any. As a matter of fact, I didn't see very many old-timers at all, and the ladies who run a local curio shop told me that it is sad but true that each spring there are fewer braids among the Blackfoots—which means that some of the old people didn't make it through the winter.

Most of the Blackfoot women still wear their hair in two braids, but not many of the teen-age girls do, and although a lot of the really tiny children of both sexes still have braided hair, among the over-ten-year-old boys I saw only one set of braids—three braids, one at each side and one down the back, the way the Piegan men wore their hair in the old days. This three-braided hair style puzzles me because, although the Chief and the other older Indians assure me that it is the traditional coiffure of the Piegan warrior, I have been totally unable otherwise to identify its origin. The really early artistic portrayals of the Blackfoots by such artists as Bodmer, Catlin and Kurtz show them wearing their hair hanging straight down, with sort of narrow bangs in the front. Sometimes the drawings show the hair gathered in at each side of the face and tied with buckskin, fur, trade cloth, or sometimes wrapped with brass wire or contained within hollow bones. This really was, come to think of it, a division of the hair into three sections, and perhaps this later developed into three braids. On the other hand, Indians were nothing if not Individualists, and perhaps these early artists sketched a limited and unrepresentative number of subjects. I do know that various pompadours and topknots were worn, and that these styles could represent the hair fashion of some powerful enemy the Blackfoot had killed, or possibly indicate his ownership of some particular medicine bundle. The very early photographs of the Chief's father I have seen all show him wearing his hair parted in the middle and falling loosely on both sides.

So much of the Plains Indian culture is of relatively recent origin, and there was so much cultural borrowing among the tribes—even among those tribes that were bitter enemies of each other—that puzzles such as this one are often impossible to solve. But since I am a linguist, not an anthropologist or an ethnologist, I have had a lot of practice in saying, "I don't know." And one of the things I do not know is why, with all the intertribal borrowing of articles relating to crafts, religion and war, there was so little intertribal exchange of language. The languages of the various Plains Indian peoples, even those of vicinal groups, are remarkable for their dissimilitude, and this fact was no doubt responsible for the development of sign language, the Esperanto of the Plains Indians. My dad, the Chief, is far and away the foremost living authority on the sign language of the Plains Tribes, and I never cease to be amazed by the very subtle shades of meaning which he and the other old-timers are able to convey through this medium. Incidentally, although practically every motion picture about Indians I have ever seen has included some noble chief's giving the sign for buffalo (you can tell the Indians from the Whites because the Indians always say "me" instead of "I" and the chiefs always express themselves in Yiddish metaphor and parable) I have never once seen the buffalo sign executed correctly. They always put in the horns, but invariably they neglect the beard: the right wrist placed to the point of the chin with the hand hanging loosely.

When the ladies discovered that I was here to visit the Chief, they surprised me with the information that Two Guns White Calf, the Indian on the buffalo nickel, was the Chief's brother. The Chief has never mentioned this fact, but this is not surprising because the

Chief is not one to bask in reflected glory. As a matter of fact, the Chief is not one to bask even in his own glory—and he has plenty of it to bask in. The Chief's father, O-nis-tái-po-kah, is generally conceded to have been the greatest—certainly the most intelligent—civil chief within the history of the Plains Tribes, and the Chief himself certainly is the greatest Indian chief of this century. Aside from his accomplishments as an orator, administrator, and diplomat (these are his present-century achievements), the Chief in the old days went on a total of fourteen warpaths or horse-stealing missions. The scalp that the Chief has tied to the handle of his brief-case is a relic of the last recorded spilling of blood in intertribal warfare on the Plains. The Chief mentioned casually one day that it is a Cree scalp (although historians have for some reason surmised that the scalp is Assiniboine) and if I could induce the old Chief to recite in detail his warpath adventures, I would have *some* book! But although the Chief is a great storyteller, he prefers to ignore his own experiences and to relate the glories of other Piegan warriors or to recite the ancient traditional Blackfoot legends.

On the way home I stopped at Stanley's place. Stanley, who was branding colts in the corral, lives in a small white frame house suspended from an immense television antenna. I could not understand why Stanley should use such a complicated brand—the largest brand I have ever seen, with very long bars running horizontally beneath the figure—but he cleared this question up nicely with, "Yah, my sister he's got his own saddles," and when I mentioned that I might drive up to Canada tomorrow to visit the Bloods (Canadian Blackfoots) Stanley said that he is a Blood and that he would like to "go along with" and visit his relatives. Some persons might get a little picky about my referring to the Bloods as "Canadian Blackfoots," but although it is true that the Bloods, the North Blackfoots and the North Piegans each have their own separate reservations ("reserves" the Canadians call them) across the line, it is also true that these three groups, along with the South Piegans of the United States, are all members of the Blackfoot Nation. The cultural ties among these separate branches of the Blackfoots are so close as to be almost indistinguishable one from the other, and certainly the speech of these groups must be considered as dialects of the same language.

Stanley, my Blood friend, lives down here with his brother-in-law, a young man named Earl Old Person. Earl is a Piegan and a member of the tribal council, and he told me that he wore his braids right up until the time he went into the army, at which time he cut them off in deference to regulation (there is a story in that, somewhere). Earl said that prior to his Army service he went to Europe with the Boy Scouts but that the Europeans would not believe that he was a genuine American Indian until he removed his headdress and showed them his braids. Earl said that this was because certain American Negro service men had considered it very funny to tell the Europeans, many of whom had never seen an Amerind, that they were "Blackfoot Indians." Earl feels extremely resentful about this, and I cannot say that I blame him. The Blackfoots are a proud people, and with all the concern currently evidenced in this country for the dignity and wellbeing of all minority groups *except the American Indian*—it is considered perfectly all right to use such unflattering terms as "injun giver" and "drunk as an Indian," but shockingly crude and even illegal to make similar statements with regard to other races or nationalities—when another ethnic group attempts to arrogate the very *identity* of the Indian, this, in my opinion, is going just a bit too damn far!

The whitefish are running heavily now in Cut Bank Creek, and the Blackfoots are catching them left and right. The fish will not take bait, so the Indians snare them with wire loops. One chap, fishing behind Earl's house, caught over fifty today. I knew that I would be supping on the inferior steak which I had bought in town, and I winced as Stanley threw two beautiful eighteen-inch whitefish to the dogs.

Ate my steak, canned greens, canned cherries, biscuits and tea. Outlined a story about Earl's braids. Fully rested now, and did not sack out until late.

THE BUFFALO NICKEL

My pursuit of Two Guns White Calf and his contribution (if any) to the design of the buffalo nickel turned out to be a Sherlock Holmes adventure of most complicated nature—but without the familiar neatly wrapped Sherlock Holmes conclusion.

One evening, following the return from Canada of the Chief and Jim, the conversation turned gradually back to the Chief's early days, and I took advantage of this circumstance by asking the old fellow to tell me where and when he was born and to explain the reason that he was so certain of his exact age. This is what the Chief said:

"Nowadays most of the Indians are born in a hospital, but I was born in a teepee. My father's band, the Skunk Band, was camped

34

Two Guns White Calf in Later Life

on the Milk River [the Teton], and I was born there on May 10, 1857. I know the exact spot where I was born because it was the custom of our people to wait until a child was old enough to remember clearly—when the child had attained the age of perhaps five or six years—and then to take the child back to the place of his birth and to rub his head in the dirt so that the memory of his birthplace would stay with him always. Most Indians of my generation did not know the exact date of their birth, but I know my birthday because when I was born there was a Jesuit priest visiting our camp and the priest recorded my birth in his book. When I was quite a bit older, this same priest visited my family once again, and it was at this time that he christened me James. I do not know the priest's name in English; we Piegans knew him by his Indian name, Marten Cap" (in all probability, Father Imoda).

I knew that the Chief's father had been Onistáipokah, who later became Head Chief of the Piegans, and that his mother had been Black Snake Woman, but I had very little actual knowledge of the Chief's siblings and I asked him if he would tell me something about his brothers and sisters.

"I had five brothers and five sisters. All of us boys were named Gun: my eldest brother, who was known as Wolf Tail, was named Strange Gun; I was second eldest, and my name was Last Gun, which was the name of my father, although later on my uncle, Run-

35

ning Wolf, gave me his name: the other boys were named Left-hand Gun, Back Gun, Cross Guns, and Own Guns."

The Chief did not see fit to name his sisters, so I did not worry the subject. Instead, I asked him whether all these children had had the same mother.

"No. My mother, Black Snake Woman, was the mother of four boys and two girls. The mother of the others was my father's second wife, Two Catcher. [These were not the only wives that Onistáipo-kah had during his lifetime—he had at least nine*—but he had these two simultaneously.] One of my half-sisters is still living; her name is Blanche Two Stabs, and she lives over at Babb."

I reminded the Chief that he had forgotten to mention his other brother, the Indian on the buffalo nickel, and here began my will-o'-the-wisp search for the true identity and claim-to-fame of the celebrated Two Guns White Calf.

"You are referring to Two Guns, but the fact is that Two Guns was neither my brother nor the model for the Indian head on the buffalo nickel. Two Guns was the son of a North Piegan man named Many Chief and a North Blackfoot lady named Red Otter Woman. My stepmother [the reference here is to Two Catcher, Onistái-pokah's second wife; she was not actually the Chief's stepmother] adopted Two Guns when he was a baby and she raised him along with her own children, but Two Guns bore no blood relationship either to myself or to any of my brothers or sisters."

Somewhat taken aback by this totally unexpected information, I asked why it was that Two Guns had become so widely associated with the Indian image on the nickel.

"Largely it was the work of Jim Hill. [Hill not only controlled the Great Northern Railway but virtually monopolized commercial tourist and vacation facilities within Glacier Park.] Hill met Two Guns at Glacier Park Lodge, and at the time that the buffalo nickel first was minted [1913], Hill and another official took Two Guns back east and told him to say that he was the Indian on the nickel. I think that Two Guns really did believe that his likeness had in-spired the design of the buffalo nickel, but actually the Indian profile on the coin is not that of Two Guns but of Two *Moon*, a Chey-enne—and Two Moon was only one of several Indians the designer of the nickel used in constructing the Indian head that you see on the nickel."

The Chief had never given me any misinformation of any kind, but his contentions were so rigidly at odds with popular local belief that I felt obligated to research the matter as thoroughly as possible.

---

* A grand total of twenty-three, I subsequently learned.

Iron Tail   *Two Moon*

The matter of identifying the Indian portrait on the nickel was (or so I thought at the time) a relatively simple one. When I presented the problem to Dr. Claude E. Schaeffer, Director of the Museum of the Plains Indian, Dr. Schaeffer informed me that there had been so much interest in this matter over the past forty years that a short statement covering the facts of the subject had been prepared by the Bureau of Indian Affairs and was available at the Blackfoot Agency Office. I called at the office of the Superintendent of the Reservation, and a secretary kindly prepared for me a Xerox copy of a 1931 Bureau of Indian Affairs news release which was displayed quite prominently on the wall for all to see.

THE BUFFALO NICKEL

June 12, 1931. Following numerous inquiries concerning the design of the Buffalo nickel, the Bureau of Indian Affairs, Washington, D.C., wishes to make public the following facts: In 1927 the Director of the Mint in a communication to the Office of Indian Affairs said that the designer of the Buffalo nickel was Mr. James Fraser of New York. He also stated that no particular Indian posed for this plate. Today the Commissioner of Indian Affairs received the following letter from Mr. Fraser:

328 East Forty-Second Street
June 10th, 1931

Commissioner of Indian Affairs,
United States Department of the Interior
Washington, D.C.

Dear Sir:

The Indian head on the Buffalo nickel is not a direct portrait of any particular Indian, but was made from several portrait busts which I did of Indians. As a matter of fact, I used three different heads; I remember two of the men, one was Irontail, the best Indian head I can remember; the other one was Two Moons, and the third I cannot recall. [The honor of being this third and forgotten Indian is claimed by John Big Tree, an Iroquois who is still living.]

I have never seen Two Guns Whitecalf, nor used him in any way, although he has a magnificent head. I can easily understand how he was mistaken in thinking that he posed for me. A great many artists have modeled and drawn from him, and it was only natural for him to believe that one of them was the designer of the nickel. I think he is undoubtedly honestly of the opinion that his portrait is on the nickel.

I am particularly interested in Indian affairs, having as a boy lived in South Dakota before the Indians were so carefully guarded in their agencies. Later the Crow Creek Agency was formed at Chamberlain, but I always feel that I have seen the Indian in his natural habitat, with his finest costumes being worn. I hope their affairs are progressing favorably.

Sincerely yours,
(Sgd) *J.E. Fraser*

It also may be added that the Indian Two Moon, of whom Mr. Fraser speaks in his letter, was an old hereditary chief of the Cheyennes, who died at midnight of April 28, 1917.*

So the Chief had been right, as always, and the question of the buffalo nickel had been resolved—for the time being. But there remained the issue of Two Guns' familial relationship, if any, to the Chief, and in an effort to clear up this point I called once again upon Dr. Schaeffer.

* I might also add that it was Two Moon who led the Cheyennes against Custer at the Battle of the Little Big Horn.

From a vault in the basement of the museum, Dr. Schaeffer brought forth the earliest existing roll book of the Piegan Reservation, dated 1904, and together we searched through the confusingly catalogued lists of names and ages and marriage records and other data. Although this document is of undeniable historical value, it contains much material that is inaccurate and many data that are the product of speculation and not fact. In most instances there was not even any attempt made to establish the birthdate of an Indian, the ages of the various tribal members being approximated as of the year 1904. In many instances, it was not possible to establish with accuracy the ages of even those Indians who had been born around the turn of the century; this was because of the fact that Indian children were not added to the rolls on the day of their birth—in most cases they were born in a house or teepee out in the hills—but on the occasion of their being registered at the agency. This might occur several years after their birth, or never. Numerous errors in the approximate dates of birth were apparent even to me, and I noted that the Chief's age—possibly because of his exceptionally youthful appearance—had been underestimated by seven years. According to the roll book, the Chief, as of the year 1962, was a mere kid of ninety-eight.

With regard to the Chief's parentage, the roll stated that James White Calf was a full-blood and that his parents, White Calf (Onistáipokah) and Black Snake Woman, had been united in Christian wedlock; this checked exactly with what the Chief had already told me. With regard to Two Guns (who went by the name of John White Calf and later by the name of John Two Guns, but who always constructed his signature by drawing a picture of two rifles and a buffalo calf), the record stated that he was the son of White Calf and Catches Him and that his parents had been married according to Indian custom. I am inclined to believe that "Catches Him" is a mistranslation of the name of Onistáipokah's second wife, "Two Catcher," also named "Holy Woman"; I have also seen her name translated as "Catches Her Horses" and "Catches Two Horses." "Catches Him" is also credited in the rolls as being the mother of the Chief's older brother, Wolf Tail (Strange Gun), but this is definitely an error: Wolf Tail's mother was yet another of Onistáipokah's wives, "Catching Each Other"—whose name I have also seen translated as "Hands Together." Whew!

I left the museum that day feeling that I had accomplished very little other than to exhaust my best source of potential information, and it was fully a year before I made any real gain toward verifying the Chief's contention that Two Guns had been his adopted brother. The records at the museum, of course, had indicated that Two Guns was a half-brother to the Chief, and Dr. Schaeffer had suggested that possibly some element of sibling rivalry had motivated the Chief in his denial of Two Guns as a brother. But this did not sound like the Chief to me, and I was determined, records or no records, to confirm to my own satisfaction the validity of the Chief's assertion.

I was not long among the Blackfoots before realizing that my best and most reliable sources of information were not official records but the older Indians themselves (although I learned too that one must exercise considerable discretion in the choice of one's informants because certain old-timers, out of petty jealousy or other childish motives, will seize upon any opportunity both to glorify themselves and to denegrate their neighbors). I also learned that even some of the best informants will hesitate to tell you that you have been misinformed about certain events—simply because they do not wish to embarrass you—and that the best approach is to pretend complete ignorance of the subject at hand. So when my discussion with an elderly Blackfoot lady began to touch on the White Calf family, I asked her simply, "What do you know about Two Guns White Calf?"

The lady said, "Two Guns was not really a White Calf. My mother was in the camp, up in Canada, when Two Guns was born, and she told me that Two Guns' mother was a North Blackfoot woman. His father was a Canadian too. Two Catching (Two Catcher) had a baby at the same time that Two Guns was born, and when her own baby died, Two Catching adopted Two Guns and raised him as her own child." (The informal adoption of children among the Blackfoots was and is a very common occurrence.)

At last I had verified the Chief's statement that Two Guns had been his brother by adoption only, but in the interim I had learned that the local legend of Two Guns White Calf, "the Indian on the buffalo nickel," was not easily to be dissipated by mere facts to the contrary. The story of Two Guns and his immortal fame had been a selling point among the local merchants for many, many years— countless tourists had purchased commercial photographs of "The Buffalo Nickel Indian"—and neither the business interests nor the civic pride of Browning was about to accept this heresy without a struggle. Two Guns definitely *was* the model for the buffalo nickel! Everybody *knew* that he was! When Two Guns had died, officials from Washington had come all the way to Browning just to attend his funeral! These officials had placed a bronze plaque on Two Guns' headstone *proving* that Two Guns had loaned his likeness to the nickel! No, no one had actually *seen* the plaque, but the plaque was there! If I didn't believe it, I could go look for myself.

Even the lady who had verified Two Guns' relationship to the Chief believed that Two Guns had been on the nickel. She declared that there was indeed a bronze plaque on Two Guns' grave, and if I didn't believe it I had but to visit the old Catholic cemetery and become convinced. Two Guns was buried right by the north gate of the cemetery, and I would have no trouble in finding his resting place.

So on a very cold and extremely windy day I drove to the southwest fringe of Browning to do Two Guns the respect of at least visiting his burial place. My first discovery was that both gates of the cemetery (if they could be called gates) were on the east side, but this fact was hardly worthy of issue and I parked my station wagon close to the northernmost east gate and began a search for the plaque-bearing grave of John Two Guns.

A careful survey of all graves within perhaps thirty yards of the gate revealed no sign of a bronze plaque or of Two Guns' name but did serve to impress me with the singular character of this cemetery. The cemetery grounds were obviously unattended. Indians customarily lavish little attention upon burial places, believing that the spirit is still living and that the body, once laid to rest, is no longer important, and among the long grass and the profusion of wild prairie flowers was an intriguing variety of graves. Most cemeteries depress me, but this was a friendly cemetery despite the gray sky and the cutting wind and with real interest I examined the mounds and depressions which signified the individual burying places. Some were marked with granite head and foot stones, some had crosses of stone or wood or even of foam plastic, many had simply a metal identification holder (upon which almost invariably the name was no longer legible), and more than a few were crowned with an ordinary fieldstone upon which the name was or had been painted. "Billy," was all that one grave spoke.

Most of the plots, including the unmarked ones, of which there were several, were outlined with small stones, and although inscriptions such as "Asleep In Jesus" and "Christ Is My Hope" assured me that the graveyard was indeed a Christian one, I noted that grave decorations included everything from flowers, both real and artificial, to small bundles of medicine sticks.

Perhaps most of all I was impressed by the variety of names represented here—there was no segregation here, that was for sure—and when I was unable to locate Two Guns' marker near the gate I undertook a systematic search of the entire graveyard, reciting in turn each legible name: Hernandez, Connelly, Morning Gun, Beaver, Blackweasel, Smith, Fitzpatrick, Wolf Tail, LaFromboise . . .

On the west side of the cemetery was a small hill, and upon this hill the full force of the wind was apparent; several headstones and even a large cross, anchored in concrete, had through the years been blown over by the unrelenting force of this wind from the west. This was not fun now, but with hat anchored firmly over ears and coat buttoned up to chin I dutifully undertook an examination of the graves on the hill. I had noted the pathetically disproportionate number of infant graves in the cemetery, some with a small headstone bearing the words "Baby———," one with a small lamb in bronze relief, but most simply a ring of small stones around the tiny, unnamed earthscar. Here on the hill I came upon a relatively recent grave—a little spot of fresh earth, embraced by the familiar stones, in which the grass and the prairie flowers had not yet taken root. In the fresh earth a narrow hole had been dug, and in the hole had been placed the playthings of a tiny child. I thought at first that the placing of the toys in a hole above the coffin might have some religious or philosophical significance—possibly motivated by a belief that they would be easier for the child to reach—but in glancing about I saw that everything, even flowerpots, that had been placed on the graves on this hill had been placed in small holes, and the reason of course was that, thus protected, the offerings would not so soon be blown away by the wind.

I continued on through the cemetery: Sharp Ears, Harper, Whitford, Baby Girl Armstrong, Monroe, No Coat, Henderson, Wades In The Water . . . I had been all through the cemetery now. I had visited every marked grave. I had scrutinized dozens of unmarked graves and had stumbled time and again upon oval rings of small stones completely hidden in the thick growth of prairie grass and flowers and weeds. If John Two Guns was buried in that cemetery, there was no bronze plaque upon his grave. If John Two Guns was buried in that cemetery, there was no identification whatsoever upon his grave. I made my way back through the cemetery to my car, and as I did so a bundle of medicine sticks came bounding down the hill to find a resting place—temporarily, I knew—against the base of a friendly tombstone.

The last chapter in the case of the missing Two Guns was a very pleasant one. After I had exhausted numerous false leads about Two Guns' burial place, Jim, my Indian brother, who had shared with the Chief a mysterious reluctance to discuss the subject, finally suggested that I consult Wilma Burd Franklin, a lady whose grandmother had been married to Two Guns. I did so, discovering to my delight that Mrs. Franklin, who had attended Haskell Institute, was not only friendly and charming but highly intelligent.

Mrs. Franklin is the proprietress of one of Browning's better restaurants, and during lunch there with Mrs. Franklin, her sister, Alfreda Burd Connolly, and another charmer named Irene Goss Mendenhall, I learned more about Two Guns in an hour than I had previously been able to learn in a year.

When I informed Mrs. Franklin that my research indicated that official agency records were incorrect and that Two Guns was a White Calf by adoption only, she said that this information coincided exactly with what Two Guns himself had told her, and so far as I was concerned, this bit of information wrapped and tied that particular issue with finality. In the matter of the buffalo nickel, however, I found that a few surprises were in store. According to the information I received that day, Two Guns had been well aware that the Indian head on the nickel was a composite portrait, and Two Guns had been informed through official channels that his likeness had contributed to the portrait through an error; although the Cheyenne, Two Moon, had been selected along with the Sioux, Iron Tail, as a model for the portrait, a mislabeling of contributory material resulted in Two Guns' being used instead of Two Moon. Although I suppose that since all parties to this dispute are now deceased, the full truth will never be known, the possibility that Two Guns actually was on the nickel cannot be discounted for the following reasons: (1) Although Mr. Fraser, the designer of the nickel, made in writing the statement that he had never met Two Guns White Calf, Two Guns was possibly the most photographed, painted, modeled and sculpted Indian in history, and the fact is known that Mr. Fraser did possess various likenesses of Two Guns; (2) By Mr. Fraser's own statement, he did not recall the identity of one of the Indians whose likeness he worked with in designing the portrait head on the nickel; (3) Although portions of the Indian portrait in question bear an unmistakable resemblance to Iron Tail (in particular the back of the head), no portion of the portrait in any way resembles those photographs of Two Moon that I have seen.

On the other hand, the face on the nickel suggests very strongly the face of Two Guns White Calf.

At any rate, Mrs. Mendenhall, who under the title of Indian Princess Dawn Mist traveled throughout the eastern United States with Two Guns in 1927, assured me that if Two Guns' being on the nickel is a fable then it is a fable of international scope. "Indian Princess Dawn Mist" (Mrs. Mendenhall is the first to giggle at this ridiculously contrived title) and Two Guns both appeared at an exposition sponsored by the Great Northern Railway in Baltimore in the fall of 1927. At this time, Two Guns, as "The Indian on the Nickel," was escorted through the U.S. Mint, was presented with a large metal replica of the buffalo nickel which he wore around his neck for the rest of his life, and was received by the President of the United States. For my money, either Two Guns really was on the nickel or else Jim Hill of the Great Northern Railway had a brass talent for promotion which beggars even his own considerable notoriety.

The possibility that there had ever been any kind of plaque, brass or otherwise, on Two Guns' grave, was immediately discounted by all three ladies present. Two Guns' burial had been a simple affair, and his grave had been marked by nothing more than one of the metal identification holders which were so common in the old cemetery.

Plenty of people had been more than willing to *tell* me all about Two Guns' famous burial place but thus far nobody had been willing actually to *show* it to me, so I was almost beside myself with anticipation when all three ladies agreed not only to show me the grave but to do so *right now*. The ladies were all on their lunch hour, and considering the possibility that I might wish to spend some time at the cemetery, they offered to take their own car.

Five minutes later I arrived at the rendezvous to find the ladies strolling about perplexedly in the vicinity of the south gate, knee-deep in greenery. I joined them. This was approximately the place that Two Guns had been buried, but Two Guns had died nearly thirty years ago (Two Guns was born circa 1871 and died March 11, 1933) and no one had had occasion to visit his grave for a long time, and there were so many graves here now and so many of the grave markers were missing and the place was so overgrown now that it was impossible to tell one grave from another. Two Guns had been buried a Methodist, not a Roman Catholic, and in former years Two Guns' grave had been easy to locate because the Roman Catholic cemetery had been separated from the Methodist cemetery by a fence and Two Guns had been buried right next to the Methodist side of the fence. But the fence had been torn down long ago, and since the fenceline could not be determined any longer, not only was it impossible to locate Two Guns' grave but it was impossible in numerous instances to know whether a grave was Catholic or Protestant (which pleased me as much or more than finding Two Guns' grave would have). The ladies were sorry, but they could not be certain which of the unmarked graves was that of Two Guns. The grave was right here somewhere, though, and perhaps the city morgue could provide an interment record and a map of the cemetery that would locate the grave more precisely.

My desire to call at the city morgue was not overwhelming. I felt that I had pursued the matter quite far enough—and I was sure that Two Guns thought so too. But two days later the unreasonable determination that makes linguists, writers and Texans dragged me to the local morgue and mortuary, an establishment which requires no description. I was in the place about thirty seconds—just long enough to become informed that there was no map or record of interment dealing with the old cemetery. The man was very sorry, but I wasn't. I had done my duty, and I was glad that it was over.

I went back to the restaurant and ordered a glass of iced tea. Mrs. Franklin showed me a photograph of Two Guns as a young man. He was astride a horse, and his wife, also on a horse, was beside him. He sure had been a good-looking guy.

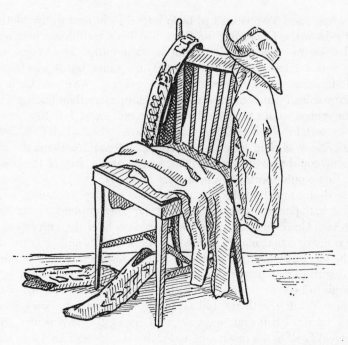

I had hoped that the Chief and Jimmy would return this morning, but they did not, so at 10:00 I picked up Stanley and drove over to Canada to visit the Bloods. The Blood Reserve is just across the border, at Cardston, Alberta. The Chief and Jim are at the North Blackfoot Reserve, at Gleichen, nearly two hundred miles away.

For an Indian, Stanley is quite talkative, and during the trip he entertained me with anecdotes and local color. Unfortunately, however, Stanley's knowledge of English is not breathtaking, and the brightness of his observations is obfuscated somewhat by a casual respect for tense, person, gender, voice, mood et al. On the way up he said, "She don't let that no liquor, that Canada—that's why she's came a here for drunk." Translation: Canada does not allow Indians to drink intoxicating beverages; that is why they go over to the States whenever they want to get drunk. Considering my very economical command of Blackfoot, though—not to mention my puisne standing as a linguist of any sort—I am scarcely in a position to be critical of friend Stanley's imperfect English. To learn a language which has no written form is a challenge in itself, but to learn a language so difficult as Blackfoot is a challenge supreme, and I find very little balm in the knowledge that few other White persons speak Blackfoot even as well as I. (Even in the old days, very few White men learned to speak or understand Blackfoot, finding it much easier to conduct their business through Cree or Assiniboine middlemen.)

But if I am inexpert in handling Stanley's native language, I *am* pretty good at handling Stanley's type of personality. North of St. Mary we had a flat tire, and I sat in the car, smug as a sultan, and graciously allowed Stanley to change the wheel all by himself—this, of course, in retribution for Stanley's having tricked me into carrying his saddle. I think that Stanley and I have an understanding now.

At first the flat and rather barren aspect of the Blood Reserve did not compare favorably in my view with the beautiful lakes and streams and hills and good grass of the South Piegan Reservation down at Browning. I asked Stanley whether he knew the size of the Blood Reserve, and he surprised me with the information that it is sixty miles long and between twenty-five and thirty miles wide—a very substantial reserve, I must say. I asked Stanley what the Bloods do for a living, and he said, "The most that she got here is farms. That irrigation water belong for the Indians. They charge them with water, but they got no water, they." As we continued northward on the Reserve I observed that the land was indeed very productive agriculturally, with many prosperous-appearing farms and ranches. From what I was able to observe, irrigation was an issue only on the southernmost portion of the reserve; to the north there was good water and fine grazing and abundant crops. The scenery could not compare to the scenery to be enjoyed on the Chief's ranch, which is located in the northwest portion of the Piegan Reservation, but the Chief lives on land which, although good for grazing, will grow nothing but rocks.

Apparently feeling that he had corralled a sympathetic ear, Stanley continued to gripe about the lot of the poor abused Canadian Indian, but I personally feel that most of Stanley's gripes are unfounded. There was a time when the Canadian Indian had an unfair shake, but this time is long since past; indeed, the United States could learn a lot from Canada about how the Indian problem (and it is a problem) could best be approached. I have examined the situation with minute care—including an exhaustive study of the Office Consolidation of the Indian Act—and when you have finished plowing through the legal terminology it all boils down to the fact that the Canadian Indian has got a *darn* good deal. The

47

559 separate Indian bands of Canada comprise a total population of some 210,000—the largest number of Indians that has ever lived in Canada during historical times. Canadian Indians have just about doubled their number since the turn of the century, and today they are increasing at a rate higher than that of any other Canadian racial or ethnic group.

Set aside for the use and betterment of Canadian Indians are 2,265 separate reserves, the largest of which occupies an area of more than 500 square miles, and although the Indian may enter freely into the contractual obligations of ordinary business and may sue and be sued, his real and personal property held on a reserve is exempt from both taxation and seizure except by another Indian. Add to this the fact that the Canadian Indian may vote at federal elections on the same basis as other citizens (in provincial elections he is governed by the electoral laws of the province in which he resides), and toss in protection by law against fraud and moral corruption, and you have the Indian living in a pretty nice place.

The thing which impresses me most of all about the situation of the Canadian Indian is the wide range of choices open to him. Some bands in the outlying regions of Canada are taking advantage of the same nomadic freedom which their ancestors enjoyed, while other Indians (Canada encourages its Indians to take advantage of the wide range of educational opportunities which are open to them) are successful teachers, lawyers, doctors, dentists, clergymen, etc. It is true that Canadian Indians are required to carry an identification card and that they are prohibited from using any form of intoxicant except for medicinal purposes, but these things are designed plainly to benefit and protect the Indian. Furthermore, a Canadian Indian is an Indian not by the color of his skin but by legal definition; should he wish to do so, any qualified Indian may relinquish his Indian status and become enfranchised as an ordinary citizen of Canada. (Enfranchisement qualifications required of an Indian are in no way different from those qualifications required of any other person desirous of obtaining Canadian citizenship, and an Indian once enfranchised has no restrictions upon his life or conduct which do not apply equally to any other citizen of the Dominion.) What else could a man ask!

My most selfish delight concerning the condition of the Canadian Indian derives from the fact that the paternalistic authority of the Minister of Indian Affairs extends even to the enforced protection of the Indian from any destruction or pilfering of his cultural and religious inheritance. Such articles as Indian burial houses, totem poles, rocks bearing carved or painted inscriptions, etc. may not be sold or destroyed or removed from an Indian reserve without the written permission of the Minister, and although the Medicine Lodge was for a time prohibited by law, all aspects of this ceremony excepting the thong torture have now been reinstated. Severe government restriction on trade with the Indians has allowed the Canadian Indian to retain much of his traditional cultural identity, whereas in the United States the Indian reservations have been just about picked clean by traders and private collectors.

Canadian Indian policy has resulted in there being many more full-blood Indians north of the Line than in the United States, and whether you like it or not, the only vestiges of true North American Indian culture are to be found among Canadian Indians (and to a much lesser extent among the relatively few full-bloods still alive among the South Piegans of the United States). It is significant, I think, that even my Indian dad, the Chief of the Piegans, spent most of his early life in Canada and started on most of his warparties from the old Blood camp on Belly River.

A public revelation of this fact invariably accelerates the consumption of Kaopectate among members of Southwestern chambers of commerce, but the "ancient Navajo crafts" of wool blanketweaving and silversmithing are neither ancient nor indigenous to the Navajo culture. The Pueblos do have a long history of weaving cotton textiles, but the weaving of wool was introduced to the Navajo by the Spanish settlers in the Southwest and the first "Navajo" blankets were probably made by Navajo slaves who had escaped from their Spanish or Mexican masters. The working of silver—again something learned from the Mexicans—was not undertaken by the Navajo until the middle of the nineteenth century, the earliest examples of Navajo silvercraft dating back only to the period of the Civil War. The famous Navajo "squash blossom" beads are known to have been constructed originally in imitation of the pomegranate, a common Spanish decorative motif which was widespread even among such ancient cultures as the Moors, the Cretes and the early Greeks. From a linguistic point of view, a translation of the Navajo word which refers to the "squash blossom bead" suggests simply "bead which spreads out"; there is no evidence to indicate that the design of this bead in any way symbolizes a squash blossom. And the equally famous "Navajo" pendant of crescent design, the "Najahe" or "Naja," is known to have been fashioned after an Old World horse trapping—an amulet, usually fastened to the bridle, which was supposed to protect the animal from the Evil Eye. This article is known to have seen common occurrence, even in the pre-Columbian period, from Serbia to North Africa.

On a portion of the Blood Reserve between Cardston and Stand Off, Stanley and I picked up two hitchhikers: Indians—girl Indians. The Blood women have a reputation for being very beautiful, and Stanley—that old married man—thought that these chicks were pretty hot stuff. They were both much too aquiline for my taste.

I noted as we drove along that the Blood Indians apparently have a fondness for two-tone houses (e.g., dark green and light pink), and when finally we reached Stand Off and Stanley directed me to stop in front of a small frame house ("She's my uncle"), the mere fact that the house was plain vanilla evoked in me the same unreasonable euphoria which I invariably experience upon discovering a small coin in a public phone booth. We entered the house to find Stanley's uncle washing his feet in a basin in the living-room, and during the ensuing introductions and the brief conversation which followed, Uncle scrubbed his toenails with a vegetable brush, wiped his feet on a towel which I think had once been either white or pink, and proceeded to rub his teeth vigorously with the same towel. Not very sanitary, perhaps, but Uncle has excellent teeth for a man of his years. Most Indians in this part of the country have horrible teeth—probably because they eat a poor diet and practice no form of oral hygiene (and because the water in this region is almost totally devoid of minerals). My Indian brother, Jim, has fine teeth, and I credit this largely to Jim's having been reared upon a diet which consisted primarily of wild game and other natural foods, including liberal portions of mineral-rich organ meats such as heart, liver and kidney.

Uncle waved good-bye with his tooth-towel, and next on the list was Stanley's father, who lived quite some distance away. The man who opened the door to us was nastily crippled, scuttling about like some pathetic, frightened crab, and Stanley volunteered the information that his father had been involved in a serious automobile wreck. Stanley also said that his father had once been an excellent singer ("Those young days before she's wreck she's very good singer"), but the old guy—not too old, really—refused to let me tape him unless I paid cash in advance, and this purely mercenary response to a predominately social gesture was sufficient to kindle my irascibility. But it would have been pointless to confront the gentleman with his rudeness and so I simply excused myself, and mine host received his measure of social opinion through the vicarious offices of a small outbuilding. "Here's that toilet, way down," Stanley informed me.

Next we visited Stanley's mother, a sad woman who was baby-sitting with her small granddaughter at a house not far away. It was lunchtime now, and the good woman offered us some of the food that was already on the table. Stanley does not know that I understand any Blackfoot, and as we plunged upon the banquet he informed his mother in Blood, which is very similar to Piegan, that I had in good Indian tradition offered him food upon first meeting. This simple gesture apparently had impressed him greatly. My glory was short-lived, however, because I helped myself to two of the small greasy meat patties from the large platter when obviously I was entitled to only one. This shocking evidence of gulosity did not pass unheeded by Stanley, and when he testily reported my *faux pas* to Mama, Mama nodded her head as though it figured and grunted, "*Náhpiquon!*" (White Man). These people are inclined to be quite captious toward the *Náhpiquon,* but I guess I can't blame them too much. The *Náhpiquon* has not always given them a very good deal.

The rest of the meal consisted of boiled potatoes, poor bread, and thoroughly execrable coffee, and hardly had I begun unenthusiastically to munch when the man of the house drove up with another Indian man in a pick-up truck. Both men were young, overweight, hungry, and artlessly miffed that their noonday pabulum was being engorged by intruders. But Stanley's mother opened a can of Spam, and everyone got enough to eat—including, no doubt, the numerous flies which invigilated the feast. As Stanley and I left, I gave two silver dollars to the little girl. These people don't really have very much, and I had taken of their food.

On the return trip, the station wagon was sardined with Stanley's relatives, all of whom passionately solicited a ride to Cardston. We also picked up and crowded in the same two girl hitchhikers. This time they looked better, as women always do late in the day.

We got back to Earl's place (where Stanley lives) just before suppertime, to find the family—including Earl's little girl who like any little girl playing grown-up was smeared from ear to ear with lipstick—glued to a very snowy TV screen. A decidedly un-Indian scene, I must say.

I accepted Earl's invitation to dine, but I did not eat very much because I did not wish to break another rule. (Stanley certainly didn't spare the victuals at my table though!) In my own set I am regarded as the very fillet of propriety: with consummate poise I tuck my napkin neatly behind my ascot; unerringly I select a spoon proper to the graceful ingestion of my apple pie; never do I fail to hand a lady her suitcase. But even the most Lilliputian of communities, I have discovered, has its own Gargantuan cipher of proprieties (against which it measures the conduct of the world), and since I am (1) sensitive enough to wish never to offend anyone, (2) neurotic enough to want people to like me, and (3) egotistical enough to think that my conduct is of interest to persons other than myself, my frequent voyages among the culturally unvarnished keep me in a perpetual blush of bumbled punctilios.

Earl, it appears, is a sort of lay preacher, and I am invited to church tomorrow. I shall go, of course. Cold tonight, and feels like snow. I am going to put my sleeping bag on top of the bed in Jimmy's room. I hesitate to trespass upon anyone's hospitality, but I know that Jim won't mind.

Jim's room is quite small—perhaps eight by ten—and it contains an incredible assortment of articles: an old bed with wooden head and foot boards; a tall, mirrored Victorian dresser, the top of which is interred in a litter of papers, magazines, photographs, clothing, car parts, a kewpie doll, and so on. The floor constitutes a veritable obstacle course of two saddles, some bridles, a hackamore, two lariats, two pairs of cowboy boots, a chair, a smoking table and a metal suitcase. I don't know exactly what is underneath the bed, but it is packed solid with something, and such additional gear as hats, cartridge belts and leather jackets are where they rightfully belong —slung over chairbacks and bedposts. Jim's .30/30 rifle leans in a corner behind the door. It is not loaded, which means that Jim is out of ammo; Jim always keeps it ready for any stray deer or elk that might wish to play bulls-eye while crossing the ranch. The last time I was up—the day I left, really—Jim shot an elk right out behind the barn. The Chief's old .38/40 Marlin rifle is here too, and it has a full magazine.

Jim's bed is exactly six feet long—a couple of inches shorter than I—but compared to the living-room floor and those insolent draughts of frigid air which creep in under the door the night long, Jimmy's creaky old sack is a perfumed boudoir—even if I will have to sleep sort of anti-godlin ("catty-corner," the Yankees would say). It appears like that everybody has got a funny way of talking except us Texans . . . and sometimes I wonder about thee-all.

Sun Dance Woman

Sunday, September 2

It was bitterly cold today. About two inches of snow, but the afternoon sun has expunged the "mostly" (Stanley's influence) of it. Up at five, ate breakfast, completed a story titled "Braids," took a bucket-bath in the kitchen, put on a white shirt and a corduroy jacket and at 10:00 went to church with Earl, Stanley, wives, kids, mothers-in-law, etc.

Church service was conducted in a small frame building close behind Earl's house. It was very cold inside the building—I still don't know why it is colder inside a house than outside—and those that had overcoats kept them on. There was no heat in the building, but somebody brought an electric heater and placed it in the aisle close by my shivering form. It helped some.

Earl began with the statement that, because of the extreme cold, a short prayer would comprise the entire service. But first we would sing a hymn. So we sang a hymn, and that went over pretty well so we sang a few more. Good old Baptist hymns, they were. Then Earl said a few words about his not preaching a sermon today, and that led into one of the longest, most tendentious—and one of the most thoroughly enjoyable—sermons I have ever heard. The congregation was most attentive, but the dignity of the occasion was marred slightly by an incorrigibly pedestrian youngster who kept trotting up onto the stage (is that what you call it in a church?) and slamming hymn books onto the floor.

Earl eased into his sermon by pointing out that this building had in past been the seat of both Christian worship and pagan rites—and a few drunken parties—and the sermon proper wound around the virtue of following a course of sobriety in the face of poverty and frustration. Earl freely admitted his own bibulous history, and indeed most of the Indian men of my acquaintance—and quite a few of the women—have had a drinking problem at some time or other. All the more credit to them, I say, for having overcome it. Even brother Jim squandered a portion of his quixotic youth in jousting with gin-mills and slaying the evil flagon.

Earl is an uncommonly articulate person, and although he made numerous supererogatory references to "The Word," "The Faith," and a few other evangelical "The's," I was greatly impressed by the general content of his message. However, he pulled the well-meant but profoundly annoying small-townism of asking the visitor to stand up and introduce himself and say a few words, and although some people no doubt enjoy this kind of thing it is one of the reasons that I hesitate to visit small churches. God knows you are there, so why turn the whole thing into a sewing bee by taking a bow! (I am reminded of the dowager who arose grandly to tell the congregation—composed largely of Texas stock-breeders and their families—how happy she was to see that so many of them had devoted their lives to "servicing" God.)

After the service, I was introduced to the members of the congregation, and this I appreciated. One man, a huge chap, is one of the Chief's sons, and I sort of wish that brother Jim would clue me in on such minor details of existence as his having a few other brothers trotting about the Reservation. I think it quite natural that I should have endowed my patriarchal Indian dad with all the purity of Montana snow, but apparently the snow drifted a bit during its younger days because my new-found brother, it was explained to me, is one of the Chief's "under-the-blanket" children. But of course this fact has no effect at all upon this chap's social status on the Reservation. Some of my White acquaintances—all of whom cleverly prearranged to have themselves born in legal wedlock, but a remarkable number of whom were premature babies—would make smoke with such petty kindling, but the Blackfoots couldn't care less. Nor could I. This man appeared to be in his fifties, which would make him about fifteen years older than Jim.

I accepted an invitation to dine at Earl's house again, but once again I did not eat much. I ate again when I got home.

Late in the afternoon, as I was heading for the spring for a bucket of water, the Chief and Jimmy drove into the yard in a venerable Chevrolet sedan. It was great to see them again after all this time. The Chief looks just about the same, but he has a cold and is pretty tired. Jim is the same: raven black hair, falling on both sides like a horse's mane, and good teeth except for the tartar. But I noticed that he has what appears to be a small white spot on one eye. This concerns me somewhat because Indians have more than their share of serious eye trouble; however, Jim assures me that his "eyesights is perfect."

Jimmy was the typical stoical Indian, greeting me as though I had been gone about four days instead of four years. But the Chief was openly overjoyed at my return, and as soon as we went inside I gave him the presents that I had brought for him: a telescope, a battery lantern, an electric clock, a large magnifying glass, a portable icebox and some other stuff. He was especially pleased with the telescope and the magnifying glass because he doesn't see very well.

We chatted and reminisced until suppertime, and Jim told me that the Sun Dance was more of a rain dance this year. The tent flooded and, although Jim took the seat cushions out of the car for the Chief to sleep on, the Chief caught a bad cold. Jim said, "Too cold for him take him up there. I thought we be back in 3–4 days, 3–4 days up maybe to week, but we was there a two week more. He got cold and kept till we got home here, but that old fella he never said mention about it. Well, like myself, if I was old guy I guess maybe I wouldn't had guts for went there in a first place."

For supper we boiled a large whitefish that somebody over at St. Mary had given to Jim. Jim says that in the old days the Indians used to snare the fish with loops of horsehair. "One time, about a week later—about one Sunday—I got strike and got two bigger even fish."

The Chief is exhausted, and after supper he immediately went to sleep on the sofa. Jim and I continued to chat, and I jotted down some of the wealth of Jim's colorful phrases.

"We blewed out tire on way back. For time there thought was going had pack him over those mountain."

"Way down north. Over south."

"Room and a board." "I need a help."

"I never et dinner all day."

"Really fed out." (Fed up.)

"You know what is it?"

"I told him a good-bye."

"Over in a Canada. In a Gleichen."

"He asked me a smoke, so just to be a good-enough I gaved him a smoke."

"Three or five."

"Could a be."

"I exactly don't know."

"Everybody don't believe me."

When I reminded Jim that I take my coffee without sugar, he said, "I don't like 'em too sweet too."

Finally Jim yawned and said, "Well, just well as do my dishes."

After we had washed the dishes I started to unroll my sleeping bag on the floor, but Jim said that I should take his bed. He will sleep in the Chief's room. As soon as I finish this, I shall accept his kind invitation. Jim and the Chief have sacked out already.

War Pipe

Monday, September 3, Labor Day

Up at six, and had a fire going in the living-room stove by the time the Chief and Jimmy rolled out. It snowed again during the night, leaving about two inches of wet whiteness through which the prairie flowers incongruously are poking their colorful blossoms.

I allowed Jim to cook breakfast—a horrible mistake! The fried eggs had black lace around the edges, like a city girl's drawers, and the pancakes were about as tender as a catcher's mitt. The Chief feels better this morning; he ate a man's share of the pancakes and eggs, and he drank his coffee with lots of *náh-pi-nuan* (sugar). But first he performed his morning toilet of re-braiding his hair and rubbing his face with cold water, and I put on his moccasins for him and gave him a new pair of wool sox.

Soon after breakfast, at about 7:30, the Chief was sitting at his table enjoying his new magnifying glass, Jimmy was washing the breakfast dishes, and I was looking out the window at the snow and wishing that my boots weren't so worn out (Jim said, "I got extra pair, but you won't fit 'em"), when two figures came walking down the road and turned in at our cattle-guard. I called Jim, and he glanced out the window and said, "Couple winos. I know 'em. From over in a Canada."

The two walkers came up to the door and knocked, and Jim yelled "Come on in it" without ceremony. So the walkers—a young man and a young woman, both in their early twenties—came in. The man was a reasonably presentable young Indian, dressed in cowboy blue jeans, black boots, a black cowboy hat and a black jacket of imitation leather. The girl was very petite, had fine bones, and would have been quite pretty had she been groomed—and if she hadn't had that Gravel Gerty voice. The boy's name is John, and the girl, as I began to suspect or at least to hope when they entered the outhouse together, is John's wife. Her name is Marie. Marie had on a black orlon pull-over sweater, pale green denim trousers, and was wearing a pair of moccasins—not genuine Indian moccasins such as the Chief wears, but moccasins of the cheap, beaded, glove-leather variety which can be purchased in any dime store. Marie was without coat, hat, gloves or sox, and it was cold outside and Marie's feet were soaked through from walking in the wet snow and Marie trembled so and her teeth chattered so loudly that I could not understand half of her comments (she talked incessantly, and used more four-letter words than Chaucer's daughter). John said nothing, but from Marie we learned that John's car, or the car in which John and Marie had been riding, had run out of gas.

About five minutes after John and Marie arrived, another walker appeared—a young Indian man, tall and thin, dressed in a black T-shirt, greasy dungarees, work shoes, and a metal helmet of the type worn by forest fire fighters. Let's face it; these kids had been out drinking all night, and this latest comer was still pretty high.

He grinned perpetually and talked unceasingly, and the absence of his upper front teeth failed to lend grace either to his appearance or to his highly insalivated sibilants. When I asked him his name he said "White Wolf", and this reply educed loud laughter from John and Marie. I later learned that this "White Wolf" routine was really a slam at the *náh-pi-quon* present (myself, of course). "White Wolf" is really named White Man. He is Stanley's brother. Jim says that Stanley—and consequently "White Wolf"—really are distantly related to him and the Chief (and so, by adoption, to me).

At first I was rather unpleasant toward these young drunks—in imitation, no doubt, of the Chief's attitude. The Chief despises heavy drinking, and when these people came into the house he immediately withdrew to a corner and refused even to look at them. Jim talked tough, as always, but actually he has a heart of soft gold and he went about fixing pancakes and coffee for the newcomers.

While the food was being prepared, Marie gave a gravel-voiced account of a rather unique velitation in which she had become engaged the previous evening. It seems that Marie, who had taken a brief furlough from the beer-guzzling, had been ensconced contentedly upon the john when some gal had strolled up and started to slug her, and little old Marie had knocked the woman cold without even getting off the pot. Marie had cut her opponent's face so badly that the cops accused her of using a knife. "Here's my knife," said Marie, waving aloft her hard little fist. Marie has Caucasian features, nice teeth, light skin, gray eyes and brown hair. I thought that she might be a half-breed, but Jim assures me that she is a full-blood Cree. (I doubt it; there are very few Cree full-bloods.)

At first, I really didn't think very much of Marie, but after she had washed her face and pulled a comb through her thick tangle of hair, she looked very young and very appealing. And when Jimmy told her that the Chief is 105 years old, her voice hushed to a reverential whisper and her face softened with the almost universal regard of the female for the very young and the very old. At that moment, a strangely ineffable quality of infinite femininity shone past the calloused knuckles and the grating voice and the tough gestures, and at that moment I would have spread my cape over a puddle for Marie.

"White Wolf", who was having a high old time for himself, giggling, and grinning from tooth to tooth, reacted immediately to Marie's interest in the Chief. He began pointing at one picture on the wall after another, saying, "That's him, that's him." Marie went along, examining the old portraits and saying, "Yeah? Yeah? No kidding?" Finally White Wolf pointed to the portrait of Jesus and said, "That's him too," and at this point Marie cocked back her fist and threatened to knock out the rest of White Wolf's teeth (his front teeth, apparently, have already gone the route of the fist). Marie said, "I owe you one, anyway, for trying to feel me up in the car last night."

Eventually, I began to have a liking for even White Wolf—despite his asinine conduct. Pointing to the model airplane on the table, White Wolf said, "Wish I had that, me. I'm be well off up sky than on earth." And for a brief moment the foolish grin failed to mask the unhappiness and frustration which, as I know perfectly well, motivate the heavy drinking of so many Indians—make that *American* Indians.

White Wolf, still wearing his helmet, sat at the kitchen table and gummed down several pancakes. John and Marie took only coffee, John downing a whole cup of coffee without removing the large enamel mug from his lips. "What are you trying to do, marry the cup?" Marie said.

Marie was shaking so badly that she had to take her coffee in quick, aspirated sips. I said, "What's the matter, Marie? Got the shakes?"

"Wise guy!" she said.

After my tough-talking brother had fed and warmed the trio of walkers, he siphoned some gas from his car into a gallon jug, gave it to them, and refused to accept the silver dollar that Marie offered as payment. Marie gave the coin to the Chief, who, thinking it a gift, did not refuse it.

The walkers left at about 9:00. It is now 12:00, and Jimmy is preparing lunch. The sum of my morning's endeavor consists of having borrowed the Chief's galoshes in order to go to the spring for two pails of water, and typing this. Jimmy spent a large part of the morning in cutting firewood, and the Chief passed the time by examining numerous articles with his new glass and by working on the whistle he is making. The whistle is made of the wingbone of an eagle. The Chief has cut a notch in the bone, and he is currently engaged in partially filling the bone with some sort of gummy-looking stuff. This stage of production, I am told, is the most difficult, because if the gum is not put in exactly right, the whistle will not blow. After lunch, we will attend the horse races down at Heart Butte. This racecourse was the setting for my story, "Horserace," and I am anxious to see it once more.

Later: At lunch today, the Chief presented me with a very old, very small pipe with a stone bowl and a hardwood stem about six inches long.* It is a miniature version of the traditional Blackfoot "peace pipe." But this smaller pipe is not a peace pipe but a war pipe. When going on a war party, or on a horse-stealing raid, the Blackfoots did not like to encumber themselves with large objects, and this pipe was carried on such forays by the Chief and by his father before him.

We drove to Heart Butte, but the races had been cancelled because of the snow. By the time we got back—a round trip of about 100 miles on poor roads—most of the snow had surrendered to the strong sunshine, but the ground was rather muddy.

We still do not have any electricity in the house, and Jim does not know why. He says that he will "tangle it up" with the light company tomorrow. "I'll told them why a hell they turn off my light!"

Jim says that this is the first sunshine he has seen since before he went to Canada. "We was over in a Gleichen a two week and didn't see a sun."

For supper we had ground beef, boiled potatoes and canned string beans. And instant tea. Jim invariably expresses an opinion in dual phrases. "That instant tea sure good; I like that instant tea." "Fella was telling me, he says . . ."

After supper, the old fellow sacked out immediately. Jim and I sat up until midnight, and I finally dozed off in a chair, was waked by my own snoring to find myself alone in the room, and crawled to bed.

* This pipe is not to be confused with a woman's pipe, which is about the same size but of entirely different shape.

Medicine Lodge

Slept soundly and was the first guy up and had a fire going and the house warm by the time Jim got up at 7:00. Jim left the door to the Chief's room open, and I could see that the Old-timer was awake, sitting up in bed. And when the water was hot and the Chief still wasn't up, I took him a cup of tea; it was only a few steps into his room, and the door was open anyway, so I didn't think he'd mind.

Without his glasses, the Chief is almost blind—he is not much better off with his glasses on—and when I touched him on the shoulder and said, "*Mah! Móyoke!*" (Here, take this!), he started and said, "*Kai-yó?*" (What's up? *Kai-yó* is actually a short form of *Kai-yáy-wah:* what is the matter?)

I said, "*Ah-say-yo-pokes-ay-y-kim-meh*" (tea), and the unaccustomed sobriety of the Chief's attitude induced me to add the (half-) wittiest quip that my limited Blackfoot could provide. "*Ps-kin-iśh-taht*" (put it in your pocket), I said, handing him the cup, and although the Chief accepted the tea and said, "*So-káh-pi*" (good), he immediately booted me gently out of the room by grunting, "*O-ó-kit!*" (Shut the door). Adopted son I may be, but I still do not know enough about the proprieties attending the presence of the Chief's medicine bundles to be welcome in my daddy's room. In

61

my own defense, I will add that I delivered the tea without looking either left or right—but I still had no business going in there.

But the Chief does feel better today, and when finally he did get up, all was forgiven and the Chief was in the playful mood that suggests his usual self. The Chief combs out and re-braids his hair each morning. Contrary to vulgar opinion, Indian men do not always wear their hair in the same style, and this morning the Chief made four braids, one behind each ear and one in front of the ear. The Chief ties the ends of his braids with a length of red flannel, and when he had finished this job Jimmy came sneaking over and pulled one of the braids around beneath his nose and accused the Chief of having a moustache; whereupon the Chief offered to knock Jim on his butt if he was not careful.

Jim says that he doesn't like meat for breakfast and that he customarily takes only a very light morning meal ("I'm not much of appetite, less if I'll get hungry could eat whole beef. Usual I just having couple coffee and a toast"). His light breakfast of this morning included fried eggs, a huge stack of his incomparably bad pancakes, and several cups of coffee from the remarkable old granite coffeepot which, despite unspeakable neglect, insists upon producing consistently marvelous coffee.

The Chief eats well, and although he frequently turns from the table to blow his nose with his fingers, this gesture does not offend. The old fellow has so much innate dignity that he could perform the same act in church without embarrassing the most fastidious of angels.

By the time the school bus from Babb went roaring down the road, loaded with Indian kids from across the mountains, we had eaten, done the dishes, and were planning to go to town. I am anxious to have the electrical service restored so that I can do some recording. The little battery-operated tape recorder ($140.00 worth) which I purchased for just such an emergency as this has failed completely. That is the last time I buy a made-in-Japan product—I don't give a damn *who* puts his name on it!

Later: Immediately after lunch, we drove to town in my station wagon. I cashed a cheque at the bank, bought some 35mm film and an immense amount of chow—including a whole side of bacon, which I don't eat. Since Jim has given me his room and bed, I figured that the least I could do was to pick up the tab—almost fifty bucks. At least we'll eat for a while. Jim has a liquor permit (Montana has a State Liquor Control Board which requires that anyone, Indian or White, must purchase a permit before being allowed to buy packaged hard liquor), so we picked up a fifth of Jim Beam bourbon. Jim said that it is the Chief's favorite, but as it turns out it is *Jim's* favorite. The Chief, who drinks very moderately, has no special preference.

While in town, I bumped into old Phillip, a gentleman whom I celebrate equally for his ponderous ventricosity, his proclivity to prevaricate, and the fact that he was the intellectual if not the physical model for "Phillip" in my story, "Horserace." Phillip is about six feet tall, but scarcely the hexapody of rhythmic graces which the word "Indian" generally conjures in the romantic imagination. He has the right-angle schnoz of a cartoon Indian, and his unreasonable avoirdupois, which cascades downward from narrow chest and shoulders to pile fore and aft below his beltline like a spent avalanche, endows him with the silhouette of a parturient kangaroo. Phillip has a peculiar sort of frantic, lumbering gait, and what he really looks like is a kangaroo which has just been rudely spun out of a revolving door.

But if Phillip's being fails to whirl me into purple raptures of description, be it noted that friend Phillip in his own good turn is something less than burdened with encomium for me. The only thing about me that ever impressed Phillip was my being from Texas. "De-e-e!" he said. "That Texas is a lo-o-ong ways over. I thought maybe you was from some state around here, like New York or Chicago."

Old Phillip does not appear to have changed much, although he has eroded to a mere 220 pounds or so, and he informed me that the government is supporting him now because he has developed "the diabetes" (this, apparently, is true). But it is *not* true that Phillip owns the gas station in which I found him lounging baronially.

Phillip also said that he remembers the last time I was up here "'bout ten or fifteen years ago." It was *four* years ago, and at that time Phillip estimated my age at "'round 'bout maybe eighteen or thirty-four." Phillip and a wandering Sioux were free-loading off the Chief then, eating and sleeping out at the ranch, and since there was no room for me in the house I pitched my tent alongside it. I remember that Phillip, who was functioning as chief cook, pot-licker and garbage disposal unit, was wearing a beautiful new pair of Justin boots and that he cursed in astonishment upon learning that the boots leaked—all he had done was to wade the creek in them. Jim told me that Phillip had received his oil lease payment (an amount that ran well into four figures) a short time before but had blown the whole pile on a couple of months of high living and so had to sponge off the Chief and Jim. The Chief is the most unreservedly generous person I have ever met, and this fact is well in keeping with the traditional generosity of the leaders of the Plains Indian Tribes.

Of course, Phillip dwells within my deep affections primarily because of the tender concern he lavished upon me when I sprained my ankle so badly. Phillip was in the corral, attempting to lasso Brownie, Jim's rodeo horse, with a loop about the size of a tennis racquet, and I, after watching him make a dozen futile tries, mildly suggested that since Brownie was used to being roped, if Phillip would just lay the rope across his withers, Brownie would stand. So Phillip did and Brownie did, and Phillip handed me the rope and said, "Here, the old man says you stake out this horse." I knew that Phillip was lying—any time he wanted to get out of work he would tell either the Sioux or myself that the Chief had ordered us to do the chore. But, anyway, I took the rope and started to lead Brownie to some good grass, and suddenly my foot went into an old grass-hidden badger hole and I fell to the ground with a seriously damaged ankle. And as I lay there writhing with pain under Brownie's sympathetic gaze, Phillip, whose sensibilities betray his previous incarnation as a Coliseum lion, came gamboling over to see the fun. Wagging a verbal finger down at me, he said reproachfully, "You better stake out that horse. That old man's goin' have mad with you."

I said, "You silly S.O.B., I think I broke my leg!" And these melancholy tidings plucked a chord (a bass chord) in the very depths of friend Phillip's overstuffed viscera. As though from an irrigation sprinkler, the muriated water of human compassion flowed from Phillip's soulful eyes, and manfully choking back a commiserative sob, he yawned hippopotamusly and said, "I'll stake out that horse. Here, you take these harness in the house." And he tossed down the tangle of bridles and hackamores and the saddle he was toting.

Being at the moment unarmed, I was unable to make appropriate response to Phillip's touching largess, and with my ankle now a swollen, discolored sack of blood I callously left the harness where it lay and hopped into the house. In a few minutes Phillip joined me, primed for round two. "You put piece of bacon rind on that foot and she's goin' was all fix up in a five minute," he said. So I, thinking that this might be some magic Indian remedy, was sitting there, a pound of bacon clapped to my ankle, when Jim came in with a rather intoxicated Indian girl. Jim shook his head in disgust, said,

"That Phillip, he don't know what's, by goz!", produced some roots from the mysterious interior of the Chief's room, and cut the roots into small pieces and added them to a basin of hot water. Then the Indian girl bathed my ankle with a soaked cloth. The girl was pretty drunk, but her hands were unbelievably gentle. It was like being bathed by an angel.

That was four years ago, but it seems like yesterday. Today, before coming home from town, I bought a pane of glass to replace the one I broke, and Jim and I stopped at the local power company office to check on our light situation. They said they'd check the line, and by the time we got home (4:30), a maintenance crew was there to install a new transformer. So now we have lights. It is 5:45 now, and Jimmy just stuck his head out of the kitchen and said, "*Ahk-so-yope*" (let's eat). "*Sey-kúhn-noz*" (I am hungry).

For supper we had fried chicken, and potatoes cooked in beef broth. The Blackfoot word for broth is new to me, but I will have no difficulty in remembering it. The word is *kó-piss*, and brother Jim kindly suggested a most efficacious (if slightly scatological) Anglo-Saxon cognate (false cognate, of course). All I have to do is change the stress. For dessert we had canned cherries and *ah-siks-eh-kim-méh* (coffee).

After supper we celebrated the restoration of electrical service by doing some tape recording. The Chief and Jim are still pretty much under the spell of the Sun Dance which they recently attended, and from them I gained a great deal of information about the Sun Dance encampment in general and the Medicine Lodge in particular. The Sun Dance this year was sponsored by a Canadian Blackfoot named Wolf Child (Mach-ku-yáy-pu-kah), and the encampment included a large number of lodges.

Among other things, I learned that although the thong torture was outlawed by the Whites around the turn of the century, it continued to be performed surreptitiously by the Blackfoots until at least as recently as the 1920's. The thong torture is a ceremony, once quite common among the Plains Tribes, in which a young man allows skewers to be passed through the skin of his chest and attached to the Sun Dance centerpole by rawhide ropes; then the man dances, leaning backward against the ropes until his flesh tears open, releasing the skewers. The thong torture has been interpreted by some as a sort of show-off demonstration of the participant's courage, but I have found no grounds for believing that this was the case among the Blackfoots. Certainly the ordeal required both courage and fortitude, but the Chief says, and he should know, that the event represented the fulfilment of a vow which the participant had made to the sun on the occasion of his requesting some special favor, such as protection in war or the recovery from illness of a loved one. Of special interest is the fact that if the skewers did not tear loose after a reasonable term of sincere effort by the dancer, it was the prerogative of any respected warrior to step forth, recite his war honors by way of qualification, and sever with a knife the strips of flesh which bound the dancer to the thongs; whereupon the severed flesh was given as an offering to the sun. Such a brutal religious gesture!—almost as nutty as having yourself lashed and wearing a hair shirt over the open wounds. Those who fast at the Sun Dance for four days take no refreshment except a small drink of water at sunrise and sunset, and since some of the old ladies and gentlemen are too frail to survive such an ordeal, it is now allowable for a surrogate faster to deny himself in their stead. There is nothing supposititious about this action; it is intended by the surrogate as a gesture of respect to the worthy old-timers and is done in the same spirit that the cutting of the flesh of the dancer formerly was conducted.

The Chief mentioned something about the Indian teepee or lodge which came as a surprise to me but which I should have had sense enough to know without being told. The old buffalo hide teepees were much smaller than their modern canvas counterparts. Hide weighs much more than canvas, and even though the Blackfoots used the lighter summer hides of the buffalo, or even split the hide to reduce its bulk, a teepee constructed of more than six or eight hides was simply too heavy for the nomadic Blackfoots to conveniently pack around. Some wealthy families, who had many horses and so could provide travois transportation for more worldly goods, had larger teepees, but these had to be divided into two or more parts because a single horse could not manage to pull the load.

The discussion moved on to the Blackfoot painted lodges, and here we really struck paydirt. Even in the old days there were only about four dozen painted lodges among all three tribes of the Blackfoot Confederacy, and the lodges were not painted helter-skelter or at the whim of the owner. The painted lodge was associated with a medicine bundle of some sort, and the designs painted on the lodges were either inspired by a vision that the owner had had or were purchased (the exclusive privilege of using the design, that is) from the previous owner. The Chief related the traditional origin of the design painted upon the Buffalo Lodges that he and Jim own, and also the origin of the Eagle Lodge.

THE TWO BUFFALO LODGES

This happened a long time ago, up in Canada, near a place on the Bull River known as Blackfoot Crossing. Two Blackfoot men, one named Holy Man and the other named Weasel Heart, were seated on a bluff above the river. The two men were partners, and they were making arrows.

In the river below the place where the two partners were sitting was a green hole [a deep place in the river, where the water is unusually clear] and suddenly Holy Man turned to his partner, Weasel Heart, and said, "I think I see a lodge down there in that green hole. I am going to go down and see what kind of lodge it is, and what it is doing there in the river." So Holy Man floated down the river on a log, and when he came to the green hole he dived to the bottom of the river. He stayed

67

under the water for such a long time that Weasel Heart began to think that he might have drowned, but finally he came up again and said, "I have a painted buffalo lodge down there."

Weasel Heart said, "I think I see another lodge down there." So he dived down into the green hole, and when he came up again he said, "I have a buffalo lodge down there too."

One of the buffalo lodges is a black lodge and the other is a yellow lodge. Today, the black buffalo lodge belongs to me, and the yellow buffalo lodge belongs to your brother, Jim. When I purchased the black buffalo lodge, many years ago, I paid for it five race horses, four beeves, many blankets and other trade goods, and also some money.

THE EAGLE LODGE

In the early days, the Blackfoots used eagle feathers in making their warbonnets and in decorating their shields and their lances and many other things. Sometimes they would capture grown eagles by digging a pit and covering the pit with branches and placing some meat on top of the branches as bait; then they would hide in the pit, and when an eagle came down to grab the bait with his claws, they would capture the eagle by grabbing its feet. At other times they would capture young eagles right from the nest, and these they would hold in captivity until they were fully grown and could provide large tailfeathers for their owners.

Eagles nest high up on the cliffs, and the way the Blackfoots captured the young eagles was to go to the top of the cliff and lower somebody down to the nest with a rawhide rope. But it was necessary to wait until the young eagles had reached a certain size, otherwise the eagles would die in captivity, so when a Blackfoot man had discovered an eagle nest he would keep watch on it until just the right time, and then he would have his partner lower him down to the nest at a time when the parent eagles were away hunting food.

One time, many years ago, two brothers had discovered an eagle nest, and the elder brother lowered the younger brother down to the nest to see whether the young eagles were old enough for capture. This happened a long time ago, and the name of the elder brother is not remembered by the Blackfoots, but the name of the younger brother was Young Bull. The elder brother was jealous of Young Bull because he thought that he had been playing around with his young wife. This was not true, but the elder brother was so jealous that when Young Bull had reached the eagle nest he pulled up the rope and left him there to die. Young Bull cried and pleaded for his brother to pull him up, but the elder brother would not listen. The brother went back to the Blackfoot camp, which was across the river from the eagle nest, and told the people that Young Bull had been killed by a bear, and pretty soon, from his place up in the nest, Young Bull saw the people breaking camp and moving away.

Soon after that, the parent eagles returned to their nest, and when they found Young Bull there they attacked him and slashed him with their claws. But when the parent eagles discovered that Young Bull was not fighting them but was just sitting quietly with the young eagles held in his lap, crying, they calmed down and did not attempt to do Young Bull any further harm.

So the eagles accepted Young Bull as a friend, and Young Bull lived in the nest with the eagles and helped to care for the young eagles, and he protected the young ones while the parent eagles were away hunting for food. At first Young Bull lived on the scraps left over from the food which the parent eagles fed to their young; then one day the parent eagles brought Young Bull a buffalo calf, and with a flint knife he butchered the calf and ate the kidney and the liver raw and then from the rest of the calf he made dry meat. From the hide he made a robe with which to keep warm.

Young Bull lived with the eagles all summer, until the young eagles were big enough to fly. Then one day the eagles left Young Bull a young goat for food, and all four of them flew away. The eagles stayed away for two days, and Young Bull thought that they had deserted him, but finally they came back with a turtle for him to eat. Several times the eagles flew away, and each time Young Bull thought that they had deserted him, but always the eagles returned.

Then one day, when the eagles had flown away once again, Young Bull fell asleep with the first fall of night and he had a dream. In his dream, Young Bull was sitting in a lodge, and the father eagle entered the lodge in the form of a man and spoke to Young Bull: "Do not worry, Young Bull. You will be returned safely to your people. Furthermore, you shall have revenge upon your brother, who left you alone to die. Your brother will suffer as you have suffered."

The eagles did not return the next day, and that night Young Bull once again dreamed that he was in a lodge. It was the same lodge that he had dreamed of being in the night before, a lodge with eagles painted on the outside. This time the mother eagle entered the lodge in the form of a woman and spoke to Young Bull: "Young Bull, you have helped me to raise my babies, and for this I am grateful. As soon as my babies are able to carry a heavy load, they will help their father and me to carry you down from the nest where you are now asleep."

On the following day the eagles returned, bringing with them two fawns which they split open with their beaks and gave to Young Bull for food. Then the eagles left again, and this time they stayed away for four nights and did not return until the fifth day. At first Young Bull thought that he had been deserted by his eagle friends, but on the fourth night he had another dream. Once again he dreamed that he was in the eagle lodge, and in his dream the four eagles entered his lodge in the form of a man and a woman and two boys that were nearly grown into men. The eagle persons spoke to Young Bull and told him that on the following day they would return to take him home, and that the nest in which he had lived so long would be changed into a lodge with an eagle painted on each side. They told him that when they returned the next day they would bring four stones, and they showed him the ceremony he must perform with the four stones. Then the eagle persons told Young Bull that he must prepare for their return by taking his flint knife and cutting his buffalo calf robe into four pieces and braiding each of the four pieces into a strong rope. They told him exactly how he was to use the four braided ropes, and then they left.

On the following afternoon, the four eagles returned to the nest, each of them carrying a stone. Young Bull had prepared the four braided ropes and had tied the ends of the ropes to his wrists and to his legs just above the knees, and now he tied the other ends of the ropes to the four stones. Then each of the eagles grasped a stone in its claws, and among the four of them they carried Young Bull down from the nest. The load was a heavy one for four eagles to carry, and they were just barely able to make it to the opposite shore of the river. The eagles were very tired, but Young Bull was safe and unharmed.

So Young Bull said good-bye to his eagle friends and started out to search for his brother. Pretty soon he met a Blackfoot man who was out hunting for horses, and the man said, "Yes, your brother is at our camp, not far from here, but he thinks that you are dead. He thinks that you were killed by a bear."

So Young Bull went to the camp and entered his brother's lodge. His brother was surprised to see him, and right away the brother made a lie: "Young Bull," said the brother, "I am glad to see you alive. I could not pull you up from the eagle nest because a bear chased me away. I thought that the bear must have killed you."

So Young Bull made a lie to his brother in return: "Yes, I was hurt by a bear, but I managed to get away alive." Then he showed the scars from the talons of the eagles and said that they were scars from the claws of a bear. He did not mention the eagles at all.

So Young Bull lived in the lodge of his brother all that winter, but never once did he mention the eagles. Then when it was early summer and the young eagles were hatched in the nests, Young Bull's brother had a dream in which the father eagle appeared to him as a person and told him it was time to go and take the baby eagles away. At the same time, the mother eagle appeared in a dream and told the brother's wife of the wicked thing he had done to his younger brother, Young Bull.

So the three of them, Young Bull and the brother and the brother's wife, went upon the cliff, and Young Bull and the wife lowered the brother down to the eagle nest. Then Young Bull pulled up the rope and said to his brother, "This eagle nest is my lodge, and you can live in it as I did. Live as well as you can, and if you care for the eagle children, perhaps you will live to return to your people the same as I did."

Then Young Bull and the wife returned to the camp, and together they made a lodge to live in, and on each side of the lodge there was an eagle painted in black paint.

I would have gotten some other teepee stories, I am sure, had it not been for the unannounced arrival early in the evening of an extroverted, loquacious Indian in his thirties—"Name by Redhorn," Jim explained. Verily doth Redhorn's tongue wag loudly and oft, and among the informations which forthwith did assail mine ears was the boast that Redhorn had been a technical adviser during the filming of Bud Guthrie's book, *The Big Sky*, which was shot here in Montana.

Redhorn "just happened to stop by," but I am sure that he knew I was here. I attempted unsuccessfully to contact the Chief and Jimmy by telephone and every other modern means when they were up at Gleichen, but the Indian grapevine (known locally as the "moccasin telegraph") informed them of my whereabouts on the day following my arrival.

Redhorn, it seems, is both an author, a linguist, and a bibliopole of sorts, and he "just happened to have with him" a printed pamphlet of his own composition:

A Guide to the Spoken Blackfeet Language into English
By
PETER F. REDHORN, JR.
Full-Blood Indian

Member of the Blackfeet Tribe
Blackfeet Indian Reservation
Browning, Montana

Souvenir Edition

All Rights Reserved

Have friends and share your happy times
and you will be happy people: Old Man.

The introduction states: "Blackfeet Indian words in this guide are written in phonetics which you read like in English." Unfortunately, however, Redhorn is not a trained linguist, and his phonetic transcriptions are far from accurate—or phonetic. He used —with somewhat less efficiency—the same technique of transcription that I am employing in this journal (because I can do it on a typewriter), merely setting down in English phonemes the Blackfoot language as it sounds to me, without regard for a valid representation of syntactical elements, and with a cavalier shrug at secondary or tertiary stress, proper syllabification, nasalization, the several types of Blackfoot stops and fricatives (although I do intend that *ch* preceded by a vowel should imply the same fricative quality that it would have in standard German), and about a million other details of linguistic import. Redhorn's little pamphlet is, indeed, a nice souvenir, but from the point of view of serious linguistic inquiry it is useless. I ran down the list of words, phrases, numbers, etc., with Jim, and Jim confirmed my suspicion that Redhorn's language background is primarily Canadian, not South Piegan.

After Redhorn just happened to leave, Jimmy whipped up some hot toddies—a good reply to the wind which pounds the west side of the house at night. Jim used tea, sugar, cinnamon, hot water, and two shots of Jim Beam Bourbon. The Chief accepted just one shot, and he took his straight. The old fellow has gone to bed now and is chanting a prayer. Jim and I are talking as I type this. We are getting to the bottom of our second toddy.

Jim just said, *"Ahk-say-góh-koh"* (good night), and went to bed. It is 10:30, and here I go too.

Onistáipokah

Wednesday, September 5

I got up at 7:00 and went outside to help Jim who had already been cutting blocks for the stove for quite some time. There was a fresh fall of snow on the ground, and when one of the dogs got in Jim's way he threatened him thus: "Get off my way, Dog, or I might liable get a snow and throwed at you." The day was already promising exceptional warmth though, and as Jimmy paused to mop his brow he said, *"Kis-tu-yáy-wah"* (it is hot). Mostly to show off my understanding of Blackfoot, I said, *"Iks-ík-tsist-tu-yay(wah)"* (it is *very* hot). In appreciative return, Jimmy added, *"I-kí-tah-mik-zis-ti-koa"* (it is a happy day), and then, knowing as he does the narrow limits of my Blackfoot, he prognosticated in English, "There won't be no snow here till this afternoon."

The Chief was last one up, and he groomed with great care. I have made a ritual of helping him with his moccasins. He washed, rubbed his face with alcohol, combed and re-braided his hair, and plucked out a few invisible chin whiskers with tweezers fashioned from the flat metal band of a packing box.

Right after breakfast, the Chief said that he wanted to go to town. I couldn't find out why—not without asking, that is, and among Indians you do not ask. One of the things I most admire about my Indian friends is that they do not ask personal questions; they assume that you have a reason for whatever you do, and that if you

74

wish anyone to become aware of the reason you will make it known. I am sure that I could live at the Chief's house for any length of time, without any questions about why I am here or why I don't get a job, etc.

Curiosity as to the Chief's destination gnawed me raw, though, and finally an opening came when Jim—after a prolonged study of the twelve-year-old calendar which has been retired on a nail above the washbasin—turned to me and asked, "What's the today?" I informed him that the today was Wednesday, September 5, 1962, and boldly followed up my advantage by inquiring why he wanted to know. He told me that some of the older Indians are eligible to receive government surplus food ("commodities," the local term is) such as rice, flour, powdered milk, lard, peanut butter, etc. The Chief was to pick up his commodities today, and this fact led into a very interesting discussion with Jim, who is a marvelous linguistic informant. Any linguist is aware that those autochthonous languages which have no written form are subject to constant and at times very rapid change, but I had no idea that so much of the Blackfoot language is of such recent—actually contemporary—vintage. As an example, Blackfoot terms for the days of the week are obviously less than a century old because they are phrases which suggest the life of the Blackfoots *after* they were confined to the White Man's reservation. Sunday is "Holy Day," or "The day upon which we attend church." Other days are identified by such terms as, "The day on which we receive our rations," "The day on which nothing happens," etc.

This was supposed to be the day on which we receive our rations, but it turned out to be the day on which nothing happens. In town I let Jim and the Chief off at the Tribal Office ("I'll jumped off here," said Jim), and while they conducted some business or other I went up to the Browning school and took some pictures of the kids on the playground. The school serves not only Browning but several neighboring communities, and all of the school children appeared to be either Indians or Swedes. The typical picture was that of a raven-tressed little Indian girl arm-in-arm with a cotton-blond playmate, and everybody appeared to be as happy and as healthy as could be—even the tiny ones were swinging high on the swings, hand-walking along the bars, and performing various other athletic feats. And something new has been added since I was in grade school: the kids crook a knee over the pipe railing along the sidewalk, grab their ankle, tuck the other leg in somehow, and whirl around like pinwheels. This appeared to be a girls' game—at least I did not see any of the boys participating. The girls—those little hams—were fighting to have movies made of themselves, but the boys, quite typically, were quick to run away. The boy with the three long braids was there, but I could not get a good shot of him. Jim says that the boy's name is Door or Dore (sp?), and that his mother rinses his lustrous long hair in tea.

After I had picked up Jim and the Chief, we drove out to the Museum of the Plains Indian, on the "skirt" of town, as Jim says. Outside the museum building there is an Indian version of Grauman's Chinese Theatre; many years ago the great chiefs of the Plains Tribes had their footprints recorded there in bronze. The Chief is the only one of these great chiefs still living, and I had a very strange feeling of anachronism—as though both the Chief and I belonged to a different period of history—as I took a photo of the Chief standing next to the footprints that he had made so long ago.

These cameras of mine are turning me into a genuine tourist, but thus far, at least, I have not begun to take pictures of *myself*.

We left the museum and went back in town and stopped at the Agency, where the Chief was supposed to pick up his commodities. I waited outside in the wagon, and pretty soon came the Chief, minus rations but bursting with a fiercely contained dignity. Nobody said word one, and in silence we drove back to the ranch and had a good lunch of porkchops (pig is *ák-sin-nee,* meaning "they grunt"), boiled potatoes, canned peas, bread and strawberry jam, and hot tea.

The Chief ate well, but in silence, and it was not until he had seated himself in his chair in the living-room and leisurely finished smoking a post-prandial cigar that he beckoned Jim and me close and launched into the fiery and truly magnificent oratory for which he has so long been famous. He sat very straight and tall, his fine, orbicular head held high. And as the thunderous old voice rumbled, and the huge old hands sculptured power and beauty in the air, the oscillatory motion of the great brown jaw added a synchronal measure of authority to the old fellow's declarations.

The Chief was speaking rapidly, and he was using oratorical forms—not the simple phrases which he and Jim thoughtfully employ in addressing me—and I could not follow the discourse. A Blackfoot word which I knew to mean *card* or *ticket* was repeated several times, and during a pause for translation Jim explained that in this case the word was being used to refer to a ration card. The Chief had forgotten to take his ration card to town today, and the Agency had refused to issue him his commodities without it, and the Old-timer had told them that he was still chief around here and that he wasn't about to osculate anybody's posterior for a few groceries and that if they wouldn't issue him his commodities without a silly piece of paper then they could take their commodities and stuff 'em. Instead of using the term *ist-tést-tin-ope:* ration card, or referring to *ní-moch-tèst-tin-àhp-pey:* my ration card, the Chief had showed his contempt for the situation by employing the word *gah-tsáh-tsis* which is usually reserved as a reference to playing cards or, infrequently, a colloquial reference to theatre tickets.

The Chief is really one of the great inspirations of my life. I find back-scratching ecstasy in the knowledge that even today, in the midst of a society which has so aptly been termed "effete and pusillanimous," this gentle, fearless old Indian chief still has the groin to tell the Federal Government where to go. Chief James White Calf of the Piegan Blackfoots will give you his love and his possessions and his life with an open heart, but all the money in the world could not buy a single hair from his stubborn old braids. Pride. Real pride! There is so damn little of it to be found.

It is really a tear-jerking realization that the Chief is almost the last survivor of a culture that will soon be gone completely. Even Jim is tossed in the tempest of this dying culture. Jim is an Indian through and through—and I could pay him no higher compliment —but he is faced with the problem of earning a decent living, and in order to do so he must either play a role of dumb Indian or become an Imitation White Man, neither of which roles suits Jimmy at all.

Because of the fact that there is so much unemployment among Indians—there simply is not enough work available—wide currency is given to the fiction that Indians are lazy bums. This burns me! Aside from the small number of street-corner loafers—and every culture and every community has its share of these—most of the Indians of my acquaintance invest a full measure of some kind of productive activity into each day. It really scorches my butt that anyone would judge an entire ethnic group by the conduct of a few drunken panhandlers, but this is precisely what a large number of persons do. They fail to take into consideration the fact that for every street-bum in an Indian community as well as in their own community there are hundreds of decent citizens at home patching the roof or washing the kids or reading the Bible.

When I left Montana four years ago, Jimmy was working at a lumberyard. I was there when the man drove up and said, "Do you want to work, Jim?" Jim, who was busily trimming cedar posts, said, "Yah, I want to work." The man said, "When can you start?" Jim said, "Right now," and handing me the axe he said, "*Sáh-koh-y-nah*, you fix Dad he's lunches." And Jim went to work. Since that time he has been a janitor, a carpenter, a painter, a laborer . . . you name it! He has also done a lot of fire fighting. The Blackfoots, as well as the other tribes in this area, are always on call to fight serious forest fires—sometimes they are flown to the scene of a conflagration as distant as Colorado or California—and they are the very best at that work.

Jim seldom if ever quits a job; the work runs out, that's all. And even when unemployed, Jim never spends an idle day. When no other source of income is available, he cuts fenceposts and firewood, hoping that he can find a buyer. I felt a tug at my guts when I discovered the other day that Jim had invested some of his few dollars in a mail order detective course—anything to try to establish himself in some sort of profession. Of course, Jim did not tell me this; I found portions of the course in his room.

Jim's real dream is to be able to lease some more land and to build up his own herd of cattle. The grass is fine here, and Jim has a pretty good string of horses, but the winters are hard and long, so Jim needs a pretty substantial loan to winter a herd the first year. He has tried to get a loan authorized by the Tribal Council, but to no avail. The Indian Reorganization Act of 1934, which was in great measure beneficial (or at least so intended) to the Indians but which also opened the door to petty political shenanigans on the Reservation, deprived the Chief of any real authority and placed him rather in the position of a contemporary European king. The Canadian Indians still retain their band chiefs, but on the Piegan Reservation it is the Tribal Council which handles business and political affairs, including the tribal funds and the employment, for whatever purpose, of tribal lands. A great deal of the best Blackfoot grazing land has already been leased to White ranchers, and this is a sore point with the Chief. He continually exhorts the Tribe to utilize in their own endeavors more of the Reservation's resources, to raise more cattle of their own. But there are racketeers even among Indians, and the Chief has a lot of opposition. Several years ago, somebody actually took a shot at him. The bullet is still in the living-room wall.

Jim did tell me that he ran for Tribal Council but did not make it. Jim is a full-blood, and the Council is controlled by the breeds, the so-called "educated" Indians, and by those Blackfoots who play up to the politicians and to the large land-holding Whites of the region.

Jim says that some of the Tribal Council members have been pretty square and have sincerely attempted to benefit the Tribe as a whole, but that a great many of the members have been no better than the law allows. The Chief is definitely unhappy with the Wheeler-Howard Act (The Indian Reorganization Act), and from what I have been able to learn, even old Senator Wheeler, who was in large part responsible for the introduction of the Act, is not exactly overjoyed with the results of this piece of legislation. The Chief states flatly that the Tribal Council since its very inception has peculated like poultry on a worm ranch, and although the Chief's claims against the Council are admittedly eristical they are certainly not totally lacking in substance. The Chief described in detail some of the more questionable episodes of the Council's reign, and some of them, including a reputed sojourn in Mexico by Council members at tribal expense, would definitely bear looking into. The Council meets tomorrow, and I am going to attend the meeting.

When the Chief had properly barbecued the Wheeler-Howard Act and the Tribal Council, he launched into a tirade against the treaties which the Federal Government has made with (perpetrated against) the Blackfoot Nation. The Chief's formal education was limited to a short period of attendance at the Fort Shaw Indian School (at which time he was already a grown man), and Jim went only as far as the fourth grade, but Jim reads omniverously and both he and the Chief are remarkably well informed on Blackfoot history and on the current political situation involving the American Indian. The Chief has very definite ideas about how the Indian's position could be bettered through various legislative acts and abrogations on the part of the Federal Government, and the old fellow does not confine his protests to monological grumbling; he directs a torrent of correspondence to both his United States Senator and the Commissioner of Indian Affairs.

The early treaties between the Plains Indian Tribes and the United States Government were, of course, not designed to benefit the Indian but to protect the White migrants and settlers who had begun to invade Plains Indian territory. The White Man was encroaching upon Indian land and the Indian was doing his damnedest to prevent it, but the probability is that most of the Whites killed by Plains Indians prior to the Civil War period had simply happened into the path of a war party which was out to war upon an enemy tribe.

The first White Man's treaty to affect the Blackfoots was the Treaty of Fort Laramie. Acting upon the naïve assumption that the primary cause of intertribal warfare amongst the Plains Indians derived from the fact that the territorial boundaries of the various tribes had never been definitely established, D. D. Mitchell, Superintendent of Indian Affairs in St. Louis, suggested to Washington that the Government should call a council of all Plains Tribes living between Texas and the Missouri River, whereupon would be concluded a unanimously acceptable definition of the territorial limits of all the tribes. In September, 1851, at Ft. Laramie on the Platte River, Mitchell held council with delegates from the Assiniboines, Hidatsas, Mandans and Arikaras (Rees). The Gros Ventres at this time were so closely allied with the Blackfoots as to be considered by some persons a part of the Blackfoot Nation, but later on, following an unprovoked attack by the Gros Ventres on a Piegan camp, the two tribes became bitter enemies. Neither the Blackfoots nor the Gros Ventres had opportunity to be represented at this council, but since a substantial portion of Blackfoot territory was located south of the Missouri, the boundaries of Blackfoot lands were defined in the treaty which the council concluded, the Treaty of Fort Laramie. In other words, the limits of Blackfoot tribal influence were outlined in a treaty which was signed not by the Blackfoots but by tribes hostile to them. The treaty was, naturally, totally ineffectual, and warfare among the various Plains Tribes continued unabated.

The first treaty council in which the Blackfoots had actual participation was held on the north shore of the Missouri, below the mouth of the Judith, during the middle days of October of 1855. (The forthcoming treaty was called "Lame Bulls Treaty," after Lame Bull, the elderly chief who headed the Piegan delegation; however, the Chief informs me that Lame Bull, known also as Lone Chief, had relatively little to do with the actual proceedings at the council and that the main Piegan speaker was a famous orator, Big Snake, whom the Piegans also called Loud Voice.) Present at the council were representatives of the "four" Blackfoot Tribes (Blackfoots, Bloods, Piegans and Gros Ventres) as well as delegations from the Flatheads, Pend d'Oreilles, and Nez Percés. A single Cree chief, Broken Arm, brought tokens of friendship from the Crees and Assiniboines, but the Crows—perhaps the bitterest of all the many enemies of the Piegans—were represented only indirectly by their Nez Percé allies. The idealistic expectation of the Whites was that Lame Bull's Treaty would establish everlasting peace and harmony among all parties involved, and one of the articles of the treaty declared that a large part of the territory which had in the Treaty of Fort Laramie been designated as belonging exclusively to the Blackfoots should now be considered a common hunting ground for *all* the tribes. Furthermore, the Assiniboines, traditional enemies of the Blackfoots, were to be allowed in addition the privilege of hunting in the easternmost portion of Blackfoot land. As might well have been expected, this arrangement worked out somewhat less successfully than the partition of Germany at the close of World War II.

Obviously all these altruistic attempts on the part of the Great White Father to bring peace and tranquility to his Little Red Brothers were not without ulterior motive. The Government wanted tribal boundaries defined in the first place so that it could then treat with the separate tribes regarding passage through and settlement upon their lands by Whites, and in Article VII of Lame Bull's Treaty we find the real reason that the United States went to so much trouble to set up the treaty council. Article VII, which I feel sure the Indians did not understand at all, provided that United States citizens should be guaranteed free navigation of all lakes, rivers and streams, and should be free to pass through and *live in* the territories designated as Indian possessions. Further, the United States would have the privilege of constructing roads of all kinds, stringing telegraph lines, and building everything from agencies and military posts to missions and schools. The Indians were to receive from the United States certain recompense in the form of goods and provisions, and education in such matters as agriculture, mechanical skills, and the White Man's religion.

There is every indication that the Blackfoot chiefs were sincere in their desire to end intertribal warfare, but this aspiration was foredoomed by the failure of the Crows to sign Lame Bull's Treaty and by the lack of control which the chiefs had over the young men of their respective tribes. For the old chiefs to tell their young warriors to suddenly cease making war and stealing enemy horses was equivalent to having the rich old men of a White community inform the young men that from now on there must be no further attempt on their part to gain wealth or to elevate themselves either socially or politically. Following Lame Bull's Treaty, incidents involving Blackfoot and White were relatively minor, but the ancient intertribal rivalries continued.

The beginning of negotiation with the Whites marked the beginning of the end of the Blackfoots as the Power of the Plains. Adhering to a philosophy which has been handed down to our modern-day salesman and advertising agency, the Whites decided that since the Blackfoots were not really the treacherous scoundrels they had been painted but were instead highly intelligent and basically honorable people, this made the Blackfoots fair game for a dirty deal. The White settlers were clamoring for more Blackfoot land, and they got it. Additional treaties were made between the United States and the Blackfoot Nation in 1865 and in 1869; neither treaty was ratified by Congress and so never became United States law, but the ceded land in question was nevertheless thrown open to White settlement. What did the Blackfoots know of congressional ratification! So far as they knew, when a treaty was made, it was made! Who can blame the Blackfoots for becoming perturbed when the payments that they had been promised upon signing the treaties were not forthcoming?

In 1871, the Congress decided to hell with the whole farcical motion of making treaties with the Indians. Thereafter there would be no treaties—indeed, from that time onward the Congress would no longer recognize the sovereignty of any individual Indian tribe. From then on, an Indian was an Indian and the only good Indian was a dead Indian and in 1873–74, by presidential orders and congressional acts, the southern boundary of the Blackfoot territory was shoved northward over two hundred miles and the land thrown open to White farmers and stockmen. No payment for the land was made to the Blackfoots, and arbitrarily the Blackfoots, the Gros Ventres, the Assiniboines, and the River Crow Indians were all placed upon the same reservation. The instigator of this congressional action was one Martin Maginnis, Montana's territorial delegate in Washington. Maginnis, who was nothing but the willing tool of Montana's land-hungry White pressure groups, has overcome stiff opposition to win my nomination as the rottenest politician in the history of Montana. In opposition to Maginnis was Blackfoot Agent R. F. May, whose courageous championing of the rights of his Indian charges resulted in his being dismissed from his post. May was succeeded as Agent by John Wood, a man with no administrative experience who had recently been a city marshal in the State of Iowa. When Chief White Calf (Onistáipokah), my Indian grandfather, who had by this time become *de facto* head chief of the Piegans, complained to Wood against the taking by the Whites of the finest portions of Blackfoot land, Wood replied that the Indians had more land than they needed and that if each Indian would cultivate ten acres of soil he could easily support ten persons for the entire year. One prominent ethnologist and historian (who incidentally has spent nearly his entire career in government employ) has referred to Wood's statement as a "common sense argument." This attitude conveniently ignores the facts that the Blackfoots were hunters, not farmers, and that the Blackfoot land in question was, for reason of soil, climate and other factors, totally unsuited to agriculture.

But still the Whites pressed for more and yet more of Blackfoot land. No sooner had the Whites succeeded in killing off the last of the buffalo herds—the great northern herd, which had grazed primarily in the Blackfoot hunting grounds—than our old friend, Delegate Maginnis, introduced into the House of Representatives a bill designed to deprive the Blackfoots of this rich expanse of grazing land and to open the area to White settlement. This time Maginnis found opposition; the Commissioner of Indian Affairs objected to the bill on the grounds that any further land cessions should be negotiated with the Indian tribes involved. The Congress, deciding that henceforth the Indian should be cheated of his lands with all due legality, acquiesced in favor of the Commissioner's position and proceeded to authorize, in May, 1886, the appointment of the Northwest Commission for the purpose of negotiating in the field with the "Sioux, Assiniboine, Gros Ventre and Blackfoot Indians of Montana" for the cession of "so much of their land as they do not require, in order to obtain the means to enable them to become self-supporting, as a pastoral and agricultural people, and to educate their children in the paths of civilization."

With regard to cession of additional lands to the United States Government, the Indians had absolutely no choice. With the buffalo gone, the Indian had no way of surviving without assistance from the Federal Government, and the only thing the Indian possessed with which to barter for Government supplies was his land.

But the portion of Indian land now sought by the Government —some 17,500,000 acres, or nearly nine-tenths of the entire Blackfoot Reservation—was immense, and the Northwest Commission was cut to the quick upon learning that the Blackfoots, under the leadership of the intelligent and knowledgeable Onistáipokah, were not eager to accept the paltry sum of 1½ million dollars for this tremendous expanse of some of the finest grazing land on the North American continent. The chiefs demanded 3 million dollars for their land (an amount still far below the going price for Montana land at that time) and in a communication to the Secretary of the Interior we find the Commissioner whining that "the Indians had been tampered with by designing white men whom we found at the Agency—men who hoped to gain some advantage to themselves, in one way or another." I have been unable to find any record of exactly who these "designing white men" were supposed to have been, nor have I located any explanation of exactly how these men might have benefited from the Indian's receiving a fair price for his land (which was to be paid for not in money but in such things as commodities, livestock, medical and educational facilities, etc.), but the Report of Negotiations of the Commissioners states that it required "long and patient reasoning" to induce the Indians to accept as payment the per annum sum of $150,000 for ten years.

According to the Chief, who in company with his father, Onistái-pokah, was actually present at this land sale, the only tampering with the Indians was done by the commissioners themselves; "long and patient reasoning" by the commission consisted in their threatening the minor chiefs, who had been assigned by the Agent to such petty posts of authority as policeman or judge, that if they did not agree to the terms laid down by the commission it would mean the loss of their jobs. This land sale, which included the sale of the Sweetgrass Hills and became the basis of what the Blackfoots later called the Sweetgrass Claim, was described to me by the Chief:

> When we sold the Sweetgrass Range it was cold weather, but there was not very much snow on the roads and I was able to drive my father to the meeting in a wagon. The meeting was held at Joe Kipp's trading post, at Old Agency. At this time my father was head chief of the Piegans, but all the minor chiefs were there as well, and everybody took a vote on how much they would ask for Sweetgrass Range. My father did not wish to sell for less than $3,000,000, but some of the others, who did not know the value of a dollar, were anxious to accept the Government's offer of 1½ million. On my father's side were Mad Wolf, Wolf Plume, Double Runner, Lone Gun, and Eagle Ribs. On the opposing side were Bear Chief, Three Sun, Calf Sitting, White Grass, Horn, Gambler, and several others.
>
> My father asked $3,000,000 for the Sweetgrass Range because he felt that when the Government offered the Indian a price for anything, the price could be doubled and the Indian still would not be getting a fair deal. But no Piegan chief ever had complete authority—not even the head chief. All the chiefs took a vote, and the vote of the head chief counted no more than any other vote. My father and his supporters were outvoted by a large majority led by Bear Chief and Big Nose [Three Sun], so the Sweetgrass was sold for 1½ million.
>
> Those who opposed my father on this issue—including Big Nose, who was band chief of the Grease Melters, and a notorious drunkard—were so ignorant that they did not even know

how much a dollar was worth. The commissioners attempted to show these men how much value the money represented by using beans. They opened a one-hundred-pound sack of beans and counted the beans into a barrel. Each bean was intended to represent ten dollars, the value of the bean being suggested by the commissioners' pointing to some article in the trading post, or to a horse or a cow or a wagon, and then showing how many beans would be required to purchase that particular item.

Then each Indian present at the meeting counted one hundred beans into the barrel, each in turn, until the proper amount had been arrived at. There were over two hundred Piegan men at the meeting, and when they had counted around only once, Bear Chief and Big Nose and some of the others said that that was all they wanted because now they had enough money to last them the rest of their lives. Then my father told them that they hadn't yet counted even half of the amount the Government had offered, so they listened to him.

When finally the amount of payment was settled, Big Nose said that he wanted the payment to be made to the Indians in cash. And then my father spoke, and I remember his words:

"Do you remember the time we were coming home from the war party down at Cree House! Do you remember how cold it was! Do you remember that we burned bunch grass to warm ourselves because we had no other fuel! If we take this payment in money and give it to the people, the money will disappear as fast as that bunch grass burned. We will see to it that the money is used in the manner most profitable to our people. We will use the money to buy for the people cattle—and horses and machinery and other things that they will need in order to raise the cattle. We do not want gardens, and we do not want any chickens or hogs or sheep. Our land is grazing land, and now that the buffalo are gone we must graze cattle."

My father had his way, and he went personally to Washington to see the President and to ask that most of the payment for the Sweetgrass Range be made to the Indians in the form of heifers and bulls, and also some big Morgan stallions to breed into our horse herds.

Finally the Government sent us a thousand heifers, but once again there was argument amongst the Piegans. My father wanted to summer the cattle on the western part of the Reservation; in this way the herd would be kept near our homes where we could keep an eye on them. But the agent wanted to graze the herd on the eastern part of the Reservation, and once again my father and his supporters were outvoted. The cattle were summered on the east side, and when we rounded them up that fall nearly half of them were missing. I don't know who stole them—it might have been Whites, or half-breeds, or the Agent himself—but the cattle were gone.

The culprit in this case almost certainly was the Agent who, like most agents and supervisors of the Blackfoot Reservation before and since, had private cattle interests bordering Reservation land. The Chief says that the Agent would not allow the Indians to brand the cattle, and that it was rumored that the Agent had his own cowboys run part of the herd off and affix to them his own brand. I do not doubt this, just as I do not doubt that Agent George Steel caused a mis-count of the Agency herd by getting the Indian cowboys drunk and having them drive the same cattle through the chutes three or four times. Even as late as the 1930's, large numbers of Indian cattle were disappearing from the Blackfoot Reservation. (This was not the only racketeering of Indian property going on at that time, and it was during the 1930's that Superintendent Mc-Fatridge was ousted from his job and sentenced to a term in a federal prison.)

From the very beginning, the Indian agent situation has been a sordid one. The agent was appointed ostensibly for the purpose of protecting the interests of the Indian, but those few that honestly attempted to fulfill this mission were summarily dismissed from their posts, particularly during the administration of President Grant. A lot of the crooked agents were bounced too, but only if their thievery became so obvious as to threaten the position of the politicians who had appointed them. The position of Indian Agent was for many years simply a political plum; the agent appointee had no knowledge of or interest in the Indian situation, his sole concern being in how speedily he could divert Indian appropriations to his own pocketbook. Often the agent did not reside on the Reservation—during one period of eighteen months, the Blackfoots were not even *visited* by an agent—and although official records and correspondence (from which so many of our contemporary "Indian experts" derive their information) are apt to sparkle with purity, the fact is that most of the employees of the Indian Service in the United States during the past century were persons of low degree. As Mari Sandoz has pointed out in her fine book, *Cheyenne Autumn*, even Abraham Lincoln, "The Great Emancipator," was so

86

concerned with human rights that he handed out the job of Indian agent as political spoils to men so incompetent or so untrustworthy as to be unsuited to any (other) governmental post. One of Lincoln's appointees to the Indian Service amassed a large fortune from a job which paid only $1200 a year.

The final Government grab of Piegan land was possibly the most hypocritical of all. In September, 1895, three commissioners met with the Piegans (the Indian tribes of Montana had since 1888 been assigned to separate reservations, and the Bloods and North Blackfoots and North Piegans had long since been subjects of the Queen) to negotiate for purchase of the westernmost portion of what remained of Blackfoot territory in the United States. The Government had by this time finally conceded that the Piegan Reservation was "wholly unfit" for agriculture, and the ostensibly altruistic motive behind the purchase was to provide the Piegans with money with which they could stock their remaining lands with cattle. The Chief, who refers to this land cession as "the time we sold the Rocky Mountains," tells me that the whole deal was whipped up in the first place by Agent Steel, by that so-called "friend of the Indian," George Bird Grinnell, and by other Whites who had become convinced that the territory in question, the eastern portion of the Continental Divide in northern Montana, contained gold in large quantities. Events subsequent to the land sale would tend to bear out the Chief's contention.

The commissioners offered $1,250,000 for the land, but once again old Onistáipokah and his supporters held out for $3,000,000. At length a compromise was reached; the Government agreed to provide the Piegans for ten years with $150,000 worth of annual benefits in the form of such things as cows and bulls, clothing, rations, mechanical implements, medicine and medical facilities, the erection of agency buildings, mills, blacksmith and carpenter shops, etc., and the payment of agents and agency employees (few persons appear to be aware that it was the Indian, not the Federal Government, who provided in one way or another the salaries of agency personnel). This agreement was in effect a ten year extension of the Act of 1888 which involved the cession of the Sweetgrass Range.

The great hypocrisy of this act, the Act of 1896, was in the failure of the United States to honor provisions with regard to the rights of the Piegans to certain privileges attaining to the ceded territory. The Act guaranteed that the Piegans should retain hunting, fishing and timber rights in the ceded portion "so long as it shall remain public lands of the United States." The Chief says that his father, Onistáipokah, believed also that the Piegans were to retain all mineral rights except those pertaining to surface deposits. But in 1898 the ceded land was thrown open to White prospectors, and hundreds of Whites scoured the region in search of gold (of which, I delight in reporting, there was none). Adding injury to insult, the Government then declared most of the ceded territory a national park (Glacier National Park), and although the question of whether the use of land as a national park removes it from the category of "public lands" is still open to dispute, the Piegans have been denied access to the resources of their former land which was guaranteed by the act under which the territory was ceded to the United States.

Probably the most tragic single effect of the White Man's intrusion upon the Blackfoot way of life was the notorious "starvation winter" of 1883–84, during which so many of the Chief's people perished for the simple want of enough food. This terrible event was a direct result of the disappearance from the Plains of the Blackfoot staff of life, the buffalo, but the occasion is rendered even more horrible by the fact that although there was adequate warning to the Whites that the Piegans were about to face a period of great privation, no measures were taken to meliorate the situation.

A definite warning that the last of the buffalo herds, the great northern herd upon which the Blackfoots relied for sustenance, was fast disappearing, came in 1879 when the Canadian Blackfoots found no buffalo north of the "medicine line" (the International Boundary). At this time the Blackfoots were still living in their traditional bands and traveling freely between Canada and the United States, and when Canadian Indian Commissioner Edgar B. Dewdney saw that his Indian charges were suffering for want of food, he issued them such provisions as he was able and advised them to cross the line into the States. This action gave the Canadian Government time to set up a program of assistance to the Indians, who by this time were dependent upon the Government for their very lives. And yet, when four years later the Indians of the United States were faced with a similar situation, Agent John W. Young of the South Piegan Reservation refused to allow his "children" to cross into Canada to participate in the annual food distribution which the Canadian Indian Commission was about to undertake.

Agent Young remains a controversial figure to this day; he has been alternately cursed and canonized by historians attempting to establish the blame for the Starvation Winter. In my opinion, Young was neither saint nor sinner. Granted that Major John Young was exasperatingly G.I. in his refusal to allow the Piegans to draw Canadian rations, the records show that in each of his annual reports after 1880 Young emphasized the increasing scarcity of game available to the Piegans and the alarmingly increasing number of Indians who were dependent upon Government rations. According to official figures, in 1881 there were 605 Indians camped near the Agency; in 1882, the number had increased to 1955; and in 1883, at which time only a small percentage of the Piegans participated in the unfruitful hunt for buffalo, about 3000 Indians were camped near the Agency in hopes of drawing sufficient rations to carry them through the winter.

Indian Bureau funds for the purchase of rations were estimated and budgeted a year in advance, and when early fall of 1883 found Young already forced to issue the Indians only ¼ rations, he earnestly petitioned for additional appropriations from Washington. In late September, a communication from the Commissioner of Indian Affairs informed Young that appropriations for the Blackfoot Agency had already been exhausted and that no further appropriation was forthcoming. Young immediately submitted his resignation, although he remained at his post until relieved by Reuben Allen the following April. In the interim, the only relief sent to the Blackfoot Agency was a small shipment of cattle which arrived in December. A sizeable quantity of bacon was also freighted in, but it was so rancid and so filled with worms that the Agency doctor condemned it as unfit for human consumption.

With regard to the responsibility of the Federal Government in this matter, several questions present themselves:

(1) Why, despite strong warnings in the form of the sudden disappearance of the buffalo north of the International Boundary in 1879 and the increasing scarcity of buffalo in the Blackfoot hunting grounds, was no legislation undertaken to stop or at least to regulate the continuing slaughter of the buffalo by White hide hunters?

(2) Why, when the number of Piegans camped near the Agency in 1883 was officially estimated at 3000 (and this represented only a portion of the tribe), was the official census of the Piegan Reservation for reason of Government appropriations numbered at less than 2500?

(3) If, as some defenders of the Government have claimed, it was not possible to freight supplies to the Piegan Agency because

of deep winter snow, how was it then possible to freight in plenty of supplies to the army posts in that area and to the trading posts which supplied the wants of the White ranchers of the region. And why did not the freighters come through in the summertime when the snow was gone? (The Chief tells me that most of the actual starvation among the Piegans occurred in the late spring and early summer, when supplies were completely exhausted.)

(4) Why did not the White ranchers, who were illegally running thousands of cattle on Blackfoot land, make some effort to aid the totally distressed Indians whose land they were using? (A few of the small White ranchers did attempt to help out, but unanimously the big cattle outfits evidenced concern only that the starving Piegans might kill some of their cows.)

(5) Why did John Schuyler Crosby, Governor of Montana, wait until August 29, 1884—at which time the Piegans had been in a state of starvation for more than a full year—before sending an indignant protest to the Secretary of the Interior against "keeping the Nation's wards within the limits of this territory in such pitiable, starving condition." Crosby concluded his pharisaical little phillipic with, "Humanity and justice demand their immediate relief." But he failed to comment upon his own lengthy delay in taking issue with a situation about which he had surely possessed a full awareness for many months.

All these questions have a single answer, and the beginning of that answer is to be found in official statements of the Indian Rights Association, which investigated the matter with admirable thoroughness. For months the Indian Rights Association labored to convince the Congress of the fearful condition of the Piegans and of the necessity for immediate action upon the matter of emergency appropriation for their relief. But not until the Association submitted an open letter to the press stating that the procrastination of Congressman John Ellis, Chairman of the House Sub-committee on Indian Appropriations, was jeopardizing the lives of hundreds of Indians, did Ellis consent to introduce a joint resolution calling for $50,000 to be made immediately available for the assistance of the Indians. Once introduced, the resolution passed both Houses of Congress in two days.

But for our real answer we must seek out the motives behind the actions (or lack of same) of such men as Ellis, Governor Crosby of Montana, and Montana Delegate Martin Maginnis. Maginnis, in company with Senator George Vest of Missouri, actually was on a tour of inspection of conditions on the Piegan Reservation on September 14, 1883 (although his real purpose in being there apparently was to seek out the possibility of further land cessions by the Piegans), and although he witnessed with his own eyes the beginnings of real starvation among the Indians, he failed to inaugurate any action which might have prevented the unspeakable suffering of the following winter.

Why did these things occur? The answer is perfectly apparent, and well known to students of the history of Montana, but so far as I know nobody has ever had the guts to come right out and say it. The facts are as follows:

(1) No effort was made to preserve the buffalo because General Sherman, who is tenderly remembered by the South and especially by the State of Georgia, decided that the best way to destroy the Indian was to remove his ability to provide for himself and so make him totally dependent upon the Federal Government. (This is a political expediency which has been employed with success since the earliest recorded periods of human society, and one which is still being expounded by various governments throughout the world —and if the moccasin fits, put it on!)

(2) Certain territorial and federal officials made no effort to aid the Plains Indian. They undertook, in fact, every effort to destroy him, because the powerful White cattlemen—and some of the Montana cattle interests were immensely powerful—wanted the Indian's land. The public officials in question were nothing more than the pawns of the cattle barons (and the mining and railroad interests, etc.) that had put them in office.

There it is, in a nutshell.

When the afternoon's discussion reached a point which suggested a possible opening for such an inquiry, I rather tentatively asked the Chief whether he remembered the Starvation Year. By way of reply, he looked at me steadily for a moment and then said, "I was already a grown man." Long moments of silence followed, and as I began to accept that the Chief quite understandably had dismissed my question, the old fellow began to speak again. At first his remarks were scattered—some of them really quite extraneous —and I knew that he was finding it difficult to discuss this most tragic event. And when finally he found the words with which to convey to me the facts of the Starvation Year, the minute details which welled from his memory and, I felt, from the substance of his very soul, suggested that the marks upon him from this awful experience had not hardened into mere scars but were still open and painful wounds.

THE STARVATION YEAR

At that time they had moved the Agency from Four Persons [Choteau] to Running Crane's place on Big Badger Creek. Now they were moving it again to Old Agency. Most of the things were hauled in two-wheeled ox-carts, and most of the work was done by women. A log stockade was being built around the Agency, and this work was done by the women too. At that time our men had good horses and they were hunters and they did not do women's work. At that time Chief Calf, also known as Buffalo Head, whose influence as head chief of the Piegans was shared by my father, Onistáipokah, died over in Canada. Chief Calf had promised to give Skunk Cap a horse, and when he broke his promise, Skunk Cap performed a secret ceremony to bring Chief Calf bad luck. Two days after the ceremony, Chief Calf died. They brought Chief Calf back home and buried him on a ridge near Old Agency. Before that year was over, hundreds of Piegans were to be buried on that same ridge.

Before the stockade around Old Agency had been completed, the Starvation Year began. The buffalo were gone. My father had led us on the winter hunt the year before, and we had found plenty of buffalo. The old men had called the buffalo with the Beaver Power, and with the power of the Thunder Pipe they had caused the direction of the wind to change so that we had a good chase and brought back many robes and plenty of meat. But this year the herds did not return, and although some of us went deep into the Crow country, we found only a few scattered groups of buffalo—barely enough to feed us on the hunt.

The buffalo were gone, and although there had been other years when we did not find the big herds, this year the old people all knew that the herds would never come again. For them, the old people, it was as though the sun had disappeared from the sky. The old ladies dug wild turnips and gathered wild rhubarb and such berries as they could find, but there was no fat with which to make pemmican for the months ahead. Some of them ate prairie dogs and foxes and badgers and anything else they could trap, and some of the old men just sat in their lodges and waited.

During a pause, I asked the Chief if the Agency had not issued rations to the Indians. He continued his fragmented but informative narration:

The Agency issued rations, but not nearly enough to keep a person alive. Each week they gave out a little flour and sugar and sometimes a small piece of meat. On Friday they would butcher maybe two or three cows from the Agency herd, and they would distribute the meat on Saturday, which was ration day at that time. But when you divide a couple of beeves up amongst about three thousand people, nobody gets very much. Thursday we called Nothing-Happens-Day, because by then all the people would be starving and just sitting around waiting for the next rations. Every day people died of starvation, and a lot of others died because they were too weak to resist pneumonia and other diseases. [Father Prando, who had established a small mission just south of Birch Creek, the southern boundary of the Reservation, reported at this time that a serious epidemic of erysipelas was proving fatal to many of the enfeebled Piegans.]

I am not ashamed to admit that it was difficult and even painful for me to ask the Chief direct questions about the Starvation Year, but I knew that this was probably the last opportunity that I or anyone else would have to record an intelligent, eyewitness—indeed, actual participation—account of this moment of history, and when Jim assured me that the Chief was willing and even anxious to relate the story to me because he wanted the truth to be remembered, I gritted my emotional teeth and asked the Chief if he knew how many Piegans had actually died at that time. The old fellow shook his head and said, "I do not know. No one will ever know. Everybody from little tots to old people died. A lot of the younger people were not even registered at the Agency because after Baker's Massacre the Piegans were afraid to let the Army know that they had children. Many times when people died, the family would just bury them and say nothing so that they could keep drawing the extra rations. Such rations as there were, the Agency distributed to the families on a per capita basis."

I asked the Chief whether he thought that as many as 500 persons might have died. He said, "More than that. Many more than that. At first they buried them, but after a while there were so many that they just left the rough boxes (rough coffins) on top of the ridge right out in the open." (The Agent's report for the year of July 1883 to July 1884 numbered only 247 deaths among the Piegans "from all causes." This report is ludicrously inaccurate! Known deaths among the Piegans during the Starvation Year numbered well over five hundred, the actual number almost certainly being in excess of 600.)

I asked the Chief whether he personally considered the Agent responsible for the Starvation Year. He replied, "I don't know whose fault it was. When the starvation began, our agent was a man we called Wolf Necklace (John Young). When he wanted something done, he did not ask the Indians the way he should have; he told them what to do as though he were talking to a pack of camp dogs. He did not sit and smoke with the old men, and when the old chiefs gave him presents, he did not give them presents in return. The Piegans did not like Wolf Necklace, and when the starvation began, many of the people blamed him. One fellow, Hump Back, tried to kill him. He shot at Wolf Necklace with a rifle, but he missed.

"My father did not blame Wolf Necklace for the starvation. My father told the people that Wolf Necklace was not giving us rations because there were no rations to give. He told the people that the officials in Washington had not sent the rations they had promised, so we should not blame Wolf Necklace for something that was not his fault.

"I remember one good thing that Wolf Necklace did for the people. Near the Agency there was a trading post—a place the Piegans called Outside-of-Town-House—and when a freight wagon of supplies for the trading post arrived at the Agency, Wolf Necklace requisitioned the supplies and distributed them to the Piegans. Shortly after that, Wolf Necklace was fired by the Government."

Actually, Young resigned voluntarily, albeit midst an audible sough of relief from Whites in both Montana and Washington. So far as I have been able to learn, Young's requisitioning of civilian property for distribution to the Indians was never officially protested, but this is no indication that the action did not occur. Civilian traders on Indian land maintained their establishments only through license by the Federal Government, and since scarcely a wagonload of freight arrived in Indian country innocent of contraband—ever since 1834 it had been illegal to sell or trade whiskey to the Indians in the United States, and in 1876, as a result of Custer's getting his pants kicked by Indians in possession of repeating arms, President Grant had issued an order forbidding the sale of metallic cartridges or fixed ammunition to "hostile Indians," including the Blackfoots—the agents of the various reservations were usually in a pretty commanding position with regard to the traders. My guess would be that Young told the trader that he could either allow the supplies to be distributed to the Indians or else face a charge of illegal whiskey trading.

Few persons are aware, I am sure, of the terrible effect of the White Man's whiskey upon the Indian. The North American Indian represented one of the very few aboriginal groups in the world whose culture contained no form of intoxicant, and the "Blackfoot rum"—actually an eight to one mixture of water and alcohol, frequently spiced with such things as red pepper, black tobacco, molasses and even gun powder—which the traders introduced to the Blackfoots was to them both physically and psychologically murderous. Drunken Indians, completely out of their minds on a few cups of traders' whiskey, not only murdered one another but died like flies from exposure and from the toxic effects of the "Black water" itself. According to the report of one agent in Montana, during the six years between 1867 and 1873, *twenty-five percent* of the Blackfoot Nation died from the effects of alcohol alone.

A year is one hell of a long time, especially when you are starving, and I could not feature anyone as tough-gutted as the Chief just sitting around all during the Starvation Year and doing nothing. I had to ask him: "Wasn't there anything your father could do to help the people? And what about you young guys—couldn't you have gone out hunting, or packed in supplies from Canada?" These questions really heated up the old fellow's eyes, and from then on I just sat back and listened.

When the hard times began, my father already had his own small herd of cattle down at Dupuyer. Right from the beginning, when the Government wanted the Piegans to become farmers, my father had refused. My father had said that it was not possible to be a farmer on the Piegan lands, so from the very first he put all he had into cattle. And my father was right. Some Piegans tried to raise crops, but they would not grow. Most of the things they planted froze right in the ground. But my father had a pretty good herd of cattle down there at Dupuyer, and they were being taken care of by an honest White man, Jim Grant, who was the father of old Dick Grant, and when the great hunger began, my father killed his cattle and shared the meat with the other old people. He even killed his horses to help feed the people. All the Piegans killed their horses. In the old days when we could not find forage for our horses we would feed the horses the inner bark of the cottonwood tree, which is soft and oily. But by the spring of Starvation Year there were no horses to feed because the Piegans had eaten them—they had even eaten their dogs and cats—so the Piegans ate the cottonwood bark themselves. That is how hungry they were.

Naturally we young men hunted for game—and not just the youngsters, either. Some of the old-timers went along, too, and every day we were hunting for elk and deer and trying to catch fish. In the wintertime we chopped holes in the ice and fished. But there is only just so much game to be found, and even before the snow came the elk had moved to the far ranges and the deer could no longer be found. The best luck I had with my old muzzle-loader was high in the mountains hunting the wild goats. The goat is very curious, just like the antelope, and we used to hunt them the same way. You make sure the wind is right so that they cannot smell you, and then you hide behind a rock and tie a piece of cloth on the end of a stick and wave it slowly back and forth. You must have a lot of patience to hunt in this manner, but if you wait long enough, the goat will come up close to see what is going on, and then you have your chance at him. We also hunted by building traps and deadfalls, and there were so many pits and deadfalls along the trails that a man had to be very careful where he was stepping. During the summer and fall we got some bears in these deadfalls, and this was always good news because we were very hungry for fat. In the wintertime we would sometimes go out for days just trying to find a place where a bear had denned up for the winter. Venison is very lean, and so is horsemeat, and we could not get enough fat.

But all the wild game we got that year put together would not have filled the bellies of all the Piegans for more than a couple of weeks. There simply was not enough game to be found, and before the Starvation Year was over we were boiling hooves and bones and scavenging across the prairie like a bunch of magpies. We even came to eat the flesh of dead wolves and coyotes, and it is strange how this came about: when the buffalo did not return to Canada [in 1879] the Canadians [Canadian Indians] came down to the United States looking for the buffalo, and the wolves came too. At that time the White men were killing the buffalo for the hide and leaving the meat or most of it lying out there on the prairie, and the wolves and coyotes had plenty to eat and were fat and had many young. There were more wolves on the prairie than you could possibly imagine, and they had lost their shyness of man; sometimes they would just sit and wait for you to finish butchering a buffalo so they could make a meal. But the joke was on the White Man. When an Indian killed a buffalo he took almost every part of it with him, leaving very little for the wolves. But the Whites left almost the whole buffalo for the wolves, and so the wolves followed the scent of the White Man, and when pretty soon all the buffalo were gone, the wolves began to eat the White Man's cattle and sheep.

So then the White ranchers had to call in wolf hunters to get rid of the wolves. You know how the ribs on a deer are; the flesh is very thin over the ribs, and if you skin a deer and leave the carcass there in the open, pretty soon the flesh on the ribs becomes almost like *kuy-yis* [meat that is preserved by slicing it very thin and drying it as rapidly as possible]. Well, buffalo is the same way, so when we got very hungry we began to hunt for buffalo carcasses from which the wolves and ravens had not removed all the meat. But soon we learned that we had to be very careful. We found large numbers of dead wolves, and we learned that the White hunters were killing the wolves by putting poison in the buffalo carcasses. So we were afraid to eat the buffalo—we were even afraid to cook the buffalo bones, because sometimes the White hunters would poison the marrow bones—but when we found a wolf dead close beside a buffalo we knew that the wolf had died very quickly of the poison and that the poison had not had a chance to spread through its body, so very carefully we cut off the wolf's head and neck and removed all the insides, making certain not to puncture them with the knife, and then we boiled the flesh of the wolf for a long time and then ate it. There were quite a few dead wolves.

You ask me why we did not pack in supplies from Canada. Well, we did. The police on both sides of the line tried to stop us, and when we got stopped we had to lie a lot, but we did not get caught often because we went only in one's and two's. Our relatives among the Bloods did their best to help us, but they had only just so much to give us and there was only just so much we could bring back. It was not enough. I crossed over on horseback and my uncle Running Wolf came back with me. We brought several parflèches of *mukáhkin* [a type of pemmican composed largely of ground dry meat, rendered fat and chokecherries] and of dried savis berries. When my uncle saw how bad things were over here, he left his horse here and went back on foot. I went over several times on foot myself, and one way or another I always managed to come back on a horse. The people ate not only the food I brought back on the horse but the horse itself. But this was not enough to stop the hunger, and by the spring of the year the people were so bad off that they were boiling their parflèches and their buckskin clothes and even their lodge covers and their moccasins.

One amazing aspect of this tragic situation is that the Blackfoots did not raid in force the herds of White-owned cattle that were grazing adjacent to and even actually upon the Blackfoot land. It has been widely supposed that the Piegans were deterred by fear of military reprisal against their helpless women and children (the Army's vicious and unconscionable massacre of defenseless Piegan women and children on the Marias River in the winter of 1870 was still fresh in the minds of the Indians), and the Chief's testimony convinces me that this supposition is correct. The Chief admitted that he personally had butchered a few of the White Man's beef calves, and he said that he was afraid to admit these thefts even to his own father. With a small, wry smile, the Chief phrased it this way: "One of the Wolves that took the White Man's stock was named Running Wolf." (The Chief had taken as his Indian name the name of his uncle, Running Wolf.)

The only really sizeable and overt effort at cattle-rustling conducted by the Piegans during this period occurred during the summer following the Starvation Winter. The Chief was in the thick of it, of course, and he tells the story this way:

When Wolf Necklace [Agent Young] was fired, we got a new agent. We called him New Chief [Reuben Allen], and we called his assistant Good Person [?] because he was very kind to the people and even gave away his own clothes to those old persons that did not have any. When New Chief arrived [in April], he called my father to the Agency Office and told him that from now on things would be different on the Reservation. But things were not different. New Chief brought only words, not food, and when the summertime came the people were still going hungry.

At that time the Agency had a herd of cattle branded ID [Indian Department], but they would not slaughter enough of these cattle to feed the people. They would kill only a few cattle each week, the same as before, and while the people starved the cattle grazed right there in plain sight. The herd was guarded by Indian police.

It got to be the middle of the summer, and still we had nothing from the Agent but promises, so four of us young men made plans to rustle a beef. We told the Agent that we were going fishing, but instead we went down to visit the Grease Melters Band to tell some of our friends there our plans. That night, when it was dark, the four of us took a cow from the edge of the herd and took it into some trees by a stream and butchered it. Then we built a fire and began to cook some of the meat.

Just as we were starting to cook the meat we heard somebody coming. Two of the fellows said that they had heard someone speak in the Flathead language, so we all hid in the brush. But it was only some of the boys from the Grease Melters, meeting us as planned.

During the evening more and more fellows showed up, until there were forty of us all together. We stayed there all night, and among the forty of us we ate that entire beef.

That night we made plans to rustle some more beef. It was decided that Curved Ribs, Flathead Eagle, and I would "borrow" some horses and run off the rest of the herd. At dawn the boys drifted out, two by two, and Curved Ribs and Flathead Eagle and I collected some horses and hid out behind a hill from about ten that morning till around five o'clock that afternoon. Then finally Curved Ribs said, "Boys, those cattle belong to the Indians. The Government sent those cattle here to feed us, and since the Agent won't give them to us we will just go and help ourselves."

So then we jumped on our horses and raided the herd. Our plan was to run off a group of twenty-three cattle that were being grazed about a quarter of a mile from where the Badger Creek Agency had been and to drive them to the fork of Blacktail Creek. There, at the fork of Blacktail, some of the other boys were to have a corral ready. We figured that by raiding at this time of day we would just about have time to drive the cattle to the corral by dark; we figured that the Indian Police, who were not mounted, would not be able to track us until the following day.

When we made our raid, the Indian Police tried to stop us by heading us off on foot, but there were only two of them guarding the herd and they were nothing but foolish old men anyway so we just laughed. At first they ordered us to stop, and then they promised that if we would leave the herd alone they would give us a beef apiece, but we laughed in their faces and drove off the whole bunch, all 23 of them.

We reached the corral in good time, and immediately butchered one of the beeves. As soon as the meat had been divided, I took my share and rode down to my father's camp on Birch Creek. I arrived just as my mother was preparing supper. I said, "Father, why don't you send out and invite all the old people in for supper. We have meat."

My father said, "Who brought meat to us?"

I said, "Your son brings you meat." I was really afraid that my father would give me a bad time for stealing the Agency cattle, but he did not. When I told him what had happened, he said, "Good! Those cattle are rightfully ours, and you had a right to take them. Perhaps our Agent will learn a lesson from what you have done."

My father asked how many cattle we had taken, and I told him that we had twenty-two in addition to the one we had already butchered. Early the next morning we moved up to Blacktail Creek and butchered the remainder of the cattle and distributed the meat to the people. But although we spent all that day at Blacktail Creek, and camped there that night, it was not until around noon of the following day that the Indian Police finally showed up. White Grass and another old man came up and told my father that the Agent wanted to see the two of us. My father told them to wait until after lunch and then we would all go down to the Agency together.

When we arrived at the Agency, the Agent asked my father whether he knew that some of the Agency herd had been run off and butchered. My father said, "Yes, I know that." The Agent asked my father why he had allowed this to be done, and my father said, "If you want to know why, step outside and look up toward the ridge and see the rough boxes that are piled there. Your answer is inside those boxes." Then my father turned on his heel and left, and I went with him.

The Chief was through talking. Nobody needed to tell me so, but when the Chief concluded his tale of the Starvation Year the story-telling was over for the time being and none of us commented upon this fact nor would (or could) we have expressed the emotional impact which the story had had on all of us, both teller and listeners. I am not an habitual smoker, but during the Chief's narration of the Starvation Winter I had asked Jim in sign language to roll me a Bull Durham cigarette. I had had trouble in finding my mouth with the cigarette, and I had burned my fingers.

Jim split blocks for the remainder of the afternoon, and I took a long walk along the creek bottom, looking for deer sign. We need meat. The Piegans are of course denied the right of hunting in Glacier Park, but they do benefit from the overflow of game from that protected area. The Reservation—our end of it, at least—is situated smack up against the Park, and on the Reservation the Indians are allowed to hunt all year round.

At supper we all ate appreciatively. Afterward the Chief related seven traditional "Nahpi" stories. I recorded them, but after the Starvation Winter they held little interest for me. We were all very tired and went to bed early.

For an hour or so I lay awake, pondering the difficulty of evoking through the literary medium a truly valid portrait of the Indian personality and the Indian life—and still getting your stuff published. Even A. B. Guthrie, a truly fine western writer, admits that his

CARL A. RUDISILL LIBRARY
LENOIR RHYNE COLLEGE

really *good* stories have trouble in finding a market, so I guess there is nothing remarkable in the fact that "Horserace," which is probably the best thing I have ever written, is still searching for a home. (My favorite rejection of "Horserace" is the one in which the editor informs me that I achieved a marvelous effect within the story but that I did not achieve this effect in the proper manner. In other words, the writer should achieve something original but he should achieve it in a perfectly conventional manner, which same is impossible.)

The basic problem, of course, is that most people—including most editors—are so steeped in misinformation about the Indian that they flatly reject any writing about the Indian which does not serve to fortify their own hard won misconceptions. The situation is not a happy one for the serious writer, and today I became so disheartened with the whole effort that I did not even type up my journal for the day. Actually, this is being written tomorrow—that is to say, Thursday. Jim and the Chief left for town right after breakfast and I have been typing ever since. It is now nearly 11:00 A.M., September 6.

Last night when I conked out, the Chief was still chanting his prayers.

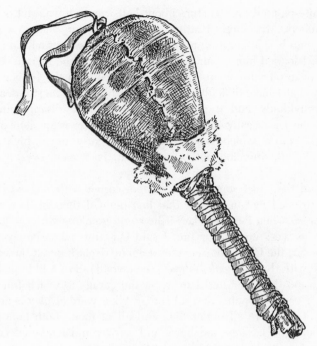

Medicine Rattle

Last night, before going to bed, Jim said, "It's going to be a cold tonight." And it was. Jim was up and had the pancakes turning when I un-sacked at 7:45. I cannot take any more of Jim's roll-your-own pancakes. They would make excellent placemats. The other day I bought a big box of Aunt Jemima mix, but Jim managed to foul up that too. I was too late to save the pancakes, but I hastily volunteered to fry the eggs—once over lightly. The Chief noticed the difference, and he said that I am now official egg-fryer. Jim liked the eggs too, and he said, apologetically, "Goddam, I can't cook! What makes me, it's always in a hurry—that's what does it [The eggs always cook too fast]." With the addition of syrup, toast, tea, and canned cherries, we had a pretty good breakfast. The Chief has his hair in two braids today. I'm afraid that his cold is worse again.

The Chief wanted to go to town right after breakfast, and since I had a lot of typing to do, Jimmy took him in the old car. I was to meet them later, at the Tribal Office. I drove in at about 11:00, stopping briefly to take some pictures at Starr School, a large, green-

and white-painted log structure about half-way to town. Met one of the teachers, Mrs. Eagle Feather, and she was very nice. A young Indian man was attempting to repair one of the swings on the playground. I loaned him a pair of pliers, and darn if the ingrate didn't try to make off with them. I am so simpatico with the Indian personality that I have difficulty in remembering that I am still dealing with individuals, and it is always an inordinate disappointment when I meet a rascally Indian. Jim says that there is an element on the Reservation which regards thievery lightly and which will make off with anything not bolted down. Isn't there everywhere, though!

I found the Chief standing on a street corner with "Popeye," the gawky drunk I met in the bar that first night. I thought they were together, so when Popeye asked if he could go along with the Chief and me as we searched for Jim, I said O.K. But when Popeye got into the car, the Chief angrily got out again, declaring that he would not ride with that "*aú-wah-tsahps'*" (screwball). So I told Popeye to get out, and the Chief and I drove to the garage to which Jim had taken his car for repairs. Several Indian tykes were at play near the garage. They were all under five, and all of them, both boys and girls, had braids. They had bows and arrows and feathered coupsticks and were playing at Indian warfare.

The three of us went to the Tribal Office, where the Tribal Council meeting was to be held in a large meeting-room. There are thirteen Council members, elected every two years, with an executive committee composed of the Chairman, the Vice-chairman, and the Secretary. In past years, the Council was unpaid, but starting with this year the members are salaried.

The Chairman ("Sherman," Jimmy calls it) was absent, the meeting being presided over by the vice-sherman. Most of the participants sat around a seminar table, but two men sat back against the wall. One of these was a White man who apparently functioned in an advisory capacity. He was middle-aged, bespectacled, and a chain-smoker, making intelligent, articulate comments with a cigarette dangling from his mouth. At the table was one very attractive Indian girl, taking notes. I am kind of hungry for some female company, and I guess I must have stared at her—with prurient arch of eyebrow and twirl of moustache, if I know me—because eventually, in typical White-girl fashion, she fiddled with her hair until I got a good look at her ring.

Dad and I, along with about fifty other observers, mostly older Indians, sat on wooden benches at one end of the room. Jim sat between us, translating. The meeting was brought to order, and what followed—excepting that it was conducted in two languages—might have taken place at any business meeting. A motion was made and carried to reimburse someone for damage to a tape recorder which he had loaned to the Council. They gave him full price for the recorder, but it was not stated whether the recorder was to become the property of the Council. It was decided that the contract of the tribal lawyer would not be renewed.

Spectators were allowed to voice grievances and opinions, and a man that looked White but who apparently had enough Indian blood to qualify as a tribal member, stood up and complained that his commercial lease on St. Mary's Lake had been snatched from under him and given to a wealthy White corporation. The man with the cigarette explained to the complainant the actualities of the lease situation.

The whole proceeding was very pettifoggerish and un-Indian, and I sighed to think that these thirteen men should control the destinies of thousands of Indians. But then, should I desire to sigh even more deeply, I need only turn my gaze toward the Great White Council in Washington.

Eventually, a discussion of real interest got under way. In the past, apparently, anybody with a drop of Blackfoot blood was able to call himself a Blackfoot Indian (when convenient) and walk off with a share of the tribal funds. The Chief is a leader in the fight to put a stop to this. The suggestion is that from now on a person must be at least one-quarter Blackfoot in order to qualify for tribal membership. If a Blackfoot man marries a White girl, the children are to be considered a part of the tribe. But if a Blackfoot girl marries a White man, the children (who are legally privileged with all the rights of U.S. citizenship) are not to have in addition those rights reserved for Indians. This, I think, is reasonable and fair.

During the discussion, the Chief arose and offered his opinions in his usual fiery manner. His oratory rocked the room, and I was very proud of the old fellow. However, Earl Old Person, who is the official translator, refused to translate the Chief's comments into English (not all members of the Council understand Blackfoot), stating that the Chief did not understand the situation at hand. I am developing definite reservations about Earl. Jimmy has had them right along.

There was an adjournment for lunch, but I did not eat because I detest cheap restaurants. After dropping the boys back at the

Tribal Office (I had had enough of the Council for one day), I went out and looked through the museum. And upon returning to town, whom should I encounter but the old Indian who was the model for "War Bonnet" in "Horserace." We remembered each other, but I had forgotten his real name. He wrote it out for me: "Plenty Treaty B.C." Although this gentleman has jet-black braids, he has lived more than seventy summers, and for a moment I toyed with the possibility that "B.C." might be an appended reference to his age. But when I asked him about it he told me that "B.C." stood for Bear Child, and then I remembered his real name: "Louis Bear Child." Jimmy later told me that "Plenty Treaty" was just another name that Louis had decided to adopt, as Indians are wont to do. Jimmy's other names are "Porcupine Bull" and "Eagle Plume." Louis Plenty Treaty Bear Child said that he predicts a storm before the week end, and since this is Thursday, I guess that must mean it will storm tomorrow.

For some unexplained reason, the afternoon meeting of the Council did not materialize, so I picked up the boys and we went home. Jimmy says that he has invited some Indian singers to the house tonight, so that I can record them. Right now I smell steak and fried potatoes and I am starving. The Chief is playing with a large black puppy which suddenly appeared out of nowhere.

I noticed that when Earl speaks Blackfoot before a group he gestures with one hand—one, two, or three fingers extended—chopping the air in vertical motions, à la Harry Truman. The Chief gestures the same way, and I wonder whether these gestures are an integral part of Blackfoot oratory. Chow time!

Later: At eight o'clock one of the singers arrived, bringing with him a woman and a small boy. He was sort of an old guy with no braids but with a stiff thatch of thick gray hair standing straight up on his head about four inches high. His name is Phillip Many Hides, and I like him, as I like most of the older Indians. Leaving the woman in the house, Phillip and the child and I went in search of the other singer, Phillip's brother. After driving about two miles west on the main road, I was directed to cut off onto a double-track which wound northward past the high aspen groves, leading finally to a small house hidden deep in the hills. I waited in the car while Phillip went inside. When he returned, a full five minutes later, he said, "He's not there. He's at his house. He lives down in the hill by the crick." It was pitch dark, and as I strove to turn the car around without backing into an outhouse or something, a kid's tricycle jumped underneath and tore the manifold loose. So we roared back down the double-track and went "down in the hill by the crick" where Phillip's brother lives.

To my surprise, we stopped at the little house at which I, upon first arriving, had made inquiries about the Chief. And to my astonishment, Phillip's brother turned out to be the skinny little Indian with the ear-lopper cap and the terrible teeth. There is no resemblance between them. Brother's name is Paul, and he brought along his wife, the retarded boy with the black birthmark, and a small boy of very dark complexion.

Back at the ranch . . . Jimmy produced two rawhide rattles from the Chief's room and handed one to each of the Many Hide brothers. The Chief said that it would not be religiously proper to play a drum inside the house, but Jimmy circumnavigated this prohibition with the fish-on-Friday expedience of pounding with a stick on the back of a chair, and while the singers made their other preparations, I attempted, with small success, to figure out who in the group was related to whom. The small boy that Phillip had brought was his grandson; the dark boy was Paul's son; the retarded boy with the patch whom we had picked up at Paul's house really belongs at Phillip's house, but I was never able to establish his exact relationship to anybody. The small boy ran around the house eating bread and butter; the dark boy sat on the sofa and picked the Chief's old Hudson's Bay blanket coat to shreds; and the boy with the patch—his name is Pete—sat in a corner and smiled.

Paul's wife, although by no means ugly, is terribly unkempt. She has absolutely no teeth, poor woman, and one of her fingernails is almost ungular in its grotesque malformation. What these people need, in addition to a little education in personal hygiene, is better nutrition.

The good woman can really sing, though, and I was somewhat startled to hear such lovely and moving music emerging from her thoroughly edendate mouth. It was Paul, that other most unlikely of musicians, who started things off, and he lived up to his boast that he had been a great singer in his day ("Sometimes when they gonna had a dances, I showed you").

The music commenced with a shaking of the rattles. Then Paul began to sing in a high quavering voice, and then Jimmy and Phillip joined in, and finally the women added a sort of minor key obbligato. All the singers had magnificent voice control, and the performance was really a very musical one.

Unfortunately, no one seemed to know the songs very well. No one except the Chief, that is, for whenever they started to foul up, the Chief would thunder in the correct phrase. Jimmy said, after a didactic interruption by his father, "Goddam! He interfered with me and now I can't get back where I'm going." The whole thing was really very relaxed and informal, though, with a lot of laughing and clowning around. At one point, Jim put a large funnel on his head in gesture of crowning himself with a dunce-cap for having goofed up. The only time that a serious note discorded the proceedings was when Paul started to sing a Cree song. The Chief got on him right away and said that he could damn well sing Blackfoot songs or not at all. So they tried to sing some Blackfoot "Crazy Dog" songs and immediately got all screwed up. "Sound like bunch drunks," Jimmy said.

I played back the songs, but the recorder had distorted the music something terrible. So I turned the damn thing off, and while the singers gave out with a few more selections I made a large pot of coffee. Paul and his wife both looked starved, so I heated up some bean soup too. At the table, Paul's wife took her soup spoon directly from her toothless mouth, plunged it into the sugarbowl, and stirred a heaping tablespoonful of sugar into her cup of coffee. Oh well, she sings beautifully. And I don't use sugar anyway.

I am afraid that the Chief's cold is no better. He sneezed loudly at the table, and Phillip said, with a tone of lachrymose poignancy, "In a old days when you sneezed we used to say your girl friend is thinking for you. Now-days we say you better get to that drug store and get you some medicine."

After I had driven all the guests to Paul's house, Jim and Dad and I each drank two hot toddies. It was still reasonably early, and the medicine songs had induced Dad into a story-telling mood, and as we sipped our drinks he told some medicine stories.

YELLOW WOLF VISITS THE SAND HILLS

This happened during the big measles [one of the several epidemics of small pox which struck the Blackfoots]. A lot of Piegans died at this time, and among them was Yellow Wolf. We cared for Yellow Wolf in the same manner that we cared for the others that had passed away: we dressed him in his best clothing and placed a blanket over him and kept him for two days in his lodge. On the second night, when Yellow Wolf's relatives and friends had all arrived and were sitting around the lodge preparing for the funeral, one of the relatives suddenly said, "The blanket is moving!" Then, as everyone watched, Yellow Wolf cast off the blanket and sat up. This is the story he told:

"When I passed away, my spirit went to the Sand Hills. I found myself sitting on a large hill, looking out upon a land that was flat and desolate. I knew that my spirit had entered the Sand Hills, and I started down the hill and across the barren plain is search of my parents.

"I had not gone very far when I encountered an elderly gentleman. He asked me where I was going, and when I told him that I was searching for my father and mother, he said, *Yes, you will find them here.*

"So I continued onward, and shortly I met with another old gentleman. He, too, asked me where I was going, and I told him that I was going down to find my father and mother. *Yes,* he said, *they are here. You will find them camped not far from here. They are in a painted lodge.*

"So I found the painted lodge, and entered it, but instead of making me welcome as I had expected, my father just looked at me and then turned his face away. My mother would not even raise her eyes to look at me. I stayed in the lodge just a short while, and since it was apparent that I was not welcome there I decided that I might just as well return to where I had come from.

"So I started back, and soon I encountered again the second of the gentlemen I had met on the way down. He was carrying a log chain and a black handkerchief. He asked me where I was going, and when I told him that I was returning to the other world—the world where my body was—he would not at first believe me. But finally I convinced him that I meant what I said, and then he put the log chain on the ground and covered it with the black handkerchief and asked me to pick them up. So I picked them up, and I found that the log chain had broken apart into separate links. Then the old gentleman placed the links on the ground and covered them with the black handkerchief, and when he picked them up again I saw that all the links had joined together again into a single chain. The old gentleman gave me the log chain and the black handkerchief and told me to take them with me back to where I was going.

"So I continued onward, and before long I met again the first of the old men I had met on the way down. He asked me where I was going, and I told him that my father and mother had not made my spirit welcome in their lodge and so I was taking my spirit back to where my body was. At first the old man would not believe me, but when I told him that I meant what I said, he was convinced. He was carrying with him a hatchet and a red handkerchief, and he said, *I am sorry that I have not any better gifts for you than this hatchet and this handkerchief, but before you leave, I want to show you something.* Then he placed his arm on a log, and with the hatchet he severed the hand from the arm. And then he picked up the hand and placed it back on the wrist and covered it with the red handkerchief, and when he took the handkerchief away again you could see that the hand was joined to the arm again. Then the old gentleman handed me the hatchet and the red handkerchief, and at that moment my spirit entered once more into my body and I found myself here in my own lodge with my relatives and friends standing all around."

The Chief continued:

From that time on, Yellow Wolf had the *Power*. One of his wives was named Pahták [Potato], and by her he had a son who was the father of the Yellow Wolf that is still living on this reservation today. One day this son asked to borrow Yellow Wolf's log chain, and Yellow Wolf told him that it was right there on the ground, covered with that black handkerchief. The son picked up the chain and it fell to pieces in his hands, but when Yellow Wolf picked up the links and covered them with the black handkerchief again, the chain was back together in one piece.

Another time, Chief Coward, who had the power to cut off his finger and then put it back on again, was showing off his power to Yellow Wolf. Yellow Wolf, who was chopping wood at the time, cut off his hand at the wrist and the hand fell three or four feet away from the arm and blood poured out of the arm. "See what you made me do!" Yellow Wolf said. "You startled me so much with your power that you made me go and cut off my own hand." But Yellow Wolf was only teasing Chief Coward, because when he picked up the hand and placed it against his wrist and covered it with his red handkerchief, the hand was joined to the arm again.

The Chief concluded the tale by saying that Yellow Wolf, who had lived to a ripe old age and had died only recently, had two daughters that were still living. Brother Jim added that actually

Yellow Wolf had died about twenty years ago. Jim said that he remembered Yellow Wolf very well. He said that Yellow Wolf, who was for some time an "Indian Police," was noted for being absolutely without fear of anything or anybody, and that Yellow Wolf always wore tied around his head, close above his eyes, a red bandana handkerchief.

THE MAN WHO CAME BACK TO LIFE

This happened on the other side of the place where Fort Benton was later to be built, but there was no Fort Benton at this time because the White Man had not yet come into the country of the Blackfoots. The Piegans were camped near the river, and during the night some Crows attacked the camp and made off with several horses, but the Piegans trailed the Crows and caught up with them and in the ensuing battle the Piegans killed all the Crows and recaptured all the stolen horses.

During the battle only one Piegan was killed. The man's name was Makúyukan, Wolf Sleeping, and he had only one wife, Chasing Horses. It was late in the morning when the Piegans returned to camp with the body of Wolf Sleeping, and the wife of Wolf Sleeping, Chasing Horses, who had been out all morning picking berries, did not appear to be at all distraught that her husband was dead. She carefully washed her berries and put them away, and not until she had done this did she speak. Then she addressed the men who were caring for her husband's body: "My husband told me that if he were to die I should do certain ceremonies for four days, and that on the fourth day he would return to life." From a buckskin bag she took out two buffalo robes; one was the hide of a buffalo cow and the other was the skin of a buffalo bull with the horns still attached. From the same bag she took out an otter pelt and an eagle-bone whistle. First she painted her husband's face, and then she placed the eagle-bone whistle around his neck and laid the otter skin crossways upon his chest. Then she said to the men, "Four of you must carry Wolf Sleeping into the river until the water is as high as your hearts. Then you must let him go, and if an otter shows his head above the water, we will know that what my husband said was true and that he will return to life in four days." So four men carried Wolf Sleeping into the river and let his body go, and immediately an otter raised his head above the water and whistled, and so the people knew that Wolf Sleeping had spoken the truth, and for three days Chasing Horses did the ceremonies that her husband had told her to do.

On the fourth day, Chasing Horses had four drummers sit on the cow robe down by the edge of the water, and she had the men place the bull robe by the water's edge. She filled her husband's pipe with tobacco, and she made sure that a man was standing ready with some *apústam* [a kind of punk made from the soft inner bark of the cottonwood tree, used by the Blackfoots in the ceremonial lighting of pipe tobacco]. Then the drummers began to play, and Chasing Horses began to blow on the whistle she had, and soon an otter raised his head above the water and whistled again, and now Chasing Horses took her husband's pipe and walked backward slowly from the edge of the water, swinging the pipe slowly from side to side and singing her medicine song. The words of the song were, "*Nit-tsí-sanni-nah-tu-yay-wah* [My paint is holy, my paint is strong medicine]."

All the people had gathered near the riverbank to see what would happen, and now they saw waves rising in the river. Then a heavy mist, almost like smoke, rose from the water, and through the mist Wolf Sleeping came walking out onto the riverbank, staggering as though he were very weary. Then he seated himself upon the bull robe that had been prepared for him, and Chasing Horses gave him his pipe, and a man lighted the pipe with *apústam*. Wolf Sleeping smoked his pipe, and everybody knew then that he was alive again.

MORNING EAGLE'S MEDICINE

On the way back from a raid against the Crows, the son of Flat Tail became very ill. Flat Tail asked Morning Eagle to doctor the boy, but Morning Eagle refused, saying that he was not a medicine man. But Flat Tail insisted. "You have the *Power*," he said to Morning Eagle. "I know that you do."

Finally Morning Eagle agreed to doctor the boy. "Place four stones in the fire," he said, "and when they get red-hot, call me and I will tell you what else to do." So when the stones became red-hot, Flat Tail called Morning Eagle, and Morning Eagle said to place two poles parallel inside the lodge and to have four men sit on each side and sing hand game songs.

When everything was prepared, Morning Eagle seated himself in the lodge and picked up the red-hot stones and began to use them for guess bones in the hand game. By the time he had picked up the second stone, the boy opened his eyes, and by the time he had picked up the fourth stone, the boy was cured.

Flat Tail had stolen two horses from the Crows, and one of them he gave to Morning Eagle for having cured his son.

The story of Calf Robe and the Medicine Coyote is especially interesting because it was told to the Chief by his father, Onistái-pokah, who was a member of the war party involved in the story. The most intriguing aspect of the tale is found in the fact that during the first part of the action, while Onistáipokah was actually present, we have a recitation of perfectly logical and verifiable historical occurrence, whereas during the latter portion of the story, during which Onistáipokah was not actually attendant upon the action, we find to enter an aspect of mystical experience which is, to say the least, remarkable.

CALF ROBE AND THE MEDICINE COYOTE

A large party of Piegans was organized to make a raid against the Crows. The first section of the war party consisted of seven men under the leadership of Ómaksapope [Big Plume]. Big Plume took his wife along with him. [Not an unusual occurrence, especially if the wife were childless.]

Ten days later, a much larger party under Áchkutaumachkan [Double Runner] and his father, Nínnaipeeksee [Chief Prairie Chicken], set out to overtake Big Plume. But they did not know that Big Plume had taken his wife with him and when they came upon a camp at which a woman was scraping a hide, they were not sure whether it was the camp of some enemies. All day long they watched the camp, but they could not recognize anybody. [Contrary to what some writers of fiction would have us believe, it was not always possible—even for other Indians—to know from a distance exactly what tribe an encampment or a group of riders belonged to. There was so much cultural borrowing among the various Plains Tribes, so much copying of enemy hair-do's and wearing of captured enemy clothing, using of captured weapons, horse gear, etc., that inadvertent skirmishes between groups from the same tribe were not uncommon.] At night some of the men of Double

Runner's party crept close to the camp in an attempt to identify the people by their language, but they could hear nothing, so at dawn they attacked the camp.

One of the Piegans camped with Big Plume's party was named Onistáiyey [Calf Robe]. Calf Robe and Machkúyee-machsin [West Wolf] and my father were all the same age, and they were all good friends. But during the attack, while Calf Robe was jumping over a log to take cover, West Wolf, his own partner, shot him through the ribs. West Wolf shouted, "My name is Woman's Moccasin" [it was common practice for a Plains Indian to take a new name on the occasion of scoring a coup against the enemy], but when the mistake had been discovered, West Wolf denied having fired the shot that wounded his friend.

When the two groups of Piegans recognized one another they stopped fighting, and they all did what they could for the wounded Calf Robe. They could not take him with them on the war party, so they doctored him and prepared a shelter for him and left him there to get better. Before they left, they prepared a quantity of dry meat for him and gave him four or five buffalo paunches filled with water; they also left him several stalks of wild rhubarb, which he used as drinking straws. Finally they cut plenty of firewood for him and also left him a large amount of *iniistan* [buffalo chips]. Buffalo chips burn slowly and leave little ash, and he used these to keep his fire going all night so that the wild animals would not enter his shelter. They also left him a dry stick with a crook in the end, and this he used in pulling the firewood inside the tent. [The word for the dry stick with a crook in it is *ahpahtohkahnikseh*, and Jim and I both had to wrestle with the translation.]

After a few days, when Calf Robe felt well enough to sit up, he heard a sound outside his shelter, and pulling aside the dark door he saw a coyote sitting there looking at him. So he talked to the coyote as though it were a person. [The Blackfoots believed that a coyote had the power to understand human speech.] He asked the coyote to please help him, so the coyote entered the shelter and licked Calf Robe's wounds and stayed with him and doctored him every day.

Finally, when Calf Robe had recovered sufficiently so that he could get about for short periods by leaning on a cane, he heard something coming toward his shelter. The coyote heard the sound too, and the coyote ran away in fear, so Calf Robe decided that an enemy must be approaching. "It is better that I should go out and meet my enemy and die like a warrior," Calf Robe thought, but when he threw aside the door of his shelter, the entranceway was blocked by a large bear. So Calf Robe spoke to the bear: "Pity me, Bear, for I am wounded and I need your help in doctoring me." But the bear did not answer. The bear grabbed Calf Robe and threw him down inside the shelter. Four times he grabbed him and threw him down, once in each direction, and the fourth time Calf Robe fainted from pain.

When Calf Robe regained consciousness, the bear was sitting beside him in the shelter, so Calf Robe reached out his hand and began to pet the bear and to plead for his help. "Pity me, Bear," he said, "for I am sick and poor and I need help." The bear did not answer, but Calf Robe could hear the coyote outside the shelter whining like a dog, so Calf Robe said to the bear, "Bear, allow your brother, the Coyote, to come into the shelter. He is my friend and he has been doctoring me." Once again the bear did not speak, but Calf Robe said to the coyote, "Enter the shelter. Your brother, the bear, will do you no harm." So the coyote came into the shelter and continued to doctor Calf Robe.

Soon afterward, Calf Robe felt that he was well enough to attempt to reach home. Sending the coyote ahead to scout for enemies, Calf Robe took his cane and started to walk as best he could. The bear walked in front of him, and the bear kept lying down in the path in front of him, and finally it occurred to Calf Robe that the bear wanted to carry him. So Calf Robe mounted the bear and rode until he could no longer stand the pain, and then the bear stopped and the coyote doctored Calf Robe's wounds and they continued onward. Three times the coyote doctored Calf Robe's wounds, and after that Calf Robe did not feel any more pain.

All this time the coyote was scouting ahead for enemies, and now the coyote came back and ran about very excitedly, so Calf Robe knew that there must be danger ahead. From a high ridge Calf Robe saw some riders coming, so he took the bear and the coyote down into a patch of thick brush where they all lay quietly. The riders were from an enemy war party, and when they passed close to the patch of brush the coyote became frightened and wanted to run. But Calf Robe made the coyote stay put, and so the riders passed and the three friends were saved.

The patch of brush in which Calf Robe and the bear and the coyote were hiding was not far from Akáhpyoyist [Many Houses: Fort Benton]. There was a Piegan camp nearby, and Calf Robe made it safely to the camp. That night, the people in the camp could hear the coyote and the bear howling, but Calf Robe told them not to harm the animals but to take them food because they had saved his life. So the people of the camp took food to the bear and the coyote.

The bear and the coyote stayed in the patch of brush for quite some time. Then finally one day the bear left, and pretty soon after that the coyote left too.

The young people of the tribe do not know this story, but the old-timers know it. Old Chewing Black Bones knows this story, and if you ask him he will tell you that it is a true story.

I had become so engrossed in the linguistic aspect of these stories that it was not until the story-telling was completed and we were all enjoying a hot drink that I paused to give full thought to the philosophical side of the narratives. "Do you really believe everything in these stories?" I asked Jim, and Jim really caught me with my cassock down by suggesting, with polite obliqueness, the phenomenal character of a prominent Christian dogma. "Well," he said, "I telling: my wife comes 'round tells me she's knock-up by a god, there's going be a big trouble in my house, I think."

Friday, September 7

When I finally rolled out, at 8:30, Jim was up and had the house nice and warm and was placidly reading a newspaper. It is snowing and blowing something fierce outside; Plenty Treaty was right. I found the two big dogs cowering in the outhouse, but the puppy is missing. 9:00 now, and the Chief still is not up.

9:30: The Chief finally got up and I moccasined him and gave another new pair of wool sox. The old fellow doesn't feel very well—his cold is worse—but he gave me a cheery, *"Ah-siks-kah-nóh-toh-nay"* (good morning). He also remarked that the radio at the Tribal Office had predicted the storm—and I guess that explains Plenty Treaty's meteorological clairvoyance. Jimmy just said, *"Ahk-so-yope"* (let's eat).

Later: Good chow. Buckwheats and eggs (rescued from Jim's irreverent hand), and the old granite coffeepot full and steaming. After breakfast I offered to give Jim a toothbrush, if he would use it, but he was remarkably disinterested. Jim's teeth are fine, but he has developed tartar deposits which, unless he starts using a toothbrush (or a foot towel), may lead eventually to serious gum trouble. But Jim is fatalistically unconcerned about the whole situation. "If these fall off, I'll get me some ghost teeth [false teeth]," he said, and that closed the discussion.

I think that the basic hygienic problems among Indians result from the combined facts that the Indians have forgotten the old methods and will not adopt (or are ignorant of) modern methods. The Chief says that in the old days the Blackfoots observed a very rigid course of personal hygiene including, for all men and boys, a daily morning bath, summer or winter, in cold water. This cold plunge, which often required that a hole be chopped in the ice, was believed by the Blackfoots to toughen them against extremely cold weather and to build their resistance to various winter ailments. The Chief says that it worked, too, and that when the Blackfoots were allowed to exist in their traditional manner—living in teepees which were lined, and floored with furs, and snug as a jug, and eating their customary diet of meat supplemented with a variety of esculent wild fruits, berries, roots and tubers—such disorders as pneumonia and the common cold were almost unheard of. But then came the White Man a-wooing with his plea of "Let me take all this away from you." And that is exactly what he did.

The Chief remembers the old days very well, and his voice took on an understandably bitter edge as he explained the extent to which the White Man's senseless slaughter of the buffalo destroyed the Blackfoot way of life. Other game could not even begin to meet the food needs of the Plains Tribes. With the buffalo gone the Indians were forced to accept the refined foods of the White Man; with no buffalo hides with which to build lodges, the Indians were forced to live in smoky, unventilated wooden shacks. Consequently, the Indians began to suffer terribly from such diseases as pneumonia, appendicitis, tuberculosis and trachoma. Additional gifts from the Whites in the form of alcohol and small pox conspired with other catastrophes to reduce the Blackfoots, once the most populous and powerful of all Plains Tribes and believed by some historians to have numbered at one time over forty thousand, to fewer than five thousand souls. The Indian was robbed of the natural resources and the *lebensraum* that were his rightful heritage, and then he was denied the wherewithal and the knowledge—and the *motivation* —to live any other kind of life.

The White attitude toward the Indian has from the first suggested all the inherent immorality of a pay toilet (what do you do if you don't have a dime, use a potted palm?), and brother Jim summed up the situation in a deliciously succinct five words. Jim's phrasing may be open to question, but I found myself unable to challenge the validity of his conclusion when he said, "They goosed the gold egg."

Despite the extensive research I have done with regard to the extermination of the great buffalo herds, I still find the facts incredible. The Chief says that he and many Indians much younger than he can remember when the great northern buffalo herd, which ranged in the region of the Sweetgrass Hills, about one hundred miles due east of the present Blackfoot Reservation, numbered in the millions and would sometimes blacken the prairie from horizon to horizon. It has been estimated that as late as 1874 this northern herd alone contained over four million buffalo, but the last successful Blackfoot buffalo hunt was conducted *only five years later*, in the winter of 1879–80, and of course by the winter of 1883–84 the buffalo were completely gone and one-quarter of the Chief's people, the Piegans, starved to death that year.

The Chief once asked me to explain to him why the White Man had been so anxious to trap all the Underwater Persons (all the beaver). I told him that it had been because the White Man was crazy and he thought that everybody should wear a hat of beaver fur. Incredible but true, the entire beaver trade, which caused so much trouble between White and Indian, resulted from a fad during which the London dandy had to wear a beaver hat in order to be in style; when the silk hat replaced the beaver hat in fashion's fickle eye, the beaver trade, around which so much of the romance of our early West has been fashioned, came to an abrupt halt. I explained all this to the Chief, but I have never had the heart to tell him the real reason that the White Man destroyed within a single decade a way of life—the buffalo culture—which probably had existed in one form or another for thousands or at least many hundreds of years. The Chief knows that the White Man did not kill the buffalo because he needed the meat; in his lifetime the Chief saw thousands of buffalo which had been stripped of the hide and left to rot and stink and fatten the wolves on the prairie. But the Chief is mistaken in his conclusion that the Whites had a great desire to own many buffalo robes. Actually, the demand for buffalo robes was never very large among the Whites. What really motivated the extinction of the buffalo was the development in 1871 of a new tanning process which turned the strong and durable buffalo hide into a material which was ideally suited for use as factory machine belts. The demand for buffalo hide then became insatiable, and within a dozen years the buffalo, the American Bison, had been slaughtered to near extinction. I have never had the courage to tell the Chief that his people and his culture were sacrificed so that some stinking machine (the older Blackfoots still refer to the automobile as a "skunk wagon") could keep on turning out beer bottles, silk umbrellas, or patent leather shoes.

11:00: Jimmy just came in with an armful of wood and said, "Goddam! It's a cold outside! Guess I got wear cap today." He asked me whether I had seen his hat, but he said it in Blackfoot and I didn't understand him at first because instead of using the word for hat (*ist-tsím-o-kahn*) with which I am familiar, he used "*o-toh-kahn-o-kós-toh-mok*," which refers specifically to a cap or hat which has a round shape. He was right about its being "a cold outside," though; I know because a short while ago I borrowed the Chief's overshoes and went down for two buckets of water. The butane tank is empty, but there is a wood fire going in the kitchen and it is nice and warm in there and as soon as my water heats I am going to take a bath. The wind is really strong outside, blowing the snow almost horizontally.

Night: Well, I'm clean! While the Chief dictated a letter to Jim (for me to type up), I took a bucket bath—what my old Texas friend, Cap Fowler, calls a "possible" bath. Cap described the procedure as follows: "First you wash down as far as possible; then you wash up as far as possible; and then you wash possible."

After lunch the Chief wanted to go to town, but when he stepped out onto the porch and felt the power of that wind he changed his mind. So instead he seated himself in a chair and sang some of his old war songs, accompanying himself by pounding on the floor with his cane, and the war songs put him in a story-telling mood so I turned on the recorder and the Chief expounded in detail the preparations which the Blackfoots made for going to war. He began by remarking that the White Man has done a magnificent job of misinterpreting and misrepresenting the Plains Indian culture. As Jimmy interjected, "Always make Indians look like bunch damn fools." This phase of discussion arose from the fact that the film, *Chief Crazy Horse,* is coming to the local flick. Indian films, and other comedies, are quite popular on the Reservation, and the older Blackfoot ladies are especially titillated by the fact that the movies always portray an Indian maiden wearing a beaded headband with a feather sticking in it. The beaded headband is itself both contemporary and ersatz, and it was at one time considered indecent of an Indian woman to adorn herself with feathers. The Sun Dance Holy Woman wore a small plume tied at one side of her head, and Blackfoot women frequently did (and still do) wear their husband's or boy friend's hats while the menfolk are dancing, but certainly no Plains Indian woman in the old days went around with an eagle feather sticking up behind her head.

Considering the relative lateness of his appearance upon the scene, the Chief's fourteen war parties constitute a rather remarkable achievement. By the time he made his raids, the Whites had begun to move into Montana and to establish military posts and to make treaties (none of which they honored) with the Indians, and so the Chief had a pretty rough time of it. He has a bullet hole in his left arm just behind the wrist, and although I have not been able to lead him into a detailed discussion of the matter, he did mention that the wound was quite an annoyance because the bullet broke the bone and he had trouble loading the muzzle-loading old rifle that he was using at the time.

With several notable exceptions—during one battle the Piegans killed more than 300 Gros Ventres and Crows—most war expeditions were made for the purpose of stealing horses and were composed of only a half-dozen or so warriors. Piegan war expeditions were not, as one authority has phrased it, "spur of the moment affairs." Usually they were planned at least several days in advance, and it was customary for the young warrior to first seek the blessing of an old man of the tribe. Sometimes the warrior built a sweat lodge in which the old man would purify him, and sometimes the two just smoked a pipe together. Almost always the older man would give the youngster a protective token or amulet to carry, and the sale of especially powerful medicine bundles or war bundles was quite a thriving business.

At length I asked the Chief to tell me frankly who the best fighters among the Plains Tribes had been, and very emphatically he replied "[píkãñi]" (the Piegans). And I guess that history bears out his opinion very well. In the early days, during the westward movement by way of the Oregon Trail, the pioneers took a southerly route around the Blackfoots (instead of following the natural course of the Missouri Valley, which would have been the logical route) simply because the Blackfoots were so powerful and so fierce that to invade their land was virtual suicide.

The Blackfoots never did engage in anything resembling full-scale warfare against the Whites, although one could not have blamed them if they had done so. Especially during the post-Civil War period, when false reports of gold in Blackfoot territory precipitated an invasion of the region by the toughs and whiskey peddlers and the brand of scurf invariably attracted to promises of quick money, the Blackfoots were very badly used by the Whites. But the only "battle" between Blackfoots and the U.S. Army occurred in January, 1870, when there took place an action which has rightfully been inscribed in history books as "Baker's Massacre." Protestations and pretensions by the Army with regard to this disgraceful episode were many, but the facts are plain enough: At the break of a bitter-cold dawn on January 23, 1870, Colonel E. M. Baker led four companies of cavalry, plus a full company of infantry and fifty-five mounted infantrymen, in a surprise attack upon the Marias River camp of Heavy Runner, a Piegan who had always been friendly toward the Whites. Of the 173 Piegans that died in this attack, ninety were women, fifty were children under twelve years of age, and only fifteen were men between the ages of twelve and thirty-seven. One soldier died during the attack, but he was probably killed accidentally by his noble comrades in arms because Heavy Runner's camp was not only totally devoid of fighting men but was suffering a severe plague of small pox. Baker claimed that he thought he was attacking the camp of Mountain Chief (Mountain Chief's boys had been raising a little hell with the Whites, which is not surprising in view of the fact that Mountain Chief's brother had been shot down in cold blood, and for no good reason, in the streets of Fort Benton).

When I asked the Chief about the Massacre, he made the following statement, displaying as always a profound knowledge of history and of the White Man's political machinations:

This is an important story. It will show you the way the Whites treated the Blackfoots in the early days, and it will show you how hard my father tried to have peace with the Whites.

At this time the Army was looking for Mountain Chief because Mountain Chief's son, Owl Child, had killed his brother-in-law, Four Bears [a White man named Malcolm Clark who was married to a Piegan woman]. Mountain Chief had been camped with his band on Bear River [the Marias River], but he had moved his camp further down the river, and Baker could not find him so he attacked the camp of Heavy Runner. He was guided to the camp by the men who had been supplying whiskey to the Indian camps on Bear River. The men were Joe Kipp, a half-breed whom the Piegans called "Choe Keepah" or by his Indian name, Raven Quiver, and three other White men the Piegans called Brown, Small Neck, and Horn Child.

All the young men of Heavy Runner's band were away on a winter hunt when Baker charged the camp. When the soldiers first showed up, Packing-Tail-Feathers-Coming-Over-The-Hill went out to meet them. He was holding up a piece of paper and a peace medal that had been given to him by Commissioner Ike [Isaac Stevens]. An officer shot him down, and then the soldiers went through the camp and killed everybody they could find, even the little children. There was big measles [small pox] in the camp at that time, and those too sick to move were burned to death in their lodges. Most of the soldiers were drunk.

The fact is quite well established that prior to Baker's attack an Indian from the camp came toward the soldiers holding up a peace medal and a paper of some sort. Up to now, it had been generally surmised, but without substantiation, that the man was probably Heavy Runner himself. The Chief is the first one to identify the man by name. An elderly Blackfoot lady offered the opinion that Packing-Tail-Feathers-Coming-Over-The-Hill was another name for Heavy Runner. The Chief says no.

The possible drunken condition of Baker's soldiers has not been pursued very diligently, but every Indian source at my disposal (and I have interviewed two ladies whose grandmothers were children in Heavy Runner's camp at the time of the attack and who hid by the river at the first approach of the soldiers) states with firm certainty that the soldiers were definitely drunk. In view of the facts that Baker's command had just made an all-night march in sub-zero weather, and they were in the company of known whiskey runners, I definitely go along with my Indian informants.

The Chief's story continues:

At the time of Baker's Massacre I was over in Canada with my father. Mountain Chief came over to join us right after the Massacre, and he thought that all the Blackfoots should join together and take revenge on the Whites for what they had done. But my father, who was Civil Chief [Head Chief] of the Piegans, would not allow this. My father said that that was exactly what the Army wanted the Blackfoots to do—to go back over to the States and attack the Army. This would give the Army an excuse to wipe out all the helpless Piegans that were more or less hostages on the Blackfoot land in the States, and that was why there were so many soldiers at Fort Shaw. My father knew that the Army was trying to make a lot of trouble with the Indians because they wanted Congress to turn over the control of Indian affairs to the Army, and that would have been the end of the Indians.

My father spent the winter on Milk River in Canada, and the following spring he went back to the States to talk to the Army. He arrived at Rock House [Ft. Benton] just as the boats were landing, and immediately the soldiers put my father under arrest and took him aboard one of the boats where an officer asked him questions. The officer asked my father whether he had come over to the States because he was seeking revenge for what had been done to the Piegans on Bear River. My father said no, but the officer kept on asking him the same question. Finally my father became angry with the officer and told him that if the Piegans were out after revenge the Army would know it by now because there wouldn't be a White man alive or a White house standing between here and the Medicine Line. My father said, "I came over here to find out why you killed our people. I do not want that there should be any more killing. I want to see my people able to go to sleep at night without wondering whether they will be killed in their lodges. And I want the same thing for the White people— especially the old people. I want them to be able to sleep without fear."

There was in fact at the time of Baker's Massacre a movement before the Congress to transfer the Indian Bureau from the Department of the Interior to the War Department. If the Blackfoots had retaliated against the Army in force, the bill probably would have gone through; as it was, when Vincent Colyer of the Board of Indian Commissioners made available to the newspapers "the sickening details of Colonel Baker's attack on the village of Piegans," the bill was squashed—and squashed along with the bill was the practice of employing Army officers as Indian agents (although all Indian agents continued to be addressed by the honorific "Major"). The whole situation suggests that the Chief's father, old Onistái-pokah, was indeed something of a diplomatic and political genius. He succeeded to an extent far greater than that of any other Plains chief in performing successfully the primary function of a civil chief, that of saving his people from annihilation.

Since the Chief was contemporary with both Custer and Sitting Bull, I asked him whether he had ever met either one of them. He said that he had heard of Custer, whom the Blackfoots called "Buck-skin shirt," but that he had never met him. And then he amazed me with the matter-of-fact statement that he not only had seen Sitting Bull but had been with a hunting party that had once captured him. The Chief has a rather low opinion of Sitting Bull (an understandable attitude toward one's enemies) but I believe every word of the story he told me because (1) the Chief does not lie, ever, and (2) historical fact bears out every detail of the narrative. Historical record places Sitting Bull at just about the time and place the Chief encountered him, and even such minor details as the kind of horse that Sitting Bull was riding (a sorrel) are given credence by history (Sitting Bull owned a large sorrel horse, and it is also generally believed that Custer's horse, also a sorrel, was captured uninjured by the Sioux after the Battle of the Little Big Horn). Further, the Sioux were especially antagonistic toward the Blackfoots at this time because the Blackfoots had refused to join with the Sioux in an all-out effort to drive the Whites out of Montana.

Actually, Sitting Bull was no great shakes as an Indian leader, but he was much publicised and since I, like everyone else, have been bombarded since childhood with propaganda about the famous Sioux, I was quite thrilled by the Chief's tale. (Sitting Bull's fame derived primarily from his world-wide travels with Buffalo Bill Cody's Wild West Show, during which time Sitting Bull peddled enough "authentic souvenirs" of the Custer Massacre to equip the United States Marines.)

THE TIME THE PIEGANS CAPTURED SITTING BULL

It is too bad that I do not remember exactly when this happened. That is where the White Man has an advantage over the Indian; the White Man writes down the time that something happens, so he is always able to remember when it took place. We Indians didn't write things down, and usually we remember the exact time of their occurrence only because they happened the same year as something else that the White Man wrote down in his books: a big battle, a treaty, or perhaps a hard winter with much sickness.

All I know is that what I am going to tell you about now happened sometime during the middle 1870's [it must have been during the spring of the year 1877]. I know this because I was a young warrior then, just in my teens, and since I am 105 years old now you must realize that this happened a long time ago.

The time had come for the Blackfoots to go on their spring hunt, and all the scattered bands joined together to set forth in search of the buffalo. There were Bloods and Blackfoots and Piegans, and we all belong to the Blackfoot Nation. There were no buffalo in the Sweet Pine Hills [the Sweetgrass Hills], so our hunting party split up and went to look for the herds. Most of them went down toward the Crow country [probably heading for the Judith Basin, a vast grazing area located roughly between the present sites of Great Falls and Lewistown, Montana]. At this time we had treaties with both the Crows and the Crees, and I went with a smaller party which headed almost due east, toward the Crees and Assiniboines. In our party there were thirty lodges of Piegans, twenty-eight lodges of Bloods, and twenty lodges of Blackfoots.

At a place called Kinnickinnick Creek, north of what is now called Wolf Point, Montana, we happened upon an encampment of Crees. A lot of them were Cree half-breeds. But at this time all the Blackfoots were at peace with the Crees, and since the Crees had found plenty of buffalo, we set up our encampment with the Crees and hunted with them.

We killed the buffalo by building a pretty big corral out of logs at the base of a little bluff about as high as a teepee. Then we ran some buffalo over the bluff into the corral where they couldn't get out. [This was a popular Cree method of hunting buffalo.] Then we killed what we wanted and turned the rest loose again. We killed most of them with bow and arrow, and we all marked our arrows so we would know who had shot that buffalo. I remember one man who stood up on the bluff and hit a buffalo in the head with big rocks until he was stunned and then ran down and cut his throat with a butcher knife. That was pretty foolish, because a wounded buffalo can be dangerous.

In the old days, the Blackfoots would run part of the herd over a big bluff maybe a hundred feet high, so that most of them would be killed or crippled by the fall. That way they sometimes got as many as three hundred buffalo on one drive. But that was before my time. On this hunt we were a pretty small party and we had a long way to go back with the meat, so we drove the buffalo into a corral and just took what we needed.

When the hunt was over, the women came down and skinned the buffalo and butchered them. The first thing we ate was the liver; we cut it into pieces and dipped it in gall and ate it raw. Then for supper we boiled the tongues and roasted the ribs beside a fire.

After we had all the buffalo we needed, we stayed around the Cree camp for a while, drying meat and caring for the hides, and that's when Sitting Bull showed up for the first time. I had never seen Sitting Bull before, but I had heard about him plenty. It was said that his medicine was strong among the Sioux, but we Piegans didn't think much of him. Before the Sioux went into battle, Sitting Bull would make medicine for them so they couldn't be killed, but the Piegans killed them anyway. I knew plenty of Piegans who had the scalps of Sioux warriors Sitting Bull had made medicine for.

Maybe the Sioux thought Sitting Bull's medicine was strong because he never told them that the signs were right for battle unless the Sioux outnumbered their enemies by plenty. Sitting Bull was a medicine man, and some people say that he was a war chief too, but warriors of our tribe who had seen him in battle said that he was a coward. They said that he always stayed in the rear, making medicine, until the battle was over, and then if the Sioux had won the battle he would ride up and help chase the survivors. If the battle went against the Sioux, he was always the first one to ride away. He always rode a big horse that wasn't much good for battle but was plenty fast to run away on. [The Sioux generally had a preference for large horses.]

Sitting Bull showed up outside the Cree camp with two war chiefs and rode up and down and made sign talk, but nobody invited him into the camp because he had a reputation for being pretty tricky. So pretty soon Sitting Bull rode away, and he sure was mad. He yelled some insults and waved his tomahawk around and spit on the ground, and then he rode away.

Pretty soon after that the Piegans and the Bloods and the Blackfoots packed their buffalo meat on travois drawn by horses and started back westward toward home. When we were traveling through the Cypress Hills, south of Medicine Hat, in Canada, Sitting Bull and a large band of Sioux warriors showed up and galloped ahead and cut off our hunting party; and Sitting Bull was really looking for trouble. He was riding a big sorrel Army horse with the Army saddle and bridle still on it, and there were a lot of other Army horses among the Sioux. And the Sioux had lots of Army equipment—saddles, bridles, canteens, swords, rifles, pistols—and some of them were wearing parts of Army uniforms, so we knew they must have had a big battle with the Cavalry. [The Battle of the Little Big Horn, which took place in southeastern Montana, was fought on June 25 of the preceding summer.]

Those Sioux were painted for war and they outnumbered us Blackfoots by plenty. [Painted for war is a Blackfoot metaphor, meaning to be in an aggressive mood; it is doubtful that any of the Sioux were wearing war paint.] And we had women and children with us, so Bull-Sits-Turning-Around, who was a Piegan and was head chief of our party, told us not to start anything with the Sioux and to avoid battle if we could. But Sitting Bull was sure acting as though he were looking for trouble, so we made a sort of corral out of the travois and the pack horses and put the women and children inside there. That was the best we could do because those Sioux had caught us right out in the open. Those women and children were sure scared.

All those Sioux had bows and arrows and lances, and a lot of them had Army rifles too. We Piegans and Bloods and Blackfoots had a few old muzzle-loaders with us, but they weren't much use in a fight [the Blackfoots had by this time been by governmental order prohibited from obtaining ammunition for those modern rifles which they possessed], but all the men in our party had their bows and arrows and lances and tomahawks, so we weren't afraid of any Sioux, no matter how many of them there were. You hear a lot about what great fighters the Sioux were, but this is because they killed Custer. The best thing the Sioux Nation ever did was to kill Custer, whom they called Yellow Hair. They say he was a brave fighter, but he had a bad reputation among the Indians for being a liar and for doing bad things to young Indian girls he captured. But the Sioux were not known as great fighters among the Plains Indians. The Cheyennes were better fighters than the Sioux, and so were the Nez Percés and the Crows, but the Blackfoots were the best fighters on the Plains, and the Piegans were the best fighters among the Blackfoots. I belonged to the Crazy Dog Clan of the Piegans, and we were the best fighters of all. This is not just a brag. Anybody who was on the Plains in the old days will tell you it is true.

When Sitting Bull and his Sioux cut us off that day they could tell there were not very many of us, and they could tell we were not a war party because we had women and children with us and because the tails of the Piegan horses were long. The other tribes called us Piegans the Bob-tail Horses, because when we went into battle our horses had short tails. But we didn't bob our horses' tails; we used to tie up their tails with strips of rawhide. The last thing we did before going into battle was to tie up the tails of our horses and then gallop around the camp.

This time I was riding my bay buffalo horse that I had marked with a hole in his ear, and when Sitting Bull started riding up and down and waving his tomahawk and calling insults and daring us Blackfoots to start something, I didn't have time to think about tying up my pony's tail. I just strung my buffalo bow and dropped my traveling saddle on the ground, because when we Piegans rode into battle we preferred to ride our ponies bareback.

Sitting Bull was acting pretty brave with all those Sioux behind him, and I guess he was still pretty mad because we didn't invite him into camp when we were with the Crees. So instead of staying in the back, he rode right out in front all by himself to make people think he was brave. He knew we were a hunting party and not looking for a fight, and so he rode up and down bragging about his big victory over the Cavalry and saying what he was going to do to us Blackfoots.

So this made us pretty mad, and some of us young warriors wanted to mix it up with the Sioux right then and there. But Bull-Sits-Turning-Around, who was the chief in charge of our hunting party, rode up and down amongst us and told us to calm down for a minute and use our heads. He knew that Sitting Bull wanted us to attack and chase him, because we wouldn't have much chance against all those Sioux with their Army rifles. Bull-Sits-Turning-Around said we weren't going to attack because we had the women and children to think about. He said that if the Sioux attacked we would dismount and make our stand in front of the place where the women and children were.

The Piegans didn't fight the way it shows Indians fighting in the movies. Sometimes we rode our horses on a raid, and sometimes we went a long way on foot and rode back on horses we had captured from the enemy. And many times when we were attacked we would dismount and lead our horses and fight on foot. The movies never show Indians fighting that way, but that was how we fought, and it was a good way to fight. You can shoot a lot straighter with your feet on the ground, and when the fighting is hand to hand you can move around a lot quicker on foot than on horseback. And when you have a good horse he helps you fight on foot as well as on his back, because it is pretty hard to put lance or tomahawk on a fellow who ducks around underneath his horse. More likely he pulls you off your horse and tomahawks you. And when two tribes are mixing it up on horseback they can't use bows and arrows very close anyway, because maybe they'll shoot one of their own warriors. Those Crows and those Cheyennes had good horses and they were good riders, but they never could lick the Piegans in a fight. And all those Sioux out there didn't want to attack the Piegans either, because they knew that even if they killed us all, there would be plenty of empty lodges in the Sioux camp that night.

When Sitting Bull saw that the Piegans and Bloods and Blackfoots were not going to attack, he kept getting braver and braver and he rode pretty close to us and sat there on his big sorrel horse and called us cowards and women. And we got pretty sick of this, and Bull-Sits-Turning-Around was having a hard time keeping some of the young warriors from riding Sitting Bull down.

With us in our hunting party was Lazy Boy's elder brother, Young Bull. He was the son of Calf Looking, who preceded my father as head chief of the Skunk Band, and he had counted coup many times. He was riding a fast gray mare and he was wheeling and circling that mare so maybe you'd think he couldn't handle her [a favorite Piegan trick of war, I have since learned]. But he was a good rider, and when Sitting Bull got pretty close to where we were, Young Bull leaned way over on the neck of that mare and headed straight for Sitting Bull.

When the rest of us warriors saw this, we gave our war yells and started toward those Sioux, but Bull-Sits-Turning-Around called us back. He was pretty mad, and he said that he was still in charge and that we wouldn't attack those Sioux and leave those kids and women. Some Sioux had started toward us, too, and Sitting Bull wheeled his horse and tried to ride back toward those Sioux, but before he got that big sorrel Army horse turned around and running, Young Bull rode around the other side of him and grabbed his bridle and galloped right back to where we were. Some Sioux had got pretty close by that time, but Sitting Bull knew that if we mixed it up then he was sure to get killed, so he signaled with both hands for those Sioux to stay back.

When Young Bull brought Sitting Bull back to where we were, Bull-Sits-Turning-Around grabbed the tomahawk that Sitting Bull was carrying and hit him on the back with the flat of it. He said, "You've been bragging about what you're going to do to us. Now let's see you do something."

Then a Blackfoot named Runs-With-Buffalo grabbed the tomahawk and hit Sitting Bull with the flat of it and said, "Now, *Stá-mek-sho-pi,* you better get ready to eat your own tomahawk." ["Eat your tomahawk" is a literal translation from the Blackfoot.] He would have killed old Sitting Bull right then and there, but Bull-Sits-Turning-Around stopped him.

All this time, Sitting Bull was making signs with both arms telling the Sioux not to attack, and he sure looked scared to death. He knew that if there was a fight he would be the first one to taste a Piegan tomahawk [again a literal translation].

Sitting Bull was carrying a riding whip tied to his wrist by a leather thong, and pretty soon Young Bull took the whip away from Sitting Bull and hit him across the face with it and then rode right to those Sioux. This man named Young Bull was one of the toughest warriors among all the Blackfoot Nation, and his name is told many times in stories about brave warriors. This time he rode right amongst those Sioux and told them in the Sioux tongue that they were not warriors just because they had licked the Cavalry. He told those Sioux that those cavalry soldiers couldn't fight, but pretty soon they were going to see how the Blackfoots could fight. Then he rode among them and struck their horses with the whip and struck some of them with the whip and dared them to do their worst. He told those Sioux that they could attack anytime, because the Piegans were ready for them. Then he told them if they did attack, Tah-táhng-iotáhngeh—that was the Sioux name for Sitting Bull—would get the first tomahawk. Then Young Bull rode back to where the Blackfoots were and hit Sitting Bull with the whip again.

All the time this was going on, Sitting Bull was making peace signs to the Sioux so they wouldn't attack, and he was making peace talk to the Piegans. He was begging the Piegans to let him go, and he was so scared I thought he was going to soil his breech clout. Maybe he did—I don't know about that, and I don't want to make a lie by telling something I'm not sure about. But we couldn't let Sitting Bull free because if we did then he would tell his Sioux to attack us. And if we killed him, then the Sioux would attack us because they were not all cowards like Sitting Bull. And if they attacked us those women and children hiding behind those pack horses wouldn't have a chance.

The place where we were was a valley, and there were three coulees that ran down to that place. And pretty soon there were clouds of dust rising up from those coulees, and everybody was watching those big clouds of dust. And when Sitting Bull saw those clouds of dust he really got scared, because Bull-Sits-Turning-Around, who was in charge of our party, told him that dust was from warriors riding down from the main camp of the Bloods and the Blackfoots and the Piegans. Bull-Sits-Turning-Around said to Sitting Bull, "You were looking for a fight and pretty soon you're going to have a good fight because here come the rest of our warriors from the main camp."

Sitting Bull had no stomach for battle when he was in danger, and now he thought my father Last Gun was coming with the Crazy Dog warriors who had taken an oath never to retreat in battle and the other Piegan warrior clans and the Blackfoots and Bloods, so he begged Bull-Sits-Turning-Around to let him go. He said he had no quarrel with the Blackfoot Nation, and he said if we let him go he would leave in peace and never war against the Blackfoots.

So everybody who was near Sitting Bull hit him with their whips and their bows and their lance shafts, and then we let him go. And Sitting Bull joined up with those Sioux and kept on riding and didn't even slow down for as long as we could see him. He just kept riding as fast as he could, with those Sioux strung out behind him and riding as fast as they could.

We were sure sorry we had to let Sitting Bull go, but if we had killed him the Sioux would have attacked, and we had women and children with us and we were few in number and Bull-Sits-Turning-Around didn't want to fight if he could help it. So we let Sitting Bull go so he could get far away before he found out that those clouds of dust were just some buffalo stampeding down those coulees. There weren't any more Piegans or Bloods or Blackfoots for a long way yet.

If Sitting Bull had been a brave man, he would have signaled his war chiefs to attack and make a fight of it, even if he was in danger himself. But he was a coward who only did battle when he was safe, and who counted coup only on dead warriors, and so he ran from a small hunting party of Piegans and Bloods and Blackfoots, and a herd of stampeding buffalo.

If I had at any time been inclined to doubt the complete veracity of any of the Chief's stories or statements, I certainly would have had my comeuppance this afternoon. When I was up last time, the Chief mentioned that not too long ago, when he was a youngster in his fifties and sixties and was chief of Indian Police, he could ride a horse at full speed and shoot snowbirds off the fenceposts with his pistol. At the time, I considered this an eyebrow-raising feat, especially since he said that he seldom missed. But today, as we were discussing guns and shooting, Jimmy suddenly said, "Oh, that's a remind me," and he went into his room and came back with a photograph that was taken last year while the Chief and Jim were paying a visit to Washington State. They had been attending a police pistol meet, and the Chief had been invited to try his hand on the twenty-yard range. And the Chief, at the age of 104, with a .38 calibre pistol he had never before fired—and not having shot any kind of handgun in many years—calmly shot the middle out of the target. Jim says that the photo and the story appeared in the Seattle *Post-Intelligencer*[*] and in other West Coast publications. A couple of the bullets had strayed slightly outside the center of the bull's-eye, and the Chief remarked that he is afraid he doesn't see quite so well as he used to. What a man! What a man! And I used to think that Winston Churchill was the greatest man of our times.

Later in the afternoon the wind abated somewhat and we all went to town. No mail. I bought a snow tire. Bumped into Earl Old Person and he asked me to come to his house Saturday night to do some recording.

Back at the ranch the fires had gone out and it was *cold* in the house. But Jim fired up both stoves and pretty soon it was *too* hot.

I had bought some steak in town, and Jim cooked it for supper. For some reason he decided to boil it, which made it gray and tough. The broth was good though, but I wish I could forget Jim's cognative association. "*Ko-píss*," indeed!

It was a long day for the Chief, and directly after supper he went to bed. Jim and I sat around and bulled as usual. Jim can be quite

* Seattle *Post-Intelligencer*, Nov. 4, 1961.

a toro-tosser, really, but I think that there is a legitimate distinction between lying and just bulling it a little—and Jim, like his dad, does not ever lie. Jim is frustrated, both vocationally and in the matter of having an outlet for his creative energies, and I believe that his bull is an outgrowth of this frustration. Jim starts off by saying what he *would have* done in a particular situation, and then pretty soon he is elaborating as though he actually *had* done it. Every guy should have a chance, dammit to hell!—not necessarily a chance to succeed, but at least a chance to fail legitimately, without having had two strikes to begin with.

During the evening I jotted down some of the gems from Jim's truly inimitable idiolect. Of course, my interest in Jim's individual speech peculiarities is not purely social—some of the best clues with regard to another person's language are to be found in the way he speaks *your* language. Jim's use of prepositions is always interesting because Blackfoot contains no prepositions in the sense that prepositions occur in English, and Jim constantly uses phrases such as: "We rode on my car"; "I played in the baseball team"; etc.

When speaking Blackfoot, Jim constantly employs a linguistic device which, in order to avoid more lofty linguistic terms, I shall call free apocopation—he leaves off the last syllable of a word whenever it pleases him—and since a single word in a polysynthetic language such as Blackfoot may incorporate not only subject and predicate but such grammatical concepts as direct object, indirect object, adjective and adverb, when Jim through analogy transfers his apocope to English he comes up with phrases such as the following:

"Cost me seven bucks for the tube and the." (tire)

"Do you got some or?" (not)

"I broked about three of my." (toes)

Most of the Blackfoots (when speaking English) say "Yah" for "Yes," but Jim frequently says, "Ee-yáh-ai." I don't know where this comes from because in Blackfoot "Yes" is simply "Ah" and "No" is simply "Sah."

Some of Jim's phrases I treasure simply for their own charm, such as these:

"I got knocked out of wind."

"He sure blewed up."

"So I did the same with he has" (the same as he did).

"Diameter of the Sun Dance Pole is about thirty-two inches around."

"I bought me room in a hotel."

"I just about couldn't couldn't move."

"Closeter and closeter."

"They tooked him away in the paddle wagon."

If I could speak Blackfoot half as well as Jim speaks English, I would sure be one proud turkey!

As we sipped our nightcap, Jim gave me some interesting information about Crow love whistles, Sioux love songs (obviously the subject had turned to women) and the Blackfoot Pipe Dance. I was delighted to learn that there is to be a Pipe Dance on Sunday next. I am invited.

P.S. I almost forgot my favorite of all Jim's *phrases du jour:* "I just about almost couldn't nearly quite reach it."

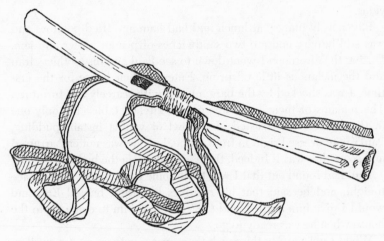

Eagle Bone Whistle

Saturday, September 8

Slept like log. Last one up. Breakfast of Buckwheats and jam and Jimmy's black filigree eggs and tea. Much warmer today. No wind, and the snow is melting. In the morning we drove to town and came back the long way, by way of Kiowa Camp. Passed two of the white crosses with which Montana marks the scene of an auto death (has the desired effect, too). Jim said a couple of Indian teenagers got drunk and ran their car off the road at high speed. "Dead as a toenail," he commented matter-of-factly, and did not waste sympathy for them. He also mentioned that Stanley's father got crippled up in a drunk-driving wreck, and that Stanley, too, has also been known to booze it up a bit.

Jim holds every man responsible for his own actions, and he wastes no commiseration on those who drink up their money and then put on a poor-devil Indian act. He says that I should not shower too much concern on raggedy little Paul Many Hides because Paul has gone through a pretty good piece of dough. Jim has held onto the little ranch through thick and thin (mostly thin), and he is justifiably proud that he has done so without asking favors of anyone ("By my own jockstraps"). Jim has never owned a car less than ten years old, so it is small wonder that he sheds no tears for the guy who hocks his warbonnet for a new car and then cries foul because he has drunk up the first payment and so loses his wagon. Jim is an exceptional guy. But then, he has the blood of chiefs in his veins.

Ravenously hungry at lunch and had ham and fried potatoes and was still hungry and ate two sandwiches of peanut butter and jam. During the afternoon I went down to see Paul and his toothless frau and the melanous little offspring. Entering their house for the first time, I was shocked by the bare interior with scarcely any furniture. The remains of their lunch was on the kitchen table (the only one in the house); it consisted of a bowl of vanilla instant pudding. Paul's wife dressed right in front of me, but she was not embarrassed and so neither was I. Indeed, there is no door on the bedroom.

Paul had found out that I was to do some recording at Earl's place tonight, and he said that his relatives live right behind Earl and would I give him a lift. I said O.K. and told him to come up to the house when he was ready to go.

When I got back to the ranch there was a note on my typewriter:

> Dick I went down to river see if
> I could found any White fish
>
> By Jim

The Chief was there, though, and during the afternoon I recorded one of his stories. I said, *"No-kits-ín-i-kòh-kit"* (tell me a story), and the Chief said, *"So-Káh-pi"* (good). Then he said, *"Nah-kóh-tsis-a-kàh-kit"* (give me a smoke), and while he smoked he thought. Then at length he nodded affirmatively, and I said, *"Ki-dáh-mai-ki-stahpsi?"* (Are you ready?) and he said, *"Ah"* (yes) and we recorded a story about a magic shield. I did not understand all of it, and Jim will have to help me with the translation. For the remainder of the daylight time, the Chief worked on his eagle-bone whistle and I typed.

Jim came home, fishless, at suppertime, and shortly after supper Paul and his crew came straggling in, looking starved as usual, so I fed them. That kid is a brat. This permissive attitude which Indians exhibit toward their young—I have never seen an Indian child punished—may be fine for building feelings of security, etc., but I think that it has undesirable fringe effects. Paul's kid needs discipline, and from me he gets it. I don't hesitate to reprimand the little B., and he minds me, too.

We arrived at Earl's place shortly after dark. Paul said that he would walk from there. Earl and family were crowded around the television set watching the Miss America pageant, and Earl, after having asked me to come down to do some recording, now proclaimed very superciliously that he was not in a mood to record. This is the third time that he has pulled something like this, and he just struck out. Someone once said, "The only time you can be nice to some people is when you are picking them up again after you have knocked them down," but I have trouble keeping this irrefutable fact in mind. Earl and his sermon about Christian living! I know quite a few good Christians, but very few of them are preachers.

Actually, though, my annoyance with Earl was ephemeral because I think I understand Earl pretty well. He is not the most erudite person in the world, but he is probably the closest thing to an intellectual to be found among the Blackfoot full-bloods, and it is to persons such as Earl that the Blackfoots must look for leadership. The transition from braids to book law is not an easy one, and somewhere in between there is almost certain to appear a measure of bravado.

Paul and company shortly came pounding on the door, rescuing me from an awkward and infuriating situation. Paul's relatives were not at home, and he asked me to drive him to the home of Phillip, his brother. I agreed.

So off into the dark wet night we went, back up the road past the ranch, way out to Kiowa Camp Road. On Kiowa we turned left, crossed the bridge over the creek, and drove a couple of miles along the main road. Then, as we were passing a double-track that cut off to the left again, Paul, who was riding co-pilot, turned to me and said reproachfully, "You was suppose turned off back there." So I turned around and took the double-track, and what a wild ride it was! There is a lot of unfenced land in Montana—immense stretches of open prairie—and after fifteen minutes of following the wagon-track over and among the rolling low grass hills of the Reservation, I had begun to share Jimmy's opinion of Paul. The windshield kept steaming up on the inside, and the defrosters would not keep it clear, so I said, "Paul, hand me that bandana in the glove compartment." Paul giggled and said, "Ya-a-a-a." I said, "Hand me the bandana, will you! The windshield is all fogged up and I can't see." So Paul got out the bandana, wiped with great industry the windshield in front of *himself*, and peered out helpfully at the dark, fog-shrouded landscape.

So I mopped the windshield with one hand and with the other tried to keep the car wheels in the barely visible track. We had cut off the main road high on a hill, and ever since then we had seemed to be going steadily downward, although the track would sometimes inexplicably take an S turn or wind up on a knoll and down again. Once we hit a rock, directly in the left-hand track, about the size of a bowling ball, and I puzzled how anyone could drive this route day after day without pausing to kick the rock aside. Finally I decided that the track had been cut by a drunk, and it probably was.

We drove for what seemed to be twenty miles—it was probably closer to ten—and then suddenly burst into the midst of a band of sheep, scattering them. The sheepherder's wagon, a wheeled, gypsy-type domicile, appeared suddenly out of the mist, lighted from within and glowing as exotically as a Chinese lantern. Dogs barked a protest at our intrusion.

As we drove along, the track would occasionally branch in two directions, but not once did Paul anticipate the advisability of telling me which way to go. Invariably I had to ask him, and invariably he was so slow in responding that I had to make my own choice. Twice it was necessary to back up and go the other way.

Finally the path crested a hill and plunged straight down toward the center of an aspen grove, the tracks disappearing under a hundred-foot long puddle or pond which reflected the car lights blindingly. I had time to ask Paul whether we were on the right track, and when he said, "Yaaah, she's it," I could not but plunge ahead and hope that the water was not as deep as it appeared to be. We were lucky. The water was half-a-wheel deep and the bottom was soft mud, but we had the advantage of momentum and as the orchestra played *Sabre Dance* the car plowed through the fifty yard tunnel of trees without drowning out the motor.

Another mile of silent disgust and I pulled into the dark, cluttered and dog-populated yard of the low-roofed log cabin that Phillip Many Hides calls home. I had been under the impression that Phillip lived close to Paul, who lives less than two miles from the ranch, and I was right. We were now once again on the shore of the creek, but on the side opposite to the ranch. There, just across the water, was Paul's shack. We had driven God-knows-how-many miles to arrive at a destination about two hundred yards away. I asked Paul how he would have gotten here if it hadn't been for me, and he calmly replied that he would have simply crossed the creek, as usual. I didn't hit him because he is smaller than I and besides he has only about three teeth left.

We went into the cabin, into a large room dominated by a fireplace and filled with stoves, furniture and people. Phillip and his wife were there, and to my embarrassment a young couple were in bed on a mattress on the floor. Another young man was present, and through a doorway leading to another room I could see yet another young Indian man. Pete, the black-patch boy, was snugly bedded down in a corner. He sat up and smiled and said hello, and I was quite startled to learn that he could talk.

It was quite obvious that Paul had neglected to announce his intention of paying a visit this evening, but everybody was very nice about it. By this time I was thoroughly fed up with Paul, but the log cabin was so thoroughly Indian that I was glad to be there. Medicine bundles were hung on the wall, a venerable pair of gray braids was nailed above the bedroom door, and the drying poles which traversed the room just below the ceiling were wealthy with parchment-like slabs of drying whitefish. The house smelled good, as do all Indian houses, but there was in the air a pungent freshness which puzzled me. I inquired about it, and one of the young men foolishly said that it was his shaving lotion (Indians don't shave). The woman of the house told me that it was some fresh mint she had gathered. She also offered me a cup of tea from the large pot on the stove. I said no thanks, but when she explained that it was the tea that the Canadian Blackfoots drink, I accepted the big enamel cup. I suppose I'd give horse-tea a try, so long as it was from an Indian pony. The tea tasted like tea.

It was late now, and we were obviously keeping everybody up, so I suggested to Paul that we had better be going as soon as he conducted whatever business had brought him out here. He said he didn't have any special reason for coming; he just thought it would be nice to take a ride.

On the way back we very nearly got stuck in the mudhole, but

I didn't say anything. I didn't say anything all the way back; I was afraid of what I might say.

Much later, after Paul had been deposited across the creek, I told my tale of woe to Jimmy. He said that I had gotten a typical dose of Paul—that Paul would try to borrow your butt if his was dirty.

Jimmy had baked two pies—a cherry and a blueberry—and we ate the blueberry. The pie, accompanied by tea and sympathy spiked with two shots of Jim Beam, brightened the evening considerably. I was tired, but the Chief was in a story-telling mood and so we did some recording until 11:30. The story the Chief told was a story of his own personal experience. It was a marvelous story, filled with pricelessly authentic detail, but it was also a very sad story, and when the story was finished I realized with most profound embarrassment that it had been I—me and my big, arrogant, White Man's mouth—that had evoked within the Old Fellow's consciousness these melancholy remembrances. Because of the Chief's cold, I had bought him a bottle of vitamin C tablets. And when he was reluctant to take them (Indians just don't like to take White Man's medicine) I thought that I was pursuing a rather clever course of proselytism by explaining to the Chief that ascorbic acid tablets are the same as rose hips (roseberries, the Indians call them). But what I really did was to put my moccasin in my mouth.

THE THUNDER LODGE

This happened not long ago, when I was living in a house I had built just below Starr School, at the juncture of North Cutbank Creek and South Cutbank Creek.

[I was able to establish the year as 1900, the year following the Chief's Christian marriage to Kit Fox Woman. I also succeeded in verifying, through elderly Indians who had been present at the time, the absolute authenticity of every detail of this story, including the unusual circumstances surrounding the several deaths which are herein described.]

There was to be a Sun Dance on the Piegan Reservation that year, and the Canadians—the Bloods, the North Blackfoots and the North Piegans—had come down to join in the celebration. But there was an argument about where the Medicine Lodge should be erected, and eventually two separate encampments were set up, one on the flat east of Starr School and the other down at Old Agency.

My father and I both set up our lodges at the Starr School encampment, and Makes-Cold-Weather, a friend of mine from the North Blackfoots, assisted Little Bear and myself in hauling in the poles for the Medicine Lodge.

When the Medicine Lodge had been completed, Makes-Cold-Weather asked me to go with him to the slaughter house in Browning to get some meat. On the way we met a rider, and Makes-Cold-Weather informed me that this lone rider was a very powerful medicine man from Gleichen [the North Blackfoot Reserve]. He said, "This man was injured, and a steel plate was placed in the back of his head, and since that time he has had great power from the Thunder. He owns the Thunder Lodge, and he has painted many people." [One of the functions of a medicine man was to paint the faces of individuals in order to insure their good health and fortune. In return, the medicine man received a gift of either money or some object of value such as a blanket or some fine beaded work.]

When the Thunder Medicine Man drew even with us, he reined in his horse close to mine and looked into my face and said, "I have been looking for you for a long time." I did not know what he meant. I had never seen him before. But when he spoke to me a chill ran up my back and I felt very strange— sort of a mixture of fear and reverence. I did not know what to say, so I said nothing. Nor did the Medicine Man speak again; for a minute he continued to look deep into my face, as though he could see right through me, and then he rode on.

Upon returning to my lodge I learned that each separate encampment had decided to have its own Sun Dance, each with its own Holy Woman. Early the next morning, when I went to my father's lodge to invite him over for breakfast, I saw that the Thunder Medicine Man had erected the Thunder Lodge on the far edge of our encampment. The Thunder Lodge is easily distinguishable because it is painted with the Thunder Paint. [The Thunder Paint is blue paint; the Thunder Lodge is painted a solid blue, with no other decoration.]

After breakfast I accompanied my father back to his lodge, and as we sat talking we heard someone singing. Stepping outside the lodge, we saw that the Thunder Medicine Man had piled his goods [his fees for face painting] on top of a nearby hill; he was seated up there, singing medicine songs, and when he saw that my father and I were looking at him he stopped singing and told me with signs that he wished me to go up there. I had a strange feeling about the man, but my father said that I had better go up and see what he wanted, so I filled a pipe with tobacco and climbed the hill. When I saw all the goods that were piled up there, I knew that the Thunder Medicine Man must indeed have painted many people.

I presented the pipe to the Thunder Medicine Man, and we smoked it together, and then the man spoke. He told me that it was not good that there should be more than one Medicine Lodge. He said that I should tell my father (he used the term, "our father") that he must use his influence as chief to convince the people that the Medicine Lodge at Old Agency should be taken down immediately and that all the people should come up and join in the Sun Dance at Starr School. I told him that he had better discuss such important matters directly with my father, and he agreed to accompany me down to his lodge.

In my father's lodge we smoked another pipe, and then the Thunder Medicine Man spoke to my father—but instead of addressing him as "father" he called him "mother." [I don't know why the Chief should have considered this point worthy of mention. The North Blackfoots address both father and mother with the same term, na-áh.* The Piegan word for father is nín-nah, the term for mother being nik-tsís-tah, and although the Piegans sometimes use the North Blackfoot word, na-áh, in reference to mother, they never use it in reference to father.] He said, "Mother, you must tell the Holy Woman down at Old Agency that there must be only one Medicine Lodge and only one encampment, and that the Medicine Lodge must be over here." My father said that he would do this immediately, and he sent Yellow Wolf to Old Agency to tell the people to move their encampment and to tell the Holy Woman to have the Medicine Lodge taken down.

But the people would not listen to Yellow Wolf, so my father went in person to talk to them. When my father had left, the Thunder Medicine Man said something that nearly caused me to lose consciousness. First he filled a pipe and smoked it with me, and then he said, "I have seen Thunder [Thunder had appeared to him in a dream in human form] and he looks exactly like you. I have promised to sell the Thunder Lodge to Iron Pipe, and for two weeks I have waited for Iron Pipe to appear. I will wait for another two weeks, and if Iron Pipe has not come to claim the lodge, the Thunder Lodge shall be yours."

* A personal or intimate form.

142

Late in the evening of that same day there was a hard, brief thunderstorm, with much lightning. [Anyone who has seen lightning on the High Plains of Montana has no difficulty in understanding why the Blackfoots regarded it as a supernatural expression; it is lightning totally different from any I have seen elsewhere.] When it was over, the Thunder Medicine Man came again to my father's lodge.

My father said, "I am sorry. I have done my best, but my arms are not long enough. ["My arms are not long enough," is the literal translation of a Blackfoot phrase which is intended to suggest something like, "my influence is not broad enough," or, "my authority is not strong enough."] The people will not camp together, and the Holy Woman will not allow the lodge to be moved."

The Thunder Medicine Man said, "I am sorry to hear this. The Medicine Lodge is not in a good place. Thunder is not happy with the way the people are conducting themselves. Misfortune will come to them."

At that time there were several Piegan children attending the Indian school down at Fort Shaw. Among them were my wife's younger brother, one of Yellow Wolf's sons, and the son of my brother, Cross Guns. I was asked to go down and bring the children home for summer vacation, so I left the next day for Fort Shaw. The journey to Fort Shaw could not be made in a single day, and as I camped that first night north of Depuyer I was waked by another violent thunderstorm. I had no way of knowing it at the time, but when I got back home I learned that upon that night the Medicine Lodge at Old Agency had been struck by lightning. No one but the Holy Woman had been killed. The Holy Woman had been killed by a bolt of lightning. [As though it were not enough that this incident is a verifiable historical fact, some years later, when the daughter of this Holy Woman sponsored a Medicine Lodge, she too was struck and killed by lightning. Once again, the Holy Woman was the only one to die.]

I was delayed at Fort Shaw for two days because upon arriving there I discovered that Cross Guns' boy had broken his hip in falling from a horse. The Superintendent of the Indian School, a man named Campbell, refused to send the boy to the hospital, and in order to borrow a buggy in which to take the youngster home I had to go all the way back to Choteau. Campbell also did not wish to allow one of the girls to go home, so I lied to him. I told him that the girl's father had died and the girl was his only heir and that it would be necessary for her to return home for the property settlement. I told him that a lawyer had told me to bring her home, and when I said this, Campbell not only let her go but insisted upon giving us rations. He also gave us eight pillows with which to make Cross Guns' boy comfortable in the buggy. [I researched this portion of the narrative with great thoroughness, and positively established as facts the following: (1) Cross Guns' boy did break his hip in a fall from a horse; (2) The Chief was forced to transport the boy by buggy all the way from Fort Shaw to his home near Browning (a distance of well over one hundred miles!); (3) F. C. Campbell, the superintendent of the Indian school at Fort Shaw, later became both Supervisor of Indian Industries for the States of Montana, North Dakota, Wyoming and Idaho *and* Superintendent of the Blackfoot Indian Reservation, and although Campbell managed by hook or crook to remain in the Indian Service for 39 years, his conduct was such that at long last, on July 24, 1929, F. C. Campbell became the subject of a special investigation by the Committee on Indian Affairs of the United States Senate.]

Cross Guns' boy had to lie on his back in the bed of the wagon, and since it would have been inhuman to force him to travel in the daytime, with the sun in his face, we traveled at night, by moonlight. We had no medicine to give the boy, but at Choteau I had gotten hold of some whiskey and we gave this to the boy to ease his pain. We dosed him with whiskey until he passed out.

North of Choteau, on a bright, moonlit night, with every star clear in the sky, we were traveling along when suddenly lightning began to flash. Drags His Robe, Heavy Breast and some other old-timers were traveling with me at the time, and none of us could figure out the reason for this sudden advent of fierce lightning flashes. We stopped and took shelter, but although the lightning continued until dawn, not a drop of rain fell and not a cloud darkened the bright full moon. It was the strangest thing I had ever experienced, and I assure you that the boy was not the only one to take a shot of whiskey that night.

At Depuyer we got some more bootleg whiskey for the boy, and finally we all made it back home. The first thing I noticed upon arrival was that the Medicine Lodge had been torn down, and the first person I encountered, a lady named Goods Stealing Woman, told me about the Holy Woman's having been killed by lightning. Goods Stealing Woman had been in the Medicine Lodge at the time, but she, like everyone else except the Holy Woman, had been spared by the lightning bolt.

Iron Pipe had arrived in time to claim the Thunder Lodge, but Many Guns, a friend of mine from Gleichen, came to my teepee and told me that the Thunder Medicine Man had saved for me a medicine drum, some medicine bells, and some other things. In order to receive the medicine articles I had first to go through a ceremony, so at the appointed time I called at the lodge of Iron Pipe. Iron Pipe's wife would not at first allow me to enter the lodge, but Many Guns explained that I was an invited guest and so the woman allowed me to take my place in the lodge.

The ceremony was conducted by the medicine man from Gleichen, the Thunder Medicine Man. I sat on his right, and Iron Pipe sat on his left. The Thunder Medicine Man lighted a smudge of juniper and then handed the smudge stick to Iron Pipe. Then he sang four songs.

The words to the first song were, "When the wind blows, that is my medicine."

The words to the second song were, "When it rains, that is my medicine."

The words to the third song were, "When it hails, that is my medicine."

The words to the fourth song were, "When the weather becomes clear after a storm, that is my medicine."

When he had finished singing, the Medicine Man took the smudge stick and with it scratched a jagged line in the earthen floor of the lodge from the place where I sat to the door; then he drew a similar line from the place where Iron Pipe was sitting. Then the Medicine Man resumed his seat, and immediately lightning flashed along the jagged lines from in front of Iron Pipe and me to the open door of the lodge.

This was the most frightening thing I have ever witnessed. I knew that this medicine man had great power, and I asked him whether there was anything in his power that was against me. He said, "No, there is nothing in my power against you. But you must never again eat roseberries; if you do, your whole body will break out in a rash the same color as the roseberries."

I said, "What about tomatoes?"

He said, "Tomatoes are all right, but you must never again,

under any circumstances, use red paint on your blanket." The medicine articles which I purchased from the Thunder Medicine Man included a drum, some medicine bells, and a small piece of metal.

Later on [in the fall of the year 1901] I went through a ceremony with Flat Tail and Drags His Robe in order to purchase a medicine pipe bundle. This bundle contained two medicine pipes. One pipe came from Sun; the other pipe came from Thunder.

During the Pipe Ceremony I used red paint on my blanket, and that same night I had a dream in which two men came to my house to visit me. They said that I had been warned not to use red paint, and since I had ignored the warning they were going to punish me by taking away my first child, my little girl. They said that they would be back to let me know when they were going to take my daughter away from me. The men did not tell me who they were, but I knew that they were Thunder and Sun.

I went with my friend Many Guns to visit the Bloods over in Canada [a customary response of the Plains Indian to an emotional crisis was the paying of a visit to a distant relative or close friend; this custom is adhered to by the Blackfoot Indian even today], and while I was in Canada word reached me that my daughter was very ill. I returned home immediately.

At that time I was still living near the main fork of Cut Bank Creek. When I arrived at my house, my father was holding my little girl in his lap. Earrings, who was an Indian doctor, was attempting to treat the child, but as soon as I entered my baby ran to me and clung to me.

That night I dreamed that the same two men came to me and told me that very soon now they would be coming for my child. In the same dream I saw a rider coming. The two men pointed to the rider and said, "We want your daughter, and we want that rider too." The rider was Mad Wolf. My daughter died the next day. Mad Wolf died four days later.

The drum that I had received from the Thunder Medicine Man had been the favorite plaything of my little girl. After my child's death I could no longer bear even to look at the drum, so I threw it into the creek.

The following year I attended a Medicine Lodge above Browning. The Holy Woman was Snake Woman, the wife of Morning Gun. There had been a flood that spring, and when

I went up on a hillside above the creek to look for wood I found the drum in the branches of a tree. The drum was completely undamaged, so I took it down to the encampment and gave it to Earrings. Earrings is buried in a house up there on the pine ridge, and so far as I know the drum was buried with him.

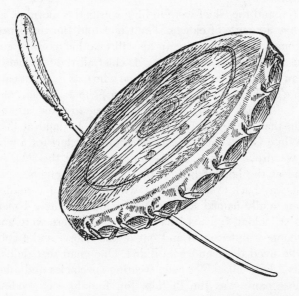

Sunday, September 9

Everybody beat me up today. I would probably be sleeping yet if I hadn't been reveilled by the ungodly sound of a dog gnawing on a bone. I thought he was outside the bedroom door, and I yanked it open with a shoe in one hand; actually, he was under the house, directly beneath my bed. So that is where the dogs go when they disappear!

I have seen a few moths around the house in past days, but suddenly this morning there were clouds of them—great fat things. I said to Jim, "I wonder where all those moths come from."

Jim said, "Me, I wonder where all those moths come from. Goddam, I wonder where they come from. They come from someplace."

Indians are very willing to participate in any experience which appears to be of interest to a friend. If I had suddenly become concerned with the reason that the moon is yellow, Jim would have participated with equal enthusiasm in this perplexity. Jim has a way of repeating things I say—of sharing my observations and opinions—and he does not hesitate to share the burden of my miseries. Now that I temporarily have a bum leg, Jim's old rodeo injuries (to his leg) are bothering him; and brother Jim finds similar experiences whenever I sleep poorly, have poor appetite, etc. This is the Indian way of participating in a close friendship. The Irish are the same way.

Both Jim and the Chief were in high spirits this morning, kidding around like a couple of clowns. The Chief told Jim that since he is Chief around here, from now on he will take his morning coffee in bed. Jim replied that the old fellow is chief all right—"Chief by the table" (an Indian metaphor for someone who eats a great deal).

At ten o'clock we drove down to "Starr School," which refers not only to the actual school building there but to the scattered residences in that area. The Pipe Dance was to be held at the home of Jim White Grass, but it wasn't scheduled to start for a while yet and so we drove on into town. Jimmy checked the P.O. box for mail, and at the hotel I bought the Chief some cigars.

On the way back to Starr School, we stopped at the residence of an Indian family named Kicking-A-Woman, and there I met some of the best looking Indians I have ever seen. There were an awful lot of people wandering in and out of the house, and I still don't know who lived there and who didn't. One chap that didn't, I am sure, was a large Blackfoot man, wearing spectacles and a baseball cap, whose name was Jim Buffalo. Jim Buffalo was good-natured and voluble, and he kidded the Chief by saying that the Chief was really a Cree, not a Piegan.

Actually, according to Jim, several of those persons present really were Crees, including one extremely beautiful girl of about twenty-one. She was really a knock-out, but her fine white teeth held a toothpick, and a cigarette dangled from her delicately formed fingers, so I don't think I'll be taking her home to meet Pater.

There was a large quantity of fresh meat hanging from the drying poles in the house, and it turned out that someone had just killed a large elk over by Kiowa Camp. As we were leaving, the host gave the Chief a chunk of elk meat.

All the way back to Starr School, Jimmy hummed Indian songs. Like most outsiders, I had always associated Indian singing with rituals—religious ceremonies, war dances, etc.—and it still is difficult for me to accept the fact that Indians sing for fun too. The Indian way of humming is merely to devoice the vowels—to sort of whisper the hi-yi-yi's. I miss so *much* by not knowing music! Music doesn't miss much by not knowing me, though, because when I secretly recorded some of the Blackfoot songs Jim has taught me, the playback sounded like background music for a Hitchcock film and I hastily erased the tape. Indian music is not so simple as it sounds.

The Pipe Dance is a religious ceremony, customarily held each year after the first thunderstorm of spring. This year, luckily for me, the dance was postponed until the present date. I have not been able to establish definitely the reason for the postponement, but there are rumors that a polio scare discouraged all public gatherings earlier in the year. I do know that the movie house was closed for a while.

But by the time we returned to Starr School, to Jim White Grass' house, people were beginning to arrive for the Dance. Cars and trucks of all descriptions—from ancient jalopies to brand new station wagons—were pulling into the yard. One car had a decal on the rear window which read, "Blackfeet Indian Reservation, Browning, Montana," and a sign in luminescent tape on the bumper which declared, "JESUS SAVES." As a matter of fact, there are quite a few "saved" Indians on the Reservation, and I do not think it particularly paradoxical that the best Christians among them are the same ones who are most faithful to the ancient Indian beliefs. In Blackfoot there are many words for God.

For a while Jim and I watched silently as the cars and trucks filled the yard and then began to spill over onto an adjoining lot, then finally Jim shook his head once, in a characteristic gesture, and said, "In old days you see at these dances there was nothing but wagons and horsebacks. Now-days you don't see." (To Jim, "the old days" refers to any time prior to the end of W.W. II, for it was not until the post-war period that the automobile replaced the horse as a prestige symbol here on the Reservation. To the Chief, on the other hand, "not long ago" means any time within his memory span, and "just recently" suggests any time between W.W. I and the present.)

When I picked up my shirts at the local laundry, the Norwegian who runs the place confided, "I came out here from North Dakota to get away from too many relatives. Then I married an Indian girl and so now I've got twice as many relatives as before." I know what he means. I am a Blackfoot by adoption only, but I have yet to meet an Indian who is not in some way related to me. However, this profusion of in-laws is attributable only in part to the endogamous social structure of the community; a fair portion of my relatives are relatives only because of the singular concept of family relationship held by the Blackfoots. As a for instance, the first person I met at the Dance—a friendly chap named Joe Scabby Robe—immediately informed me that we were kith and kin. As I got the family portrait, Joe Scabby Robe is Earl Old Person's brother-in-law; and since Stanley White Man is also Earl's brother-in-law, and since Stanley is some kind of distant kin to some branch of the Chief's family (by one of his wives, I guess), and since I am now the Chief's son, that makes Joe Scabby Robe and I something-or-other. Which means that I am also related to the only orally deprived child on the Reservation, because Joe was leading by the hand the first thumb-sucking Indian kid I have ever seen.

But, relative or not, Joe Scabby Robe is a willing and capable informant and I like him. The wind was rising all the time and the clouds were moving thick in the sky, and Joe pulled up the collar of his maroon nylon jacket and pointed far off to the northeast and said, "You see that big hill down there with the clouds on top? That means storm. We call that hill 'Sweetgrass Hill,' us Indians, and we say when Sweetgrass Hill has got a hat on, that means storm."

This led to a discussion of the unusual weather that the Reservation has been seeing lately, and Jimmy said, "Corn to [according to] some people says, it's that Adam bomb. I don't know what the real made it, but we sure having a funny weather."

As we talked, some friends of Jim drove in and parked nearby. And as soon as the car had stopped, Jim called out, "Hey, when you was driving that car your wheels was going round." Now this was probably the most un-funny remark ever made by an Indian (or anybody else), but everyone in the car laughed heartily. And this brings up an important point: the popular belief that Indians are cold, stoical, sober-sided and full of stiff and pompous dignity could not be further from the truth. Indians have marvelous senses of humor; they love to laugh, and even if your quip is not at all funny, your Indian audience will laugh in appreciation of the fact that you at least made the effort at affability.

Strangely enough, Indian humor is neither as sadistic nor as scatological as the humor of Western Whites. The Western White frequently finds humor in physical or mental deformity or in the various biological processes of both men and animals. This, I am convinced, derives from the days on the frontier when a deformity or physical malfunction was a very serious thing because it meant that you could not pull your own weight; there was no room for sympathy in the frontier struggle for survival. But the Indians have been leading a rough existence for a much longer time than the Whites, and their humor has mellowed to a gentler flavor (although I am told that the good ladies—*as usual*—can spin some pretty curly yarns).

Indians are especially fond of linguistic humor, including puns and quidproquo jokes, and Joe Scabby Robe immediately seized upon the moment of Jim's effort to tell me one:

"Once a White man was hunting elk with a Blackfoot guide, and when the White man saw an elk on a far-away ridge he raised up his gun to shoot. But the elk was too far away to shoot at yet, so the Blackfoot Indian he said, '*Kick-kah, kick-kah.*' *You* know that '*Kick-kah*' means 'wait' in the Blackfoot language, but that White hunter he didn't know that, so he says to that Indian, 'Kick 'im hell! I'm goin' shoot him.'"

As Jimmy and Joe and I stood chatting, several people came up and asked to be introduced to me (Jimmy says that I am getting to be quite well known on the Reservation, especially among the old-timers). Finally there approached an older woman whom Jimmy introduced as Mary Ground, the lady that was sponsoring the Pipe Dance. Mary Ground has a rather light skin, gray-blue eyes, and she speaks flawless English. Despite her being dressed in a fine Indian costume, with beautifully beaded, shin-length moccasins of smoked buckskin, I thought at first that she must be White or of mixed blood. I still do not know for certain, but I soon learned that Mrs. Ground speaks Blackfoot beautifully, enunciating all the difficult Blackfoot sounds with a clarity that was a revelation to me. Especially interesting was her articulation of the alveolar nasal semivowel [n], which in the Chief's idiolect is sometimes indistinguishable from the lateral alveolar semivowel or bilateral continuant [l].

After a brief chat, Mrs. Ground said that the Pipe Dance ceremony would not start for about another hour, so Jim said, "Shit, I'll had me little nap," and he went to the station wagon, slumped down in the front seat, pulled his hat down over his eyes and went to sleep. Mary went back inside the house; the Chief was already inside, talking with some friends; Mrs. Scabby Robe had taken the child to the outhouse, and this left Joe and me on our own. This was fine with me, because Joe was an eager and knowledgeable source of local color and information and in talking with him about Indian religious beliefs I became more than ever impressed with the tolerant and unhypocritical way in which the Blackfoot Indian finds room within the framework of his philosophy for both the

Christian dogma and his own spiritual inheritance. Joe told me of the time that a sixteen-year-old Indian girl had seen a vision of the Virgin Mary. The Virgin had asked the girl to sponsor a Sun Dance (an Indian religious ceremony) at a certain time and place, promising that Jesus would attend the ceremony. So the Sun Dance was held, and afterward, in solid rock, were found the footprints of Jesus, showing where he had stood during the ceremony.

Our religious discussion finally led into a discussion of Indian burials, and Joe Scabby Robe turned and pointed south, across the creek, to a high pine bluff about two miles away. "You see that pine bluff?" he said. "Just below the ridge, in that open place among the pines? You see that little house up there?"

Now that he had pointed it out, I could see the house quite clearly.

"That's an Indian burial house. That's where old Earrings is buried." And Joe told me that a long time ago, before there was a road across this part of the Reservation, a man named Earrings had been returning from the Agency with supplies when he lost his way in a blizzard and froze to death. He was buried, in the Blackfoot tradition, in a small house constructed especially for that purpose, with his personal belongings left lying close about him in case he should need them in the other life.

I asked Joe whether it would be all right for me to visit the burial house, and he said sure. He even told me how to get there ("You could go that way there, or either go that other way").

Most of the Pipe Dance guests had arrived now, although an occasional late arriving car or truck would still appear. The house was overflowing with people, and numerous children (Indian children invariably go where their parents go) raced in and out and around the house and visited the outhouse in two's and three's. Joe Scabby Robe went off to find his wife, and I set out to locate the Chief, entering the house by way of the back door which led directly into the big kitchen. The kitchen was crowded with women and children. Mary Ground was there, stirring a huge cauldron which toiled and bubbled on the large woodstove. Also on the stove-top was a two-gallon granite coffeepot. To the right of the kitchen was a small room containing a bed upon which several small children napped. Beyond the kitchen was the main room of the house. I could see the Chief and most of the other men in there, but since this was obviously the room in which the Pipe Dance was to be performed, I did not feel free to enter alone and without invitation.

As I stood uncertainly there in the kitchen, feeling rather like the only man at a lingerie sale, a roundish, Mrs. Murphy-type Indian woman went charging back and forth, bowling over kids and frequently bumping into people and things. I ducked her several times, but finally she smacked solidly into me, and placing her hand on my chest she smiled an apology. I looked down into her eyes and could tell immediately that she was stone blind. Jimmy entered at that moment. He explained that the woman was Mrs. Amy White Grass, wife of our host, and he led me into the other room.

The room was quite large—about 25 × 30, I think—and all of the furniture except a stove in one corner had been removed, leaving the place bare except for some rather incongruous wall decorations: the inevitable Indian family portraits, a medicine bundle, a large framed picture of Jesus, and a really huge and very dirty old toy poodle. The Chief was seated on the floor at the far end of the room, to the left of a very old-appearing, cadaverously thin Indian man with wispy white braids. Jimmy explained that the old man's name is Dan Bull Plume and that he was to be chief functionary during the ceremony. Next to the Chief sat old Plenty Treaty (B.C.), and on across the room and down along the adjoining wall sat Indian men shoulder to shoulder. As Jim and I entered, a place was made for us and we hunkered down to join the tight-packed row of men.

To the right of old Dan Bull Plume, and down along the wall opposite the men, the women sat. Most of the women were dressed in Indian costume, but a few had on plain dark cotton dresses. None of the men was dressed in a complete Indian outfit, although most of them had on moccasins and several wore necklaces of claws or beads or shells. The Chief had on his moccasins, of course—he never wears shoes—and he was wearing his shell necklace and the copper and abalone shell earrings which have pierced his ears for at least three-quarters of a century. (In the old days the Blackfoots had their ears pierced by a hot awl.) In his hand the Chief held a fan made from the wing of an eagle.

Eventually, Mary Ground entered and assumed a place to the immediate right of Dan Bull Plume, four drummers seated themselves cross-legged in a row in front of the women, those who could not find seats on the floor crowded into doorways or behind the stove, and the Pipe Dance ceremony got under way.

My attempting to describe in detail the Pipe Dance would be equivalent to a pagan's trying to describe High Mass at Saint Peter's. The ceremony began with Dan Bull Plume's suddenly bursting forth with a very rapid and forceful chant; then almost immediately the drums came in, and then followed a lengthy series of religious rituals which were, of course, Roman to me. The experience was somewhat akin to my first attendance, as a small boy, at an Italian Opera; I didn't understand half that was going on, but I thoroughly enjoyed every minute of it. I especially enjoyed the drumming. Each of the four drummers held in his left hand a flat, tambourine-shaped drum. The top of the drum was covered with horsehide; the bottom was open, criss-crossed with rawhide thongs which held the drumhead tight and which also provided something by which the drum could be held by the drummer. The drum was struck with a single padded drumstick, and the tempo was fast. The rhythm consisted in a hard beat and then a soft beat—like a rapid heart—and at the end of a sequence (or whatever the musical term is), the final soft beat would be skipped, the music ending with *hard beat, pause, hard beat*. No two drums were of exactly the same size or pitch, and they all sounded in perfect unison and the effect was magical. Once again I felt cheated because I have no real knowledge of music.

One of the drummers was Phillip Many Hides; another was a blind old Indian named Fish. The other two were strangers to me, and I was pleasantly surprised to see that one of them was a very young man—not many of the younger Indians participate actively in the old Blackfoot ceremonies.

The most striking ritual of the Pipe Dance ceremony is the un-wrapping of the Medicine Pipe. The Medicine Pipe—actually a large and highly ornate pipe stem, without a bowl—is kept wrapped in cloth and wound with buckskin thongs and can be opened only at a religious ceremony with the proper ritualistic procedure. The procedure included chanting, drumming, much symbolic pointing and gesticulating with the Pipe, and the burning of sweetgrass. A braid of sweetgrass and a pair of wooden tongs made from the bifurcate branch of a sarvis berry bush are included in the wrapping along with the Pipe. The tongs were presented to Mary Ground, who used them to transport a burning ember from the stove to a flat stone on the floor in front of the functionary. With much chanting and gesticulation, old Dan Bull Plume shredded some of the dry sweetgrass over the hot coal, producing a sizeable amount of sweet, pungent smoke.

The Medicine Pipe itself, when finally exposed to view, was a beautiful thing. Over three feet long, it was marvelously decorated with such things as ermine tails, colored feathers, fur, beads, tiny brass bells, human hair, etc. The Medicine Pipe itself is not used for smoking, but during the ceremony another pipe (the long, stone-

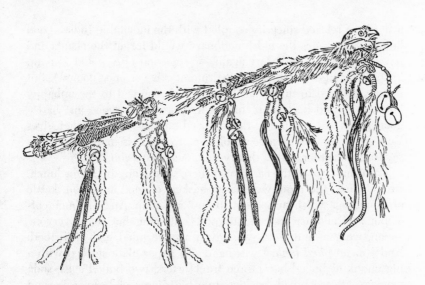

bowled, peace-pipe variety) was passed around and puffed on by both men and women. In addition to puffing on the pipe, the smokers blew the smoke into their hands and made a gesture of cleansing their bodies with it. They passed me by, though, and I was rather wounded by the slight, I must confess.

Actually the Pipe Dance ceremony was conducted as a series of separate events, with breaks between them. During the breaks, everyone was free to talk and joke and practically everyone, male and female, rolled Bull Durham cigarettes. It is fascinating to see those gnarled old fingers perform so expertly the delicate task of rolling a cigarette. I can't do it. The Blackfoot word for Bull Durham, incidentally, is *Stá-mek-shay-ahp-stá-kan*—which suggests that in Blackfoot, as in language generally, the tendency is toward ease of utterance. The Blackfoot language (typically) also contains several alternate terms for the same product (Bull Durham), one of which (*Áh-boot-ski-nahp-stahk-kan*) translates as "Cow tobacco." Cigarette is *Ìk-ka-móne-nape* or *Móne-yee-mahn*, depending on whether you roll your own or smoke tailor-mades. The secret of speaking fluent Blackfoot, I have decided, consists in three simple rules: (1) never use the same noun more than once a year; (2) if you must use the same old noun twice, pronounce it differently or at least change the vowel stress; (3) when in doubt, calculate by the sun and divide by the moon.

The outstanding aspect of the Pipe Dance was the over-all

attitude of relaxed sincerity coupled with the inevitable Indian good humor. Sometimes the old functionary would forget the chants and have to back up and start again, or someone else would foul up in some detail of ceremony (the drummers never once goofed), but nobody seemed to think that he would be damned to the unhappy hunting ground because of his error. Instead, everyone just had a good laugh at himself and then carried on. The Indian belief gives God credit for having a sense of humor, which is more than I can say for some other, rather dreary religious persuasions.

About midway of the ceremony, there was a long break for lunch. Brought into the room were large baskets of food and a big kettle of something which turned out to be berry soup. And the huge coffeepot and another tremendous pot containing hot tea. Everyone —man, woman, and child—was given a plate piled high with food. And I mean *piled high*. I was handed a paper plate stacked with a big chunk of boiled beef, three frankfurters, two boiled eggs, soda crackers, grease bread, cookies, two big pieces of berry cake and an orange. This in addition to a mug of tea.

I was having too much fun to be really hungry, so I gave away (to the kids) everything except the berry cakes, which were delicious, and the tea. Then Mary Ground sought me out and handed me a paper cup filled with the thick berry soup. It was marvelous— slightly tart, the way I like things—and I drank it all and went looking for more. The soup, the main ingredients of which are juneberries (serviceberries) and bitterroots, is almost identical to something the Swedes call fruit soup. When I was a fumbling undergraduate— before I became a fumbling graduate—I wrote a paper attempting to suggest a valid relationship between Algonkin, of which Blackfoot is a subdivision, and Old Norse (an idea which did not originate with me but which I still consider worthy of pursuit). My instructor ridiculed my sophomoric efforts, suggesting, with typical Germanic vitriol, that I should instead attempt to prove that the Blackfoots were the Lost Tribes of Israel. But he (aha!) had never tasted berry soup. (I had not attempted to trace the origin of the Blackfoots themselves but only certain aspects of their culture.)

After lunch, the ceremony continued, and during the afternoon the actual dancing took place. Only the men danced, and each man danced individually. The dancing of the American Indian today follows a pretty universal pattern, I think. At least I cannot distinguish the dancing patterns of the Sioux, the Crow, the Cheyenne, the Arapahoe, the Shawnee, the Pueblo or the Blackfoot one from the other, and this of course can be attributed to the same wide cultural borrowing which has made the Sioux war bonnet an ubiquitous addition to the costume of the American Indian generally. Even the Blackfoots now wear the Sioux-style headdress; the true Blackfoot eagle-feather bonnet had the feathers standing straight up all around. The feathered trailer on the Sioux-style bonnet, now seen from coast to coast, and on tribes that formerly never wore a headdress at all, originally came from the Mandan Indians of the upper Missouri. The Mandans gave their women to the White Man and their culture to the other Indian tribes, and so now the Mandans are no more.

Of course, it was pretty difficult to detect any choreographic individualism at the Pipe Dance because most of the dancers were very old and could achieve little more than a rhythmic stamping of the feet. Dan Bull Plume danced, supporting himself with a heavy cane. Fish, the blind drummer, danced as well as a sightless man can. And the young drummer, whose name, I learned, is Joe Horn, danced magnificently. Borrowing the Chief's eagle-wing fan, and obtaining an identical fan from another old man, Joe held the fans, one in each hand, stiff-armed straight out before him. At each strong drumbeat, he dipped the wings downward with a quick motion of his wrists, and the movements of his feet were so subtle that he gave the impression of being propelled around the room by the power of the wings alone. It was a strikingly graceful performance.

The Chief later said that neither he nor Jimmy had danced because the ceremony was not properly presented. Many of the formal rituals were missing, and a great deal of the chanting was not according to Chief Hoyle. The Chief is so religiously tolerant that I had never suspected him of being so kosher with regard to the Indian religion. Actually, the Chief is the only Blackfoot left who knows the old songs and ceremonies in their entirety and who can officiate with real authority at Blackfoot religious ceremonies. These young kids of seventy and eighty are just not with it.

The final portion of the ceremony consisted in the granting of blessings by the chief functionary. Those that were ill, and those desirous of remaining well, knelt before old Dan Bull Plume and to the accompaniment of chanted prayers had their faces marked with vermillion earth paint.

I'll say one thing for myself: I'm an adaptable son of a gun—at least linguistically. When the Pipe Dance was over and we were getting into the car, I heard myself say to Jim, "That berry soup was the best they're had I liked."

Jim, with perfect understanding, replied, "Yah, and that what-his-name's was a pretty good too."

At the roadway I said, "Which way at?" And my improved command of language inspired Jim to a (for an Indian) lengthy and detailed response.

"Home back to ranch," Jim said. "We don't had went back in town some more. Me, I don't like that town on a Friday, Saturday or a Sunday too. Too much of a crowds and drinking, and we ain't got much of a gas too, this car. You ain't got it no spare tire, too. We'll have flats we're be up a shits crick."

My perspicacity, on occasion, astounds even myself. With scarcely a pause for contemplation, I deduced that Jim did not want to go back to town but that he preferred instead to return directly to the ranch.

The wind was raw and wet now, and after we had the ranch stoves going, Jim said, "I know what let's make some—hot drink." So we had hot toddies and as we drank them the Chief rested on the sofa and Jimmy gave an hilarious account of the time that Oral Roberts, the evangelist, had attempted to induce him to give up tobacco. Roberts asked Jim what his religious beliefs were, and Jim answered, "Me, I believe the Christian way—Methodist and Catholic and Baptist—and I believe the Indian way, too." And Jim was not kidding. As the Chief once phrased it: "There is more than one trail through the forest, and sometimes many trails go to the same place. And how can you know which is the best trail unless you have traveled them all!"

For supper we boiled the elk meat and it was exceeding tough. Jim and I promised one another that we would get an elk or at least a deer before I leave ("Shook on that!").

The Chief went to bed at nine, but Jim and I sat up and talked. Jim told about (1) The many wealthy women he could have married ("She lived on the outskirt of town, but I never did went back, not me"); (2) How he always managed to draw a killer horse at rodeo bucking contests ("Goddam, I got buck off quick that sona-bitchers"); (3) The time he was chased by a white bull ("He wouldn't take it no skairts, that bull. I thought for minute was going had my goddam"). My leg hurt a great deal all day; so did Jim's, naturally.

The Chief prayed steadily from nine until after I sacked out at 11:30.

Burial House

Monday, September 10

Slept soundly until eight. The Chief and I rolled out at about the same time, and like the iron men we are we faced shoulder to shoulder our matutinal penance—Jimmy's cooking. Jim's pancakes are never exactly a gourmet's delight, but this morning they were so bad that even Jim couldn't eat them.

"Goddam!" Jim said, after I had sadistically invited him to sample one of his own creations. "I must a forgot the something in the pancakes. Twice of a sometime [once in a while] I'll did that. Think I'll eat another two couple slice bread instead."

The Chief, who has the digestion of a boa constrictor, continued to eat as though the pancakes were fit for human consumption. I took "two couple slice bread" and made an egg sandwich.

The Chief wanted to go to town right after breakfast, but I insisted upon a half-hour in which to take a bath and put on clean clothes. Jimmy washed to the waist, and I noted that, although his face and hands are a deep copper color, those portions of his anatomy which are kept fully clothed are quite light. I am convinced that the darkness of an Indian's skin is the result of a pigmental response to the elements.

159

In town, Jim and the Chief got off at the garage at which Jim's antediluvian truck is being revivified. Jim is extremely anxious to get the truck going because he wants to start bringing the winter supply of wood in from the mountains.

I went to the post office, where I met Plenty Treaty (Louis Bear Child). We chatted for a while and Louis told me that he, too, is related to brother Jim. Exactly what the relationship is, I was not able to determine. Louis said, "She married my aunt and it's a baby of Jim," and although I am a fair linguist, I think, this threw me completely. I told Louis that I thought it was going to snow again, and he said, quite seriously, in a very hushed voice, "Don't talk about snow or the snow-maker will hear you. I'm the guy ain't going squeal on anybodies, but that snow-maker hears you he's going snowed on you in a future time."

When I got back to the garage, Jimmy and the Chief and the truck were gone, and not being able to locate them around town, I headed back for the ranch. Just before reaching the Starr School Bridge, where the creek swings across to the north side of the road, I noted a cattle gate on my left. The gate gave access to a double-track which, according to my translation of Joe Scabby Robe's instructions, headed off in the general direction of the pine ridge on which was the burial house. So under the enigmatic gaze of a large Hereford bull I let down the gate, drove through, put the gate up behind me, and ventured along the track.

The track wandered like Exodus across the short-grass prairie, gently rising and falling with the land, but always pointing generally upward and to west-south west. I drove slowly, through scattered groups of beef cattle that stared in stupid immobility and then invariably at the very last instant kicked high their heels and scattered from the track in sudden, momentary panic. Then after perhaps four miles the track climbed abruptly among steep-sided hills, leveled briefly again, and burrowed suddenly into a grove of gold-turned aspens. The track went on, twisting out of sight among the trees, but I stopped the car and climbed out to reconnoitre. I was deep among the hills now, and by my calculations the high rise on my right was the south side of the ridge on which stood the burial house. A goat path led around the side of the hill to my left, and I began to follow it, soon finding myself treading rather adventurously the belt-line of a slope that plunged precipitously to the creek far below. This part of the creek was totally isolated from roads and human habitations, and there, almost directly below, some beaver were building a dam. The noon sun was shining with friendly brightness, the wind was a strong but not unpleasant carrier of outdoor smells, and in a relaxed and happy mood I sat for several minutes there on the slope-steepness, allowing the willing cleanness and un-hurried reality of out-of-doors to enter into myself.

I continued on around the hill, and there, sure enough, in the lea of the ridge, in a small open place among the pines on the north-east side, was the burial house. It was a small, pitch-roofed cabin built of pine lumber that had weathered to a silvery gray. The little house had no windows at all, and I could tell that the open entrance-way had never owned a door. All around the outside of the building, logs had been coupled together, Lincoln-log fashion, barring the doorway to a height of about 3½ feet.

The burial house was much smaller than it had appeared from down at Starr School—it was only twelve or fifteen feet square—and once again I marveled at the tremendous distances which lie at eye's command here in high, dry Montana. Turning, I could see every detail—miles away—of Jim White Grass' house. Children were play-ing in the yard down there, and white chickens strutted about.

I walked to the doorway of the burial house and looked in. The sunlight was very strong, revealing every detail of the interior of the little unwindowed house: the sturdy pine plank floor, the weathered but undecayed walls, the roof that was still tight and protective after all these years and through which no small shaft of sun betrayed an entranceplace for snow or rain. My first impression was one of surprise, for this small gray house was the burial place of not one but four. On the far right, in an uncovered, casket-like box, was the stripped and white remains of something that had once stood tall, and I knew immediately that this had once been a man called Earrings. The glistening white bones, to which small pieces of dark and desiccated flesh still clung, were tossed in disarray as though by animals. A few shredded rags alone testified that Ear-rings had been placed here fully clothed.

Against the far wall, behind Earrings, was a small closed casket large enough only for a child. And there were two other boxes, both open. On the left, clothing was yet nearly intact on the shrunken form of a half-grown boy. The body appeared undisturbed, except that one of the skeletal legs was twisted grotesquely sideways, pro-jecting over the side of the box a brown, brogan-type shoe—un-walked upon.

Directly in front of me, with most of the clothing torn away, was the almost perfectly mummified remains of another adult, lying straight and with the dark, claw-like hands at stiff repose over the

161

withered, ustulate rib-cage. The floor of the burial house was an incredible litter of rags and papers and bones and a shoe or two. In the air was a faint sweetish smell.

None of the human remains here on the hill had a head, and this puzzled me until, turning from the doorway, I saw glinting in the sun nearby a shiny metal can with the word "COLA" lettered on the side. And then, of course, I knew that some tourist or some student of anthropology must have told quite a tale as he displayed the souvenirs that he had stolen, ghoul-like, from the burial place of human beings.

I did not remain very long at the burial house, and I did not go inside, and although I had brought two cameras I did not take any pictures. At first I had experienced nothing really unusual up here on the ridge, but now, as I angrily kicked the Cola can and stood in arms-akimbo embarrassment for my race, I began to sense the presence of something unearthly. I did not see anything; I did not hear anything but the wind; but I felt something—something that did not welcome my presence here. And suddenly I realized that although I could not say that I saw or heard anything, neither could I swear that I *did not* see or hear something. It was a very strange sensation, and one not entirely comforting. I wanted to be gone from this place, but with Anglo-Saxon stubbornness I forced myself instead to sit down under a pine tree and to look for a long minute at Starr School and at the pick-up truck which moved slowly down the road below, trailing close upon itself a thick, sciuroid tail of dust. I noticed that Sweetgrass Hill, far to the northeast, was not wearing a hat this afternoon.

If I were a smoker, I should have lighted a cigarette and smoked it very slowly. But I am not, so before rising to go I ostentatiously and with deliberate slowness untied and then re-tied my shoes. Then, instead of taking the trail back around the side of the ridge, I climbed to the very ridgetop. The top was bare of trees, and many years ago someone had piled there a large cairn of flat rocks—purple, pale green, pink, all the colors of the stones of Montana. The view from the cairn was magnificent, but I stayed for only a moment. After all, I had told nobody that I was coming up here. My car was hidden out of sight in the aspens behind the ridge. I was miles from the road. The fellows would worry about me. Besides, it was now mid-afternoon and I had not yet eaten lunch.

I started down the slope toward the aspen grove in which the station wagon was parked. The going was very steep, and I slipped a good deal. It was easier to go down fast, in sideways bounds.

What if the car would not start! The Presence was still with me, and growing stronger—more angry.

I reached the car and started it and turned it around with no difficulty, and as I started back down the track, the Presence moved with me—not inside the car, but not outside, either. But it was there. I felt it, and I felt a chill move like a cold quick centipede up my back, and still I did not see or hear a thing. And then suddenly I smelled the thick pungent odor of burning sweetgrass—smelled it unmistakably and very strong, but only for a moment. Then it was gone.

I was driving faster now, still among the hills, and then again came a brief but thick and undeniable fragrance: tobacco smoke— the smoke of a strong cigar, I thought. Then the smoke was gone, but not so the Presence. The Presence was there and the Presence was very strong, and in the heat of the day I felt the gooseflesh rise. Then once again the brief strong waft of tobacco smoke. Very real! And then nothing. I had reached the prairie now, and as the final whiff of smoke faded away, the Presence faded too—not all at once, but gradually, fading back to the hills.

No cows barred the track on the way across the prairie to the road, and when the cattle gate had been raised again behind the station wagon, I turned left on Starr School Road and drove slowly back to the ranch. In passing by Jim White Grass' house, I looked left across the creek to the pine ridge beyond. Yes, there really was a burial house up there.

The Chief was asleep on the sofa and Jim was absent. On the cardboard from my morning's clean shirt, a note was written in large script:

> Dick we couldn't found you around town
> I thought you went home. I went after
> wood be back this evening.
>
> > Jim

There is your "lazy Indian" for you. When Jim got his truck back he went for wood not later on, not tomorrow morning, not when the Social Security check comes in, but *right now*.

I was really hungry, and I ate the boiled elk and boiled potatoes that Jim had left on the table and also downed three sandwiches of peanut butter and honey.

The Chief woke up shortly after I finished eating, and although I was very anxious to have his reaction to my experiences at the burial house, I was forced into a realization that I don't know Blackfoot from Tocharian. Without my bilingual brother there to translate back and forth, I found it impossible to convey to the Chief any concept more subtle than "me Tarzan, you Jane." When the Chief asked me what time it was (*"Tśe-tòk-tòk?"*), I was able to convey the information to him; when I brought him a hot drink, I was able to say, *"Ki-tau-wan-ahks cheh-estú-y-simsk";* but that was about the height of my linguistic attainment for the afternoon and I did not even attempt to discuss in Blackfoot the philosophical connotations of the open house burial tradition. I spent most of the day typing, and the Chief played solitaire. He is very sharp at cards.

Jim came back at six o'clock, loaded down with cottonwood logs. Jim calls a cottonwood a "cotton tree," and he refers to the logs as "toothpicks." Jim proudly called the Chief out back to view the woodpile, and the Chief smiled and said, *"So-káh-pi."*

Jim was very tired ("This the most goddam tire in my life I ever was. I couldn't hardly walk"). So I prepared a simple supper of bean soup and sandwiches, and we all retired to the living-room and the close comfort of the Simmons stove. Jimmy, that sensitive soul, actually apologized for being late to supper. He explained that he had to drive slowly with such a heavy load of logs ("I didn't want too damn fast going down that pass there"), and that he had stopped at Kiowa Camp for some tobacco ("I says what the hells, I says it a goddam, I'm going to buy me some smoking—I'm all out of smoking").

It might be well to interject here the fact that, although Jim and many other Blackfoot men of the younger generation habitually express themselves in a salty English barnacular worthy of Captain Kidd, profanity is not indigenous to the Blackfoot language. The process of "linguistic degradation," wherein a word becomes identified with the object or the action which it describes and thus becomes (to the unwashed ear) a "bad" word, does not function in Blackfoot. The Blackfoot Indian, in his *primitive ignorance,* regards the human body as a perfectly decent and inculpable member of the natural world; the Blackfoot does not see his body as a sexual fetish, and he considers neither any portion of his body, nor any of his bodily functions, nor any of the terms which describe those functions, to be in any way reprehensible. And since the Blackfoot does not take it upon himself to decide the relative purity of his neighbor's conception, or to determine in advance the post-mortem destiny of another person's soul, it was left to the super-culture of the

White Man to elevate the Blackfoot Indian even unto the artful employment of profanity and imprecation. And even when a Blackfoot is cussing a veritable English blue streak, chances are that he does not, even today, understand the traditional implications of the *náh-pi-quon* phrases he is using; more than likely he believes that he is employing terms of strong emphasis, nothing more.

About the worst thing you can call someone in Blackfoot is *i-mi-dés-ki* (dog face), and since this is a term the Blackfoots formerly used in reference to the White soldier (because of his moustache?), Blackfoot may well be the origin of that term as now universally applied to the American infantryman.

The only home-grown expletive I have ever heard the Chief use is, "*I-mi-táu-chi-kahn!*"—a word which he employs with purely humorous connotation and which could perhaps best be translated as referring to the vernacular portion of a dog.

I told the Chief about my experiences up on the pine ridge (Jimmy translating) and the Chief considered it all unremarkable enough; however, he could not explain my having smelled cigar smoke. (Cigar is a word that the Blackfoots got from the Whites. The Blackfoot *tsi-kái-yeh* is quite obviously the French *cigarre* expressed in Blackfoot phonemes. Another Blackfoot word for cigar, which Jim usually but not always pronounces, *Bo-tsíp-stahk-kan*, translates as "all tobacco.")

Jim explained that the Blackfoot word for ghost is *stúh-aw* and that the burial house on the ridge is referred to by the Indians as the "ghost house." The Chief was surprised to learn that someone had made off with Earrings' head, because this is definitely a recent occurrence, but I learned that grave-robbing is nothing new to the Reservation. The traditional Blackfoot method of burial was the scaffold or tree burial (chiefs and men of prominence were sometimes left at rest in a teepee high on some hill or ridge), and the Chief explained the reason that the burial house came into existence among his people. The Blackfoots left the earthly remains of their departed loved-ones wrapped in a robe and tied to a scaffold which was placed either in a tree (usually by a stream or on a bluff above a stream) or atop a cairn of flat stones. The Blackfoots believed that when the body had served its earthly purpose of transporting through life the spirit of an individual, the body should return to the earth and so nourish the earth to the creation of new life (this is certainly a philosophy much more beautiful than the White Man's encasing the dead body in a vault in order to "protect" it from any possibility of its renewing the soil which had given it birth). But the

White Man, who considered the Indian burial scaffold to be "indecent" and "unsightly," not only forbade the Blackfoots the privilege of burial according to the Blackfoot belief but actually went about tearing down those burial scaffolds which already existed. So the Blackfoot, understandably reluctant to inter his loved-one in a closed grave from which, according to Indian belief, the soul could not escape, secretly began to construct small burial houses which he hoped would pass in the White Man's observation as ordinary places of residence. This worked all right for a while, and at one time there were many burial houses on the Reservation—the Chief's father was placed in a small house atop a large, barren hill just to the southeast of Starr School—but during the 1930's the W.P.A. was sent onto the Reservation to "improve and beautify" the land and the bastards tore down every burial house they could find. They were supposed to give the remains decent burial, but in most instances they were too lazy to do this and after pocketing whatever valuables had been placed in the burial house along with the deceased, they tore the place down and scattered the remains like so much garbage (little did they know that the Indians preferred this to burial). But the Indians did *not* prefer that the W.P.A. workers steal the skulls and trade them to saloonkeepers for drinks. One saloon in Cut Bank, a town just across the Reservation line, had a collection of such Indian skulls lined up behind the bar until, I am gratified to report, decent persons of both races forced their removal.

Earrings' burial place apparently was protected by its very remoteness and difficulty of access, and so far as I have been able to learn it is the only "ghost house" left in this part of the Reservation. The Chief remembers Earrings very well, and with his impeccable honesty he told me the true tale of how Earrings bit the dust. It happened about fifty years ago, in the fall of the year during an unseasonable cold spell such as the one we have been having lately. Earrings was coming from town all right, and although he was carrying supplies he was also carrying a plentiful supply of extract—most of it inside himself—and he got drunk and passed out and froze to death. An empty extract can was lying nearby when they found him. (I'll bet he was the drunk sonofagun that chased me down the hill.) The Chief does not know the identities of Earrings' gravemates, and he did not know that they were there in the ghost house. [I was later able to identify them as certain of Earrings' relatives.]

The conversation dwelt throughout the evening on Blackfoot religious beliefs in general and on Blackfoot burial customs in particular. The Chief informed me that Schultz was buried by the

Blackfoots, at his own request, in the Indian manner. This was undoubtedly James Willard Schultz, a fur trader during the latter portion of the nineteenth century who lived from time to time among the Blackfoots and who wrote some three dozen books of varied worth about the Plains Indians. He was buried down at Two Medicine, next to a Blackfoot chief named Red Eagle.

During the course of our discussion, the Chief told once again about the belief of the Blackfoot Indian that after death his spirit resides in the Sand Hills (Jimmy translates it as "Big Sandy"), a rather desolate region in the Province of Saskatchewan. The Chief says that you can track the spirits in the Sand Hills, but that at the end of each set of tracks you always find the same thing—a dead mouse. If this belief isn't enough to jar even the most smug *Náhpiquon* amongst us, it certainly should be because it strikes pretty close to home. No matter what kind of tracks you make through this world, Buster—barefoot, moccasin, wagon track or Cadillac—when you go you can't take any more with you than the humblest mouse that ever got caught in a five-cent trap. I can already visualize a story based on this concept. Title: "The Trail of the Mouse."

It is late now, and the Chief does not feel at all well. Jim and I are sitting up with him. I am typing, and Jim is lamenting the fact that he has only a fourth grade education. He is aware that Indians should learn to make better preparation for the future.

Just read over the part about my feeling the Presence as I came down from the burial house. It is difficult not to dramatize an experience such as this, but I have sincerely attempted not to. I have tried to record what happened—what I felt and thought—as objectively as possible, for to do otherwise would be to cheat myself. When an experience is set down on paper, the written description of the experience becomes, in time, the experience itself; consequently, to distort in any way the written record of an experience is to cast away irretrievably a portion of one's life. This fact was impressed upon me very strongly on the occasion of our recent visit to Heart Butte. The Heart Butte racetrack had provided the setting for my story, "Horserace," and I had passed an entire afternoon at the Heart Butte track and I had thought that I knew the place in its every detail and that I could never forget it. But when finally I went there again, I went as a total stranger. Nothing was familiar. It had been necessary in my writing to alter certain details of the scene in order to meet the symbolic demands of the story, and I found myself now searching not for those features of terrain which

167

exist at Heart Butte but for fictive landmarks which I, myself, had constructed upon the written page.

There remains, of course, the possibility that the sensations which were evoked within my personal self by a visit to an Indian grave house are subject to a perfectly rational scientific explanation—psychology, and all that. Perhaps the entire experience was, as my malaproptic old pal, Ernie, once expressed it, "A figleaf of the imagination." But then, to quote good old Ernie once again: "Life is truer than fiction."

My experiences high up there on the pine ridge were, in some measure, extraordinary experiences, but I do not apologize for having had them and I certainly do not reject the actuality of their occurrence. ("There are more things in heaven and earth . . .") But although many aspects of such experiences must be viewed and reviewed in the light of other noons—one must not jump to delusions about such things—there is one aspect of today's adventure which I am able to regard with absolute certainty: the prickle of horripilation which arpeggioed my spine as I came barrelling down the hill from the ghost house—*that*, brother, was the real McCoy.

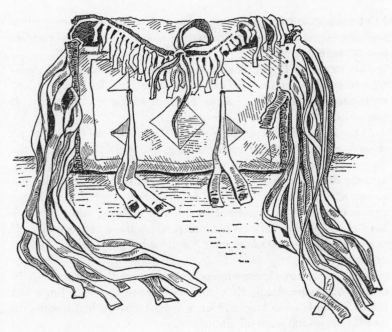

Medicine Pouch

Last night before sacking out, Jim and I decided that the Chief would benefit from a hot drink—purely medicinal, of course—so Jimmy whipped up his famous concoction of hot water, sugar, cinnamon and bourbon. Jim drank one too, and I conferred unanimity upon the compotation by doing likewise, but I put honey in mine instead of sugar. The first one was good, and the second was better, and the third sent me beddy-bye *muy pronto*.

I was up before seven, but Jim, who cut wood all day yesterday and then sat up with the Chief until 4:30 this morning, was up before I. He is anxious to go out and get more "toothpicks." The wind is strong from the west this morning, and both Jim and I think that we are going to get more snow.

At breakfast, Jimmy achieved the impossible—he made the pancakes worse than ever before. Poor old Jim just doesn't seem to get the point: it is the *eggs* you cook once over lightly, *not the flapjacks!* This morning's argilliferous atrocities had the consistency of kindergarten paste, and after employing one to repair a crack in the plaster, I thriftily set the rest aside for use in sealing envelopes.

I did manage to salvage the eggs, though, and I downed my portion with a grim resolve to start insinuating more roughage into the diet around here.

This morning, Jimmy finally located the remarkable cold medicine in search of which he has been ransacking the house. I had anticipated some exotic Indian nostrum of herbs, roots, etc. It turned out to be a bottle of Dristan.

At 8:00 a large band of sheep—*i-mák-ski-nah* or *i-má* (glottal stop) *-ki-nah*—came down the road, flowing like quicksilver under the direction of two magnificent sheepdogs which raced back and forth keeping their charges away from the creekbank and, thankfully, out of our spring. I think that these must be the happiest dogs in the world; they have an important function to perform, and they work hard at it, and they take an obvious pride in the excellence of their performance. I wonder how long it will be before somebody tries to unionize them.

I grabbed the movie camera and got some fine shots of the dogs in action. And when finally the road was clear to the west, Jim asked me to fix Dad "some lunches" when he got up—we had decided to let him sleep—and went off after wood.

After Jim left I felt a sudden depression, and I realized that it was because I need a woman—even just to talk to. So I grabbed two buckets and went to the spring for some water, and then I went out back and split blocks for an hour. The wind was very cold and extremely strong, and as I worked I told myself once again that I must be realistic and make plans to go south pretty soon.

With Jim gone, it was up to me to take on the charwoman chores, so I washed the dishes and cleaned up the kitchen (otherwise known as the James White Calf, Jr. do-it-yourself botulism kit). Why none of us around here ever comes down with a dose of the trots, I do not know—probably because no self-respecting bacillus would be caught alive in our kitchen. But anyway, I got the oilcloth on the kitchen table as clean as you could without sandpaper, and scraped as much dirt off the floor as you could without using a carpenters' plane, and then retired to the luxury of a "possible" bath. I can work out-of-doors all day without feeling dirty, but fifteen minutes of housework and I feel unspeakably filthy. So upon completing my bath I put on a clean white starched shirt for morale's sake.

The Chief got up at 10:00, feeling somewhat better, and I put on his moccasins and fixed "some lunches." I said, *"Kee-estún-non áhk-so-yope"* (we are going to eat), and the Chief, to whom my attempt to learn Blackfoot is a source of constant delight, wagged his head in approbation and said, "So-káh-pi!" (good).

12:30: The wind is really strong now. It just blew out a pane of glass in the living-room. I put another blanket on the Chief, who is lying on the sofa and coughing badly. He smiled his thanks and said, "So-káh-pi." The Blackfoots do not have a word for "thank you" —not exactly, that is. A Blackfoot acknowledges a gift with, "ni-tsi-tsíks-y-maht-tsi-tisp" or possibly "ni-tsík-ku-tak-tsi-tak," which translate roughly into "glad to have it." So-káh-pi means good, but it is a utilitarian phrase which is frequently used to express gratitude. When the Chief says, "Ik-so-kahpi," he means "that is very good"; when he says, "Kéet-so-kah-pio," or "Kén-yai-yay-so-kàh-pi" he is expressing something like "well, now, I think that is very nice indeed." Blackfoot speakers do not always pronounce a word the same way—any more than speakers of English do—and a change of stress in Blackfoot can carry with it a connotative difference equivalent to that implied by a stress variation in English. Add to this the fact that the Chief's advanced age and incomplete dental structure cause him to articulate in a manner quite different from that of brother Jim, and you begin to get some idea of the barriers I am forced to hurdle in learning Blackfoot (you may also get the feeling —and correctly so—that I am currently not too boastful about my linguistic attainments).

1:00: The wind is really blowing out there now, and I am rather enjoying it. When one of Hemingway's characters, a wine connoisseur in *The Sun Also Rises,* was asked why he did not write a book about wines, he replied that all he wanted from wine was the drinking of it. Today, all I want from life is the living of it. The literary allusion is undoubtedly an attempt to reestablish my personal identity. So is the starched white shirt. In order really to get to know and understand the American Indian (or anybody else, for that matter) you must relinquish your personal self to his way of life, to his very way of thinking and feeling. But my inability to communicate really effectively with the Chief in his own language has caused me to draw up short and face the fact that I am not really a Blackfoot Indian and never could be. I *am* a human being, however, and it is the common ground of humanity upon which I am able to meet the Chief and Jim and my other Indian friends.

So today I am a *Náhpiquon,* and a rather lonely one at that. But certainly not a bored one. Life may not always be a piece of cake, but never—if only for the fact that it *is life*—does it become boring.

Part of my afternoon was passed in just thumbing through old magazines and mail-order catalogues, and although this type of reading is not to be recommended as a steady diet, it certainly is revelatory of a basic difference between the personality structures of Whites and Indians. A great deal of modern advertising is obviously directed by the knowledge that the White person, whether male or female, has become so confused by the rapidly changing roles of both men and women within the framework of our society that he is no longer quite certain of his own identity and will consequently grab at almost anything that promises to reestablish him in the eyes of his peers as belonging to the proper gender. The Indian, on the other hand, although he has in large measure been deprived of his cultural identity, still possesses in very strong degree that sense of sexual identity for which so many Whites are groping; such phrases as "A real MAN's smoke," and "Banking with a feminine touch," mean absolutely nothing to an Indian, and Indians in general are very poor targets for advertising of this sort.

Regarding Indian women (and I do my share of regarding), I believe that the Blackfoot woman of today is definitely a happier person than her White sister, and I feel sure that this same contrast existed in the old days. The Blackfoot wife was never the slave or chattel that she has been pictured as being. True, Blackfoot marriages usually were arranged affairs, but the arrangement had the same social and economic basis that most modern White marriages have, and a Blackfoot girl could refuse to accept her family's choice of husband if she wished. And a Blackfoot girl was not bought or purchased by her husband; gifts were exchanged between the suitor and the bride's family, and the more expensive the gifts the suitor could provide, the better were his chances for receiving the blessings of his future in-laws, but the final choice was up to the girl.

Certainly the Blackfoot woman was expected to do her share of work, and the classier were her domestic attainments the more desirable was she as a bride; but the teepee and its furnishings were the property of the wife, not the husband, and for good cause a Blackfoot woman could tell her husband to get out of the teepee and stay out. Even the meat that the husband provided, after the wife had turned it into dry meat or pemmican, belonged to the wife. But the Blackfoot society was structured around the family unit, and if a Blackfoot woman started to get uppity with her spouse, she darn well better have some relatives she could depend on for support.

White women generally shudder at the thought of polygamous marriage, but the Blackfoot ladies rather enjoyed the idea. There was considerable labor involved in tanning hides, building a new lodge, making moccasins and clothing, picking berries, gathering wood, hauling water, preparing food, and taking care of the children, and so far as a Blackfoot woman was concerned, the more wives the merrier. A woman's husband traditionally had first claim on her younger sisters as his additional wives, and if a woman had no younger sisters she frequently shopped around and located her husband's second wife for him. There was less work for her to do this way, and she always had somebody to talk to.

For about an hour this afternoon I just sat and watched the flies flirt with the flypaper. In case the world would like to know, about twice as many flies light on the concave side of the paper as light on the convex side, and about two out of every five flies that light manage to get free again. Maybe I should compile a compendium of my observations. After all, Mr. P. gained immortal fame by revealing that a hungry dog will salivate when it thinks it is going to get fed —a fact which could have been gleaned from any farm boy.

At four o'clock, Jim came in with an immense load of wood, and his return left me free to go to town to check the mail. When I got back, at about six, Jim said that he and Dad had already "lunched around," so I opened a can of vegetable soup and made a jam and peanut butter sandwich. I brought the Chief several large cans of pineapple juice and a couple of pounds of white seedless grapes. I think he needs more of this kind of food. He ate some of the grapes and went immediately to bed. While I was taking off his moccasins, it occurred to me that he has been wearing the same sox for more than a week—and God knows his feet have not touched water—but the wool sox smell as fresh as the day I first put them on his feet. I hate to imagine what my sox would be like after a week of constant wear. I have never yet encountered an Indian with an unpleasant body odor, and I credit this in part to the fact that Indians are total strangers to nervous perspiration—they *never* become flustered, no matter what the situation. Well, hardly ever.

After the Chief retired, I imitated Jimmy's effort of several days ago and baked two pies—just to see whether I could do it. One was cherry and the other blueberry. We ate the cherry one as soon as it was finished, and it was not too bad for a first effort. During our postprandial discussion, Jimmy let slip the fate of the leather jacket and the tooled pistol holster that I gave him during my last visit. The Blackfoots have something called a "give-away dance," during which they vie with one another in seeing who can give away the most (just take a typical *White Christmas*, turn the whole thing around backward, and you come up with the general idea). I never

173

did discover where all the stuff ends up, but undoubtedly, as do so many Blackfoot social functions, the dance centers around some sort of charity drive. Generosity, especially among the families of chiefs, was a primary virtue among the old-time Blackfoots, and from what I gathered, Jim came away from this dance in his moccasins and jockey shorts.

9:45: Jimmy has gone to bed. He must be exhausted, poor chap. And I am alone again and pretty introspective and analytical and am playing a tape of Cisco Houston singing folk songs.

No booze. I gave the last shot to the Chief this afternoon.

Wednesday, September 12

Last night I washed up and sacked out at 11:00. Three more puppies have appeared, and also a very small, very tough yellow kitten. The pups whined all night, waking me several times, and each time I waked I could hear the Chief chanting (praying). He must have prayed nearly the night long.

Jim was first up again. I was second. The Chief slept till eight. I talked Jim into having oatmeal instead of pancakes for breakfast, and I am sure that the Chief feels better because he ate a large bowl of oats and drank a glass of pineapple juice.

It was very cold out this morning, and when I went down for water I found that three horses had broken through the ice on the spring and were standing knee-deep therein. One was a beautiful pinto stallion, and my admiration of the animal turned the breakfast conversation to horses. The horse, of course, was a very important part of modern Plains Indian culture. I say *modern* because there were of course no horses on this continent until the Spanish brought them, and it was probably not until the eighteenth century that the northern Plains Tribes started employing horses for domestic use. The Blackfoots, situated as they were way up in Canada, probably were the last of the Plains Peoples to obtain the horse (in all likelihood from their enemies to the south, the Shoshoni) and indications are that the Blackfoots went horseless until the very late 1700's. Up until that time, the Blackfoots' only beast of burden was the dog, and the Blackfoot word for horse, *puh-no-káh-mi-tah,* actually means "elk-dog" (what the word really implies is "elk that does the work of a dog").

But if the Blackfoots were somewhat late in obtaining the horse, they were anything but dilatory in adapting to its employment—especially in warfare. As I get the picture, not only from history books but from the Chief, many of whose stories refer back to the time "before we had horses," the Blackfoots were for some time taking a shellacking from the horse-owning Shoshoni to the south and the gun-using Cree to the east. But when the Blackfoots finally got a good supply of horses (by stealing them from the Shoshoni) and a fair number of guns (obtaining them by any means, fair or foul, by way of the Cree) the Blackfoots in an incredibly short length of time pushed aside all opposition—Cree, Shoshoni, Flathead, Kootenai, Crow, Assiniboine—and extended their range from northern Saskatchewan southward as far as the present Jackson Hole region of Wyoming. (Blackfoot raiding parties sometimes traveled remarkable distances, and there is good evidence that on occasion they ventured as far as Mexico.)

The Chief, in his narratives, gives credit for the Blackfoot military success primarily to the gun, not the horse, although during his youth the possession of fine horses was *the* thing, and most of the Chief's war parties were horse-stealing raids. The Chief says that the importance of the gun in Blackfoot history is the reason that so many Blackfoots have the word "gun" as a portion of their name. In the old days, of course, the Blackfoots recognized no surname, but since the White Man has forced upon the Indian a patrilineal appendage to his given name, one finds today upon the Reservation such family titles as, Found A Gun, Takes Gun, Morning Gun, Dog Taking Gun, Cross Guns, and literally scores of others.

This business of Indian names is pretty rugged for the linguist, and for several reasons. In the first place, the old-time Indian man invariably had more than one name during his lifetime—sometimes several names simultaneously—and if this didn't mess things up badly enough, the White Man consistently did a lousy job of translating Indian names into English. Officially, the name of my Indian dad is "James White Calf," and the reason is that $E = MC^2$. The following simple explanation will suffice: The Chief's father, Onistáipokah, was called "White Calf" by the White Man, although Onistáipokah does not mean "White Calf" but rather "Sacred Calf Child" (when an Indian name contained the word calf, cow, or bull, the reference was to the buffalo, not to the White Man's beef). Old Onistáipokah's other name—not his *last* name, but just another name which he took upon the occasion of achieving a war coup—was Sáh-ko-y-nah-mach-kahn, which the White Man translated as "Last Gun" but which actually means something like "The-last-one-to-come-running-and-capture-a-gun-from-the-enemy." This is the name the Chief gave to me, although he and Jimmy usually shorten it to "Sáh-ko-y-nah," which cuts off the "came running" part. So . . . Onistáipokah (who was also called Bear Hat, Bad Head, Now-He-Has-It, and several other things) became known as "White Calf" instead of "Sacred Calf Child," and his son, my dad, had the misnomer tacked onto him by the Agency rolls. And the pay-off came when I saw a picture of my Indian dad on an old Glacier Park advertisement which bore the title, "CHIEF JIM WHITE CALF (Ah-pe-so-mika)" . . . Ah-pe-so-mika does not mean White Calf! Ah-po-nés-tah means White Calf. Ah-pe-so-mika is a very poor rendering of Ah-pée-so-mach-kahn, which means "Running Coyote" but is usually translated as "Running Wolf" and which is the Chief's rightful name. In addition, the Chief was christened "James" by a priest, and also, he once mentioned, he took the name of Och-koh-neép-po-wah-tah when he scalped an enemy he had killed. This latter Indian name means, "Everybody-Talks-About," and I think it exquisitely appropriate that there is no indication of *who* everybody talks about. All right, *whom!*

My nameless Indian friend at today's breakfast table told me that the Blackfoots did not believe in ruining a good horse by breaking him too roughly. They did not want their horses fully broken because that made them too easy to steal, and Indian methods of horse-taming included riding a horse in water deep enough so that he could not buck, and tying a buffalo hide to his tail and having three or four men sit on the hide (which sounds like quite a job) until the horse wearied of trying to drag them around. I told the

Chief that I had read somewhere that Indian horses were trained to be mounted from the right side, instead of the left side as is the case with White-trained horses. The Chief laughed and said that in his day an Indian didn't have time to go running around from one side of a horse to another and a horse that couldn't be mounted from any side—including from the rear—could damn well cost you your life.

In discussing the ownership of horses as a measure of wealth, the Chief mentioned that his brother Wolf Tail, who had been very wealthy and had even owned a partnership in a bank later in his life, had at one time possessed nearly a thousand horses. This revelation answered a question which had been puzzling me. Since Wolf Tail was old Onistáipokah's eldest son, he would in natural course have inherited chieftainship of the Piegans when his father died. But the old Chief had been so anxious that not Wolf Tail but my dad succeed him as head chief that he had an official document prepared, in the custom of the White Man, specifically stating his wishes in this matter. The document, which was officially filed with the Bureau of Indian Affairs in Washington, was drawn up in 1897,

On October 29th 1897 for to know I will put my boy where I am standing and same time he supports the Blackfeet Indians for their rights.

The reason why I am putting my boy to be Chief of the Blackfeet Indians is because I am pretty old for my age.
And I am always glad to know that he fights for our rights and he sticks with it until he gets what he is fighting for.
The reason why I put my son to be Chief of the Blackfeet Indians is to be friends with everybody with is heart and to do right for the Blackfeet Indians.
And same time I put my boy to be Chief because he sure fights for the Indians rights and at the same time he fights for us old people rights.

And at the same time I wanted my boy to be friend with everybody even whites or redskins with his heart.
So I told my boy to be friends with our Superintendent here on the Blackfoot Indian Reservation to do right for for the Blackfeet Indians and at the same time to get the Blackfeet Indians a good start to build nice homes for themselves in case that they die so they have homes for their children.

I am Chief White Calf and I am the Chief of the Blackfeet Indian Reservation so you know I said what I said in here. So now I gave my boy to be Chief in the Blackfeet Indian Reservation.
And if my boy is smart enough to do same thing in future time in case he gets a boy.

This is what I said and I am Chief White Calf of the Blackfeet Indian Reservation.

Chief White Calf

****

six years before the old Chief passed away in Washington, D.C., still fighting for the rights of his people. The Chief has already given me a photostatic copy of the official proclamation of his chieftainship.

In order to understand the significance of this document, one must have some knowledge of the social and economic structure of the Blackfoot Nation as it existed in the century past. Especially must one have some acquaintance with the Blackfoot system of government and the hierarchy of chiefs under which the Blackfoots lived. The movies usually portray a band of Indians being ruled over by a single chief whose primary pastime is to lead his warriors off after as many enemy scalps as he can lay his scalping knife on. This is bunk. In the first place, the taking of enemy scalps or in most cases even the killing of the enemy was not the most laudatory of feats among the Plains Indians. Indians—the Blackfoots, at least—were considerably more practical than that. Like all cultural groups, they had some damn-fool ideas, but they were much more interested in possessing something useful or necessary to their existence—a gun or a horse—than in having somebody's old second-hand hair. (It was the Blackfoot women, not the men, who displayed the scalps during a victory dance, and oftentimes they were simply thrown away afterward—unless the hair might be used in decorative work.)

Insofar as the chiefs were concerned, a war chief was generally of his own making and he might or might not have much influence in the tribe; there were many war chiefs in every Indian band, and each one was subject to fall from favor should his medicine fail to work and his followers (who might be only a few of his own relatives or clan members) take a drubbing by the enemy. War chief was a step in the right direction, though, and if a war chief displayed consistent qualities of wisdom and good judgment as well as bravery he might well earn the position of *band chief* or *civil chief*, who was the real leader of the tribe.

The band chief had a lot of influence in the tribe, but he also carried a tremendous weight of responsibility. Not only did he sit at the head of the council of war chiefs of his band, but he made decisions regarding where and when the camp would be moved, where and when the buffalo hunts would take place, etc. It was also the responsibility of the band chief to see to it that when the camp moved, all persons, including the aged and the infirm, were provided with horses so that they would be able to move their belongings at a pace that would not delay the group in general. This was why horses were so important to the Blackfoots, and why the ability to steal horses from the enemy was the primary key to social and political advancement among all the Plains Tribes. It is also of importance to know that not only was a chief expected to be able to obtain horses and guns from the enemy, he was expected to be very generous in loaning or giving these articles to those who lacked them. Especially the head or civil chiefs were often quite poor simply because they had given so much of their material accumulation to other persons. This great burden of obligation which the civil chief bore in the name of his people was one reason that some war chiefs actually refused to accept the position of civil chief: they were too stingy, and of course when this fact became known the tribe would not have retained them as civil chiefs anyway. Generosity is still highly regarded among the Blackfoots, and even today the stingy Indian is regarded with contempt. Obviously then, since the Chief's older brother Wolf Tail retained in his personal possession the fantastic number of one thousand horses, the man was not overly burdened with charitable tendencies. And that is why old Onistáipokah made sure that my Indian dad, who is generous to a fault, became civil chief in his stead. Little could the old Chief have known that in 1935 the Wheeler-Howard Act would deprive his generous and capable son of any real authority and place tribal control instead in the hands of a tribal council.

The fact that the Blackfoots and Plains Tribes in general were directed in the more important aspects of life by the authority of a civil chief, does not in any way imply a sequacious leaning on the part of Indians. The civil chief controlled the destiny of his people only so long as the strength of his personality and the obvious correctness of his judgments served to vindicate his authority. The American Indian was and is an individualist in the most trying connotation of the word; no single person ever held total sway over any Plains Tribe. Every Indian battle ever fought was conducted not as a single concerted effort under the master guidance of a single commander or strategist-in-chief, but as the coincidentally combined efforts of numerous small groups or individuals, each fighting as he damn well pleased. This is true even of such supposedly masterminded military operations as Chief Joseph's withdrawal to the Canadian line and, especially, the Battle of the Little Big Horn. It is, from the point of view of the Indian at least, a damn shame that the Plains Indians couldn't have stuck together. Even today, one of the main problems of the American Indians is that they cannot stick together and function politically as a single force. The Plains Indian constituted the best light cavalryman the world has ever known—excepting *nobody*—and if he could have united against the invading Whites he could have smashed them for so long a period that eventually they would have had to leave him alone. I do not make this statement fancifully or romantically; I make it factually, and any student of the history of military affairs will agree with me.

Another point: merely because there was so much generosity among Plains Indians—or because the old-time buffalo drive was a communal affair—this does not imply that the American Indian lived in a communal society. The Indian was much too much the individualist for that. Free enterprise was the standing order of the day, and although generosity on a voluntary basis was considered commendable it was by no means obligatory. If you wanted to hide yours under the mattress, that was your business, and even among the most generous there was a lively competition to see who could get the most loot with which to *be* generous.

This individualism among the American Indians is every bit as apparent today as it ever was, and it is one of the reasons that the American Indian earned a reputation for being a notably courageous and resourceful fighting man during World War II and the Korean conflict. It is also the reason that Communism has never been able to establish even a toe-hold among the Indians. I would bet everything I have against a sack of corn that there is *not one single full-blood American Indian Communist* in this country, but obviously I could not make that same wager with regard to other American "minority groups" (I have yet to meet *anyone* who belongs to a *majority* group).

Communists have been quite openly prowling about every Indian reservation I have ever visited, and their lack of success in proselytizing the Indian is really so total as to be funny. You would really have to know Indians personally in order to get the full picture, but the experience of a Communist organizer who showed up on the Blackfoot Reservation a short while ago suggests a reasonably comprehensive view. Our Commie pal went the usual route of cornering the Blackfoots individually and in small groups and telling them how badly they had been exploited by the White Man (which was true enough) and how much the Communists were going to do for the poor abused Indian, etc. So the Blackfoots all nodded in agreement and said, "Yah, Pardner, you sure said a right. Yessir, we sure been exploited, sure enough." In other words, the Blackfoots, who are almost orientally polite to any stranger, agreed with everything the Commie had to say, and the Commie was so flushed with success that he immediately planned a huge Communist rally in Browning and even hired a hall for the purpose. And when the great hour arrived, not one single Blackfoot Indian—not even the winos who had been promised free drinks—showed up at the meeting. By a strange coincidence, each and every Blackfoot had suddenly found it necessary to visit an uncle over in Canada or a nephew down at Heart Butte.

What this all adds up to is that the American Indians—at least the Blackfoot full-bloods, whom I know as well as I know my own family—*do not want a free hand-out.* What they want is a chance to earn their own way, doing the work and expressing the talents which they rightfully feel could make a contribution not only to the perpetuation of their own culture but to an enrichment of the culture of the Country and the Nation in general. I will add that from my own observations I have decided that the Blackfoots do not need to be given *more;* they need intelligent and honest assistance in utilizing those resources which they already possess. And they need to be protected by law (by a complete reorganization of the Bureau of Indian Affairs) from the leeches, both White *and* Indian, who have long been skimming off the cream from the Indian milk bucket.

We tried to eat my blueberry pie at breakfast this morning, but it was a sickening glop of cornstarch, etc., and I threw it to the dogs. After a more or less steady diet of Jimmy's rejected pancakes, those dogs will eat anything. Incidentally, the father of the pups showed up today, that scoundrel! He is a scroungy and obsequious hound, certainly not deserving of a selfless and dedicated wife such as poor little Coyote. I saw Coyote come home with a big belly full of food —apparently a rabbit she had caught—and regurgitate the whole thing for the benefit of her hungry pups.

After breakfast, Jim went off after more toothpicks. And while I was in the kitchen grimly attacking the señora chores, Paul Many Hides—he of the corduroy cap and the fulgent, smaragdine smile —came a tap-tap-tapping at my (*chambre*) door. Paul had his wife in tow (I am sure she has only one dress, and no underwear), and when I called out, as Jimmy does, "Come on in it," they came on in it and I gave them the rest of the breakfast coffee and since they both looked as hungry as Coyote's pups I threw in icebox privileges (figuratively of course, because we do not have an icebox). Paul's wife sat at the table and ate oatmeal and milk and soft toast, but Paul, who apparently had taken my invitation a bit more literally, nibbled about the kitchen like a mouse. (When Paul at last saw fit to quit the cupboard, platoons of emaciated rodents were seen to take indignant departure, satchel in hand, via casement and postern.)

Everything has its end, though, and at length Paul assumed (total) occupancy of the living-room sofa, enunciated an appreciative belch, rolled a cigarette with some of Jimmy's Bull Durham, and expressed his desires of the day. They were: (1) to sell me some sort of medicine bundle; (2) for me to drive him over to St. Mary (about thirty miles away on the other side of the mountains); and (3) to keep the rest of Jim's tobacco. Jim has admonished me to lavish no solicitude upon wee, sleekit, cowerin', timorous Paulie ("He's just lazy to work, that's all") so I turned Paul down on all counts.

When Paul left, he threatened with evil glint of tooth and eye to return anon. But he did not, and the Chief and I ate lunch together alone. Afterward, leaving the Chief contentedly playing with the pups—they all love him, and so does the kitten (who hates me)—I walked over the hills to a log cabin on the creekbank owned by Joe Kicking-A-Woman. Joe's cabin is typical Indian—a yard full of dogs and walls loaded with family portraits—but for some reason Joe's yard has a rustic turnstile instead of the customary gate.

I had thought the old-fashioned scrubboard to be just about vestigial by this time, but in the kitchen of the house Joe's wife was industriously bent over one. In the large single other room of the cabin, several Indian men were casually and without any apparent plan nailing sheeting to the roof beams. Nobody was at all conversational, so with slightly disjointed proboscis I went home to play in my own yard.

Jim came in at 3:00, having dented the front of his truck slightly ("Made too damn short of turn"). He said, "I be here rest the day, so might well's a go town if you wanted." So I went to town, picked up a letter from Margaret, bought a new hat, bought some smokes for the Chief, and bought a jug of Jim Beam on the strength of Jimmy's liquor permit.

Back at the ranch, a rather disconcerting discovery awaited our hero. I had noted that the water in our spring was full of tiny specks, but today, waiting for them to settle to the bottom of the dipper before drinking, I observed for the first time that the damn things are self-propelled. Jim suggested that from now on we get our water from the creek, so in the truck we drove to the edge of the clear-running creek and came back with a milk can full of nice, clean water.

By suppertime the wind had stopped blowing entirely, and the air was still and suddenly very warm. Nobody had much to say, so we all gravitated to the sack at 10:00.

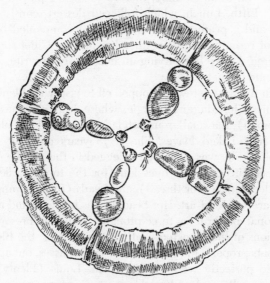

Medicine Wheel

Thursday, September 13

I suppose we all have times when we feel like retreating to some murky corner, assuming the fetal position, and waiting hopefully for a better *mañana*. I still do not have the stories I want, and I was not comforted to learn that there is a linguist living in a nice comfortable motel in Browning and paying his informants by the hour and getting all kinds of information. Perhaps I should apply for a linguistic grant, but I prefer to be my own man. Things may not be going too great at the moment, but I still would rather be a skinny stallion than a fat gelding.

This morning was very warm, with no wind at all, and I was up and had the stove going and breakfast ready when Jim and the Chief got up at 6:30. Everybody was uncommunicative at breakfast, and as soon as they had eaten, Jim and the Chief took the truck and went to town. I took a long walk along the creek as far as Paul Many Hides' house. Nobody at home there, so I walked back along the creek bottom, examining the colorful stones and pebbles. I finally picked up two stones, but for their texture, not their color (and no doubt Freud's boys could manufacture some significance out of even that small gesture of preference).

I took advantage of the warm day and the empty house to take a bath and put on clean clothing, then for dessert I played a tape of Beethoven's Fifth. Lunch, which followed dessert, consisted of tomato soup and a peanut butter sandwich—accompanied by liberal quantities of resentment that neither Jim nor the Chief showed up. It is now 2:30. I have been trying unsuccessfully to write, and I am tired, but I am going to town.

Later: On the way to town I stopped off to visit with Plenty Treaty B.C. and his wife, Maggie. Maggie, whose Indian name is Sikáki (Black Woman), is a small, roundish lady with cheeks as plump and brown as fresh-baked loaves. She is 78 years old, but certainly doesn't look it. She was sitting cross-legged in the middle of a bed, making moccasins of white buckskin (for the top), parflêche (for the sole), deer sinew (for thread), and beads (for decoration). Her moccasins are works of art. Her beadwork is intricate and always in the traditional pattern (a three-pronged design, representing the three divisions of the Blackfoot Nation—the Piegans, the Bloods and the Blackfoots proper). Maggie does not wear glasses, but apparently she can see perfectly well without them. Louis (Plenty Treaty) said that he needs a pair of bearskin moccasins for ceremonial wear, and he showed me a piece of bearhide that he is keeping for the purpose of making them. Maggie cannot help him out because it is taboo for her to touch bearskin. The situation suggests that probably Louis is a *Kyái-aht-so-mi-tai* (bear dog), of the Crazy Dog Clan (*K'náht-so-mi-tahks*).

Snapped a picture of Louis and Maggie and then took Louis on to town with me. Could not find the boys. Had no mail. I searched for them in the Tribal Office which contains a long hallway with the following rooms designated, front to rear, by prominent signs: Tribal Chairman, F.H.A., Realty, Tribal Secretary, Employment, Housing, Chairman, Court Room, Ladies, Mens.

Dropped Plenty Treaty back at his house and went on back to the ranch. Jim and the old man were there, and I was just in time for a supper of hamburger, fried potatoes and tea. I spiked my tea with bourbon but soon wished I hadn't. After supper Jimmy took the telescope I had given to the Chief and went outside ("In case if I see anything") and almost immediately spotted three mule deer heading down toward the creek about a mile away. So we jumped into the truck and barrelled down the road and across the prairie and skidded to a halt on a bluff about a hundred feet above the wooded creek bottom. The deer had gone into the trees below, and while Jimmy jacked a cartridge into the chamber of the old Marlin .38/40, I, half gassed and with eyes as blank as Orphan Annie's, skidded down the embankment in an attempt to flush the deer up the far side. It was a long-shot chance and it didn't pan out, and after several minutes Jimmy called to me to come on up. The deer had cut back and followed the creek bottom for about half a mile before climbing out on the opposite bank. We could see them making for the wooded ridge behind the Many Hides place.

The Chief laughed loudly when Jim and I described our Laurel-and-Hardy attempt to slay the wily deer, and the situation induced him into a story-telling mood. First he added to the hilarity by telling about his first buffalo hunt.

THE FIRST BUFFALO HUNT

When we were kids, when we were starting to get into our early teens, we would tag along on the buffalo hunts to watch the men kill buffalo. One time my partner, Night Shoot, and I, riding double on Night Shoot's old iron gray horse, went along on a buffalo hunt and roped a buffalo calf. We made a loop in the end of the rawhide rope we were using for a bridle and we roped the calf with the loop, but almost as soon as we roped the calf he pulled the rope away from us and so he was running wild leading our horse on the end of the rope.

Men were chasing bunches of buffalo all over the place, and the calf kept trying to get into the middle of a herd, and I was so scared I was crying. I told Night Shoot to jump off and save himself, but he said that he would stick with me—even though he was as scared as I.

Pretty soon a bunch of buffalo came over the hill being chased by several men. Among the men was Woman's Moccasin, who had already killed his buffalo. He rode up to us, and we pleaded for him to help us, but he refused. He said that we wouldn't eat all that day and night and all the next day, and that sooner or later the calf would lead us into the center of the herd where we would surely be killed. He was only teasing us, but we didn't know this and we begged him for help. "If you love your father and mother and brothers and sisters, help us!" we said, but still Woman's Moccasin refused.

"You boys are crazy for roping that calf," he said. "Sooner or

185

later you are going to get into the middle of the herd and be killed for sure."

Later on, Woman's Moccasin stopped the calf by hitting it in the head with a stone, and we were so grateful for being saved that we kissed him. We begged him not to tell on us, but he did. He told the whole camp, and the people sure did laugh at Night Shoot and me.

This experience cured Night Shoot and me of roping buffalo calves, but a couple of years later we got our first real buffalo. We got hold of an old flintlock rifle and joined a buffalo chase. We didn't get any buffalo on the chase, but we managed to sneak up on some that were on a pine hill. We killed three of them.

Next he told a story which convinced me once and for all that Indian warfare, even as any other kind of warfare, was not only a tragic waste of human life but was filled with treachery, double-dealing, and the antics of glory boys who were anything but the Noble Warrior.

TRAITOR'S CAVE

One time, when the Piegans and the Snake Persons [Shoshoni Indians] were at war, a member of a Piegan war party got left behind. Toward evening it began to rain, and the Piegan sought shelter in a cave. It was very dark in the cave, and although the Piegan could not see, he had a feeling that someone else was in the cave with him. Then the Piegan felt a human hand take his hand and press the palms together [a sign of friendship], so the Piegan accepted the sign and then asked in sign language who the other person was. The other person took the Piegan's hand and made a wiggly line along the palm with his finger [the sign of the Snake Indians, or Shoshonis]; then the Piegan took the Snake Person's hand and made the hand into a fist and moved the fist in a circle next to his cheek [the sign of the Piegan, signifying that they used paint on their cheeks]. The two men were enemies, but they had made a sign of peace and so they spent the night in the cave together as friends.

Early the next morning, the Shoshoni signed to the Piegan that he wished to challenge him to a hand game. The Shoshoni said that he would bet his gun and his scalp against the gun and the scalp of the Piegan. The Piegan agreed, and the two men

186

played the hand game until at last the Piegan won; whereupon the Shoshoni handed the Piegan his gun and then lay face downward on the ground and allowed the Piegan to scalp him. The Piegan scalped only one braid of the Shoshoni, cutting a small circle of skin from the scalp where the braid joined the head, but the Shoshoni cried with pain and the Piegan sang a victory song. The words of the song were, "Now the Snake Person is crying."

Then the Piegan bound up the wound of the Shoshoni, and when they parted, they parted friends. The Piegan made the sign for parting [both fists held together and then pulled apart], and then he made the sign for brothers [two fingertips held to the mouth, suggesting that they had been nursed by the same mother]. Then the Piegan told the Shoshoni that he would reward him for the gun and the scalp, and the two men made plans to meet secretly at a certain place.

When the Piegan got back home and told how he had taken the gun and scalp of a live enemy, nobody would believe him. The Shoshoni told his story, too, but nobody would believe him either. Later on, it was discovered that the story was true.

Neither of the men told about their plans for a secret meeting, however, and when finally they did meet, the Shoshoni told the Piegan that he had come for the reward he had been promised. So the Piegan said, "I will pay you back with a gun and a scalp. I will take out a war party of two men, and I will tell you where you can ambush us. I will pretend to shoot at you, but I will not hit you. But you must kill only one man of my party, and take only one gun."

So the Piegan took out a war party of two men, and the Shoshoni ambushed them and killed one man and scalped him and knocked the other man unconscious and stole his gun. Some time afterward, the Shoshoni did the same favor for the Piegan: he led a war party out and allowed the Piegan to kill one man and capture one gun. The two men planned a third meeting, but by this time people were starting to get suspicious and the two traitors decided to quit before they got caught.

The story-telling was progressing nicely when suddenly Jim became ill and staggered outside and threw up violently. I had mentioned that I wasn't feeling very well today, and at first I thought that Jimmy's, "Me, I don't feel so good too," was just one more of his empathic responses. But he was really sick, and as he came rather unsteadily back into the house he said, "I ate some onions in town for lunch. Every time I ate onions I gets sick." Then he said, in a single unpunctuated sentence: "I been sick before eating those onions and if I get sick again well whose fault is it it's mine."

Jim pluckily carried on with his translation of the Chief's stories, though, and I was thankful that he did because the results were outstanding. Many so-called "experts" and "authorities" on the Blackfoot culture have voiced the incredibly off-base conclusion that because the Blackfoots never brought more than an occasional few beaver pelts into the trading posts, the Blackfoots were not good trappers. The fact is that the small water-dwelling animals (the "Underwater Persons," of which the "Beaver Persons" were the leaders) were nearly as important in Blackfoot religious life as was the Sun. On occasion the Blackfoots would take the pelt of an Underwater Person for employment in religious ritual, but they did not trap beaver on a commercial basis, and those beaver pelts that were brought in by the Blackfoots for purposes of trade with the White Man invariably had been captured from White trappers or from the Crees or from other tribes that had no religious prohibitions with regard to trapping the Underwater Persons. It is easy to understand, then, why the Blackfoots raised so much hell with trappers, White or Indian, who invaded Blackfoot territory.

To my best knowledge, the Blackfoots were the only Plains Indians who placed so much credence in the existence of underwater spirits, and I have my own theories on this subject. All of the Algonkin Indians, including the Blackfoots, are known to have lived at one time in the Northeastern region of North America, and it is generally believed that the Blackfoots were the first of the Algonkin groups to take up residence in the Northwest. And I personally believe that the Blackfoot Underwater Persons are a religious inheritance from early Eastern Woods Indian culture. (The Cheyennes also believe in underwater spirits, and the Cheyennes, like the Blackfoots, are of Algonkin origin.) I have long observed a Norse influence upon Algonkin culture, and this observation is fortified with regard to the Blackfoots by the Blackfoot belief in not only the Underwater Persons (the water animals, the water birds, and in some instances even frogs, turtles and lizards) but in disembodied underwater spirits which appear to the Blackfoots in visions in the form of human beings *with blond hair and blue eyes.*

It is quite logical that since the Blackfoots departed from the East Coast at such an early time (they lived for some generations, it is believed, in the region of the Great Slave Lake) that early Algonkin culture should have been retained by the isolated Blackfoots in a form more pure than that found among those Algonkins who remained in the East and were thus subjected to the cultural influence of other Indian groups and of course to that of the various European groups which colonized in that area. I am especially intrigued by the fact that even today some of the older Blackfoots, when crossing a body of water, will offer gifts to the spirits upon whose domain they are trespassing. Usually the offering to the Underwater Spirits is in the form of tobacco—a sack of Bull Durham or a cigarette—but this gesture certainly evokes thoughts of the ancient mariners (not only the Norsemen but the Ancient Greeks) pouring libations upon the waters in petition for a safe voyage. Even today, the Underwater Spirits are very real to those Blackfoots who cling to the old beliefs, and although some of the younger Blackfoots do not hesitate to trap the Beaver Persons and the Otter Persons, the old-timers still prefer to purchase their ceremonial water-animal skins from the barbaric Crees.

There is certainly a great deal of factual information with which to link Blackfoot culture to that of the ancient Norsemen (e.g., the Blackfoot sweat lodge is identical in appearance and function to the rustic Scandinavian sauna bath, and the Blackfoots switch themselves with a buffalo tail exactly as the Scandinavians smack themselves with birch branches), but our best clues as to the origin of the Blackfoots exist probably in Blackfoot legend. Tonight, after we had discussed the Underwater Persons, the Chief told me a richly interesting history of an event which had taken place "a long time ago" (when the Chief says a long time ago he means a *really* long time ago) when all the Blackfoots lived "far to the north." This legend may imply, among other things, the first breaking away of the Piegans from the main body of Blackfoots. The hero of the story is a man called Round Scabby Robe, who received his power from the Underwater Persons, the Beaver Persons. The word "Piegan"—which most writers transcribe from the Blackfoot as "Pekuni" or "Pecunnie" but which is correctly pronounced either [pikãni] or [píkãni] according to linguistic environment—means Scabby Robe.

WHY THE PIEGANS KILL THE SNAKE PERSONS

A long, long time ago, when all the Blackfoots lived far up in the North, they did not kill the Snake Persons [the Shoshoni Indians] or make war on them. Each year when the waters became warm [probably in July or early August], the chiefs of the Blackfoots and the chiefs of the Snake Persons would meet at the Big River. [The Chief used the term, Ó-mach-k'tai: Big River, and since this is the Blackfoot name for the Missouri River, I believe that the reference was to the Missouri and not to the body of water located west of the Rockies which is today known as Big River.] When they met in the water of the Ó-mach-k'tai, the chiefs of the two nations would count coup by touching each other lightly with their lances. Each time they touched one another they would shout their coups back to their own camps, and that night each camp would have a victory celebration as though there had been a real battle instead of just a friendly ceremony. The next day, the two nations would exchange gifts, and then each would go its separate way, singing.

It was customary in those days that when the Blackfoots had a dance each girl should dress in the manner of her husband or sweetheart; in this way, everybody could tell whose woman she was. The men displayed their war honors by decorating their belongings with the white winter skin of the weasel [the Blackfoots believed the weasel to be the most courageous of all wild animals], and by wearing in their hair the feathers of the hawk and of the eagle. But since it was not proper for a woman to wear feathers, the Blackfoot ladies attended the dances with their hair decorated instead with braids of *ah-pu-tú-yis* [white grass].

There was at this time among the Blackfoots a young man known as Áh-pi-koh-koh-mì-nim-mah: Round Scabby Robe. Round Scabby Robe was pretty much the camp buffoon; he was not a good hunter, he had no war honors, and his only robe was a scabby old hide which he had cut into the shape of a circle. Round Scabby Robe was too poor to take a wife, but he was secretly in love with the youngest wife—the "far-away" wife—of the head chief, and she in turn was in love with Round Scabby Robe.

[Although a Blackfoot man—especially if he were a chief—might have several wives, his various spouses were not considered to share positions of equal privilege in his lodge. A definite hierarchy of both social prestige and household authority existed among the good ladies, top dog being the "sits-by-him," wife (so called because she was the one who sat nearest her husband at social and religious functions). Next in line was the "takes-care-of-him" wife, and so on down the ladder until we reach the poor gal who was required to perform the meanest labors of teepeekeeping and who was obliged to sleep next to the door and who for obvious reasons was known as the "far-away" wife. The far-away wife almost invariably was the baby sister of one (or more) of the other wives. Frequently she was a mere child and a wife in name only—more of a ward, really—and she was available for marriage to any young chap who could cough up the right price. If our friend Round Scabby Robe had had the hots for one of the head chief's top echelon wives, he would have been in hot water; however, as we shall see, his romance with the young far-away wife had a happy ending.]

No one in the camp was aware of the love between Round Scabby Robe and the chief's far-away wife until one night at a dance the girl appeared dressed in the manner of her lover. All the people began to gossip then, and when Round Scabby Robe saw his sweetheart dressed in a scabby old robe, with no braids of *ah-pu-tú-yis* in her hair, he felt so ashamed that he asked his partner to go with him down to Bull River, where the beaver lodges are. Then he told his partner good-bye and said that he was going to pass the winter in the lodges of the Beaver Persons.

When Round Scabby Robe entered the lodge of the Chief Beaver, the Chief Beaver, who is Chief of all the Underwater Persons, asked him why he had come there. He said that he had come to spend the seven moons of winter with the Beaver Persons, so the Chief Beaver made him welcome.

The Chief of the Beaver Persons gave Round Scabby Robe a shell formed like a plate. The shell contained seven berries, and the Chief Beaver said to eat the berries. So Round Scabby Robe ate the seven berries, and immediately there appeared upon the shell seven more berries. Each time the seven berries were consumed, seven more appeared.

Then the Chief Beaver gave Round Scabby Robe a drink of water in a large shell shaped like a drinking horn, but each time that Round Scabby Robe drained the shell of water it was immediately filled once again to the brim.

Then the Chief Beaver said, "You cannot eat all the berries because they represent the savis berries which grow all along the banks of the river, and there is no end of the savis berries. And you cannot drink all the water because it represents the water in this river, and the water flows unceasingly."

So Round Scabby Robe passed the seven moons of winter in the lodge of the Beaver Persons. He became good friends with everyone, but he grew especially fond of a small white beaver which was the youngest son of the Chief Beaver and which soon became his constant companion.

When springtime came and Round Scabby Robe was preparing to leave the Beaver Lodge, the small white beaver called him aside and whispered into his ear: "Do you see those medicine bundles over there? And do you see that small stick amongst them? Well, when you leave our lodge you must take that small stick with you. That small stick represents myself, and I have gotten used to you as a friend and so you must take me with you when you go. My father will offer you your choice of any of the medicine bundles and all the power that goes with it, but you must accept nothing but the small stick which represents myself and my power."

Sure enough, as Round Scabby Robe was preparing to leave, the Chief Beaver offered him his choice of any of the medicine bundles, and when Round Scabby Robe said that he wanted only the small stick, the Beaver Chief attempted to dissuade him from his choice. He said, "You cannot make use of that stick. I will give you other gifts instead." But Round Scabby Robe insisted that he desired only the small stick.

The Chief Beaver made a ceremony then, and sang three songs, and then he offered Round Scabby Robe a bundle which contained the pelt of an otter (*ém-moon-i-sey*). Round Scabby Robe refused the bundle, saying that he wished only the small stick. Three more times the Chief Beaver performed ceremonies and sang songs, and in turn he offered Round Scabby Robe bundles which contained the pelt of a beaver (*ksísk-stah-ki*), the skin of a loon (*máht-sey-i-sèy-pi-eh*), and the skin of a turtle (*spoo-pí*), but each time the bundle was refused. Round Scabby Robe spoke to the Chief Beaver: "I am honored that you offer me these medicine bundles and the great powers that they possess. But I am a simple man and I cannot accept such fine gifts. I can accept only the small stick."

The Chief Beaver said, "You have spoken well. And you have chosen well, for the small stick which you have chosen possesses the most powerful medicine of all. You shall have the stick, but first I shall teach you two songs which you must sing in order to evoke the power of the stick."

The words of the first song were:

In the spring of the year we come out
from our lodges, and if we see enemies,
we dive back down beneath the water.

The words of the second song were:

In the spring of the year we come out
from our lodges, and if we see enemies,
we do our best to save our lives.

Then the Chief Beaver said, "When you meet your enemies
you must first sing these songs, and then you must chant four
times, *yuh! yuh! yuh! yuh!*"

So the Chief Beaver gave Round Scabby Robe the small stick,
but first he wrapped the stick in cattail leaves and admonished
Round Scabby Robe never to place the stick upon the ground
but always to place it on a buffalo chip. He said, "If ever the
stick touches water or swampy ground it will immediately turn
into a young beaver, so never allow the stick to become damp
unless you wish to evoke the full power of the Beaver Medicine
which the stick represents."

Round Scabby Robe accepted the stick then, and as he was
about to leave the lodge the small white beaver came and whispered once again into his ear. He said, "Soon you will have occasion to use the power of the stick. When next the Blackfoots
and the Snake Persons meet at the water of *Ó-mach-k'tai*, Big
Top, Chief of the Snake Persons, while pretending to touch the
Blackfoot Chief with his lance, will treacherously attempt to
kill him instead. You must save your chief by meeting Big Top
in the water and fighting him. Sing your medicine songs, and
tie the small stick across your chest, and then Big Top will not
be able to harm you because my power is too strong for him.
Big Top will be wearing his hair in two braids, and at the front
of his head he will have a large topknot decorated on the one
side with white shells and on the other with black shells. After
you have killed him, you should take his scalp. If you do these
things, you will become a great warrior and a chief."

So Round Scabby Robe returned to his people, and he told
his plans to his partner. He said, "Partner, Big Top is going to
try to kill our chief, but I am going to save our chief's life by
meeting Big Top in the water and fighting him. After I have
killed him I will take his scalp, and since you are my partner
I will share the scalp with you. Some of our other warriors will

attempt to take the scalp from me, but I will fool them by employing the same trick which the Beaver Persons employ in fooling their enemies. Our people will be waiting down the river from the crossing where I will kill Big Top, and I will dive under the water headed downstream. But underwater I will turn and swim upstream instead, so you must wait for me upstream."

And that is the way it happened. Big Top charged the Blackfoot Chief, but Round Scabby Robe made his ceremony and rushed into the water to fight with Big Top. Big Top threw his lance, but it glanced harmlessly off the small stick that Round Scabby Robe was wearing across his chest, and then Round Scabby Robe killed Big Top with a flint knife and scalped him and divided the scalp with his partner.

That night the Blackfoots had a victory dance, and as Round Scabby Robe's sweetheart danced she carried the scalp of Big Top. She was very proud.

After the dance, Round Scabby Robe gave the scalp to the head chief and said, "I want your far-away wife to become my sits-by-him wife."

The head chief said, "You are a great warrior and someday you will be a great chief. I am proud to have you for a relative."

From that time on, the Blackfoots and the Snake Persons were enemies, and since that time they kill one another and take one another's scalps.

Since the English translation of the Blackfoot word for "Piegan" means "Scabby Robe," I assume that in Blackfoot legendry Round Scabby Robe is given credit for having established the Piegan Tribe of the Blackfoot Nation. No further mention was made by the Chief of the partner with whom Round Scabby Robe shared the scalp of Big Top, but it is possible that in Blackfoot legend he was first chief of the Bloods (who refer to themselves as the Many Chiefs, not the Bloods), the third major division of the Blackfoot Nation. If so, this portion of the narrative has been lost in the telling.

I was in a veritable rapture of fascination over receiving so much priceless material from the Chief, and the Chief was obviously enjoying telling the stories, so I asked him if he would tell me some of his own warpath experiences. He appeared willing enough, and at last I learned the story of his first war parties.

Red River Cart

MY FIRST WAR PARTIES

When I was about fourteen years old, I was outside of camp playing around with my bow and arrows when I saw a party of men led by Running Buffalo heading south. I thought that they were just heading down to visit some of our camps further down the river, so I followed them. They were on foot, and every once in a while they would stop and rest; whenever they rested, I would rest too, but I kept a good distance behind them.

Finally when the party stopped for the night I joined them in their camp. One of the men said, "Why did the boy come along! If anything happens to him, his father will make it very hard on us." But finally they decided to let me come along.

We circled down through the Sweetgrass country, but we did not have any luck. We went back home without getting any horses or meeting with any enemies.

When we got back home, my father asked me where I had been and I told him that I had followed a party which I thought was on the way down to visit some of our own camps. My father said that the party I had followed was a war party and that I was very fortunate not to have run into any enemies.

It is extremely doubtful that the Chief did not have a full awareness from the very beginning that he was following a war party; probably he had overheard the plans for the war party and had been all prepared to follow along. The reason that he will not admit, even today, that he knew what he was doing derives from the traditional ritual which attended a Blackfoot boy's going on his first war party. The ritual (which is very similar to the coming-of-age routine which contemporary fathers and sons usually go through) was roughly as follows:

(1) The boy would ask permission of his parents to go on a war party, knowing full well that the parents would withhold their consent.

(2) The parents would invariably forbid the boy to go to war, expecting that the boy would go anyway (if he did not go, the suggestion was that he had not as yet attained sufficient manhood to make his own decisions).

(3) When the boy returned from his first war party, he would explain to his parents that the whole thing had been a misunderstanding and that he had too much respect for them to intentionally disobey their wishes.

(4) The parents were now proud as hell of their warrior son.

In other words, everybody was lying like hell and everybody knew it and everybody knew that everybody knew it.

The Chief continued:

My first real war party took place a few years later. Tripod was the leader. We started from the Blood camp on Belly River, over in Canada. We were all on foot, and we were headed down to steal some horses from the Crows. About half-way between Belly River and where the Gros Ventres are today, there is a short cut across the mountains, and as we were crossing over we saw a rider coming toward us.

Tripod told us all to take cover, so we hid out and watched the rider coming closer. When the rider came to where we were, Tripod saw that he was a Gros Ventre, so he shot him. The Gros Ventre was knocked from his horse, and the horse bolted and ran so that we never did catch him.

The Gros Ventre was only wounded, and he jumped immediately to his feet. Tripod ran out of the brush, and after quite a fight he finally killed the Gros Ventre. After that we did not go on down to the Crow country. We turned around and went back to Belly River, making the entire journey on foot.

The first war party during which I captured any horses took place when I was about twenty years old. At that time we were camped south of the Milk River, and from there Heavy Breast led a war party to Round Brush, up in Canada. We made a successful raid and captured several horses from the Crees. The only weapon I carried on this war party was a knife.

The first war party on which I was the leader started from Belly River, over in Canada. On this party there were three of us: Running-With-Guns, who was just a kid, Narrow Belt, and myself. We started out on foot, and the first night we made it as far as Magrath, where we camped. Our next stop was west of the Sweetgrass Hills, and from there we made it to the east side of the Sweetgrass Hills, to a place where Bad Head had been killed many years before.

We moved on to Purple Lake, and there we took a break to rest up. We called this lake Purple Lake because on its east side there is a cliff from which we used to dig our purple paint. The clay from this cliff colors the water of the lake purple, and the water is not drinkable.

While Running-With-Guns was on lookout at Purple Lake, he saw something which he at first thought to be a large bird. But when we got closer to the creature we saw that it was a steer with very wide horns. [This incident is quite famous among the Blackfoots. The steer was a Texas longhorn, obviously a stray from a Texas trailherd, and it was the first longhorn to be seen this far north.] We killed the steer east of Purple Lake, and built a fire and camped there long enough to smoke and dry the meat. The reason we used to dry our meat was that dry meat will not spoil when you pack it. Fresh meat will spoil on you, and you can pack a lot more dry meat with you anyway.

From there we went on to a place called Many Berries. There had once been a Medicine Lodge there, and it had been known as the Raspberry Medicine Lodge because the side of the hill there is covered with raspberry bushes. There is a stream there which leads into a small lake, and there we managed to kill some ducks.

While Narrow Belt and I cooked the ducks, Running-With-Guns went up onto a hill to keep a lookout, and pretty soon he signaled for us to come up there. We left our guns and clothing and meat and went up onto the hill, but immediately I sent the other two fellows back down to bring all of our belongings up into the brush on the hill. Some people were approaching, and we could tell that they were Crees because they had a two-wheeled cart [a Red River Cart] with them.

The Crees camped by the lake, and after a while one of them walked down the creek with his rifle—maybe he was going to try to shoot some ducks. Finally he crossed the creek to the place where we had been cooking the ducks. We had drowned out our fire, but the Cree found the fresh entrails of the ducks. He was right down below us, and we all had him covered with our rifles. But he could not see us, and apparently he decided there was nobody around here any more because he walked back down the creek and the Crees made ready to camp for the night.

We hid out all night, planning to make off with the Cree horses at daybreak, but late in the evening the Crees broke camp and headed out. We could not see them, but we knew they were leaving because we could hear the creaking of the cart. We started to follow them, but when we couldn't hear the creak of the cart any longer, we figured that they might have stopped to try to ambush us, so we took to the brush again until daylight. The next day we started to trail the Crees, but at Round Brush the tracks led into a patch of timber. We were afraid of an ambush, so we turned around and beat it out of there.

We went back and slept in some brush to the east of the place we had killed the ducks, and then we headed north to look for more Crees. At Medicine Hat we found some Cree camps, and I made off with four horses.

Narrow Belt and the boy [Running-With-Guns] started back with the horses while I stayed back and scouted around to see whether I could find some more. Finally I saw a brown-and-white pinto dragging a rope. A White man was chasing the pinto, trying to catch him, but every now and then the man would fall down. I think he was drunk. When the horse came near the brush where I was hiding, I rode out and caught him and made off with him. The White man fired several shots at me, but I was too small for his bullets. When finally I caught up with the other fellows, I gave the pinto to the boy and told him that he could tell people that he had stolen the horse himself.

We camped below what is now Taber, Alberta, by a stream we called Many Red, and from there we went north to the place where Lethbridge is now located. At that time the survey work for the Lethbridge townsite had just been completed.

The survey crew had gone, but they had left behind some bread. The bread was mouldy, but we were so hungry that we ate it anyway.

From there we followed the creek down to a place called Red Painted Rock, and from there to a Blackfoot campground known as Many Chief. We hid out our guns and staked out the horses and entered the camp. My grandmother, Holy Rags, and my aunt, John, were in the camp. Most of the people in the camp were women and girls; they were picking berries.

My grandmother had started to cook some food for us when a half-breed interpreter from the States came in and wanted to know what we were doing there. He said that the Mounties wanted to know. My grandmother knew that we had been on a war path, but she told the interpreter that we were some of her relatives visiting from another camp. The interpreter said that we had better leave right now—I think he was afraid we might raise hell in the camp, or else he was jealous of the girls there—but my Aunt John said that it was pretty late now and it would be better if we left early in the morning.

Early the next day some Mounties came through, and when they and the interpreter had crossed the stream on the ferry, we fellows took our guns and horses and went to where the old Blood Agency used to be. The Blackfoots called it Many Surrendered. The Agent at this time was called Big Bear.

Once again we hid out our guns and horses, and went into the Agency. There were a few Blood camps in the area, but not many. We found out that most of the camps, including that of my uncle, Running Wolf, had moved down east. The Agent asked us where we were from, and we told him we were from one of the camps down east. He told us we had better go back home, so we went and got our guns and horses and went down to Running Wolf's camp. That is to say, Narrow Belt and I did. Running-With-Guns' people were camped near Many Surrendered, so we left him there.

So we got home safe with all our horses. I gave the best of my horses to my uncle, Running Wolf, and I also gave one to my sister, Weasel Tail Woman. I gave the others away too, but I can't remember who I gave them to—I think I gave them to my female cousins.

I felt that in these last stories the Chief had really warmed up to his task, but as I sat in confident expectation of learning even more about the Chief's early life, I learned instead why it is that so many ethnologists and anthropologists are a bit buggy.

The Chief's next story consisted of the following statement:

At the time I was chosen to cut the centerpole for the Medicine Lodge at the Sun Dance [a very great honor, granted only to warriors of outstanding achievement] I recited the following war honors:

I took the scalp of a Cree.

I stole all the horses of Little Shield, a Gros Ventre, and brought them back to Canada. [Not to be confused with the Blackfoot war chief named Little Shield.]

I shot a horse from under Night Eagle, a Chippewa chief.

One of our men got left behind during a war party against the Crows, and I went back and saved his life.

The maddening aspect of this little narrative was that any one of these events, if told in detail, would undoubtedly be a much better story than the others the Chief told me tonight. But he did not elaborate upon these achievements, and I dared not ask him to.

The Chief, as always, was obviously more interested in reciting the old traditional Blackfoot tales than in telling of his personal adventures; he is saddened by the fact that very few of today's Blackfoot youngsters display even the faintest interest in the old legends, and he wants me to record them so that they will not be lost to future generations. During the evening he remarked that the man who is "buying stories" around town is not getting anything for his money but a bunch of tall tales. I believe this, because the Chief and Chewing Black Bones, a Piegan nearly as old as the Chief, are the only ones left who really know the old stories. Old Chewing Black Bones is a bitter old warrior who has very little use for the White Man; he will speak with Father Mallman, with a young White man whom he has adopted as the Chief has adopted me, and with a few other Whites whom he has learned to trust, but for a strange White man to attempt to approach him would be entirely fruitless. And neither the Chief nor old Chewing can be bought.

The Chief explained that he learned the old traditional and historical Blackfoot tales as a youngster by having the old-timers recite them to him, over and over, until he knew every word (rather in the same manner that the Rig-Veda was passed from generation to generation in India, but of course lacking the formality which attended this linguistically important ritual of the ancient Brahmin religion). The Chief said that the old-timers had been very patient and generous but that sometimes they would tease him, and he illustrated the nature of this teasing by relating an actual incident.

THE BATTLE AT SIX PERSONS

A group of us youngsters were sitting around listening to some of the old-timers tell stories. There was Looking For Smoke, Big Spring, Morning Eagle and some others. Morning Eagle was telling us about the time that a Blackfoot war party was fighting against some Crows at a place called Six Persons. The Blackfoots were doing all right for themselves until they ran out of ammunition, at which time six of them got killed. Finally Morning Eagle said, "I see plenty of ammunition around here," and he began to point to various small sticks that were lying around the ground. Then he took from his pocket a piece of milkroot that was just about the size of a bullet, and placing the milkroot in his rifle he shot it as though it were a bullet and killed a Crow. Then all the rest of the Blackfoots placed sticks in their rifles and fired them, and pretty soon they had the Crows on the run.

When Morning Eagle finished his story, he took a black handkerchief from his pocket. He said, "This black handkerchief is my gunpowder. I think I will throw it into the stove and make the stove explode." When he said that, all of us youngsters became frightened and ran outside. Those old-timers sure did laugh at us.

Inevitably during the evening the conversation would return to Blackfoot religious beliefs and ceremonies, and at length the Chief stated that he would like to have a Beaver Ceremony if only he had the money to pay for the feast. The Chief is the only living "Beaver Man" (he owns the sacred Beaver Bundle, and is the only person qualified to conduct the Beaver Ceremony), and I am anxious to see the ceremony performed and so I handed him the twenty dollar bill I had in my wallet and promised to give him a like amount tomorrow if that would make enough to pay for the feast. My dough is going fast, but I do want to see the Beaver Ceremony—and I know that it will mean a lot to the old Chief, too.

The Chief said, "*Sokáhpi*," and he presented me with a very old little wheel made of buckskin-covered wood. The wheel has four spokes, made of large old Indian beads strung on sinew, and the buckskin is painted with small Indian designs. The wheel was given to the Chief by his father, and Jimmy had trouble translating the name for the wheel because the term is no longer used. The closest Jim could come to the actual translation of the term was "wheel for rolling."

The wheel was employed by the Blackfoots in a type of gambling game, and I taped the Chief's explanation of how the game was played. The wheel would be rolled along the ground toward a log, and the contestants would attempt to toss arrows through the spokes of the wheel. The objective was to toss the arrow through the spokes as close to the log as possible, the winner being determined by the position of the arrow in relation to certain beads. Each bead —the beads were of various colors—represented a horse that the owner of the wheel had stolen from the enemy, and the game was really very ritualistic and complicated.

We all stayed up until 12:30, and everyone was very happy and conversational. The Chief has been quite aware that nobody has been very joyful around here lately, and he said that this sudden metamorphosis to conviviality has resulted from our decision to have a Beaver Ceremony. The Chief also confided that I have made quite a hit with Mary Ground, the lady who sponsored the Pipe Dance. She was quite pleased that I enjoyed the berry soup so much. She, incidentally, had prepared it.

I gave the Chief the red flannel shirt that I had bought for him.

My thoughts this A.M. were Grimm—Jakob Grimm, that is. Actually, Jake was quite a guy—personal librarian to the King of Westphalia, instructor at the University of Göttingen, appointed by Friedrich Wilhelm (King of Prussia) to the Academy of Sciences in Berlin, an authority on the beginnings of law and religion among the Germans, and a very important linguist. Jakob Grimm's book, *Deutsche Grammatik*, in which he formulated previous observations by Rasmus Rask concerning the almost regular shifting of Indo-European stopped consonants in Germanic languages into what has become known as "Grimm's Law" (the first Germanic consonant shift) was an invaluable contribution to linguistic science. And in view of the fact that Jakob's brother, Wilhelm, was also a person of rather considerable scholarly and cultural attainment, I think it speaks ill of our American educational system that 99.44% of our college graduates know the Grimm brothers only as the authors of some fairy tales which were the by-product of their study of Germanic philology and mythology.

What got me wound up on this subject is my current suspicion that as a linguist I would make a great writer of fairy tales. I am still kicking around the word for "moose," and when I asked Tom Many Guns about the matter he informed me that there are several ways of pronouncing the word and that each pronunciation carries with it a slightly different meaning. He said that when the word is pronounced with an additional strongly stressed "u" [sikstisùú] this suffix adds the meaning, "having a big nose." I tried this pronunciation on the Chief, and he recognized it immediately as meaning precisely what Tom had suggested. At linguistic conferences I used to sit in complete awe of the abilities of Pike and some of the other great linguists, and the more I fumble around at field work of my own, the deeper my respect for these men becomes. Apparently I have neither the ability nor the dedication to do fantastic things such as spending several months in some jungle just to prove the existence of an additional tone level in some obscure tonal dialect, and my only resentment against the really top linguists is that none of them is here to help me figure out Blackfoot.

Actually very little has been done with the Blackfoot language—mostly a few vocabulary lists, such as the one by Uhlenbeck and VonGulik, and they are all open to improvement. The really important aspect of a language is its structure, and in this direction I am strictly on my own. But actually I like it better that way. Since no work on the Blackfoot language at all was done until the post-Civil War period, and since my own informant (the Chief) is a native speaker of that period, I would be a fool to rely upon anyone's linguistic observations save my own.

For some reason, practically everyone except trained linguists assume that simply because a culture did not achieve a high degree of technological or artistic proficiency, it follows that the language of that culture was rudimentary and crude. Such is definitely not the case. Blackfoot, for instance, although it has produced neither works of poetry or prose nor even a written form (aside from a few symbolic or decorative pictographs) is a language which lends itself in the spoken form to the most intricately precise and most colorfully imaginative of employments. Aside from its marvelous store of metaphors (which are my special love, and which bring a tear to my eye along with the knowledge that there is no Blackfoot Poet Laureate) my special interest at the moment revolves around the existence in the Blackfoot language of personal forms. Broadly expressed, I am interested in the connotative implications—implied variations in meaning and/or emotional expression—which derive either from the use of ordinary expressions in special situations (with notable difference in pronunciation or stress) or from the use of extraordinary words in ordinary situations.

Now that we have decided to have a Beaver Ceremony next Sunday, there is a noticeably closer and warmer fellowship among Jim, the Chief and myself. The Chief chanted prayers all night, and Jim, who was up first and waked me with the sounds of his fire-building, says that the Chief was praying for me. The Chief did not get up until 8:30, and separately and out of hearing of each other, both Jim and the Chief said good morning to me in an entirely new way. Usually they say, "*Aì-siks-kah-nóh-toh-nay*"; this morning they both said, "*Aht-sahpi-náh-koh.*" "*Ahk-sah-pén-a-koh,*" I know, means "Good daylight," and this apparently is a variant of the same word-phrase. Whether this new phrase has any special semantic significance—whether it is a personal form—I have yet to determine. Frankly, I doubt it.

With the addition of tomato juice and canned cherries, the usual breakfast of pancakes and eggs was much improved. And after having eaten, after we had all slicked up—Jimmy helped the Chief to groom, plucking out his invisible-to-me chin whiskers and braiding his hair into four pigtails—we all went to town in my wagon.

The Chief spent the entire morning sitting in the Tribal Office. The Tribal Office used to be the Tribal Store, and the place is still a country store-type meeting place for the tribal members. Out front is a large room with benches all along the walls and with a large storefront window looking out upon the sidewalk. The Tribal Office is the Forty-second street and Broadway of the Reservation; if you stay there long enough, you will eventually meet whomever it is you are seeking. The Chief was waiting for the old-timers to drop in so that he could invite them to my Sunday coming-out party, the Beaver Ceremony.

I passed the time in chatting with my Indian friends as they came by, and I was greatly annoyed when a White American escorted a group of Norwegian tourists into the place and began offering the proud old-timers a quarter to pose for a snapshot. Naturally the tourists were supposed to get in the picture too, bless their little passport photos. The whole situation had a definitely calefacient effect upon the seat of my pants, but what really incinerated my saddlepad was the way the man went about it—holding the quarter up between thumb and forefinger the way one holds up a cookie to a child, or a biscuit to a dog, and speaking in an indulgent, cajoling, pidgin English manner. The Blackfoots as a group are extremely courteous and will go to almost any length to avoid hurting a person's feelings. But when the occasion demands, they can be as rough as corncobs, and for a moment I manufactured a blissful vision of this particular *Náhpiquon* scattering quarters frantically as he hot-footed it down the road, getting his hind-end barbered at every jump by the tomahawk of an armiferously aroused Blackfoot Indian.

Most of the old-timers either left immediately or smiled tolerantly and put on a me-no-speakum-English act, and when our boy tourist guide appealed to me for assistance—I look more Scandinavian than the tourists did—it gave me much emotional wampum to play dumb

Indian too. I answered him in Blackfoot (*"Tah-key-táu-wah-nisht"*:
What did you say?), and one of the few photos I would really
treasure would be one of his face at that moment.

When Fish Wolfrobe, the blind man, who has a magnificent "typical Indian" face, found out what was going on, he pulled down his
hat and turned angrily to the wall. The Chief completely ignored
the whole thing.

At noon we came home and lunched on a stew of my own concoction—a stew being the only solution I could devise to the problem of rendering chewable the remainder of the tough, half-dried
elk meat.

I said, "I don't know how this is going to taste, but we'll soon find
out."

Jim said, "We'll soon found out!"

The Chief went to bed right after lunch and slept until 7:30 this
evening. I do not think it was my stew that forced him to bed, however. He still has a pretty bad cold, and I know that he did not
sleep last night because he prayed until dawn.

I, too, attempted to sleep during the afternoon, but as soon as I
had dozed off, the kitten, which obviously had climbed to some high
place and awaited just such an opportunity, landed with a thump
on my chest. I awoke like a fireman, of course, and after tossing the
kitten out I tried to go back to sleep but the flies would have none
of this. No matter how many I slaughtered, there was always one
left to make a Kamakaze dive at my nose, so finally I gave it up and
spent the day hunting arrowheads along the creek. Jim went down
to help Joe Kicking-A-Woman work on his house.

The Chief was well rested after his long nap, and following a late
supper of ground beef and fried ham and fried potatoes the old
fellow told me some really marvelous stories. The story-telling lasted
until 11:00, and including Jim's translations the tales occupied a
full 7″ reel of ½ mil tape. For once, I was overjoyed to discover, the
tape recorder worked perfectly.

THE MYSTERY OF THE OWL PERSONS

The Chief is aware that I have attempted to become a student
of Plains Indian life, and he began this evening by asking whether
I had ever heard of any band or society of Indians known as the
Owl Persons. I said that I had not, and he told me the following
story:

206

I once was with a good-sized war party led by Many Medicine Lodge. As we approached Round Brush, we saw some riders duck into the heavy timber of a creek bottom in order to hide from us. We, too, were mounted, and we rode slowly along pretending that we had not seen anything. Then when we neared the point at which the riders had entered the creek bottom, we broke into two groups and pretended to be having a sham battle. When one group had worked its way across the creek, we charged into the timber from both sides and killed every single one of the men hidden there. The only Piegan killed in this battle was a fellow who got hung up in his stirrup and was dragged to death by his own horse.

I do not know for certain which tribe these enemy riders were from, but I think that they were Crees. The only feathers worn by any of them were owl feathers—even their arrows were fletched with owl feathers—so thereafter we always referred to them as the Owl Persons. I never did see any more of them, and today you don't even hear them mentioned. So I guess we must have wiped out the whole lot of them.

Mystery was definitely abroach of the evening, and the Chief's next story was,

THE STORY OF MAGIC SHOOT

This story is about a boy from the North Blackfoots, a boy who became known as Àh-péek-skoòn-nàki [Magic Shoot]. When Magic Shoot was getting big enough to start going on war parties, his father offered to give him a gun, but the boy refused the gun with the comment that it was not the one he was looking for. For a long time Magic Shoot went on war parties without a rifle, and although he captured several guns from the enemy, he always gave them away because they were not the gun he was looking for.

Then one summer the North Blackfoots had a Sun Dance at which some of the young men were playing the wheel game. One of the fellows was losing steadily, and when he sent his partner back to his lodge to bring him some more things with which to wager, he told him he might as well bring along his old flintlock rifle so that he could wager that too.

As soon as Magic Shoot saw the old rifle, he said, "That is the gun I have been looking for. I will give you my finest buffalo horse in trade for that gun." The gun wasn't worth looking at, so its owner agreed to the trade.

Some of Magic Shoot's friends called him aside then and said, "That buffalo horse is the finest in our band—you were always the first one to kill your share of buffalo. Why did you trade that fine horse for that no-good old gun?"

Magic Shoot answered: "I traded for this gun because it is the gun for which I have been searching for such a long time. This gun was showed to me in a dream. An old White man named Big Pemmican showed me the gun. He told me that I should search until I found the gun, and that when I did find it he would come to me in another dream and show me the ceremony of using the gun. Then he said that when I had learned the ceremony I would become a great warrior and a chief."

Shortly after Magic Shoot had obtained the gun, he went on a war path. He took the gun with him, but he did not take any bullets. But since the war party did not meet any enemy, he did not have occasion to use the gun anyway.

Then one day Magic Shoot and his partner went on a war party all by themselves. When they were out in the open they were attacked by a large number of Crows, and Magic Shoot's partner began to sing his medicine songs in preparation for dying. But Magic Shoot said, "Don't worry, Partner, and don't think about dying. I will kill every Crow that charges us."

"How can you do it?" his partner said. "You don't even have any bullets for your gun!"

"Don't worry!" Magic Shoot said. "I'll do it all right!"

Just then a Crow warrior charged the two Blackfoots. When the warrior got pretty close, Magic Shoot struck the butt of his rifle on the ground and yelled, "Haugh!" Then he raised the rifle and fired and knocked the Crow warrior from his horse. He did the same thing again and again, and after a while the Crows did not charge any more.

After that, Magic Shoot did the same thing on every war path. He never carried bullets with him—one time his father offered to give him some bullets, but he refused them—but he always killed more of the enemy than any of the other fellows did.

Finally Magic Shoot grew old, but before he passed away he gave the gun to his brother and told him how to pray for the power to use it. Then the brother was able to shoot the gun without bullets, just as Magic Shoot had done.

"Magic Shoot" is my favorite of all the traditional stories or legends that the Chief has thus far told me because I think I can account for its origin. Many Indian legends are of course based upon actual happenings, and my primary clues with regard to "Magic Shoot" are located in the facts that the magic rifle in the story was a muzzle-loader—a flintlock—and that the rifle was presented to Magic Shoot (via a dream) by a White man. The rest, my dear Watson, is elementary, as shall be revealed in the statement of fact which follows:

The process for loading a flintlock was (1) to prime the frizzen pan [to place some powder in a small pan, located just in advance of the hammer (the "cock"), so that the spark produced when the hammer—at that time really a sort of vice-like holder for a piece of flint—struck steel (the "battery") would be conducted by way of a small opening into the firing chamber of the weapon]; (2) to pour a charge of powder down the muzzle of the gun; (3) to wrap a bullet in a patch of linen, place it in the muzzle of the rifle or musket, and seat it upon the powder charge by ramming it down the barrel with a rod carried for that specific purpose. The weapon might now be cocked, aimed and (sometimes) fired.

Obviously the process of loading and firing a flintlock weapon was so laborious and slow that a man who had discharged his piece against Indian attack was in real danger of being overwhelmed before he could once again complete the complicated routine of powder and ball and patch and ramrod. An Indian archer could flight perhaps a dozen arrows for every well-aimed bullet the White Man could send his way, and many a White bit the dust swinging an empty rifle. However, the White frontiersman in Indian country soon learned that if he was to survive he must take advantage of all possible shortcuts in reloading, so he devised a rather clever and highly effective method which, lest the Indian should beat him at his own game, he attempted to keep secret.

The barrel and frizzen pan had to be charged with powder—there was no way of getting around that—but this operation could be carried out in a very few seconds. The real bottleneck was in the lengthy procedure of patching a bullet and ramming it down on top of the powder charge, so this procedure was eliminated. Since the bullet was designed to be patched in linen, it was of necessity smaller in diameter than the gun bore into which it was to be placed. Without the linen patch the bullet would run freely down the barrel, and although the lack of a patch meant a loss of both velocity and accuracy, the result was still adequate for close engagement. The usual procedure was for the rifleman to pop a few bullets into his mouth, moisten them with saliva, and spit one down the barrel after he had inserted the powder; the employment of this method multiplied the rate of fire enormously, and many an Indian who charged confidently upon a White man's empty gun died with a look of astonishment.

In using a "spit bullet," however, the rifleman was well advised to bear in mind that the missing linen patch served not only to seat the bullet snugly upon the powder but to cleanse the barrel of residue from the previous shot. A fouled barrel could mean that the bullet would not seat deep enough, and since a bullet midway of the barrel instead of on the powder charge where it belonged could mean an exploding gun, a good precaution was to rap the gun butt sharply on the ground in order to insure a proper seat for the spit bullet. This, of course, is why Magic Shoot, who had learned the White Man's secret but was keeping it from his pals, always struck the butt of his gun on the ground before firing. I suspect that what has come down to us as a shout of, "Haugh!" was originally the sound of Magic Shoot spitting a bullet down the gun barrel. Undoubtedly Magic Shoot's prowess with his rifle, along with the mystical aspect of the story, has been embroidered in the repetition of many tellings.

The adventures of Magic Shoot, which pretend to no living witnesses, can with at least some degree of confidence be set down as conventionalized embellishments upon an actual happening, but the Chief's next story, a story about the famous Piegan White Quiver, and his equally famous fog bundle, presents in both literal and figurative terms a somewhat mistier issue.

One of the more frangible hinges of the cultured intellect is a propensity to intrude into areas of human experience which are impervious to rationalistic mapping. Such headlong assaults upon the integument of mystical occurrence are a good bet to cockle the most tranquilly sophisticated brow, and the attempt to explain away the ability of White Quiver to command certain forces of nature—specifically, his power to whip up an instant fog—has scored my own intellectual visage with Neanderthal furrows of perplexity.

If White Quiver were, like Magic Shoot, a mythical or mythico-historical character from some cobwebby corner of Blackfoot legend, I could undoubtedly categorize his achievements on the basis of some cozily self-satisfying intellection. But such is not the case. White Quiver was a real person. He was, in fact, a contemporary of the Chief. And since the historicity of his fabulous accomplishments has been verified not only by members of his own tribe but by the enemies against whom he exercised his prowess, White Quiver's mystical powers cannot be attributed to the transmogrifying effect of verbal circulation but must be taken at face value.

An additional note of personal interest attaches to this story through the fact that the Chief, himself, was both a witness to and a participant in the actions here described. White Quiver, who was the most celebrated of all Blackfoot horse-raiders, preferred to conduct most of his forays as solo performances. When he did agree to lead a party, he was careful to choose as his companions only the bravest and most accomplished of warriors; therefore, since the Chief was elected a member of a White Quiver war party, it follows that the Chief had by this time risen high in the regard of Blackfoot connoisseurs of the fine art of horse-histing.

WHITE QUIVER DISPLAYS THE POWER OF THE FOG BUNDLE

This war party was led by White Quiver and Under Bull. Other members included Weasel Head, White Antelope, Makes-Cold-Weather, Flathead Eagle, White Eagle, White Running Wolf, Chewing Black Bones, and myself.

We started from Big Badger Creek, near Old Agency, and headed down to steal some horses from the Crows. We were all well mounted, and we made good time. Our first camp was west of Great Falls, and by the end of the third day we had reached Beaver Head [a butte located at the confluence of Pryor Creek with the Yellowstone River].

We located a Crow camp on the Elk River [the Yellowstone River] near Saw Mill [Saw Mill remains to this day the Blackfoot name for Billings, Montana]. At break of dawn we ran off a goodly number of Crow horses, but although we made all haste toward the north, the Crows overtook us at a stream north of Elk River which we called Deer Creek [possibly Big Coulee Creek].

When we spotted the Crows, we were high on a hill. When we spotted them coming they were still about from here to the bridge [perhaps three miles] away, and since the Crows outnumbered us by so many, I thought that probably we would simply cut out the best of the horses and make a run for it. We had just given the horses a wind break, and chances were that, unencumbered by a large horse herd, we could have outdistanced the Crows quite easily.

But White Quiver had other ideas. He said, "There is no reason to run. I will make a ceremony and cause a fog to come. The fog will be so thick that the Crows won't even be able to see us."

White Quiver seated himself upon the ground and opened his war bundle and took out an eagle plume. He asked that some dirt be brought to him, and when the earth had been brought he mixed it with spittle. Then he took the eagle plume and the dirt mixed with spittle and made a ceremony in which he sang a medicine song. The words to the song were, "I want a fog." [Although Plains Indian songs may be quite long, they are composed largely of conventionalized meaningless syllables (vocables, if you prefer), the actual sentiment of the song usually being expressed in one or more short phrases. This particular song is associated with the Circle Pipe Bundle, a Blackfoot Medicine Pipe Bundle considered to possess such extraordinary power that its ownership must at all times be shared by four persons.]

The day was clear and bright, but as soon as White Quiver conducted his medicine ceremony a heavy ground fog began to appear. The Crows reached the hill where we were and began to surround us, but soon the fog was so thick that we simply drove the horses right past them. Eventually we arrived home safe, with all the horses.

Nothing—but *nothing*—that can be conceived of in the human imagination is impossible. With this concept firmly in grasp it is possible to approach even the most exotic aspects of Plains Indian culture with an open mind (not, prithee, with a hole in the head, which appears to be the approach of those ethnological flaneurs who trip once around an Indian reservation and immediately have the whole deal rationalized on the basis of some sciolistic and totally inapropos Freudianism).

But although I like to feel that I have succeeded in sloughing off the residual fripperies of an undergraduate minor in psychology, it would be insipidly hypocritical of me to disown an occasional effort—albeit a tentative and provisory effort—to reconcile the miraculous powers of Blackfoot "medicine" with the conventional "truths" of my own academic background. For instance, when the Chief told his next story, I found myself quite ready to attribute the superior athletic prowess of an elderly Blood Indian to a factor so prosily scientific as "self-hypnotism."

This happened the first year they had the Calgary Stampede. The officials of the event invited several tribes of Canadian Indians to attend, and among those who accepted the invitation were Using Belt and his partner, two elderly Blood Indians from Cardston.

During the Stampede, a young White athlete from Calgary issued an open challenge to Whites and Indians alike to race against him over a distance of one quarter of a mile. No one would accept the challenge, so some White men began openly to challenge the Indians. They asked the Indians who the fastest runner amongst them was, and they all answered with the name of Using Belt.

Although Using Belt was an exceptionally well-muscled man, he was by no means a youngster, but the White men thought that it would be a good joke to see this old Indian run against their finest athlete. They told Using Belt that if he would run against the White boy they would give him one hundred dollars even if he lost, so finally Using Belt agreed to run.

The White men offered to lend Using Belt a pair of track shoes, but he refused to accept them. He said, "I was not born with track shoes on my feet. I will run the way I was born—with bare feet."

At this time the Indian interpreter for the Mounties was a man named DeRouche. Through DeRouche the sergeant in charge of the Mounties asked Using Belt whether he really thought he could defeat the young White athlete in a race. Using Belt said, "I am not running this race in order to lose. Compared to me this White boy is a mere baby. I will beat him."

The race began, and at first the White boy ran easily ahead of Using Belt, sort of jumping around and making fun of the old Indian. Then, after they had gone about one hundred yards, Using Belt slapped himself on the thigh and immediately began to run very fast. The White athlete began to run in earnest now, but Using Belt slapped his thigh again and again and he won the race by a considerable margin. Beyond the finishline of the racecourse was a tall board fence. At the end of the race Using Belt did not stop running but continued to go at full speed until he ran right into the board fence and was knocked backward and lay stunned upon the ground. It took a few minutes for him to come around, but he was not injured.

The betting on the race had been very heavy. The odds had been heavily in favor of the White man, and the Indians had all bet on Using Belt. But now the Whites refused to pay off. They said that Using Belt could not have run that fast unless he had used some sort of medicine [a stimulant].

The Indians called the Mountie sergeant, and when the sergeant questioned Using Belt, Using Belt said, "No, I did not take any medicine. When you want a horse to run fast, you whip him; when I was running in the race I became a horse and so I whipped myself, and there is no rule against whipping a horse in a race. I won the race fair and square."

So the Mounties made the Whites pay off on the bets, and the Indians made a lot of money. Using Belt, who had bet everything he owned, won $600.00. Most of the other Indians who had won money on the race came over and gave Using Belt a share of their winnings, so altogether he had close to $1000.00.

My attempt to obtain additional verification of Using Belt's unusual achievements brought me into correspondence with Mr. Fred Kennedy, Publicity Executive of the now famous Calgary Stampede. Mr. Kennedy was kind enough to reply to my inquiries, that portion of his letter bearing upon the issue at hand reading as follows:

"On the question of the foot races between the Indian runner and several Calgary athletes in the old days, the following may be helpful. These match races had nothing to do with the Calgary Stampede. As a matter of fact they were held many years ahead of the first Stampede in 1912. This Indian was either a Blood from Cardston or a Black Foot from Gleichen, and my understanding is that he was never beaten in these matched races, over long distances of ground."

Usually I have to lead the Chief into recitations of his personal warpath experiences, but this evening, without the slightest nudge from me, the old-timer followed the story of Using Belt with two pages from his own calendar of coups. These were *good* stories.

THE BLACKFOOT TEA PARTY

This happened while we were camped on the Belly River, in Canada. About sixty of us young men had a meeting down at

Little Shield's camp. We drank tea all night, and by dawn the plans for the war party were all agreed upon. In six days' time we would all meet at the Pine Tree and start from there. The leaders would be Little Shield and Hog Coat.

[Jim was undoubtedly correct in translating the Blackfoot word *I-náh-kah-wote-tàhni* as "Little Shield," but I think that *Ák-sin-nee-so-kàht-simi*, which Jim translates as "Hog Coat," might better be expressed as "Pigskin shirt." For the time being I will go along with Jim, though, simply because his translation is a few letters shorter than mine (after working with Blackfoot proper nouns for a while, you will accept almost any compromise in order to shorten them a bit). For example, Tripod, a gentleman who appears in this and several other of the Chief's stories, has intimidated me into the most cowardly of linguistic compromises. The Blackfoot word from which I derived the English noun, "Tripod," is *Ni-táu-pi-sai*, a term which makes reference to the tripodal affair from which a cauldron or kettle is suspended over a fire. Both Jim and I had a wrestling match with *Ni-táu-pi-sai*, and since in literal translation the word would mean something like "One person cooking meat for a long time in a kettle suspended from a tripod," the gentleman in question will henceforth meekly be referred to as plain old "Tripod."]

Four days after the tea party, six of us went to Little Shield's camp to make sure that we would not be left behind on the war party. When we arrived at Little Shield's camp, we found that Chief Little Shield was not there. [The leaders of Blackfoot war parties frequently departed in advance of the appointed time. The reason for this was that large groups of warriors, especially on horse-stealing raids, were not desirable; surprise attack and quick get-away constituted the essence of success on these missions, and since there was invariably a surplus of volunteers for any war party led by a well-considered taker of horses, the leader's problem was first of all to get away unencumbered by too many followers. The Chief (my dad) was at this time very young and relatively inexperienced, and young and inexperienced warriors were those least desired in the company of experienced war chiefs. As we shall see, the Chief's fear of being left behind was perfectly well justified. Indian chiefs came in all sizes and varieties; Little Shield was a war chief, which meant only that he had sufficient prestige as a warrior to command a substantial following on raids.] Little

Shield's wife told us that the war party had left four days before, on the night after the tea party.

Little Shield's wife fed us, and then we went back to the camp of my mother's brother, Running Wolf. The six of us had decided to have our own war party, and I asked Running Wolf to paint me. He did so, and we left his camp that night. [Running Wolf painted the Chief's face and probably his hands and other portions of his body as well, and it is also possible that he painted his blanket and his weapons; this action was intended to endow the painted one with good luck on the war party and with protection from the enemy.] The members of our war party were Big Ribs, Blackfoot Shorty, Hollering Owl, Tripod, myself, and Shake A Leg. [I translated this last name as "Shakes His Foot," but since in Blackfoot the same word may be used to refer to both the lower leg and the foot, I shall go along with Jim's translation of "Shake A Leg."]

We traveled hard all that night, and hid out the next day near a stream. At dusk we started out again and traveled all night, and at dawn, as we neared the Writing-on-Stone in the vicinity of the Sweetgrass Hills, we saw smoke. We crept near in order to see who was camped there, and we found that it was the party of Little Shield—a total of seventy-six men. We had caught up with them in two nights of traveling. [Undoubtedly the Chief's six-man group had made excellent time, but subsequent events suggest that they had overtaken Little Shield so quickly because Little Shield had been dawdling along trying to find some way of cutting down the size of his much-too-large war party.]

We joined Little Shield's party, and after going two or three miles further the whole outfit camped for the day in the Upper Sweetgrass Hills. That night we went as far as the place where Red Tailfeathers had been killed some time before, and there Little Shield said, "This is where the butterfly will alight." [This ancient Blackfoot metaphor, no longer in use, directed me into a rather lively linguistic chase. The Chief explained that the phrase, "This is where the butterfly will alight," means, "This is where we will pitch our camp," but Jimmy had never heard the expression before and the Chief was unable to suggest any explanation of its origin. I was so intrigued by the problem, however, that I gave it no rest until finally, with the help of an elderly and highly intelligent Piegan lady named Ist-stán-nìt-niki (Kills Instead) I was able to determine that the correct interpretation of the metaphor in question is, "This is where we will *sleep*," and that the phrase derives from a Blackfoot belief that the facial structure in the region of the eyes of a sleeping person resembles a butterfly with wings outstretched (and by George it does!).]

When we started traveling again, we had gone only a short distance when Little Shield called a halt and addressed the party. He said, "Men, I think that our war party is much too large. We started out to steal some horses from the Gros Ventres, but we must remember that those Gros Ventres are pretty smart boys. Those Gros Ventres sleep with their horses in their fists [another metaphor, the meaning of which is quite apparent], and I do not believe that a party of this size has any chance of catching them napping. We might get a few horses, but I feel it unlikely that we could capture enough for all of us to have a share. So why don't we split up into four separate parties! One party could go to Medicine Hat and raid the Cree camps, another could go to the fork of Kinnickinnick Creek, the third could go to Round Brush, and the fourth to the Yellow Mountains."

When Little Shield said this, Tripod, who was the leader of our party, said, "I think you are right. There are six in our party, and we will head down across the Yellow Mountains [the Judith Mountains] and steal some horses from the Crows."

Then Curled Up spoke, and he was angry. He said, "It suits me fine not to go any further with Little Shield. This party has been crawling along like old women moving camp. I am ashamed to be with this war party, and I will go my own way from here. Furthermore, I'll bet that I will be the only one to bring horses back home. What is going to happen to the rest of you will be a sorry thing, and when I get back home with the horses I have stolen I will mourn for you."

We didn't wait to hear any more arguing. The six of us pulled out immediately and started down toward Crow country, and before long we saw somebody following us. It was Middle Legs [actually, the name means that this fellow always sits with his legs pointed toward the center of the gathering], and now that he had joined us there were seven in our party.

We continued on toward the Crows, and pretty soon Shake A Leg spotted somebody else following along behind us. We waited for the man to catch up. It was Greasy Breast, and now that he had joined us, we were eight in number.

We traveled all that night and before dawn had reached the Bear Paw Mountains. Our plan was to hide out in the Bear Paws during the day, so we made our camp.

As dawn broke, we discovered some cattle grazing in a valley down below us, and Tripod said, "I want some of you boys to go down and kick one of those beeves." [The Piegan word, *Si-káhk-sin*, meaning literally "to kick," was at this time used as a slang term for "shoot." What Tripod actually said was, *So-káhp-si-kàh-kit* (Kick 'em good), meaning to shoot the beef dead with the first bullet.] While Shake A Leg, Big Ribs, Blackfoot Shorty and Hollering Owl went down and kicked a beef, the remaining four of us stayed up on the mountain to keep watch. We ate some of the beef for breakfast, and smoked and dried the rest of it.

We kept traveling generally toward the south until we reached the fork of the Yellowstone. Here, Shake A Leg suggested to Tripod that we had better turn around and start back north. Greasy Breast was against turning back until we had found some enemy horses. He said, "The reason I followed you boys is that you always have good luck on your raids against the Crows. Why do you want to go back home empty-handed?" Tripod explained to him that we were so far from home now that we had very little chance of making a successful raid. Even if we did take some horses (and we had not as yet even located a Crow camp) we would have to run the horses so steadily in order to get safely back to our own territory that most of the horses would probably play out and have to be left behind. Tripod said that we were not giving up, but that we would turn around and see whether we could locate some horses up around Havre.

We went steadily northward then, eventually reaching the eastern edge of the Bear Paws. Our plan was to proceed westward toward Havre, but first Tripod went ahead to the top of a high ridge to scout for possible enemies.

Tripod was on top of the ridge for quite a while, and when he returned he said that he had spotted some sort of camp over to the west but that he could not make out whether it was an enemy camp or just some of Little Shield's party. He asked me to go up on the ridge to see whether I could identify the camp, and when I had gone about fifty yards he called me back and gave me his field glasses to use. I lay flat on the top of the ridge, scanning the camp with Tripod's field glass, and soon I was able to determine that the camp was composed of Gros Ventres, and that they had quite a few horses.

When I reported back to Tripod, he said that since I had discovered the horses I would be allowed to take first choice of them. It was now about noon, and since we would not be able to steal any horses until after dark, I went back upon the ridge to keep watch on the Gros Ventre camp. The horses were at present grazing right next to the Gros Ventre camp, but since the Gros Ventres might stake out the horses away from the camp toward evening [so that they would be more difficult for enemies to locate in the darkness], the plan was for me to relay to the rest of our party any information as to where the horses might be found. If the horses were to be left near the camp, I was to lie facing the camp; if the horses were to be hidden on the north side of the camp, I was to lie facing north. I was to face in whatever direction the horses were taken so that our men could start moving in that direction in order to find exactly where the horses were.

The Gros Ventres staked their horses out on the north side of their camp, but we knew exactly where they were and as soon as it was properly dark we made off with them. First we each took a horse to ride: I took an iron gray, Tripod a gray, Big Ribs a sorrel—each man took a horse. Then we drove off the thirteen remaining horses, of which I was to have my choice of five.

We knew that the Gros Ventres would be after us for sure as soon as they discovered that we had taken their horses, so we traveled without stopping all the way to the west side of the Bear Paws. There, in a little swamp by a pine hill, we decided to hide out until things cooled off a little. The same four fellows that had killed the first beef killed another one nearby, and for five days we hid in the swamp.

Finally one night we pulled out and made it as far as Big Rocky Creek. We arrived just at daybreak, and spent the day there. After traveling all of the following night we again reached the place where Red Tailfeathers had been killed. We were going to stop there, but the morning fog was so thick—almost like smoke—that we figured it would be safe to keep on traveling. After we had gone quite a ways further, Shake A Leg spotted some riders. But the fog was still quite thick, and when Shake A Leg signalled to us we took a course opposite to the direction in which the riders were heading and so were not seen by them.

Finally we got home safe, with all the horses, to our starting point at my uncle Running Wolf's camp on Belly River. I gave the iron gray horse to Running Wolf, and also gave away the rest of my horses.

Lazy Boy in Later Life

LAZY BOY'S MEDICINE DREAM

Three of us—Lazy Boy, myself, and my brother, Cross Guns —started from above Old Agency. We were on our way to steal some horses from the Crees, and we were all mounted. I was riding a roan horse, and my brother was riding a buckskin. I don't remember what kind of horse Lazy Boy was riding.

We made our first camp at *Ai-yo-ko-want-sìn-nàht-sin*. [This word is a real beaut (or, as it turned out, a real butte); Jimmy could suggest only that it described a geographical point and that it had something to do with entrails, and only after much time and labor was I able to determine that the word referred to a butte which was pock-marked in a manner such that it resembled a tripe.]

The following morning, while Lazy Boy was still asleep, Cross Guns and I spotted a calf down below and we went down and killed it. [The Chief explained here that each member of a war party was expected to be able to take care of himself, and that if somebody overslept, the rest of the party would just leave him there and go on their way.] We butchered the calf and packed the meat back up onto the butte to smoke it, and upon returning to our camp we found Lazy Boy seated upon a hill singing medicine songs. We asked him why he was singing, and he said that he had just awakened from a bad dream. He said, "I dreamed that the enemy attacked us and that you fellows ran off and left me. I managed to escape with my life, but the enemy captured my blanket. This dream is bad medicine, so we had better call off this war party and go back home."

Cross Guns and I told Lazy Boy that we would not accept his medicine dream. We told him that we had killed some fresh meat at our first camp and that that was good medicine. We told him that he could go back home if he wished, but that we intended to continue on the war party as soon as we had finished drying the meat.

We breakfasted on fresh beef and then smoked the remainder of the meat over a fire in preparation for our journey. All the while we ate, and all the while we smoked the meat, Lazy Boy attempted to talk Cross Guns and me out of going on a war party. When we had packed our gear and started toward the northeast, Lazy Boy tagged along for a while, still trying to talk us into going back home, but eventually we convinced him that we were determined to go to Canada to take some Cree horses. Lazy Boy turned back then, and Cross Guns and I continued onward and made our next camp at The Drummers [a point somewhere west of the Bear Paw Mountains, so called because beaver were formerly so numerous here that the slapping of their tails on the water was described as sounding like drummers; apparently this place has some great religious significance for the Chief because he refused to reveal its exact location, saying that both Jim and I were "too young to know"].

The next day we camped at River Bend, and from there we made it to the Bear Paw Mountains. About half way between the Bear Paws and the Wolf Mountains there is a small tributary of the Missouri River which we called Middle Creek [Cow Creek], and it was at Middle Creek that we discovered a Cree camp. We lay high on a butte overlooking the camp, and although we could view the camp clearly we could not see any horses. There was a small horse corral near the camp, but since there were no horses in the corral we knew that the Crees must have hidden their horses out somewhere.

As we lay there upon the high butte, I spotted something on a wooded hill between the Cree camp and our own position. I pointed the object out to Cross Guns. "It is only a burnt log," he said, but I insisted that it was a man. I was right. Shortly thereafter the man got to his feet and started moving cautiously away from the Cree camp back toward the hills, and he was immediately recognizable as Night Gun. Night Gun, a Piegan, walked with an unmistakable limp, and for this reason he was also called One Short Leg.

Night Gun was a member of a six-man war party which had preceded Cross Guns and me by a few days. The other members of his party were Arrow Topknot, Strange Bird, Coat, and Mike Day Rider. Mike Day Rider, who died just recently, was the father-in-law of Paul Many Hides. There was one other member of the party, but I cannot remember who it was. With the exception of Night Gun (One Short Leg), all the members of this party were afoot. Night Gun had gone on horseback because he could not otherwise keep up.

Cross Guns and I went down to speak with Night Gun. We asked him where the rest of his party was and he told us that they were out trying to locate the Cree horses. He said that his party had been trying to locate the Cree horses for two nights [they could not do much exploring during the daytime for fear of discovery], but without success.

When we told Night Gun that we, too, were after horses, he said that his party would make a bargain with us. If Cross Guns and I located the horses first, we were to meet the other party at this spot, and if the other party found them first, they would wait for us here. In any event, we would share the horses and all go home together. Cross Guns and I agreed to the plan, but we did so with tongue in cheek. We knew perfectly well that if the other party found the horses they would cut out for home without the slightest concern for anyone but themselves.

It was broad daylight now, so Cross Guns and I returned to the top of the butte to rest and keep an eye on the Cree camp until darkness should make it prudent for us to move about once again. Upon reaching the top of the butte, we were amazed to find that the Cree horses were now in the camp corral. We watched the camp like hawks then; undoubtedly the Crees had a hiding place for their horses, and if we could discover the direction in which the horses were herded as evening approached, we could probably locate the animals after dark.

But darkness came and the horses were still in the camp

corral, so Cross Guns and I crept up to the corral ready to run them off. The horses were not there. The Crees were smart enough to take their horses out to their night hiding place when it was too dark for any possible watchers to see what was going on, and my brother and I spent the whole night in a futile effort to find where the animals were hidden. We could find nothing in the brush, or along the creek where you might expect to find horses hidden, but toward dawn we thought we heard horses on a flat toward the south of the camp. Sure enough, we found a deep little wash that the Crees had converted into a corral by stretching ropes across in two places. We could have taken the horses right then, but it was already breaking daylight so we holed up for the day and made off with the horses the following night. Of the total of eleven horses, I allowed Cross Guns to take six and kept five for myself.

By traveling nights and hiding out days, we made it home in five nights.

Almost invariably the Chief ends his story-telling sessions with, "*Kèn-yai-au-wah-nay-náh-pi-quon.*" This translates literally into, "That's what the old White man says," but the satirical connotation which encompasses the phrase's true significance is missed completely until one becomes acquainted with the circumstances which gave original coinage to the expression. It all happened as follows:

Iron Breast, also known as First-To-Grab-A-Gun, married a woman of whom his father, old Tearing Lodge, did not approve. The woman was virtuous and hard-working, her only defect being that her hair was prematurely gray, but old Tearing Lodge was very unkind in his criticism of his daughter-in-law, complaining that his son had married a gray-haired old woman who was fit for nothing.

One night Tearing Lodge was seated in his teepee, smoking and talking with some of the other old men, quite unaware that his daughter-in-law, who had spent the afternoon repairing the old man's robes and clothing, was seated quietly in the shadows. After a while old Tearing Lodge began to say unpleasant things about his daughter-in-law, and finally the daughter-in-law spoke up. She said, "Why does Tearing Lodge say such unkind things about me? I have never harmed him in any way."

Now, this put Tearing Lodge in quite a spot, but the old fellow was equal to the situation. Pretending that he had not heard his daughter-in-law speak and that he was still unaware of her presence in the lodge, he addressed himself to his old cronies: "Yes, gentlemen, as I was saying . . . All of these unflattering remarks about my daughter-in-law are merely things I overheard an old White man saying. Yes sir, that's what the old White man says."

This is a true story, not a fabrication, and the Blackfoots with their universal appreciation of humor quickly adopted Tearing Lodge's face-saving comment as a part of their everyday speech. *Kèn-yai-au-wah-nay-náh-pi-quon* may also be expressed as *Nàh-pi-quon-sáu-wah-nay* (which means the same thing), and sometimes the final syllable is changed from *quon* to *quax* (which merely changes "man" into the plural form, "men"). At any rate, "That's what the old White man says" has become an integral part of Piegan life, and it is this same phrase that the old-timers laughingly employ to end a street-corner bull-session.

The Chief, Jim and I have all been sipping hot toddies during the story-telling, and I think that by the time I finish this we will all be ready for the sack.

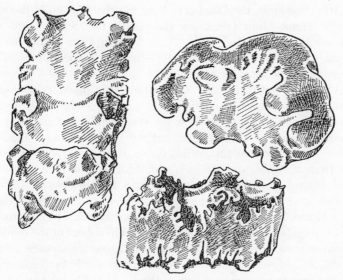
Buffalo Stones

Saturday, September 15

Both Jim and the Chief were up before I this morning. The Chief feels much better, and there was much joking and carrying-on around here including a mock boxing match between Dad and Jim. At breakfast, Dad chewed Jim out about his horses; Jim has about fifteen head out on the range, but only six are in the pasture.

I am to receive a Medicine Pipe in conjunction with the Beaver Ceremony (presumably in a separate ceremony), and in the Blackfoot tradition my relatives (Jim, in this case) are required to give to the present owner of the Pipe (the Chief) certain gifts, among them a horse. The Chief says that this is his chance to get his hands on that fine buckskin mare of Jim's. For "buckskin," the Chief used the term *och-t'kói-miu* (yellow-colored horse). He might instead have said, *sík-ku-ah-si* (black-tailed horse), or, *In-nu-kóh-ku-yi* (elk-colored horse), but by any name the buckskin would be a magnificent animal—and of course the transfer of ownership will be in fact just a formality. Jim and the Chief make a big thing of who owns what on the ranch, and they are constantly attempting to con one another out of things. But this is merely the affectionate mock-competition common to men friends of all races. Both the Chief and Jim are extremely generous, and they would cheerfully give one another—or me—anything they have, without question or comment.

After breakfast, the Chief asked me to drive him up to the ranch of the Home Guns (these are the people that Stanley said were named "Hommagunna"). They have quite a large house, and the Chief wanted to hold the Beaver Ceremony in their place so that there would be room for everybody.

As we got out of my car at the Home Gun place, twelve—count 'em, twelve—dogs of remarkably diverse ancestry came yipping around. A chickenwire gate on the door kept the dogs out of the house. It kept the Chief and me out too, and the Home Guns, who were just eating breakfast, yelled for us to come in—without getting up from the table or missing a mouthful. We unlatched the gate and entered, and Mrs. Home Gun, still gobbling away, jerked a thumb over her shoulder and said, "There's a chair back there." The Home Guns shattered a rigid Indian tradition by not inviting us to the table, and not one of the several members of the family so much as stood up or offered an introduction to the stranger in their midst. After several minutes of silence, broken only by the smacking of lips and the slurping of coffee, the Chief made his request, and Mr. Home Gun, who is overweight, surly, and who wears tinted glasses like the King of Saudi Arabia, refused peremptorily without even looking up from his plate.

It was his right to refuse, but it is no man's right to be so incogitably discourteous. I was angry enough to clean out the place, but the Chief, who surely must be some sort of saint, merely said "So-káh-pi" and with gigantic but totally unostentatious dignity arose and walked out the door. Resisting a huge impulse to spit on the floor, I followed him out. The Chief never mentioned the incident, either then or later, but all the way to town I sputtered my disgust to brother Jim.

(Advice to the Peace Corps: It is a mistake to attempt to get along with *all* members of a community. Not only is it impossible, but the attempt will alienate those whose friendship and respect is worth having. "He that is a friend to everyone is a friend to no one," somebody once said.)

In town, I cashed a cheque at the bank and then we all went to Buttrey's store to buy the food for the Beaver Ceremony feast. Buttrey's has just replaced their old store with a new superduper-type market, and today was grand opening day—replete with several junior chamber of commerce-type White men that had come to town to usher in this great step forward toward ?.

One young supersalesman type had a microphone in his hot little hand and was talking things up and cracking smelly jokes and generally attempting—in the inevitable indulgent White Man way—to impress the Indians. The Indians were terribly *un*impressed. There was a big crowd of Blackfoots present, all right, but most of them were bearing the pain just to see who would win the free prizes. After several yawn-producing attempts to build up an aura of suspense (the Indians just kept on rolling Bull Durham cigarettes), the cat with the microphone finally came through with the facts. Sam Spotted Eagle had won an electric toaster (I hope he has electricity out at his place); Tom White Weasel had had the extravagant good-fortune to win a badminton set (a Blackfoot Indian with a badminton set, yet!); Cecile V. Elk had gotten herself a new coffeepot; and my old pal, Louis Plenty Treaty Bear Child, had walked off with a new fly rod.

The little fellow with the mike kept directing your kind attention to the new meat counter "in arrears of the store," and Jimmy and Dad and I, no longer able to resist the force of his mellifluous persuasions, finally went "in arrears of the store" and purchased a large quantity of boiling beef, some roundsteak, and a beef tongue.

The butcher, a White man, was a nice enough guy. But I suppose that in our society I qualify as a sentimentalist because I classify supermarkets along with neon lights, paint-by-the-numbers landscapes, and artificial insemination of human beings. The meat department (for all of being "in arrears of the store") was very slick and modern, but I could not help thinking back to my hometown and to Mr. Meyer, the German butcher, who was huge and had an accent and was moustached like the Kaiser and was as clean as God, and who made his own link sausage and headcheese. Mr. Meyer, who never surrendered to the use of an electric bone saw because it made the meat look white, and who always cut off the first slice of liverwurst or bologna and threw it away (or gave it to my dog, Jerry), would have absolutely shuddered at meat pre-packaged in cellophane or plastic wrap. Mr. Meyer was always scraping his cutting block with powerful two-handed sweeps of a wire brush, and the floor of Mr. Meyer's shop was always covered with lots of nice, clean-smelling sawdust, and people came from miles around, passed by rows of supermarkets with their plastic wrap, to buy their meat from Mr. Meyer. Furthermore: I am convinced that icecream tasted much better when it was made in boy-cranked home freezers, or scooped by hand from mysterious depths behind marble countertops and packed firm and heaping into cardboard quart containers. Talk about getting Christ out of Christmas! I am convinced that there is an even more insidious—and equally successful—attempt to get the human out of humanity.

A number of my Indian friends were at the store, and when I said "Ó-keh" to them I was exchanging greetings not with Indians but with friends. It was a good feeling. I talked for a moment with Mrs. Fish Wolfrobe (Mínaki: Berry Woman), the wife of the blind man. She is in her sixties, I think, but still very beautiful, and if I could find a younger version of Mrs. Wolfrobe, I would soon have, I feel sure, more relatives than the man at the laundry.

After shopping, we went over to Mary Ground's house and asked her whether she would be willing to assist at the Beaver Ceremony— to make the berry soup, etc. She said she would be glad to. She and Jimmy and the Chief conversed in Blackfoot for several minutes, but they talked so rapidly and used so many short forms and personal forms that I could catch only enough to know that they were talking about me. Jimmy afterward explained that Mary, who is a widow and could easily be my grandmother, had said that she has set her cap for me and that she is going to put a love potion in the berry soup so that I will come to town more often.

Mary suggested that we ask Jim White Grass if we could have the Beaver Ceremony at his house at Starr School. On the way back to the ranch we stopped and asked him, and Mr. White Grass, who is a remarkably fine person, never without a smile, readily complied. We drove on to the Ranch then and lunched on boiled steak, boiled potatoes, tea and grapes. And then we went back to town and picked up Mary Ground and dropped her off at Buttrey's to do some more shopping for the feast.

While Mary shopped, we drove out to a section of town known locally as "Moccasin Flat" in order to invite Tom Many Guns to the ceremony. On the way, we appraised everybody's woodpile, finally agreeing that ours was second in size and quality only to that of Jim White Grass. On the way back, we passed by a fenced field thickly populated with headstones and religious monuments. Brother Jim asided the remarkable intelligence that this was a graveyard.

When we stopped at the store to pick up Mary and the groceries, Paul Many Hides, who is always going someplace but apparently never gets there, trotted up to the car with his wife and child ("My boy she's a seven years, changing eight now. Be on December"). Paul was looking for a ride home, but since we were to transport Mary—and an enormous amount of food, blankets, pots, pans, kettles, etc.—to Jim White Grass' house, we did not have room for Paul's crew. The Chief wants to start the ceremony early so that we will not miss the races that are to be held at the Starr School racecourse tomorrow afternoon, and Mary will spend the night at the White Grass home. I don't want to miss the races, either—I am still anxious to determine just how accurate my rendition of the event in "Horse-race" really was.

Saturday evening: Boiled tongue, green beans, boiled potatoes, bread and tea and canned blueberries.

I: "The tongue is not bad, Jim."

Jim: "It is?"

Joe Morning Gun, a close neighbor, stopped by, and of course the Chief invited him to stay for supper. Mr. Morning Gun is older, tall and slender, and very courteous and mild mannered. His black hair, which he wears rather long and parted in the middle, is covered when out-of-doors by a wide-brimmed, high-crowned gray sombrero. He is an Indian of the old school, and I like him very much.

Jim and the Chief are inordinately proud of my increasing facility with the Blackfoot language, and at supper they showed me off quite shamelessly to Joe by using my Blackfoot name exclusively and by asking me, in Blackfoot, to pass them everything on the table—whether they could reach it or not and whether they really wanted it or not. So I ate with one hand and with the other kept passing the bread (*nah-pai-yén*), the sugar (*náh-pi-nuan*), the salt (*ist-ik-tsíp-o-ko*), the pepper (*áp-stah-kai-po-ko*), the catsup (*ish-pó-yópe*), etc. The literal translation of the Blackfoot word for pepper, by the way, is "tobacco taste" or "it tastes like tobacco." The word for catsup, *ish-pó-yópe,* which is also used to refer to mustard and to similar table sauces, translates as, "you use it when you eat."

Many of the foods that were introduced to the Blackfoots by the Whites have the prefix, *náhpi,* attached to them, but although *náhpi* is one of the first Blackfoot words I learned, I still don't know exactly what it means—and I have decided that nobody else does either. I first encountered *Náhpi* as the schizoid old gent who is the central figure in Blackfoot mythology (in the Chief's story, "Why the White Man Will Never Reach the Sun," the *Náhpi* image is composed of two separate characters, one named *Mokáhki:* wise, and the other named *Mut-tsáhp-tsi:* crazy or stupid; but in the common run of *Náhpi* stories—and there are hundreds of them—*Náhpi* appears as a single character who is alternately clever enough to create the world, and stupid enough to get into all kinds of dutch with the very animals he has created). My search for a valid English translation of the word *náhpi* (which most scholars have translated as "old man," but which translation does not satisfy me) turned up "old man," "old White man," "crazy old White man," and a few others. One informant suggested that the phrase does not mean "old White man" but rather "White old man" (there is a significant difference between these two translations) and I would be inclined to go along with him if only for the reason that sometimes the Blackfoots in their prayers to the sun will refer to the sun not as *Nah-tóh-sey* but as *Náh-pi*. "Old White man" would refer to an elderly Caucasian, whereas "White old man" could refer to an elderly (hence, in the Indian belief, wise) man of any race.

A further shred of evidence is present in the fact that when a Blackfoot wishes to refer to a Caucasian, he takes the term *Náhpi* and adds the suffix *quon* to it. I think that I am fairly safe in saying that in its broadest application, *quon* means "man" in the sense of "person," but of course things are not that simple. I haven't really studied the thing out, but my observations thus far suggest that *quon* functions as sort of a restrictive diminutive and that when stuck onto the end of a noun it carries the meaning that the noun in question is one part of a larger group. Perhaps a good translation of *quon* would be "son of." For instance, while the term for the Blackfoots as a group is *Siksikáu*, the term for an individual (male) of the Blackfoot Nation is *Siksikáiquon*. "Dog" is *imitái*, and "puppy" is *imitáiquon*. (The Blackfoot term for a half-grown dog is *seh-súmp*, but let's not get into that!) At any rate, I am a *Náhpiquon*, but in regard to whether this means that I am a "Sun-person," "The-son-of-a-foolish-old-white-man," or something in between, your guess is as good as mine.

The Blackfoot term for whiskey is *náh-pi-ò-kee*, a form combining *náhpi* with *och-kée*, the Blackfoot word for water: hence, the usual translation of, "White Man's water." After supper we all had a shot, and this was the first time since my arrival that the Chief was the one to suggest a drink—undoubtedly out of hospitality to our guest.

Our guest, Joe Morning Gun, left early, and for an hour then I recorded the Chief's telling of the origin of the Beaver Bundle. The Bundle contains, among numerous other things, an albino crow and the dressed skins of many animals, and according to this tale the whole thing started right over the hill from the ranch, at Lower Saint Mary Lake. The story of the origin of the Beaver Bundle is in some respects reminiscent of the story of Round Scabby Robe, but the Beaver Bundle story points up much more strongly the relationship in Blackfoot religious belief between the Underwater Persons and the Sun.

THE ORIGIN OF THE BEAVER BUNDLE

A long time ago there was a Blackfoot trapper and hunter who traveled about killing bear and buffalo and other large animals, and capturing eagles and trapping the small animals for their fur. One time he camped on the north side of Lower Saint Mary Lake, above the place where the bridge is built today. Years ago you could see the circle of rocks where the trapper pitched his lodge, but now the rocks have disappeared.

One evening the trapper returned from checking his trapline to discover that his baby son was crying and that his wife was not in the lodge. He searched for his wife but could not find her. He could not even find her trail, so finally he decided that a bear must have killed her and carried her off.

That night, as the trapper sat in his lodge trying to comfort his baby son, a spirit person in the form of a man entered the lodge and spoke to him. The spirit person said, "I am here because I pity your poor child. Do not worry about your wife. She is in the lake, in the lodge of the Underwater Persons, and she is safe. I shall return to visit you again." Then the spirit person left.

On the following night the spirit man returned to the lodge and spoke to the trapper once again: "I have come to tell you what to do to get your wife back. In the lake is a small white beaver, the son of the Chief of the Beaver Persons. If you succeed in capturing the white beaver, your wife will be returned to you. I shall return again to tell you how to go about catching the beaver."

The next night the spirit man came into the trapper's lodge

and said, "Here is what you must do in order to catch the small white beaver. First, take the manure of the elk, the deer, and the buffalo and mash the manure up fine and rub it all over your body to disguise the human scent. Then dig a pit near the water and cover the pit with brush. Hide in the pit, and when the small white beaver comes out of the water, catch him with your hands. But do not injure the beaver. After you have caught the beaver, I shall return to tell you what to do next."

So the trapper did as he was advised. He killed his scent with manure and hid in a pit near the water, but the white beaver did not come. Once a light-colored beaver came near, but it was a large beaver and not pure white, so the trapper decided that it was not the right one. Finally one day the geese swimming on the lake became startled and took flight, and the trapper could see that the geese had been startled by the wake of a small white beaver that was swimming toward shore. The trapper waited until the white beaver had come out of the water near the blind, and then he captured the beaver and carried it home to his lodge.

That night the spirit man came to the trapper's lodge for the fourth time. He said, "You have done well to capture the son of the Beaver Chief. If you want to get your wife back, you must hang onto the white beaver at all cost. The Beaver Chief will send word that if you release his son, your wife will be returned to you. But do not let the beaver go. Sooner or later the Underwater Persons will come out of the water to bargain for the release of the white beaver, but do not let the beaver go. And do not leave your lodge. Instead, when you hear the Underwater Persons coming out of the water, clear a place in your lodge for them to sit, and do not release the small white beaver until the Underwater Persons have returned your wife and have given you other gifts besides." The spirit man told the trapper what gifts he should ask for.

That night the trapper heard someone come out of the lake. It was one of the Underwater Persons—one of the water animals—who had taken on a human form. The water animal spirit entered the lodge and found the trapper seated with both the baby and the small white beaver on his lap. The spirit said, "I bring a message from our chief. He says that if you will release the little beaver, his son, then he will return your wife to you."

The trapper said, "No, I don't think so. Tell your chief that my baby is very lonely for his mother, and so I will keep the small white beaver so my baby will have a playmate until his mother has returned."

The water spirit person left then, and pretty soon the trapper heard a lot of people coming out of the water singing a medicine song. These were not real people that he heard; they were the water people, who had all assumed human form. There was the Chief Beaver, chief of all the water animals; there was the loon, which is chief of all the water birds; there was every animal and bird from the lake, and when they reached the shore they were joined by some of the animals which live on the land. The elk and the buffalo and the coyote and the fox and the badger and several other land animals all took on human form and joined in the procession. Likewise did some of the land birds join in. The song they were singing was,

> This is our holy walk
> We are starting our holy ceremony.

When the trapper heard the spirit persons singing their holy song, he cleared a place in his lodge for them, and after the spirits had marched four times around the lodge they entered and sat down. Leading the procession was the Chief Beaver, and with him was the trapper's wife. The wife was carrying a bundle.

When he had seated himself, the Chief Beaver said to the trapper, "We have returned your wife to you unharmed; now return my son to me."

The trapper said, "No, it will not be so easy for you. You have caused many tears in this lodge by taking my baby's mother away. You owe me something for that. My wife will sit on my right hand, holding both of our sons, and you will sit upon my left hand and tell me what presents you will pay me for the return to his people of the small white beaver."

So the Chief Beaver sat at the left of the trapper and sang seven songs. The songs that he sang were:

> I have the tailfeathers of an eagle.
> I have the pelt of a black coyote.
> I have the pelt of a red fox.
> I have the pelt of a fisher.
> I have the hide of a white buffalo calf.
> I have the pelt of a marten.
> I have the hide of a cow elk.

Each time the Chief Beaver sang a song, he took an object from the bundle that the trapper's wife had carried into the lodge, and placed the object in front of the trapper. When he had finished singing, he said, "This is the sacred Beaver Bundle; I am transferring it to you in exchange for the return of my son."

The trapper said, "It is not enough. What other things will you add to the bundle?"

Chief Beaver appealed to the other spirit persons to help him out, and one by one the animals and the birds stepped forth and sang seven songs and added something else to the bundle. Most of them added their pelts to the bundle, and the loon, chief of the waterbirds, gave his skin. Some of the other birds gave their feathers or their skins too. Last to contribute were the turtle and the frog. The turtle had no songs to sing, but he borrowed some songs from the lizard and put them in the ceremony. The frog stood up then, but he had no songs to sing so the turtle knocked him over backward. "You do not belong in this ceremony," he said. When the turtle knocked the frog down, the frog lay on his back holding up seven fingers. Nobody knew what he meant by this, and when they asked him for an explanation he said, "I have no songs to contribute, but I will give you seven winter moons during which the pelts of the animals will be prime." So although the turtle and the frog do not have any songs, they are represented at the Beaver Ceremony. The turtle and the frog and the lizard are painted on the hide which is spread upon the floor of the lodge before the Beaver Bundle is opened.

The trapper said, "What else will you add to the bundle?"

The Beaver Chief said, "I have already contributed my pelt, as have several of the other Beaver Persons, but now I will also give a whistle which can be blown when the bundle is opened." Then the elk and the otter stepped forth and said that they would also give whistles.

The trapper said, "The Holy White Buffalo Calf has given his pelt to the bundle, but the other Buffalo Persons have given nothing. What will they give?"

The buffalo calf said, "I will give my hide as an inner wrapping for the bundle." The buffalo cow said, "I will give my hide as an outer wrapping for the bundle." Last of all the buffalo bull said, "I will give my hooves." Toward the end of the Beaver Ceremony we sing songs about *Kip-pi-táh-key* [Moon], *Nah-tóh-sey* [Sun], and their son, *I-pi-sú-ahts* [Morning Star]. But there are many of these songs, and they are very long, and if we do not wish to sing them we pick up the buffalo hooves and start dancing instead.

The trapper said, "I am still not satisfied," and the Chief Beaver replied, "I have only three things left to give. I will put into the bundle my *it-tśi-wahn* [gambling wheel]; you should gamble with this wheel only before you go to war, so that you may have good luck. I will also put in a small stick that has been chewed by a beaver; when the Beaver Bundle is opened, he that is the first to take possession of this stick will have much good fortune. Finally, I will give you the seeds of the tobacco plant; put these seeds into the ground, and each year as you return from your travels to the place the seeds were planted you will find tobacco to smoke during your ceremonies."

The trapper said, "It is enough," and the Beaver Chief painted his face for him and transferred to his ownership the Beaver Bundle.

Then the Spirit Man—the spirit that had first come to the trapper in human form in order to tell him how to get his wife back—entered the lodge. He was leading two dogs, a male and a female, and the male dog was drawing a travois. He said, "Whenever you move camp you should carry the Beaver Bundle on the travois pulled by this dog. I am also giving you a female dog, so that dogs may multiply and you will never again have to carry your own burdens while moving camp."

The spirit person who took on a human form in order to help the trapper was really the Sun. Each night, when his day's work was done, he took on the form of a man and came down to earth to help the trapper get his wife back and also to advise him about obtaining the Beaver Bundle from the Underwater Persons. When the trapper found out who the Spirit Man really was, he took for himself the name, Nah-tòh-sey-i-néy-pey: Brings Down The Sun. He was the first Blackfoot ever to have this name.

Finally the Chief leaned back in his chair and said, "*Kèn-yai-au-wah-nay-náh-pi-quon,*" signifying the end of the Beaver Bundle story. But it was still early, and we all felt conversational, and we chatted on about ships and sealing wax. The Chief said that he thinks I am a pretty good son, so he is going to will me some of this Montana land that I love so much. I was deeply touched, and I gave him my red-handled knife.

Then the Chief spoke to Jim, and Jim went into the Chief's room and came back carrying an extremely old pouch of buffalo hide. I recognized it as a Blackfoot man's medicine pouch, quite large, painted with Indian designs, and with fringe more than two feet long. The Chief opened the pouch and showed its contents to me one by one. There were four large rattles of hardened rawhide—very, very old; a lock of hair from a buffalo tail; a small piece of hair-on buffalo hide which served to line the bottom of the pouch; and a sueded buckskin sack, colored with *nits-i-sahn,* a dull-red paint which the Blackfoots produce by burning a certain kind of clay, containing four buffalo stones (*I-nís-kim*). The buffalo stones are the darndest things I have ever seen. They are natural formations—not altered in any way except to be colored by *nits-i-sahn*—and although I was able to identify three of them as fossils and the fourth as probably an odd-shaped stone of sedimentary origin, it required very little imagination to see them as the Indians do, as tiny buffaloes. The pouch and its contents were an inheritance from the Chief's father, and his father before him. They obviously meant a great deal to the Chief, and I admired them lavishly. I nearly flipped when he told me that they were mine.

Before I could recover from my astonishment, the Chief spoke to Jim again and Jim went again into the Chief's room and returned this time holding a bundle carefully wrapped in old trade cloth and tied with strips of buckskin. I learned that the bundle contained two Blackfoot Medicine Pipes, two pairs of rustic wooden tongs, some sweetgrass braided into a queue, *nits-i-sahn* paint, and several other articles. I had thought that I was to receive a Pipe tomorrow, after the Beaver Ceremony, but instead I received it tonight.

The Medicine Pipe is not to be confused with the so-called "peace pipe" which was a smoking pipe and was a rather common article among Plains Indians. The Medicine Pipe, which is really one portion of the Medicine Pipe Bundle, is a purely religious article and cannot be smoked.* According to best authority, there were never more than seventeen Medicine Pipes among all three tribes of the Blackfoot Nation, and it is a rare privilege nowadays even to see a Medicine Pipe, let alone own one.

No two medicine pipes are exactly alike; the owner of each pipe

* I know of only one exception to this rule. During the Sun Dance, if a very special prayer is to be offered to the Sun, the Sun Pipe may be fitted with a bowl and smoked by those inside the Medicine Lodge. Such occasions are very, very rare.

can be identified by the way he paints his face, and the ceremony of transfer of ownership of a Pipe is inimitable to the individual Pipe. I have heard of a pipe transfer ceremony which required four days of ritual, and of another which consisted only of the singing of four songs. The transference of this Pipe to my ownership occupied a time somewhere between these extremes—slightly less than four hours.

Attempting to describe the ceremony would be like trying to describe in words the quality of any other religious experience—it simply cannot be done. If you have been there, you know; if not, you will never know. It is very reassuring, in a way, to realize that there are still, in this day of movies, television (next comes the feelies, I guess), some experiences which cannot be realized vicariously—which must be *lived*.

First there was the burning of sweetgrass and the ceremonious unwrapping of the Pipe Bundle. And then, for three hours, ritual followed ritual, each movement and gesture established by long tradition—the entire ceremony accompanied by a ceaseless chanting by the Chief. The Chief is the only living Blackfoot who knows in its entirety the proper ceremony for transferring ownership of the Medicine Pipe, and I was humbled, as I sat there on the floor before him, by the realization that in all probability I was the last person, Indian or White, who would receive a Piegan Medicine Pipe with full traditional ritual.

I was emotionally very receptive to every aspect of the Pipe Transfer Ceremony—and the feelings which the ritual evokes in the participant are truly singular—but I could not make an intellectual grasp on much of the proceeding because I did not understand its significance, and I must confess that several times during the long hours of gesture and chanting my thoughts wandered. I thought—irrelevantly, perhaps—about one of the most profound paradoxes of modern society: that so many people are cynical about human experience without ever in their lives having had the guts or the sensitivity to participate—really—in a human experience. And if you are cynical about human experience you cannot but be cynical about religious experience, because a truly human experience—a human relationship—is in every sense a religious experience.

I find myself unable to articulate my feelings on this subject, and in a way I am glad. Because any experience which can be clearly articulated has not been fully assimilated. No brave man can define courage, and no one capable of real love can tell you what love is. More important, he does not feel the need for definition; the need, if that be the term, is for realization. Knowledge, sometimes, is a poor substitute for knowing (I think I got that from Kahlil Gibran). Faulkner felt this, I think. Sherwood Anderson must have been aware of it, and Jack London. Steinbeck knows it, and I think Hemingway, toward the end, caught a glimpse. I sicken myself when I have to drag in famous names in order to fortify my convictions. Really, I just defeated myself.

One more rambling thought: where the hell do people think they are going? I am thinking now of the "religious" do-gooders who are so preoccupied with some vague never-never pursuit of eventually converting the whole world to their own particular religious belief that they haven't time to show a little love and concern for the people they *actually meet* in the *now*. This observation is of course subject to limitless ramifications, but the pinnacle of egotism, I think, is in believing that you—not your neighbor—are "saved." I suspect that more than one joker is going to strut confidently into the lobby only to discover that he has no reservation after all.

The final portion of the ceremony consisted in my having my face painted with red earth paint by the Chief. Then the Chief asked me to choose one of the Pipes. I said that either one would be fine, but the Chief insisted that I must make a choice and so I chose the nearer of the two. The Chief presented the Pipe to me, showed me how to wrap it properly, and advised me that the Pipe must never be unwrapped without the proper ceremony. Such an action would bring much ill-fortune. The Chief said that the last man of his acquaintance to sell a Pipe without adhering to proper ritual went blind a short time later.

The Chief gave me, along with the Pipe, two necklaces. Both are very old, and each is composed of beads and shells strung on a dull red-colored piece of buckskin. One necklace has seven blue beads, a dentilium shell, and a queue of human hair; this is the Sun Dance Necklace, worn by the Holy Woman and the Medicine Man at a Medicine Lodge celebration. The other necklace is made of three large Indian beads and a different variety of shell; this one, for which the Chief traded a racehorse, many, many years ago, is associated with my Medicine.

Just as the ceremony concluded, there was a thump in the kitchen and immediately the kitten strutted into the living-room with a mouse in its mouth. The mouse was not as big as the kitten, or even half as big; but the mouse was *so* big, and the kitten is so *tiny,* that Jimmy said, "Look up [look out], cat, or that mouse is goin' ate you up." The kitten is a female (I have just decided), and now that she

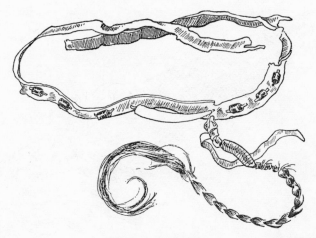

Sun Dance Necklace

had an audience she proceeded to do the dreadful things that cats of all breeds do to mice of all descriptions.

It was 12:30 now, and the Chief was exhausted from the lengthy ceremony, and after a cup of Sanka he and Jimmy went to bed. I was tired, too, but sometimes I find it hard going to bed without a wife. This is not supposed to sound especially virile—tonight I would have kept my wife up all night just talking. But I have no wife, and so I am sitting here alone typing this. Life, I have decided, is, in at least one respect, like death. Neither is realized all at once; each is realized, rather, in scattered little bits and pieces. I experienced a lot of living today—and a little of dying too, I think.

But now it is very late and I am tired enough to kick Liz out onto the floor. So, *Kèn-yai-au-wah-nay-náh-pi-quon!*

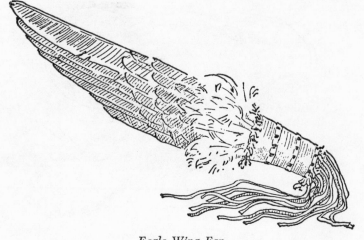

Eagle Wing Fan

Sunday, September 16

This morning dawned rather chilly and slightly overcast. I was up at 6:30 sharp, but Jim and the Chief had already been up for some time and the Chief was industriously putting the final touches on his bone whistle.

I said to Jim, "What kind of bone did you say that is?"

Jim said, "Of eagle."

By the time breakfast was ready the Chief had the whistle blowing just fine, but neither Jim nor I could get a sound out of it. "How a hell he makes that thing poof?" Jim said. "It's all in the *embouchure*," I said, and Jim agreed.

After breakfast, we all washed up and got ready for the Beaver Ceremony. Jimmy fixed the Chief's hair in the three braids of the old-time Piegan warrior, and the Chief put on his new red shirt and his new wristwatch. Last night, after the Chief had given me so many treasures, I wanted to give him something in return and so I took off my wristwatch and slipped it onto his arm. He said, "*Sokáh-pi*," and this morning he wore his new watch proudly. He put the watch on backwards, and I notice that he still tells time with his big pocketwatch. He probably can't even see the face of the wristwatch clearly enough to know what time it is, but so what! He is none the less pleased with it, and I am happy that he enjoys wearing it.

During his grooming the Chief went through the ritual of plucking out his chin-whiskers. I offered to assist him and he handed me the tweezers, but I couldn't find anything to pluck. Jimmy doesn't have to shave very often either. The lucky dogs.

Jim cooked the eggs this morning and they were incredibly bad. I offered some to the kitten, and after one taste she backed away from the plate shaking her head and spitting—obviously possessing a perfectly justifiable preference for mouse heads.

Joe Morning Gun and his wife came by right after breakfast and had coffee with us. Joe was wearing a nice blue suit, and his hair was freshly cut, clipped straight around above the ears. His wife had on a blue dress (Indians like the color blue) with circles on it, and she was wearing a very large and unusual Indian necklace.

The Chief and the Morning Guns rode to the Beaver Ceremony in the station wagon with me. Jimmy said that he would follow in the truck: "I'll take you over [overtake you] at Starr School." The back of the wagon was loaded with paraphernalia for the ceremony, all of which Jimmy had carted out of the Chief's room. The Beaver Bundle, which was packaged in a *nitsisahn*-painted animal skin, is quite large—larger than a man's suitcase. In addition to this we took several medicine rattles, also colored with *nitsisahn;* some wooden bowls, from which we would eat our food; an ancient horn spoon, with which the Chief was to eat his portion of berry soup; and several large, *nitsisahn*-colored hides which would be spread upon the floor of the ceremonial room and upon which the contents of the Beaver Bundle would be spread.

When we arrived at Starr School it was still early in the morning, and at Jim White Grass' house three small children were asleep in the little bedroom off the kitchen. Our blind hostess, Amy White Grass, and Mary Ground were busy in the kitchen preparing heaps of food for the feast, and when finally the children tottered sleepily into the room Mary said, "We got a lot of work to take and do. You kids eat them beans and bread and butter and drink some coffee and get from underfoot." Patty, the tiniest of the children, is a perfect-featured little doll of about three. She had on a red leotard, red tennis shoes, and a pink dress.

Soon the people began to arrive, and soon the house was overflowing with people, and soon the Beaver Ceremony had begun. The setting was nearly identical with the setting for the Pipe Ceremony of a week ago, but the ceremony itself was quite different. The Chief, of course, conducted the ceremony (in addition to being a Chief, he is a "Beaver Man"), and assisting him, seated on his left, were Plenty Treaty B.C. and Fish Wolfrobe. I was delighted to discover that the two female assistants, seated on his right, were Mary Ground and Maggie Bear Child (Plenty Treaty's wife).

I am an observant person, I think—or at least I try to be—but when I observe people it is usually a conscious and sometimes a strenuous act on my part (occasionally there is the embarrassing moment when I am caught staring). But I have discovered that my Indian friends, who usually appear not to notice anything or anybody, are actually more observant than I—in fact they don't miss a thing. Jimmy was one of the functionaries at the ceremony—he sat cross-legged and cut tobacco with a knife on a brass tack-decorated wooden cutting board, and he filled and lighted the long ceremonial pipe and performed various other functions. I didn't think he took special notice of anything or anybody. But when later I asked him to explain some of the rituals—who had done what when and why—my omnipercipient Indian brother was able to give me the most intimate detail of anything that had happened at any time during the ceremony. I would have liked to take some pictures and do a tape of the ceremony, but, feeling that this would be a tourist-like intrusion, I did not seek permission. But I wanted to include in this journal the names of the people present at the Beaver Dance, and when later in the day I asked Jim to help me out, he was able, without the slightest hesitation, to name them all. On the Chief's left, in correct order, were Louis Bear Child, Fish Wolfrobe, James White Grass, Tom Many Guns, Henry Little Dog, Charlie Horn, Joe Morning Gun, James White Calf, Richard Last Gun (myself), Juniper Old Person, Jim Buffalo, Paul Many Hides, and Francis Redhorn. To the right of the Chief: Mary Ground, Maggie Bear Child, Mrs. Tom Many Guns, Mrs. Fish Wolfrobe, Mrs. Charlie Horn, Mrs. Joseph Morning Gun, Mrs. Jim Buffalo, Mrs. Molly Arrowtop, Mrs. Phillip Many Hides, and Mrs. Henry Little Dog. All these people were seated on the floor, and there were others that could not find seats and so stood in doorways or along the walls. I was relieved to see that not everyone sat cross-legged because I am currently unable to sit in this manner—I can fold under one leg at a time, but not both at once.

The four drummers all sat cross-legged, and they were positioned, as at the Pipe Dance, in a row in front of the women. But this time the drum rhythm was not a pulsing, heart-like, hard-soft beat. This time the drumming was a rapid steady pounding. But it was much more than that. Perhaps a musician could explain how the drummers achieved such an unusual effect with their steady pounding drumming. I cannot.

And at the Beaver Dance Ceremony the pounding of drums was accompanied by the sound of rattles. There were four rattles, played at various times by different men—sometimes the Chief had one in his hand. But the rattles were not shaken in the air; they were pounded on the animal hides that covered the floor, so there was the double sound of the rattle striking the hide and the pebbles chattering inside the rawhide rattle. And then, too, there was the piping of the eagle-bone whistles. (The striking of the rattle upon the hide is a symbolic representation of the beaver's striking the water with his flat tail as a signal of danger; the blowing of the bone whistle represents the beaver's whistle-like warning sound.) The Chief had his whistle hung about his neck on a buckskin thong, and Plenty Treaty and Fish Wolfrobe had similar whistles. At special times, the whistles would inject a series of shrill peeps into the music, and the over-all effect of the drums, the rattles, the whistles, and the chanting was spellbinding—truly fascinating.

There is a theory, rather widely held in music circles, that American jazz derives not from African Negro music but from the music of the American Indian. I would be inclined to go along with this theory. Indians are the most musical people I have ever met. And although my opinion admittedly is unqualified, it is not prejudiced. I think that Keely Smith is the greatest female singer of popular songs, and I held this opinion even before I found out that she is an American Indian. And I did hear jazz—really good jazz—in the music of the Beaver Ceremony.

When everyone had taken his place, and the hides had been spread on the floor and the Beaver Bundle had been placed before the Chief, the ceremony began with the burning of sweetgrass on some earth which had been poured onto a hide and then flattened and swirled with the fingers into a pattern which, I feel sure, was symbolic. The sweetgrass was shredded by the Chief over a hot coal which had been carried in by Mary Ground with a pair of wooden tongs and placed on the earth on the hide. The long series of rituals which followed are, like the rituals of the Pipe Dance, defiant of description, but I think it interesting that women play such important roles in Blackfoot religious ceremonies. Interesting too is the fact that, with the exception of the carrying in of the coal, female functions are always carried out by groups of women, whereas the men usually dance singly.

I had somehow gotten the idea that I was to be number one debutramp at this here cotillion, but not so. I was just one more Blackfoot, and actually I preferred it that way. I was allowed to participate fully in all the ceremonies, and when the men, one by one, got up to dance—including the Chief, that old rascal—I in my turn danced too. Fish, the blind man, who was wearing a really terrific Indian belt, danced also, but of course he had to be led onto the floor and he could dance only in one fixed place.

During the really formal dances, the women always danced in groups of four—four being a number of some great religious significance among the Blackfoots. I think this derives from the four directions, for I noticed that as the smoking pipe was passed along, the old men all blew the smoke four ways. The pipe was of the large ceremonial variety, with a stone bowl and a stem about thirty inches long so that it was necessary to hold the bowl at arm's length while smoking. The pipe was passed from one man to another down the line from the Chief, and as it approached I asked Jim whether there was any special way in which I was supposed to smoke it. Jim said not to worry but to watch him and do exactly as he did. So I watched Jim very carefully. And when he handed me the pipe I dutifully scratched my crotch, coughed in the face of the man on my left, and took four puffs on the pipe.

The ceremony was adjourned for the feast, and once again there was plenty for all, and once again I lapped up a bowl of Mary's berry soup and looked around, bright eyed and waggy tailed, for more.

After lunch came the big moment: the sacred Beaver Bundle was unwrapped by the Chief. I had expected a great deal, and I was not disappointed. The chanting and ritual which accompanied the unwrapping were spine-tingling, and I found it easy to imagine that I was seated in a Blackfoot lodge of not 1962 but of perhaps a hundred years ago. And the contents of the Beaver Bundle were, to me, breath-taking. There were in the bundle, in addition to the albino crow—the whiteness of which had been reddened somewhat with vermillion earth paint—a large number of the most beautifully cured animal pelts I have ever seen. There were beaver, otter, mink, weasel, ermine, marten, and many others. Each pelt had been fleshed out even to the head and toes, and I had never before fully appreciated the efficacy of the Indian tanning procedure. I do now, for sure.

There were numerous other articles contained in the Beaver Bundle, and each article was in some way employed ceremonially as it was taken from the wrapping. Four women performed a dance structured around the significance of the four buffalo stones. Four women did the Beaver Dance, each holding a beaver pelt to her chin and holding in her mouth a small stick, in imitation of the beaver. And there was a lively number called the Prairie Chicken Dance, in performance of which the women held blankets over their heads and spread their arms wide in imitation of the movements of prairie chickens. For some reason the Prairie Chicken Dance caused quite a stir of excitement among the womenfolk, and one woman (Cecile Horn) who had been standing in a doorway pulled her coat up over her head and moved out onto the floor to join the dancers. Almost immediately, another woman did the same thing.

The Blackfoots always manage to include in their religious cere- monies some occasion of pure fun, and today it was the Buffalo Dance—a real fun dance if such there ever was. The Buffalo Dance was the only co-educational dance of the day—boys can't have much fun without girls, let's face it—and if you want to have your own buffalo dance you need only music, people of both genders, and some buffalo hooves, polished and split and strung together on raw- hide thongs so that they rattle nicely.

During the Buffalo Dance, both men and women remain seated on their respective sides of the room. Only one person at a time dances, the dancing beginning when a man takes the hooves and carries them twice around the room and on the second go-around tosses the hooves to a woman; then the woman dances twice around and tosses the hooves to a man, and so on back and forth until everybody has had his turn at dancing. But of course there is much more to it than that. The dancing is performed in imitation of the mating of the buffalo, and as the men dance they prance and stomp and grunt and lower their heads like bull buffalo, and the dancing women project the coyness and seductiveness of the buffalo cow. There is no set pattern for dancing—everyone is free to im- provise and to dance as originally and as entertainingly as he can, and this is where the fun comes in. The whole proceeding radiates a tone of merriment and good humor, and when a man dances up to a woman she will shake her head in mock protest and flap her blan- ket or skirt at the "bull" to frighten him away. And when a woman dances close to a man he will grunt and hook his buffalo horns at her in an attempt to discourage her overtures—or else, with humor- ously exaggerated dignity, he will pretend to ignore her completely.

It was Mrs. Tom Many Guns, dressed in a beautiful Indian cos- tume of predominating blue, with blue beadwork on her moccasins and a fine blue blanket over her shoulders, that received the hooves from Joe Horn, the young drummer. (Joe had been replaced at the drum by Fish Wolfrobe, who is blind and so could not see to engage in the Buffalo Dance.) Mrs. Many Guns tossed the hooves to me, and so now it was my turn on the floor. I danced once around, stomping and hooking my horns at the ladies and rattling the hooves at them, and they laughed and pretended to be terrified by the overpowering masculinity of this fierce big bull and with threats and gestures they shooed the bull away. And the second time around, amid shrieks of delighted approval, I suddenly tossed the hooves to Mary Ground, one of the oldest ladies present—whom I had ignored completely the first time around but who had been my intended mate all the time.

The next man to receive the hooves tossed them to Maggie Bear Child, and that Maggie Bear Child—small and round and seventy-eight years old and cute as a button—is a living doll. Maggie directed her attention toward Jimmy, and those two really put on a show. Little Maggie danced as gracefully as a fawn and as coyly as a girl. She was alternately seductive and aggressive, and Jimmy was very fierce and threatening—or petrified with fear—and they both stomped their feet and hooked horns at one another, and finally Maggie backed off and charged Jimmy with little dancing steps and they butted their heads together and Jimmy at last was subdued in horn-locked combat.

Brother Jim danced then, and he is probably the best dancer on the Reservation. As a boy, Jim traveled widely, giving exhibitions of Indian dancing, and I was slightly put out that he had not worn his dancing moccasins but instead had on the same old work shoes in which he had cut wood for the breakfast fire. But if need be, Jim could dance better than the rest of us in hip boots, and he proved it now by prancing and stomping and charging and retreating and shaking his mane and hooking with his horns and spinning in small circles and hopping wounded on one foot—all with magnificent manly grace and with perfect regard for the rhythm of the tireless drums.

Everyone took his turn with the hooves, and I wish that all the world could see the Blackfoot Indians as I saw them during the performance of the Buffalo Dance—graceful and gay and creative and warmly human and thoroughly wonderful. I loved them all—with the possible exception of one Ned Sparks-type Indian who, as he had done at the Pipe Dance, came late and hung around the kitchen until he had been fed and then left. I am sure he is not a full-blood because he has a face like a weak cup of tea—with lemon.

The Beaver Dance Ceremony was over after all us Blackfoots, one by one, had knelt before the Chief and had our faces painted with vermillion earth paint. Jimmy admonished me to make certain that when I arose again I should turn to the right and not to the left. I still don't know why, but after I had knelt and the Chief had painted my forehead and nose and cheeks and the part of my hair and had chanted a prayer for me, I was careful to do as Jimmy had directed.

Anyone who thinks that Blackfoot Indians stand around with their arms folded under their blankets, feeling sorry for themselves or otherwise wasting time, could not be more mistaken. Despite lack of educational and employment opportunity—despite lack of money and everything that lack of money implies—the Blackfoot of today holds to the perdurable courage and zest for living which is his heritage.

"Idleness is the devil's workshop," my grandmother used to say, and the devil would find very little working room among the Blackfoots. There is always something cooking on the Reservation. Last night there was a dance in town, this morning there was the Beaver Dance, and this afternoon, as soon as the ceremony was completed, everybody went barrelling across the prairie to the Starr School racetrack.

The racetrack is only about a mile behind Jim White Grass' house, and the Chief and Jim and I got there in time for the first race. I parked the station wagon between two other cars, and as I got out, an intoxicated younger-generation Indian stuck his hand out of a car window (why is it that all drunks want to shake hands!) and asked me who I was. I shook hands and spoke to him in Blackfoot and left him staring in the wide-eyed, drop-jawed posture of disbelief that only a drunk can portray. He was very young, and the only drunk I saw at the races.

Almost the next person I met was Stanley White Man, leading his palomino racehorse. I said, "Are you going to race the palomino, Stanley?"

Stanley said, "Yah, she's going ride her for me." Which, as anyone knows, meant that Stanley was going to enter the horse and that he had hired a jockey (male) to ride her for him. Stanley's horse lost.

The races were all match races, run over a straight, quarter-mile course. The finishline was flanked for many yards with cars and trucks, and the bet-takers were busily conducting business on the hood of an automobile. I was really quite pleased that I had represented the event so accurately in "Horserace."

The Chief was laying down bets along with the best of them. Indians love to wager, and Jimmy says that they even bet on whether someone will snare a whitefish on the next attempt, sometimes betting a dollar a loop. The Chief, by the way, is an excellent judge of horseflesh, and he won a few bucks today.

Last time, down at Heart Butte, I did not take any pictures of the races, but today I came well prepared and shot a full roll of 35mm and two reels of 8mm movie film. A "Stick Game," one of which invariably takes place along with the horseraces, was in progress a short distance from the track, and since the stick game had constituted an important symbolic element of "Horserace," I took some movie shots of this one. The stick game is an Indian gambling game in which two lines of people—each side representing a team —sit facing each other. To the accompaniment of a very rapid drumming, and a constant, unisonous chanting by all the players, two sets of small bones, one in each set marked with a black stripe, are shuffled and concealed in the hands of two of the participants. The object is for the opposing team to guess in which hands the unmarked bones are concealed, the guess being made not vocally but by intricate gestures of the fingers and thumbs of both hands. Score is kept by the passing back and forth of small sticks, the first side to have ten sticks being the winner. The stick game is, like all Indian games, a very graceful and rhythmic thing. Jimmy immediately joined the game, but the best player was Ray Many Hides, one of Phillip Many Hides' sons. Ray is a fine young chap, and one of my favorites among the younger Indians.

As I raised the camera from the game to get a shot of the onlookers, a lovely teen-age Indian girl hastily shook out her long hair and touched it with an infinitely feminine gesture in preparation for having her picture taken. This kind of grabbed at me because I recognized the girl as one of the older kids that had been at the Beaver Ceremony. I had felt strangely drawn to this lovely little creature with the sensitive face and the shy demeanor. I had fallen immediately in love with her large, moist, doe-like eyes, and I had wondered that she did not enter into things but rather spent the entire time in the kitchen, her jean-clad legs dangling from the high table upon which she sat. And then finally she got up to leave, and I could tell then that her blue jeans masked a badly crippled leg.

When the films are developed, I am sure that I will have a fine photographic record of both the horseraces and the stick game, but there is no escape from the suspicion that by taking pictures I have somehow cheated myself. Somehow the presence of the cameras places me outside of things, and although I will always be able to recapture now exactly how things *looked*, I do not have the *feel* of how things *were* that I carried with me after the Heart Butte races. What I have done, actually, is to limit myself, for now I will have to deal with mere facts . . . Before, I could deal with something more meaningful than facts—and more durable: concepts. They tell me that Spinoza would walk down the street reading a book, and, after reading a page, would tear it out and throw it away. I think I understand why.

I did, however, finally get some good photographs of the boy with the three long braids. I concocted a very clever scheme for getting him to pose for me: *I asked him*. His full name, I learned, is Roy Rides-At-The-Door (Indian name: Sitting Calf), but the family name now has been shortened to simply "Door." He and some other boys were playing with a football near the racetrack, and they felt that they had been munificently rewarded when I threw them several long spiral passes.

And I was not the only one taking pictures today. There was a White man at the races, loaded down with several very expensive cameras and much equipment, and at first I felt a rather hypocritical resentment against this *Náh-pi-quon* who was so nervily intruding upon the private recreations of us Blackfoots. As I turned from conversing with the Chief, the man suddenly snapped a close-up of me, and this puzzled me until he approached and asked me why my face was painted. I had forgotten about the vermillion. He explained that he was a photographer for National Geographic, and he turned out to be a pretty nice guy—although he couldn't throw a football very well.

After supper, the Chief went immediately to bed and prayed loudly as Jim and I finished the booze and talked. I moved from one chair to another as Jim told about Indian Owl Dances and then launched upon an interminable account of his great shyness as a boy. "My face was starting to feel getting hot, so I says a myself I say a goddam its, you got start coming out of that goddam bashful."

I had surmised that because the Chief always wraps his braid-ends with strips of red flannel it followed that he is fond of the color red, and so I had bought him a red shirt. But from Jim I learned that I had been mistaken. The Chief wraps his braids in red in adherence to tradition, but he regards red as being too loud a color for a man's clothing. He prefers shirts colored blue or gray (he dislikes the color black, especially in the matter of a hat), and Jimmy told me that he wore the new red shirt to the ceremony today only to avoid hurting my feelings. How characteristic of the grand old fellow to undertake such a sensitive gesture!

At eleven o'clock I awoke to find myself lying on the sofa. Jim had gone to bed, and I did likewise. Another very full day.

Monday, September 17

"*Sixty-sou.*" It sounds like a French merchant haggling with a Yankee tourist, but actually, "*Sixty-sou*" is the Blackfoot term for moose. We got a moose today.

I slept soundly last night, and it was fortunate that I did because this was to be an eventful day. The morning dawned clear and warm, and we were all up early, and immediately after breakfast the Chief expressed a desire to go to town. Jim's truck had a flat tire, and he had no spare, so we all piled into the station wagon and headed for Browning. We had gone only a couple of miles when Jim suddenly broke the silence with, "Hey, look a there," and following the direction of his finger I saw a large, dark animal, moving parallel to the range fence about a hundred yards to the left of the road. The animal was about a quarter-of-a-mile ahead of us, and as we drew abreast of it, Jimmy said, "It's a moose! By goz, it's a moose!" And without further conversation we went into action. I stopped the wagon by a line pole, and Jimmy tumbled out and ducked behind the pole to keep an eye on the moose while I went back for the rifle. "Gun that sonabitcher down!" Jim said with hushed excitement. "Floorboard the bastard!" And with the Chief still imperturbably occupying his place in the rear seat, I roared back down the unpaved road, skidded badly as I turned in toward our cattle guard—almost crashing through it—and, leaving the Chief seated calmly in the car, grabbed the old .38/40 Marlin rifle from behind the door in Jimmy's room, cussed my inability to find Jim's skinning knife, snatched two butcher knives and a file from the kitchen, and barrelled back down the road again.

Jim was standing by the pole, waiting, but no moose was in sight. I felt certain that the moose had high-tailed it back into the hills, but as Jim got into the car he said that the moose had continued on down the fenceline, apparently trying to find a break in the fence through which it could cross the road and reach the thick woods of the creek bottom. The creek was only about five hundred yards from the fence; the wooded hills in the other direction were several miles away across the slightly rolling prairie.

The moose was just over the next rise, trotting steadily along the fence, and when we were nearly abreast of the animal I stopped the wagon and Jim and I got out. I had not drawn even with the moose for fear of panicking it into a retreat back across the prairie, and as Jimmy jacked a cartridge into the chamber of the old octagon-barrelled rifle and took aim, the distance between the moose and the gun muzzle was about 250 yards, and increasing all the time. Jimmy fired, and the heavy .38 calibre bullet kicked up dust at least forty feet in front of the moose. Jim fired again. Another clean miss, but this time the bullet-dust—once again far ahead of the moose—caused the animal to turn and trot nearly fifty yards back toward us. Then the moose stopped still, and at a distance of not more than 200 yards Jimmy fired again and for a third time missed cleanly. In disgust he handed me the rifle and said, "Here, you try him."

The .38/40 is not a good cartridge for long-range shooting. The bullet is heavy and the powder charge is light, and the .38/40 has the recoil of a .22 and the trajectory of a slingshot pellet. The .38/40, like the .44/40, is a cartridge so short that it can be fired not only in a rifle but in a pistol. In the old days this was a desirable situation because it meant that the plainsman needed to carry only one kind of ammo for both rifle and pistol, but by modern standards both of these cartridges are considered obsolete for rifle use.

I estimated that the moose was just under three hundred yards away now, and taking a guess that the slow-moving old .38 calibre bullet would probably drop around 30–36 inches at this distance, I held just behind the top of the moose's hump and squeezed the trigger. The bullet struck visibly about twenty-five feet to the right of the moose, and immediately the trouble was apparent. "Damn sights are off a mile, Jim," I said, and throwing the rifle again to my shoulder I pointed, not aiming with the old buckhorn sights, and squeezed off another shot. After what seemed to be an incredibly long pause, I heard the solid whump of the bullet striking; but the moose, no more affected than if he had been stung by a bee, trotted in a quick little circle and then stood still again. Another shot, another "whump," and still the moose did nothing but trot searchingly up and down the fenceline. Both bullets, we later discovered, had scored solidly in the heavy muscle of the moose's shoulder.

I handed the rifle back to Jim, and Jim threw off another quick shot and this time the bullet struck the moose mid-way of the lower left rear leg, breaking the bone cleanly. "Come on," Jim said, as the moose circled pathetically on three legs, and with Jim holding the rifle ready—the old Marlin holds fourteen cartridges, so we had plenty of shots left—we moved cautiously toward the moose. When we reached the range fence, the moose was standing quietly a hundred feet the other side of it. Those heavy .38 calibre soft-point slugs are devastating at point-blank range, and Jim hit the moose with a perfectly placed neck shot and the moose went down on its side with the sound as of a tree falling. The moose lay there and raised its head and looked at us as we cautiously crossed the fence and approached, and Jimmy ended it all, thank God, with a shot to the head. We circled the moose at close range then, carefully staying clear of the huge hooves which still struck out spasmodically—piston-like—for one kick from those immensely powerful legs could easily kill a man. But the eyes were clouding over now, like embers dying, and Jim said, "That smoked him up," and we went back to the station wagon and we cut off the road and drove along the fence until we came to a cattle gate. And we lowered the gate and drove through, and then back along the other side of the fence to where the moose lay quiet now. And the moose seemed unreal lying there on the prairie so far from the forests and the marshes that a moose calls home.

The taking of the moose was not an heroic adventure. The Chief says that in the old days the two animals that the Blackfoots really feared were a grizzly bear and a bull moose in rut. But the fact remains that in most cases the shooting of a moose is about as heroic as the shooting of a cow in a pasture. So far as Jimmy and I are concerned, we slaughtered some badly needed meat, nothing more. The Chief says that a moose is the only game animal that he has never killed, and both Jimmy and I wish it could have been he that shot this one.

When the Chief walked up to the moose, he said immediately and without hesitation that it was a young bull, two years old. It was a fairly big Shiras moose—much larger than a horse—but the antlers were not remarkable. The Chief says that in the old days the Indians used to make serving platters of the flat, dish-like antlers.

The Chief remarked matter-of-factly that we had gotten a moose because we had sponsored a Beaver Ceremony yesterday. (He has already revealed that one of the functions of the Beaver Bundle in the old days was to call the buffalo to the Blackfoot hunting grounds.) I told him that when I had tried peyote, down in New Mexico, I had seen a vision of a young bull moose with small antlers. And indeed this was true. Under the influence of peyote I had seen a phantasmagoria of beautiful and brilliant colors, most remarkable of which was a singular and delicate shade of blue (it occurred to me this very instant for the first time that blue is the favorite color of the Blackfoots—I had not made the association before). Next in the vision was a three-dimensional cross, and finally I saw the head of a very dark young bull moose—identical to the head of the moose we got today.

The Chief passed my peyote experiences lightly, obviously convinced that the moose had been presented to us because of our sponsoring of the Beaver Dance Ceremony. Of course, I would not argue the matter with him, and indeed there is much ground for the Chief's conviction. The Beaver Ceremony is in part a prayer to the Great Spirit to make game abundant, and the fact that we took a moose early the next day is definitely remarkable. But, out of regard to my peyote experience, why did we get a young bull moose instead of one of the more plentiful animals such as deer and elk? This part of the Reservation is not moose country—this was the first moose to be taken in these parts within the memory spans of all the old Indians to whom I talked. But, to return once again to the Chief's point of view, why was it that we, of all the thousands on the Reservation, took the moose. That moose must have traveled many miles, crossing several ranches, in order to appear at just the proper time almost in our backyard. To me the whole affair represents a fascinating enigma; to the Chief it is a perfectly logical and apodictic sequence of related events.

The shooting of the moose was the easy part. The real work was in skinning and butchering the huge creature. For years I carried in the woods a sheath-knife with a short, nicely curved blade, and never did the opportunity come to use it on anything larger than a deer. And now that I was faced with the necessity of skinning a moose—probably the most difficult of all North American animals to de-hide—there was no proper knife to be had. There were the two butcher knives, with blades too long and too straight for skinning, and there was in the station wagon the horn-handled little machete with the twelve inch blade that I had picked up in Old Mexico. Moose hide is exceeding tough, and when green it will dull a knife in no time, but we didn't have a whetstone with which to re-sharpen our blades and so had to make do with a fine-grained file. But you can do what you have to do with what you have to do it with, and we did a reasonably quick and efficient job of skinning the moose. But it was I and not brother Jim that was the stoical Indian; Jim was very excited and in a great hurry and he managed to cut several small holes in the skin.

Before the skinning, of course, came the chore of removing the entrails, and it was during this phase of operations, even more so than during the skinning, that I wished for a good knife. I did most of the work with the little red-handled pocket knife that I had given to the Chief. The Chief was sort of straw-boss ("Big Push," Jim said) on the job, making suggestions (good ones, too) and occasionally taking a few cuts with a butcher knife. Most of my share of the actual skinning was done with the little machete. It had a nice curve, and I found that by holding the back of the blade instead of the handle I could do a good job with it—but my hand got awfully tired.

When the skinning was nearly finished, a pick-up truck slowed out on the road, stopped, turned around, and began to follow the marks of the station wagon on the grass leading to the cattle gate. "Home Guns," Jimmy grunted, and no one spoke again until the truck had parked close by the moose. It was Mr. and Mrs. Home Gun, the people that had been so rude when asked to participate in the Beaver Ceremony. But now they were all ooh's and ahh's and smiles and I restrained my reaction only out of respect for the Chief. The Chief was, as always, courteous and unperturbed, but largely he just ignored them.

Mrs. Home Gun at least made a gesture of assistance. She picked up the idle butcher knife and split open the paunch, dumping out about a bushel of green fodder, and shook out the tripe and divided it neatly in two. I noticed that she was dividing everything—liver, heart, kidney, kidney fat, lungs—into two equal piles. Her husband stood around grinning foolishly behind his tinted glasses and did nothing but get underfoot. Once, for no good reason, he gave a sudden tug at a front quarter, causing me to cut myself, and at this point my patience ran out and I told him to get the hell out of the way.

All the 35mm film had been shot at the horseraces, but there was still half a reel of 8mm left and Jimmy asked me whether I would take some "moving" of the moose. The Chief wanted me to get in the picture too, so I decided to evoke a minor miracle and make Mr. Home Gun useful. When I told him I wanted some pictures of the moose, he grinned and immediately assumed a great-hunter pose behind the carcass. I explained, with short phrases, that he was to take the picture, not star in it, and after an unbelievably long time I finally got him to point the camera in the right direction and press the right lever. So I thanked him, stated that in my opinion he was a true "semi-colon" (my own mixed-company euphemism for "half-ass," which was of course wasted on him), and he flashed an ophidian grin, slithered over to the truck, and coiled attentively there in the shade while the rest of us did the work.

At last the moose was decently skinned and caped, and Jim and I quartered it and loaded the gigantic quarters into the station wagon. As I had known he would, the Chief gave the Home Guns one of the piles of meat—one-half of the lights—that the woman had set aside. I didn't like it, and neither did Jim—we had plenty of friends that needed meat—but Jim just shrugged and said, "It's the Old Fella's moose." In spite of myself I had to admire the old Chief's attitude of returning good for evil. No wonder he has lived to be 105 years old. However, since we had no room in the station wagon for the head and cape of the moose, I saw to it that the Home Guns carried it to our place in their pick-up. When we got home we found it in the front yard, where they had thrown it, but Jim smoothed my hackles a bit by suggesting that I should not judge all the Home Guns by those few I have met. He said that they comprise a rather sizeable clan, that some of them are very fine persons, and that one of the older family members, now deceased, had been a true friend to the Chief.*

* I later learned that there might be any number of reasons that a Blackfoot would refuse to participate in a religious ceremony at any given time. I also learned that Mr. Home Gun was not a well person. A couple of years later, following serious abdominal surgery, he became as nice a guy as you could hope to meet. I even learned to like his wife, which, since it turned out that the Home Guns, like practically everybody else on the Reservation, are my relatives, was a fortunate circumstance.

A couple of years ago, Jim bought a secondhand freezer. It is a very large freezer, and we were able, after some additional butchering, to get most of the moose into it.

Then we went down to the spring to wash the tripe and liver and to scrub off the moose blood that was caked up to our elbows. While we were there, a car came speeding down the road from town, skidded through our open cattle gate, and careened to a stop. For all their hurry, neither of the two men in the car apparently had any intention of getting out, so Jim and I unbent from our labors and went up to the car. The car was unmarked, and both of its occupants were dressed in civvies, but the driver, for all of the smile and the cigar clenched in his teeth, had *cop* written all over him. Obviously these people were here on business, and my first thought was that I must have broken some kind of law by helping Jim with the moose.

Jim knew the man with the cigar, and he introduced us by name, and after a few moments of inconsequential chatter, during which the cigar man kept addressing me by the wrong name, old Cigar abruptly asked to see my identification papers. I asked him upon what authority he made the request, and he got out of the car quickly then and flashed a card holder at me and said that he was a Federal Marshal. The other man meanwhile got out of the car and came around behind me. I asked the Marshal why he wanted me to identify myself and he said that there was a federal warrant for a man answering my description. He was still pointedly addressing me by a name other than my own, and I had just about decided to reciprocate by calling him Marshal Dillon when he introduced me to the other man, his deputy, and I'll be a moose if Deputy didn't have a crippled right arm. Not wanting to push things too far, I asked what the warrant charges were, and the Marshal said desertion and several other things and he showed me the warrant. The warrant was for a 22-year-old that had deserted from the army, and I fitted the description of the desperado only in that I was from Texas. So I showed the Marshal my identification and told him what I was doing here, and he said oh yes he had heard of me. He also remembered the last time I was up here, and this surprised me. If you want to get lost, don't go to an Indian reservation—I'll bet there is not an Indian for 100 miles that does not know of my presence here.

So we all parted friends, and after Marshal Dillon and Chester had galloped off to further adventures, Jimmy and I went back to the house. It was now 2:30 in the afternoon, and we had been working steadily since early morning without food and we were starved. So in the Indian tradition we ate hugely of the fresh liver of our kill. Jim also cooked some fresh kidney, and although he made no preparation of the kidney except to slice it thinly and pop it into a frying pan, the kidney was mild-flavored and delicious. So was the liver. The Chief ate as much as we did.

We still had not gotten to town, so after eating, Jimmy and I put on fresh shirts and we all boarded the station wagon again. As we were crossing the bridge at Starr School, a load of young Indian men in a car with Canada plates charged down upon us from the rear and passed us at dangerous speed. "Bunch drunks," Jimmy muttered, and as usual he was right. An empty quart beer bottle went flipping out a window of the car almost at that instant, and I was already beginning to slide into the reflective mood which comes to me with twilight and I thought both of the scene in "Horserace" in which Phillip throws a beer bottle out the window of a moving car and of the dramatic juxtaposition of the two cars here on the road to Browning—one car occupied by two fine Indians who had worked hard all this day to bring in the winter's supply of moose meat, and the other car filled with Indians who had spent the day in getting drunk. How antipodal can you get!

"Give everybody a bad names," Jimmy growled, referring to the drunks, and once again he was right.

There is something about bringing in the family meat that allows a man to feel that he has earned the right to sit for awhile and smoke his pipe. Ordinarily I don't smoke anything, but today, seated in the Tribal Office waiting for Jim and the Chief to conduct their business, I puffed rather smugly on a small cigar. There was leisure in which to pass the time of day with those friends that were there, including Mary Ground and Mrs. Charlie Horn, and I made one new acquaintance—a big, black-sombreroed Indian man with no eyebrows whose name is Paul Running Crane. (In the old days, some Indians plucked out their eyebrows along with their chin whiskers.)

There is, in this day and age, something infinitely inspiring and tragically anachronistic about a functional female breast. Seated opposite me at the Tribal Office was an Indian girl of about twenty, holding her baby, and during the course of the afternoon she casually raised her blouse and gave baby an early supper. The girl was much too aquiline—almost accipitral—to be really pretty, but she was very wholesome and as she affectionately and efficiently nursed her child she became, in a way, quite beautiful to behold. She did not have on her face the ecstatic expression that mothers in women's magazine ads always have—that would have been obscene, I think. But she was contented and unselfconscious and very feminine during the entire proceeding, and it gave me a nice warm member-of-the-family feeling to be there. Too many White women nowadays regard their breasts as something with which to fill out a sweater—they wouldn't even consider nursing their babies—and this attitude, I feel sure, must represent some gross but socially acceptable form of perversion.

We started home at 5:00, and upon arrival Jim and I took the ten-gallon can and drove down to the creek for water. A small, wiry Indian man of undeterminable age was fishing there, accompanied by four dogs. Jimmy made proper introductions, but Joe Young Eagle was very shy and almost immediately he went splashing knee-deep across a gravel bar, followed by his faithful dogs. Jim said that Joe is pretty much of a hermit, and that he walks wherever he goes, often walking to town—about twelve miles cross-country, as the Indian trots—strolling around for awhile, and then walking home again.

Jim fried some moose shoulder for supper and it was tough as hell. I asked him why he didn't cut some steaks from the more tender and flavorful hindquarters, or broil some of the huge tenderloins, and he replied that he is saving the hindquarters for drying.

At supper, Jim casually mentioned that he was married for two years since I was up here last (I guess it was an Indian style marriage, because Jim said that when the woman started to drink too much, Jim divorced her by packing up her things, taking them into town, and handing them to her). Jim said that tomorrow we will have tripe, an Indian favorite. If it is going to be anything like the venison tripe that old Phillip put on the table four years ago, no thanks! Phillip said, "White people don't know how to cook tripe —they clean it up too much so you can't tell what you're eating." Phillip's method of preparation incorporated a careful avoidance of cleaning the tripe (or anything else) too scrupulously. Phillip's recipe consisted in yanking the stomach out of a deer, slitting it open, shaking it a few times, and cooking it as little as possible. Phillip's tripe was brown and smelled like manure and I don't know what it tasted like because I couldn't get it past my nose.

The Chief was very sad at supper. The moose meat—he has not eaten moose in sixty years—brought back a lot of memories. It must be kind of rough to be the last of your generation, almost the last of your culture, but the Chief's only complaint is his poor eyesight.

He says that he could still do everything he used to do, if he could only see well enough.

After supper, the old Chief lay on the couch with closed eyes, clearly wishing to be left alone with his thoughts. So Jim talked to me as I typed. With his usual prefatory, "Do you ever remember," which means, "are you familiar with," "have you ever been to," etc., Jim informed me on the various techniques used in fighting forest fires. Then we recorded some of the word forms that have been puzzling me. Sometimes a Blackfoot word contains a sequence of two or more unvoiced consonant clusters, and it is very difficult to pick this up in normal conversation, especially when it occurs at the beginning or end of a word and is unstressed. There was no booze left, so Jim had coffee and I drank numerous cups of tea.

Everybody to bed at 11:30.

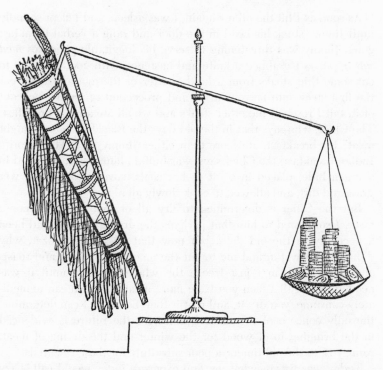

Paid the penalty for having drunk all that tea before going to bed last night. Was called outside during the wee (wee-wee) hours for a tea-pee council—a privy council, if you please, although I did not go that far. I hated to get out of my nice warm sack, of course, but once outside I would not have traded the experience for all your silver and gold (plumbing). The moon was on the wane, and it was lighting with cold fire the edges of the black clouds, and the wind was chill enough to make you know you were alive and a part of all this. It is easy for me to appreciate why Faulkner never surrendered to reality-killing comforts of civilization such as air-conditioning, and why D. H. Lawrence always wore thin-soled shoes—so he could feel the real earth beneath him. If I ever am called into the service again, I will be fighting for the right of a man to stand at night on a Montana prairie, far from the binoculars of virtuous old maids, and do what he has to do. So you get a little frost on the family jewels, so what! But I doubt that any woman could understand this. Women are made, I guess, to squat over china pots.

As soon as I hit the pillow again, I was asleep, and I slept soundly until Jimmy stuck his head in the door and rang a verbal breakfast gong. Jimmy was threatening to serve his inevitable pancakes *med sylt uppå,* so I grabbed a knife and hastened with good appetite to cut some thin steaks from a hind-quarter of the moose. Jimmy cut the first steak into narrow strips and proceeded to fry the hell out of it, but I rescued the other steaks and we all ate a huge breakfast. The Chief, who says that in the old days the Blackfoots ate "straight meat" for breakfast, ate more than either Jimmy or I. The favorite Indian breakfast, the Chief says, was buffalo hump-ribs, wrapped in a green hide, placed in a pit of hot coals, covered over with wet grass and dirt, and allowed to cook slowly all night.

But the Chief is determined to dry all of that delicious moose meat. I suggested to him that perhaps the drying of meat had been a necessity in the old days, but now that he had a freezer, why didn't he allow Jim and me to cut the moose into steaks and roasts and wrap them and just freeze the whole business until it was needed. No deal! When you have more meat than you can immediately consume, you dry it, and that is that. So far as I can determine, the only concern of the older Indians for the future is evidenced in the bringing in of wood for the winter and the drying of meat. Money is, to the old-timers, a poor substitute for these essentials.

Today was warm—what my film exposure index would call "hazy sun"—and I didn't want to stay in the house even long enough to wash, so I took my bath in the back yard. The hills are fully gold with aspen now, and the far ridge behind the house shines sun-clinquant against the sky. I will really miss this Montana scenery.

After I had washed, Jimmy said, "Dad wants going in town now," so we piled into the wagon and arrived in town shortly before ten o'clock. Jim and Dad went off somewhere, saying that they would be back "in a few minutes," and when they at last did reappear at 12:30 Jim led the way into a greasy-spoon diner and ordered cheeseburgers for himself and old Iron-gut. I have no passion for cheap restaurants, so I passed up the greaseburgers in favor of some white grapes which I purchased "in afores" of Buttrey's chrome-plated new store (which goes to show that *anything* is good for *something*). I had passed the lonely interim in snapping pictures around town, and I had been especially attracted to the local constabulary because it was they that had sicced the Feds on me. One of them was so grossly abdominous that when he sat on a table at the Tribal Office he was taller from back to bellybutton than from the seat of his pants to the top of his straw hat—and I have a picture to prove it. I asked Jim whether this local Nero Wolfe had always been so corpulent, and Jim said, "Him? No. In the [his] thirties he was skinny guy—just ate a too much dinners." I also learned, at long last, the real name of "Popeye," the tall, rubber-eyed character with the fist-flattened nose and the no front teeth. Name by "Wesley," yet!

The Chief and Jimmy disappeared again after lunch, so I was once more on my own. I am still in my post-moose mood of contemplation and introspection, and I find the more simple background of Indian life a convenient scale against which to measure the actualities and illusions (and dis-) of my own existence. I have finally decided what is wrong with the Hemingway phrase, "All I want from wine is the drinking of it." I want more than that: I want the sharing of it. I guess I am feeling lonely, or incomplete, or something. At any rate, although I love the Chief as a father, and Jim as a brother, and although I have much affection for my other Indian friends, I need an even closer and somehow different relationship with someone—a woman, obviously. (In recent days I have more than once been offered a chance on an Indian blanket—otherwise known as the sport of teepee-creeping—but a daily reading from that most inspirational of best-sellers, *The Power of Positive Wassermans,* has time and again yanked me like a yoyo back from a fate worse than affluence.) Anyway, that is not the kind of relationship I am referring to. My libido bulges with muscles, but it is tempered by a belief that when the sexual relation is entered into for the sole purpose of obviating a physiological exigency—without any real emotional involvement—a marvelously meaningful human experience is thereby lowered to the status of defecation. "Love me, love my other loves," is my motto, and what I am searching for is a bride that won't mind sharing her nuptial couch with everyone from Shakespeare and Mozart to Deborah Kerr and Licia Albanese—not to mention one slightly used Indian Chief.

There is a phrase on my writing pad that puzzles me. I jotted it down this afternoon, while waiting for the guys to return, but now I don't remember quite what was going around in my head when I wrote it. It states, "True intelligence approximates total logic." Maybe if nobody else understands it either, and if I repeat it often enough, I can become known eventually as a great philosopher. In fact, it wouldn't surprise me if I were to be offered a full professorship at good old Moo U. (Texas A&M).

Jim and Dad came back at 4:00 and I bought some grub and a jug of booze and a tank of gas, and we came home. The grapes didn't stay with me very well, and by supper I was starved and ate a hell of a lot of moose meat. I was quite surprised that both Jim and the Chief were enthusiastic about the mustard greens, stewed tomatoes and canned apricots that I added to the menu. I had supposed them merely tolerant of the fruits and vegetables which I have been forcing upon the table, but in future I shall no longer hesitate to act as dietitian.

The Chief ate marvelously, grunted away from the table, and immediately went to sleep on the sofa. Jim spun some tales until eight o'clock, at which time the Chief arose refreshed and ready to tell us some stories about early and contemporary Indian politics. Most of the stories were fragmented or, at best, anecdotal, but the one story that did have any form was really a good one: this story concerned a diplomatic mission to Washington which the Chief and Plenty Treaty had undertaken in 1935. Although the narrative was at times very funny—most of the laughs were at the expense of Mr. Plenty Treaty, I am afraid—I prized it less as a sample of the Chief's humor than as an indication of his fantastic memory for detail and his remarkable powers as an orator (I think that the Chief's comparing his pockets to arrow quivers should be set down among the great oratorical metaphors of all time).

THE BIG CLAIM

The Government owed us several million dollars for some land that they had taken from us, and for many years we had been trying to collect what was owed to us. Finally we hired a lawyer in Washington, D.C. He was the same age as I, and we Indians called him Bear Head. [Bear Head would be Mr. Serven, of the law firm, Serven, Joyce, Barlow and Goodman.]

It all happened this way: One day Bob Hamilton, the official interpreter for our tribe, informed me that there was to be an important meeting down at Helena. For the previous four years we had been attempting unrelentingly but without success to present our claim before the Federal Government, and this Helena conference was the result of a communication which I had sent to [United States Senator] B. K. Wheeler. B. K. Wheeler and his [law] partner were to be at the Helena meeting along with Bear Head and another official from Washington whom we called Morning Eagle. Also to be represented at the meeting were the Flatheads, the Gros Ventres, the Assiniboines, the Sioux and the Crows. Delegates from the Piegans included, besides myself, Big Spring, Wolf Plume, Rides-At-The-Door, and several others.

The meeting at Helena had been arranged in order for the Indians to receive information from the Washington officials regarding the proper way to go about presenting our Big Claim, but instead of giving us advice, the officials asked us a question. One of the officials stood up and said, "If any among you can answer this question, let him speak. The Blackfoots were once a great nation, but they are no longer great. They are few in number, and so are the other tribes represented here. How, then, do you propose to fight your claim against the mighty United States Government?"

Our delegation talked together then, and Wolf Plume said, "We came here to receive advice, but instead of giving us advice the White Man has given us a question. What shall we do? Who will answer for us?"

At this point I got up and went outside to get a drink of water. I had a little money in my side pants pockets, but while I was outside I took everything out of my side pockets so that they were empty. Then I went back inside and announced that I would speak for my people. I said, "You have asked us a question, and although I do not know whether I can answer your question satisfactorily, I will try. I am not able even to read or write or to speak your language, but I will do my best to answer for my people.

"In the old days, when we made war on the other tribes, and conquered the land you later took away from us, our warriors carried a bow and two quivers full of arrows." I pulled my side pockets inside out, and continued: "These are my quivers. In the old days my quivers held arrows, because in those times we fought with arrows. But nowadays one can no longer fight with arrows; nowadays one must fight with money, and you can clearly see that the quivers which should hold the money with which to fight for my people are empty. If you want me to be able to fight, then fill my empty quivers. Fill my empty quivers with money, and then I will be able to fight."

For a minute nobody said anything, and then B. K. Wheeler's partner said, "I will put one hundred dollars into your quivers so that you can fight through representatives in Washington." Then B. K. Wheeler gave one hundred dollars, and so did the other official, Morning Eagle. Then the Gros Ventres put in fifty dollars to provide stationery and other supplies that we would need. Finally it was agreed that I would go to Washington, with Bob Hamilton as interpreter, to put our Big Claim before the Government.

So the meeting was over, and our delegation went back to Browning to prepare for our mission to Washington. But before we were ready to leave, Bob Hamilton, our interpreter, passed away.

Bob Hamilton's death left me without an interpreter, so I asked several English-speaking Blackfoots to go to Washington with me. At various times, certain individuals agreed to go, but at the last minute every one of them backed out. Finally one night I gave a Medicine Smoke, a ceremony among the men. Louis Bear Child, also called Plenty Treaty, was present, and it was to him that I spoke: "You speak English well, and I want you to go to Washington with me to assist in representing our people. Do not refuse, as I ask in the name of our people. I know that you are a poor man and that you cannot afford to make this journey, but if you will agree to go, my young son, Jim, and I will pay your expenses out of our own pockets."

Plenty Treaty agreed to go, and we informed our Superintendent, Mr. O'Hara, that we wished permission to go to *Sikkoi-yis* [Black Lodge], which is our Blackfoot name for Washington, D.C. Mr. O'Hara, whom we called Good Dancer, agreed to let us go, and one very cold winter day, with a blizzard blowing, my boy Jim drove Plenty Treaty and me to the railroad depot in a sleigh. At first the ticket agent would not sell us our tickets; he called Good Dancer on the telephone and asked him whether we had permission to leave, and only then did he sell us our tickets. [Technically, to this very day no American Indian can leave his reservation without the specific permission of the superintendent; this fact, along with numerous others of similar nature, might profitably be made known to those *ignorantes* who are currently militating for a strict adherence by the Federal Government to the very letter of the old Indian treaties.] Then my son Jim shook hands with us and wished us good luck, and we started on our journey.

I had a lot of respect for Plenty Treaty for making the trip with me, but when we got on the train I felt sad because the poor chap was dressed so shabbily. His shoes were far too large for him, and his toes were sticking out of holes worn in the shoe tops; he was wearing an old leather jacket that was nothing short of pathetic, and his cap wasn't worth owning. At that

266

time he did not have any braids, but he needed a hair-cut very badly. He certainly did not look like a diplomat on his way to Washington, and I was so embarrassed by his appearance that I would not go to the dining car but instead had our food served in our compartment.

When we got to Chicago I had Plenty Treaty telephone Washington and tell our attorney, Bear Head, that we would be arriving the next day. The train was supposed to arrive in Washington the following morning at 10:00, but it did not get there until the middle of the afternoon.

As soon as we stepped off the train, a Colored chauffeur in a maroon uniform approached and asked whether I was Mr. White Calf. Plenty Treaty told him that I was, and he drove us in a big car to a place where a number of officials were waiting to have lunch with us. Bear Head was among them, and he greeted us and said, "We have been waiting for you since morning, and we are about starved. Before we do anything else, let us eat." I glanced at Plenty Treaty. He had not brought even a spare shirt, and by this time he was so disheveled that I was truly embarrassed for him. But there was no way of avoiding the situation, so we went ahead and ate lunch with the officials.

When the food was served, Bear Head turned to me and said, "Which way do you want to eat, White Man style or Indian style?"

I said, "The way you eat is up to you; as for myself, I will eat Indian style."

Then Bear Head asked the other officials in which manner they preferred to eat, and they all said that they would eat Indian style. So that is the way we ate our food, not using forks but just knives and fingers. It was a good meal, but I noticed that every once in a while some of the officials would sneak a glance at Plenty Treaty. He was really a pitiful sight.

After the meal, I told Bear Head that I would be in his office in two hours' time to talk about the claim money. Then I took Plenty Treaty out and bought him some new clothes and threw his old rags in a garbage can. Next I took him to a barbershop, and you wouldn't believe that a haircut and a new suit of clothes could make that much difference in a person's appearance! By the time he walked through the door into Bear Head's office, Plenty Treaty had become a very handsome man indeed.

From Bear Head's office, Plenty Treaty and I went to the office of John Collier, Commissioner of Indian Affairs. We were accompanied by Bear Head's son, Four Bears. [According to my best information, "Four Bears" was Mr. Joyce, the young assistant and adoptive son of Mr. Serven, or, as the Blackfoots called him, "Bear Head."]

When we arrived at Mr. Collier's office, I said, "Mr. Commissioner, I did not come here to complain about the Superintendent of the Blackfoot Reservation or about the Bureau of Indian Affairs here in Washington. I came here for the sole purpose of obtaining the claim money which is the rightful due of my people." Collier appeared very annoyed and very impatient. He said that I should turn around and go back home and that he would see to it that the money was sent to our people in due time. I said, "No! I will not go back home without that claim money in my pocket! You know as well as I that my father, who was Chief White Calf before me, died right here in Washington some time ago. [Actually, the old Chief White Calf died in Washington in 1903 in the private chambers of the President.] If necessary, I will die here too. I will stay here until my money runs out, and if I have no more money I will take an old blanket and sleep in the streets and eat garbage. But I will not leave Washington without that claim money! I will die here, if there is no other way, and if I do die here, the whole world will know that two Chief White Calfs died in Washington fighting for the rights of their people. The whole world will know that the Old Chief White Calf and his son, the New Chief White Calf, both died in Washington trying to collect the money that is the rightful property of their people." Once more I repeated it to Commissioner Collier: "Remember, my father died right here in Washington, and I will do the same. I will starve here before I will turn around like a whipped dog and go home." Then I walked out of the room.

When we got back to Bear Head's office, Bear Head asked us what had happened in the Commissioner's office, so I told him to ask his son, Four Bears. Four Bears told his father everything I had said to the Commissioner, and then he turned to me and said, "You've really got old Collier thinking now. You've really got him hanging on a nail. I'll bet he'll call you tomorrow."

The next morning between eight and nine o'clock, Collier called on the telephone and asked me to come back to his office. So Plenty Treaty and I went to Bear Head's office and from there the same three of us—Plenty Treaty, Four Bears and I—went back to Collier's office. As soon as we arrived, it was apparent that Commissioner Collier had changed his attitude; he met us at the door with a handshake, and he acted very friendly and congenial. "Well," he said, "have you changed your mind yet about going home?"

I said, "No, I have not!" Then I picked up a book that was on the top of his desk and said to him, "Listen to what I say! The White puts his laws and his treaties and his promises in a book, and then when they no longer sound good to him, he simply erases them." I picked up a pencil and marked four Xs on a piece of paper on his desk, and then with the other end of the pencil I erased the four Xs. "That is what the White Man does," I said. "He uses whichever end of the pencil happens to please him at the moment. But that is not the Indian way. The words I spoke yesterday are not on paper; they are in my mind and in my heart, and they cannot be erased away. And my words are the same today as they were yesterday."

Still apparently in a pleasant mood, the Commissioner led us from his office and showed us through a small Indian museum in the building. Then he took us back to his office, took a key from his desk drawer, and showed us into another room which contained a safe. Opening the safe, he took out a small metal box, and handing me the key he told me to open the box. I did so, finding that inside the box was a piece of blue paper—a cheque—which the Commissioner asked me to take out and hand to him. Then Commissioner Collier pointed at me with the cheque and said, "You were lucky. You got what you came for. When you go home, you will be taking the claim money back to your people."

Each of the Blackfoot Tribes represented at the Helena meeting got a share of the claim money. The Piegans had a pretty good share to begin with, but the Government held out a lot of money. They charged us for everything they had given us from the Treaty of 1855 right up to the present time. They made us pay for the gifts they had given the chiefs in the old days before I was even born, and they went so far as to charge us for the time they moved the Rocky Boys onto our land without our permission. Then the lawyers took out ten percent for their share, and we didn't have much left.

Commissioner Collier told me that there was one hundred dollars apiece for each member of our tribe, and he asked me if I wanted to take the whole amount back to the people. I told him no. I told him that I would take eighty-five dollars for each Piegan and leave the rest of the money in Washington to draw interest. Later on I tried to get the rest of this money, but by that time the Tribal Council was handling business affairs for the Tribe and the money had disappeared. Joe Brown, the mixed-blood chairman of the Council, said that the money had been used to buy horses and wagons for the old people, but I never saw the horses or wagons.

Records of transactions between the United States Government and the various American Indian tribes can at times be very difficult to obtain. Aside from word of mouth verification by the Blackfoots that the Chief did indeed go to Washington in 1935 and obtain $85.00 for each tribal member, my many attempts to obtain specific information relating to the Blackfoots' "Big Claim" earned only two pieces of evidence. The following brief and at times uncertain information is from the Social and Economic Branch, Office of Civil Archives, Washington, D.C.

The publication entitled *Report with respect to the House Resolution Authorizing the Committee on Interior and Insular Affairs to Conduct an Investigation of the Bureau of Indian Affairs* (Union Calendar No. 790, House Report No. 2503, 82nd Congress, 2nd Session, 1953) shows that on July 10, 1925 the Blackfeet, Blood and Piegan Indians filed with the United States Court of Claims, a claim for $71,338,278.10 (Docket No. E-427). This amount was claimed as the value of lands taken and as reparation for the loss of hunting and fishing rights. The claim was allowed on April 10, 1933 and a judgment of $622,-465.57 was awarded to the Indians (81 C. Cls. 101).

Although the claim was allowed in 1933 rather than 1935, this probably is the claim in which you are interested. According to the *Report* the Blackfeet had filed only one other claim. On August 9, 1951, the Blackfeet and Gros Ventres filed a claim with the Indian Claims Commission (Docket No. 279). It is possible that the judgment of $622,465.57 was not paid to the Indians until 1935. The part of the award that was actually paid to the Blackfeet is not given in the *Report*. Since the Blood and Piegan Indians are part of the Blackfoot Confederacy, the judgment may not have been broken down.

Another and more enlightening document (from an unofficial source which I shall not divulge) was an onion-skin copy of a report entitled "SUMMARY OF GRATUITIES CHARGED AGAINST 1935 JUDGMENT, BLACKFEET." The first page of this document reads as follows:

PURPOSE OF PAYMENTS	AMOUNT
1. Excess paid for purposes enumerated in Articles 9 and 10 of Treaty of 1855	$ 58,535.29
2. Gratuities from October 17, 1855 to June 30, 1873	130,616.16
3. Gratuities from July 1, 1863 to June 30, 1927	2,765,239.61
4. Gratuities from 1910 to 1915 (during period Rocky Boy's Band was attached to Agency—percentage chargeable to Blackfeet	130,530.27
5. Balance of amount expended for surveying and allotting lands on Blackfeet Reservation	73,343.47
6. Amounts expended for purpose enumerated in unratified Treaty of July 13, 1868	852,036.71
7. Education of Indian children at non-agency schools	21,854.10
Total	4,032,155.61

With regard to the above cited statistics, I feel that the following statements are in order:

With regard to sections two and three (2. and 3.), an obvious overlapping of time periods exists.

With regard to section four (4.), the "Rocky Boy's Band"—a polyglot assortment of displaced Canadian Crees, Chippewas and mixed-bloods—was allotted land on the Piegan Reservation without the consent of the Piegans; following lengthy and vehement pro-test by the Piegans, the Rocky Boys (so named after the Chippewa Chief, Rocky Boy) were removed from Piegan territory, but the United States Government charged *the Piegans* with the expense of moving the Rocky Boys onto the Reservation, surveying and al-lotting them land, issuing them commodities and other benefits, and, as if that were not bad enough, further charged the Piegans with the expense of moving the Rocky Boys *off* of Piegan land. The Rocky Boys are now located on a federal reserve south of Havre, Montana.

The second page of the document is headed, "BREAKDOWN OF GRATUITIES DEDUCTED FROM BLACKFEET SHARE OF 1935 JUDGMENT," but although the first summary deduction (1.) was specific in regard to the amount right down to the last twenty-nine cents, no further breakdown of this deduction is offered. Deduction Number Two (2.), however, is offered in greater detail, and is so enlightening as to be worth passing along.

2. Gratuities from October 17, 1855 to June 30, 1873   130,616.16

Clothing	419.00
Provisions	3,205.62
Work & Stock Animals	430.00
Feed & care of Livestock	292.50
Hardware	14.72
Fuel	518.00
Pay of Misc. Employees	280.25
Agricultural aid	210.75
Misc. Agency expenses	11,777.07
Agency Bldgs. & Repairs	1,201.80
Pay of Interpreters	3,663.52
Pay of agents	16,344.26
Presents	3,223.54
Transportation, etc. of supplies	89,034.23
	130,616.16

This breakdown is largely self-explanatory, but certain of its features should be given careful note. (1) The Piegans were charged $3,223.54 for "Presents." A present, in my book, is something you *give* to a person, not something for which you send his grandchildren a bill. (2) The total declared value of all goods supplied to the Piegans (the "Blackfeet") during this period, including clothing, provisions, work and stock animals, hardware, *and* "presents," was $7,292.88, whereas the charge to the Piegans for "Transportation, etc. of supplies" was $89,034.23—*more than ten times the value of the goods that were transported.* And brother, that is either one hell of a big transportation charge or one hell of a big "etc." (3) In view of the fact that the fuel for which the Piegans were billed was not fuel which the Indians used but fuel used by Agency employees,

I find it rather hard to swallow an additional billing of $11,777.07 for "Misc. Agency expenses."

As I read on through the additional three pages of "BREAK-DOWN OF GRATUITIES DEDUCTED FROM BLACKFEET SHARE OF 1935 JUDGMENT" it became apparent that the poor Piegans had been "Misc."ed and "Etc."ed to death. The next section ("3. Gratuities from July 1, 1868 to June 30, 1927"), which overlaps "2.," cuts the charge for "Presents" down to a mere "$567.10" but more than makes up for this oversight with other charges. In this section, a total of thirty-four separate charges against the Blackfoot share of the claim judgment are made, resulting in a loss of income to the Indians in the staggering amount of $2,765,239.61. A fair sampling of the charges in this section follows.

Fuel	34,826.79
Agency bldgs. & Repairs	99,925.39
Pay of Misc. employees	166,420.46
Misc. Agency expenses	43,822.78
Transportation, etc. of supplies	376,939.06
Indian dwellings	38.50

Four more sections follow, all pretty much the same, but perhaps the most pathetic charge of all is right here in section three (3.), which includes the period of the Starvation Year. At the bottom of one of the pages is a charge of $1,344.40 for "Burial of Indians." First the Piegans were starved to death, then they were forced to accept methods of burial which were in conflict with their religious belief, and then they were forced to pay for their own funerals. God help us!

It is now almost 11:00 P.M. We drank our bourbon during the story-telling. The Chief has gone out back to touch second base before retiring. By the time he gets back, I should have completed the typing of these few pages, and I think that by that time we will all be ready to roll in. I have reached that linguistic plateau at which, from now on, the learning of Blackfoot should be relatively easy.

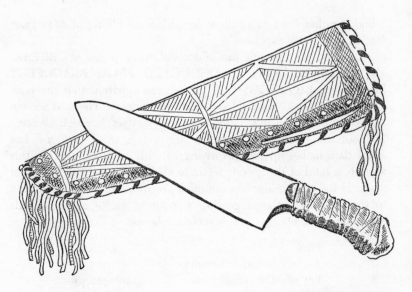

Wednesday, September 19

Slept late again. Jimmy woke me up, and when I stumbled grumpily into the kitchen the Chief was already at table, eating oatmeal. Jim had fried the rest of the kidney and liver for my benefit, but all I wanted was oatmeal and canned cherries. Jim fixed the flat on his truck and went off to help Joe Kicking-A-Woman fix his house —very neighborly, but rather impractical in view of all the fixing-up that needs to be done around here.

At ten o'clock I was in the kitchen taking a bath when the kitchen door suddenly opened and in walked Joe Morning Gun's wife, carrying in one hand a large butcher knife. She smiled and said good morning and started clearing the kitchen table, and there I was— about as inconspicuous as a lighted chandelier. Mrs. Morning Gun was not in the least embarrassed, and neither, I keep telling myself, was I. That is why, substantially abetted by a lubricating layer of wet soap suds, I suavely donned my vestments in a casual three seconds flat!

A few minutes later, Joe came in—also carrying a butcher knife— accompanied by the Chief. The three of them sat at the kitchen table and began with great industry to prepare of those delicious hindquarters of moose for drying. The meat is not cut off in slices— it would be impossible to slice it thin enough. Instead, the meat is cut off in a rather thick chunk, and the chunk is then held in the hand and scored with sort of accordion pleats so that when hung over a drying line the whole thing unfolds into one large, almost transparently thin sheet. Agnes Morning Gun is a real expert at the cutting. Before beginning, she knotted her long braids behind her neck so that they would not dangle in the meat as she bent to her work. The Chief is pretty good too, and he is cutting away very efficiently—apparently in seventh heaven. I don't recall ever having seen him quite so contented. Somehow he reminds me of those sheep dogs (no derogatory implications, certainly)—happy in the capable performance of a useful occupation. Frankly I have no special sympathy for our unhappy "senior citizens." I know plenty of older people—Cap Fowler and the Chief, for instance—that lead happy and meaningful lives, and all of these happy oldsters have one thing in common: they have developed the ability to be interested in something besides themselves. If you are miserable at 65, it is a pretty good bet that you were miserable at 45—and at 25—and for the same reason. If you spend your whole life catering solely to your own physical appetites, and if and when these appetites pall—and they are bound to—then you are left floundering in the lumpy emotional bed of your own making. And whose fault is it but your own! "They buttered their bed and they can lay on it," Ernie says. (Ernie and brother Jim really must get together sometime.)

Mrs. Morning Gun says that in the old days the smoking of meat while it was drying served a double purpose: it helped to cure the meat and it kept the flies away. This comment was apropos of the swarms of flies that have invaded the house since the arrival of the meat, especially since Jimmy has left the tripe uncovered in the pantry (perhaps to ripen?). I don't care; I just won't eat any. Jim, by the way, showed me a better way to kill flies. Instead of smacking them with a folded road map, I now snap them with a strip of innertube. It is more sporting this way, and I don't break so many things. Thus far today I have killed exactly one million. Joe M. G. said, with reference to the flies, "It don't spoil it that meat."

I certainly like the Morning Guns, but we have a serious problem in communication. My Blackfoot is pretty pidgin, and so is their English. The Blackfoot equivalent of "Gee" is "D-e-e-e," and this is the usual response of the Morning Guns to my questions and comments.

Agnes said, "Did you ever cut that dry meat next day have him over again?"

I said, "How do you cook dry meat?"

In reply, the Morning Guns laughed good-heartedly. Joe said

"Y-a-a-a-a-a," and finally Agnes added, "That old man sure can cut that dry, an' a he was young."

12:30: I just said to Joe, "Ask the old man what he wants for dinner."

Joe said, "Y-a-a-a-a, that's goin' a do it."

The old Chief is certainly enjoying himself, and doing a fine job with the meat to boot.

1:00: The drying lines across the kitchen are filled now, and the large washtub in the center of the table is nearly filled now with concertinaed pieces of meat. I have been alternately typing and doing yard chores. There are drying lines strung across the interior of the large wood shed out back, and this, no doubt, is where most of the moose meat will hang to dry.

Later: At 1:30, Mrs. Morning Gun cooked some deliciously tender moose meat for our lunch. She cooked it in a covered frying pan, with a little water. I opened a can of greens and a can of apples—delicacies for the Morning Guns. Apparently they are flat broke. I was able to understand Mrs. Morning Gun's explanation that the main source of income for them has long been the seasonal picking of fruit in Washington State. Now that they are older, they can no longer procure this kind of work. Agnes also told me that she is a first cousin of old Home Gun, and some distant kin of the Chief. She also informed me that Mary Ground is Amy White Grass' mother, that brother Jim's mother was a first cousin of Plenty Treaty B.C., and that Maggie, Plenty Treaty's wife, is the mother of Paul Many Hides. I was rescued from being related to Paul only by the fact that Paul is Maggie's son by a previous marriage.

But the greatest delicacy of the day, for the Morning Guns and for the Chief, was something that the Chief fetched to the table after we had begun to eat. It looked to me like a large white softball, but the Chief explained that it was kidney fat from the moose. Everyone was downing the kidney fat with such relish that, although it reminded me of the paraffin we used to chew as children, I finally ventured to try some. It tasted like the paraffin we used to chew as children, and, as had been the case with the paraffin, I finally had to spit it out.

The Chief and Agnes Morning Gun ate the moose meat in the old Indian fashion, holding a piece in the hand, clamping the teeth over a portion of it, and cutting the portion off close before the lips with a sharp knife. Joe, who has no teeth but is very handsome for all that, ate very fastidiously with a knife and fork.

After dinner the meat-cutting began again, and since I was not needed—or especially desired—at this endeavor, I heated a tub of water on the kitchen stove and began to wash out some clothes. Paul Many Hides came wandering in then, and immediately he dragged a chair into the middle of the kitchen floor—right in everybody's way—and seating himself in it he leaned back, crossed his legs, and gave a perfect imitation of a dog waiting for a bone.

Paul regards my washing as an idle pastime. "Yah," he said disdainfully, "I got two women down the house been washing all day." This was probably a lie because there is nothing at Paul's house to wash. It occurred to me that I had never seen Paul without his earlopper cap on. More and more, he puts me in mind of a character out of Pogo.

At three o'clock I drove into town to check the mail. None. I bought the Chief some cigars, and when finally the road was cleared of a large band of sheep I started back to the ranch.

On the way, I stopped for a brief visit with Plenty Treaty and Maggie Bear Child. Louis (P.T.) showed me a "sweat teepee" that he has built on the creek-bank—actually a small, dome-shaped lodge, about 4½' high, made of a bent-willow frame covered with hides and old blankets. A sweat lodge is a diaphoretic device—the Indian version of a steam bath, with the steam being produced by the pouring of water over hot stones. But Plenty Treaty explained its function thus: "If a fella feels distressing, is good go in there and take a tub bath—you know, really luke warm. It limbers my everything."

Maggie was making moccasins again, and when I admired her beadwork, Louis showed me his beaded pipebag. "Yah, I had that a long time ago," he said, meaning that the bag is very old.

I felt that I knew Louis well enough now to tell him about my experiences at the Indian burial house, but his reaction was very blasé and un-Indian. About my having smelled sweetgrass smoke, he said cynically, "Yah, well maybe somebody was burning that sweetgrass down below somewheres and that smoke blewed up the hill there." Louis believes that both aspirin and Bufferin are deadly poison, but he is a great fan of Oral Roberts. He swears that Oral Roberts cured him of both stomach ulcers and cancer of the stomach, and he says that he can produce two doctors who will testify both to his former condition and to his miraculous recovery. "Could a be," as brother Jim would say.

Meanwhile, back at the ranch, Jimmy had not returned, and the meat-cutting was still in progress. Agnes Morning Gun told me that one of the nails that anchor the drying lines had pulled out of the wall, draping Paul with moose meat as a Christmas tree is draped with tinsel. But Paul was still sitting there, still smack in the middle of the floor, still with his ear-lopper cap on, still looking like a dog waiting for a bone.

Jimmy came in at six o'clock, and at supper we all feasted on moose ribs, greens, bread and tea. The others ate a lot of the kidney fat, but I didn't even try. Paul, who was at the table gobbling away while the rest of us were still trying to locate enough chairs for everybody, said, "Me an' that fat is a good friends. I sure like 't." The ribs were flavorful, but not nearly so tender as the afternoon steak—possibly because the ribs were boiled.

After supper, Joe and Agnes started home. They were carrying quite a load of meat, so I volunteered to drive them in the wagon. This turned out to be a bad move, though, because the several dogs that had followed the Morning Guns to the ranch and lain around all day didn't catch on at all. They thought their masters still inside the house, and they hung around all night and howled.

After dropping off the Morning Guns, I picked up Jim and the water can and headed down the road toward the creek. Shortly we overtook Paul, traipsing down the road in the gathering dusk, a slab of moose meat chucked over one shoulder. I slowed down and pulled over to the side of the road behind Paul, and Paul was so intent upon his journey, and the evening wind had so effectively muffled the approach of the car, that I could not resist creeping up close behind Paul and blasting the horn; whereupon Paul leaped a good five feet sideways, simultaneously turning his startled face almost completely to the rear, like an owl. Poor Paul. He is the kind of guy to whom you do things like that. (In spite of everything, though, I cannot help liking the little rascal. Paul may not be equal to the more genteel aspects of social intercourse—and his incessant ululating for alms can become wearisome—but Paul is honest, and I have the feeling that he would be quite generous if ever he had anything to be generous with.) We dropped Paul at his lane, and completed our errand.

Scarcely had Jim and I returned to the ranch and unloaded the water than a station wagon full of drunks drove into the yard (drunk is *áu-wah-tsì-o*) demanding meat. The word about the moose has certainly gotten around. But the Chief has already given away nearly half of the moose to friends, and the drunks got nothing.

After supper I cleaned up my little machete and gave it to Dad, and darn if he didn't trot out and present to me his old war-path knife. The knife, a gift to the Chief from his father, is very large and heavy. The blade, which is marked, *"Village Blacksmith, Watertown, Wis.,"* is twelve inches long, two and three-quarters inches wide, and three-eighths of an inch thick. The Chief says that he

Weasel Tail in Later Life

used the knife primarily to dig fox holes when he got caught out on the open prairie, but that about fifty years ago he loaned the weapon to a man named Weasel Tail who killed a bear with it. (Weasel Tail was one of the most famous of Piegan* hunters, and I own an old photograph of him. The photo bears a striking resemblance to Maggie Bear Child, and upon inquiry I learned that Weasel Tail was, indeed, Maggie's father.) According to the story, Weasel Tail was charged by a grizzly, and he struck the bear in the mouth with the knife, knocking out some of its teeth and killing it "right now," as Jim says. I fully believe it, the knife being that formidable.

The bear-killing incident reminded the Chief of the time that Mad Wolf, a devil-may-care warrior, had killed a bear with a knife just for the hell of it, and this led the Chief into telling me some great stories of horse-stealing efforts against the Flatheads and Kootenai in the old days.

* Weasel Tail was born a Blood, but while still a very young man he took up permanent residence among the South Piegans.

MAD WOLF, THE FEARLESS

Mad Wolf was the sort of chap that would do *anything*. He was immensely brave, but he was such a hell-raiser that you never knew what he was liable to do next. He would do such things as jumping astride of a sleeping horse, or leaping off a bluff into a deep snowdrift. Once, when he discovered some buffalo bedded down in a deep drift beneath a bank, he slid down the bank, landed on top of a young bull, and stabbed the animal to death with his knife. Another time, when he and his partner, Dusty Bull, were stealing horses from the Gros Ventres, Mad Wolf did something that would have cured me of being his partner for good: Mad Wolf had already rounded up the horses he wanted, and when Dusty Bull was cutting loose a horse tied to a lodge [especially valuable horses were sometimes tethered with a rope that was passed through the door of the owner's lodge and fastened to a lodgepole], Mad Wolf called out in Gros Ventre, "Hey, in there! Somebody is cutting loose your horse!" Dusty Bull and Mad Wolf had quite a time getting out of that one.

On the war party I am going to tell you about, Mad Wolf was the leader. This was also the first war party of which Yellow Wolf was a member—you remember Yellow Wolf, the man who visited the Sand Hills. The party left from right here, and crossed the mountains into Flathead territory. As we were heading down the western slope of the mountains, we spotted a young bear coming up the trail toward us. Mad Wolf said, "I wonder what that bear would do if he found me lying in the middle of the trail," and while the rest of us hid in the brush, Mad Wolf stripped down to his breech clout and moccasins and lay down in the middle of the trail with his knife in his hand. Mad Wolf lay very still, and the bear almost stepped on him before realizing that he was there. The bear jumped back, but Mad Wolf continued to lie perfectly still and in a short while the bear came up and began to sniff of him. At length the bear began gingerly to paw at Mad Wolf, and at this point Mad Wolf suddenly plunged his knife into the bear's underside and ripped the animal open. The bear fled back down the trail, its innards dragging along outside its body. But the bear did not suffer for very long; Mad Wolf soon overtook it and finished it off with his knife.

When we came down out of the mountains we were in Flathead territory, but Mad Wolf did not attempt to screen our approach by staying in the woods or sticking to the shelter of coulees or creek bottoms. He led us right across the open flat, and the first thing we knew we ran smack into a Flathead camp.

We were in a small valley, with steep cliffs on one side [probably the Swan River Valley], and as soon as we knew that the Flatheads had spotted us we made it to the base of the cliff and started digging a trench. Since we were unmounted and could not escape, the Flatheads were in no hurry to attack us. Leaving a loose semicircle of guards to keep an eye on us, most of them went back to the camp to prepare for the battle. One of the Flatheads who could speak our language called out, "As soon as we finish praying with our war bundles we will charge you and kill you all."

Mad Wolf shouted back, "I hope the Flatheads will die as bravely as they speak." By this time we had finished our trench and were lying on the ground in front of it, waiting for something to happen.

Finally the Flatheads mounted a charge, and all of us except Mad Wolf jumped into the trench. Mad Wolf stood right up in the open, firing his rifle as calmly as if he were doing target practice. He was the only one shooting, but each time he fired he knocked down a Flathead, and the Flathead charge was broken before it carried anywhere near our trench. Mad Wolf was completely untouched by the enemy. He turned to us and said, "Why don't you boys give me your weapons. You aren't using them, and I will need them. When the Flatheads charge again, I will make a clean sweep of them."

But the Flatheads had no intention of losing more men in an open charge. Leaving just three men—one on each side and one in front—to keep an eye on us, they went back to their camp and devised a pretty clever scheme of attack. Taking down their lodges they tied all the lodge poles in a bundle, wrapped the lodge covers around the outside, and rolling this mobile fortalice ahead of them they advanced once again upon our position, shooting as they came.

We jumped back into our trench and returned the fire, but from down where we were we couldn't see anything except that big roll of poles and lodge covers coming toward us. Mad Wolf, on the other hand, was standing as before, right up in front of the trench, and from that position he had a good shot at whatever Flathead straightened up to shoot over the barricade. He knocked over a couple more of them, and they stopped moving toward us. One of them called out in our language, "You have killed several of us, and we can't even hit you. Who are you, anyway?"

Mad Wolf called out, "I am Sái-yeh [Mad Wolf]."

The Flathead said, "Mad Wolf's medicine is very strong. Mad Wolf is our friend. If Mad Wolf will allow us to gather together our things, we will leave this place."

Mad Wolf said, "You have not seen the power of my medicine yet. You said that you were going to kill all of us, and now I say that as soon as I sing one medicine song I am going to charge and kill every one of you." To show he meant business, he put a bullet into a Flathead who lay wounded beyond the fortalice.

At this the Flatheads broke into a complete panic and fled the field and the camp without taking anything except the horses they ran away on. We helped them on their way by charging out of our trench and firing at them as they retreated.

Mad Wolf said, "Come on boys, I'll give you some new moccasins." [This meant that the enemy had been routed so completely that they had left all their belongings behind, including their lodges; the top portions of the lodge covers, which had been rendered waterproof by constant exposure to the smoke rising from the fire in the center of the lodge, were prized as material for making moccasins and raincapes.] We took all the loot we could carry, and the rest we destroyed. We even broke up the lodge poles.

WILD HORSE ISLAND

When the White people began to settle in the Flathead Valley, they discovered that a good-sized island near the southwestern end of Flathead Lake, about a mile from the south shore, had horses on it. The Whites named this island, "Wild Horse Island," but the horses that they found on the island were not really wild. The horses had been put there by the Kootenai Indians. Early in the spring, while the ice was still strong, the Kootenai would drive their best horses out to this island. They did this because they knew that as soon as the passes were clear, the Blackfoots would be coming across the mountains to see how many horses they could capture.

On the war party I am going to tell you about, there were eight of us. The leader was a Piegan named Strong. The others besides myself were, Eagle Head, White Antelope [this was Jim's translation; a more accurate rendition would be, "Cream-colored Antelope"], Elk Chief, Calf Robe, Taking-Fine-Gun [also called Good Gun] and one other. It is strange that I cannot remember the name of the other man, for he was one of the two members of our party that were killed by the Kootenai. But I am getting ahead of my story.

It was in the early summer. We crossed the mountains on a trail that ran down through where Kalispell is today [Kootenai Pass], and when we spotted some horses on the big island in Flathead Lake, we built a raft. [When describing the building of the raft, the Chief used the phrase, *Iks-ík-tukes-i-mish-tí-au-wax*. This describes the action of several men building a raft by laying several logs parallel to one another and fastening them together, but both Jim and I had trouble in translating the phrase because in contemporary Blackfoot the pronunciation of it would be quite different; today it would be, *I-ti-kún-a-aks-tush-tí-au*.] At first we pushed the raft along with long poles, but presently we could no longer touch bottom with the poles and so had to paddle.

There were six of us on the raft—we had left two men on shore to guard our weapons and other belongings—and when we finally reached the island we set about capturing the horses we wanted. The difficult part was to catch the first horse,

283

and when we finally roped him we used him in catching the others.

We started back with the raft, swimming the horses behind us on the ends of ropes. I don't know exactly how far the island is from the shore, but it must be around a mile or more. At any rate, the water was cold and a lot of the horses got tired and drowned before we got them to dry land. One fellow had fashioned a rope halter for a horse and was trying to hold the tired horse's head above water, but as we neared shore the horse played out and in final panic closed its teeth on the man's hand. We freed the man's hand by prying the horse's jaws open with the elk-antler handle of a riding whip, whereupon the horse drowned. We managed to bring only four horses safely to the mainland.

Upon returning to shore, we discovered that our blankets and weapons and supplies were undisturbed where we had cached them but that the two men we had left on guard were missing. Deciding that the two men had gone on ahead, we started back, but before long we found one of the men lying dead, killed by enemies. This was the fellow whose name I cannot remember. We began a search for the other fellow, Taking-Fine-Gun, and pretty soon we heard someone moaning in a patch of brush and discovered that it was Taking-Fine-Gun. He had been shot through the jaw, but with signs he told us that he had stolen a brown horse from the Kootenai and that he had the animal picketed in some brush nearby.

We found the brown horse and placed the wounded Taking-Fine-Gun on it and started for home. We decided to go back by way of Cut Bank Trail, traveling slowly out of regard for the wounded man. At first Taking-Fine-Gun could take no nourishment except water, but after a couple of days he was able to ingest some soup that we had prepared for him by boiling the blood of a deer.

When we reached the eastern side of the mountains, at a place where we had built a sweat lodge some time before, Taking-Fine-Gun signed that he did not wish to go on with us but that he preferred to wait here until his father, Iron Coat, should come to take him home. We attempted to convince him that he had better go on with us, but we could not, so finally we covered the frame of the old sweat lodge with brush to give him shelter, and went on home.

We got home all right, and Elk Chief went back with Iron

Coat to show him where his son was. Just as they arrived, a "real bear" [a grizzly] was coming out of the shelter. The bear had killed Taking-Fine-Gun, and Iron Coat killed the grizzly in revenge for his son's death. Iron Coat said that Elk Chief could have the horse that Taking-Fine-Gun had captured.

When the two men returned and told of the death of Taking-Fine-Gun, Calf Robe said to Iron Coat, "I am sorry that your son is dead, but he should have stayed with the rest of our party. If he had done so, he would be alive right now."

Eagle Head said, "Calf Robe is right. We did our best to care for your boy. We did not want to go off and leave him, but he refused to come with us. It was not our fault that he was killed."

The three men who cared for Taking-Fine-Gun on the way home from the Kootenai country were Elk Chief, Eagle Head, and Calf Robe. All three of them lived to be old men, and it was not until recent years that they passed away. Calf Robe [O-nis-tái-yay] also went by the name of Home Gun [Ách-yah-pin-nah]; he was the father of Pete and Dan Home Gun, and also of Jim and Paul Home Gun, now deceased.

Although in telling the next two stories, "The Kootenai Ambush that Backfired" and "Bob-tailed Horse 'Guesses' a Kootenai," the Chief employed the pronoun "we," the Chief himself did not participate in these adventures; he used "we" merely to refer to "the Piegans." The employment of the first person plural nominative pronoun when relating an historical event involving one's tribe is a device commonly used by the Plains Indian, and this fact may explain why so many of our junior anthropologists keep turning up junior-age "veterans" of intertribal wars.

THE KOOTENAI AMBUSH THAT BACKFIRED

Knife,* Iron Coat, Turned-Up-Hat, and Mad Wolf were the leaders of a war party that started from right here on Cut Bank Creek and crossed the mountains to where Kalispell is today, on a trail where Cut Bank Chalet was later built, in order to steal some horses from the Flatheads.

We located a Flathead camp and took some horses, and as we were returning home, heading down the eastern slope of the mountains toward the Creek here, we found two dead Blackfoot men. The men had been killed just recently, and Iron Coat and Turned-Up-Hat became quite frightened. Turned-Up-Hat

* Knife, who was also known as Looks-Like-A-Bear, Onistáipokah, and several dozen other things, was the Chief's paternal grandfather. He was the owner of one of the very rare Blackfoot "bear knives."

said, "We had better leave the horses here and take to the timber. This is the only trail we can take, and if we try to get the horses through we will be ambushed for sure."

Mad Wolf spoke up then and said, "No! These horses belong to us. We stole these horses fair and square, and we will not give them up. We will wait until the old-timer [Knife] catches up. He knows this trail as he knows the palm of his hand, and he will know what to do."

When Knife caught up, he said, "Just around the next bend is a fall of dead timber. If there is an ambush waiting for us, it will probably be there. Mad Wolf and Iron Coat will cut through the timber and come up behind the fallen trees to see whether there is anybody lying in wait for us there. We will give them a head-start, and then we will move slowly up the trail. But first let us picket the horses here for the time being."

Mad Wolf and Iron Coat sneaked through the brush around behind the timber fall, and they found two Kootenai men lying there with their rifles pointed up the trail. The two Piegans were able to get within fifty feet of the Kootenai men, and then they both fired together.

When Mad Wolf and Iron Coat fired, one Kootenai fell dead and the other fell badly wounded—and then all hell broke loose. Some other Kootenai warriors, apparently convinced that they were surrounded, broke from their hiding places in the trees; some Kootenai women, hidden in the brush, began to wail; and the rest of us Piegans, with old Knife in the lead, made a screaming charge down the trail at the sound of the guns.

Knife ran up to the wounded Kootenai, took his gun from him to count coup, and then stabbed him to death with his knife. Meanwhile, we were chasing the rest of the Kootenai. We killed a few more of them, but most of them escaped into the brush. We captured some women, but we gave them to the Sun. [They released the prisoners as an offering to the Sun, praying that at some future time the Sun would be as merciful to the Piegans as the Piegans had been to their prisoners.]

BOB-TAILED HORSE "GUESSES" A KOOTENAI

A war party led by Bob-tailed Horse started from right here on Cut Bank Creek and crossed the mountains to the west to raid against the Kootenai. Near Saint Ignatius we found a Kootenai camp, and we hid out until after dark, at which time we had planned to steal some horses.

Darkness came, but instead of everybody going to sleep, some of the men gathered inside a lodge and began to play the stick game, also called "hand game." We waited for quite a while, but the stick game continued late into the night because one of the players was so clever that nobody could "guess him" [i.e., they could not determine in which hand he held the unmarked or "guess" bone]. The longer the game continued, the more angry Bob-tailed Horse became. Finally he said, "I'll guess him!" and walking up to the teepee he stepped inside and shot the man right through the head. Then he stepped outside and began calmly to reload his gun.

Not a single Kootenai man came out of the teepee; I guess they were too scared. The rest of the camp panicked and made for the brush, and we took all the horses and got away clean.

I attempted to lead the Chief into reciting some adventures in which he, himself, had played a more central role, but I did not have very good luck. The Chief definitely resents being prompted in his story-telling in any way, and although he obliged me with two tales, both were tearfully disappointing in their brevity.

Eagle Ribs, Tripod and myself left from Old Agency on foot. It took us twenty days to get to Medicine Hat, where we stole some horses from the Crees. I took a mouse-colored horse with one glass eye. When we got back home, I gave the horse to Yellow Plume, who had married my sister, Lonely Woman.

Five of us—Brave Rock, Long-tongue Bird, Buffalo Berries, Morning Howler and myself—started from Belly River in Canada. In five nights we got to Round Brush, where we stole nineteen head of horses from the Crees. On the way back we took a shortcut and made it in three days. I took the pick of the horses, and the finest of all—a buckskin—I gave to my father. I also gave a horse to my sister, and one each to two girls, Pretty Owl and Isabelle.

At ten-thirty, just as we were all going to bed, the Home Gun girls knocked on the door and said they wanted a ride home. I guess I am as bad as the Chief, because I got dressed and took them home. And I was so awakened by the night air, and so angry with myself for having catered to their damned arrogant whim (they were afraid of range cattle, they said) that I stayed awake most of the night. "Maybe they was looking for some meat, too," Jim said. And he laughed.

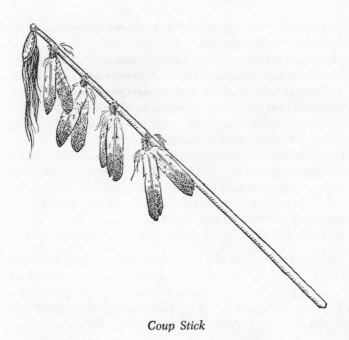

Coup Stick

Thursday, September 20

(*Ni*)*táh-kau-tote*(*eh*) means, "I am going to build a fire." Jim said it, and I said, "*So-káh-pi*," and after the fire was built, Jim cooked breakfast.

But I dined largely on erudition. I am still working on the word *sixty-sou* (*sík-sti-su* would be better, I think), and at the morning meal I raked Jim and the Chief over various syntactic, semantic and paradigmatic coals in an effort to determine exactly what the word really means. It means "moose," of course, but in literal translation it would be "black" something-or-other. *Sik* means "black" (although it can also be used to suggest "night"), but the closest I can come to a translation of the remainder of the word (-*sti-sú*) is, "heading for the center of the place where all the people are."

Jim says that his nearest approach to an English translation of *sík-sti-su* would be, "Black-going-to-town." Agnes Morning Gun, whose pronunciation of the word is different from Jim's (she sounds it as *sik-sti-sú-eh*), interprets *sik* as an adjective instead of a noun, and she does not believe that such syntactic elements as verb, preposition or object are present or implied within the phrase at issue; her translation is simply, "Black town."

On the third hand—and all linguists seem to have at least three, plus several thumbs—Mary Ground believes that the best translation of *sík-sti-su* would be "Black (or Night) Walker," or "Black (or Night) Trotter." Mary recognizes the "going-to-town" element, and her suggestion is that its use in Blackfoot is figurative in the same sense that the phrase is used in English to denote great industry or speed. Blackfoot is affluent with metaphors and other figures of speech, and the language is so highly developed structurally that the most subtle connotation—the faintest difference in shade of meaning—can be made known, but there are a dozen separate linguistic reasons for my thinking that on this latter point—the "going-to-town" part—Mary's deduction represents the product of a sincere but naïvely conceived effort at logical analogy.

Of course I am not being critical of Mary or of any of my other informants; none of them would recognize a grammatical term or a linguistic symbol if it snapped at their ankles, and they cannot be expected to. The ability to speak and understand a language does not imply the ability to conduct a descriptive analysis of that language, and a Blackfoot Indian cannot be expected to discuss bound morphemes with any more authority than that with which the average Spaniard (or American, or what-have-you) is able to expound upon the optative use of the subjunctive. Granted that this fact may somewhat roughen the linguist's road, it also gives him a reason for being.

It is now 9:45 A.M. and the Morning Guns have been here for a little over an hour, helping Dad cut the rest of the meat for drying. The wind is from the north this morning, and it is much colder. I like it this way. I curse the wind when it blows, and I pine for it when it does not blow—that is the Swede in me, I guess. We have a fire going in the living-room stove (*Ni-káu-tote:* I built a fire). I have unlimbered the typewriter. Finally did locate my ballpoint pen, though, and Jim responded with, "Hey, you found your writing-stick again!" Right after breakfast, Jim and Joe Kicking-A-Woman went off to haul in some toothpicks; they are going to split the wood 50/50. Breakfast was moose steaks, oatmeal and coffee.

Night: Jim was back for lunch. We had boiled moose ribs again, but the gastronomic monotony was relieved (I don't think!) by Jim's munificent insistence that Agnes also serve boiled potatoes, store-bought potato bread, and "kitney fat" ("an' so force").

After lunch the Chief re-braided his hair into two plaits, and at 12:30 he and Jimmy wheeled into town to participate in some mysterious and undoubtedly crafty political conspiracy. The Morning

Guns departed at the same time, and since the house was both empty and warm—an unaccustomed combo—I should indeed have been both lax and addlepated had I not treated myself to a thorough bath. The wind continued moderate but steady from the north. Range horses kept drifting down from the hills, and by mid-afternoon I could count well over one hundred. This means a norther, I think.

Drove to town at 4:00. Letter from Margaret, such as it was. M is of that peculiar school of female logic (although the school is co-educational) which holds that it is just fine for a man to want to write but that there is something vaguely odd about his wanting to go out and find something to write *about*. Her comments caused me to think of that pithy bit of verse—I think it is by Wissler—which states:

> Traveling light, to a woman,
> Is a carefully worked out plan
> Whereby all bags and packages
> Are carried by a man.

So far as I am concerned, if anyone wishes to delude himself into believing that security consists of something you hide under the mattress so that nobody will filch it from you, that is his privilege. But for myself I reserve the right to believe that the only true security consists in your ability to adjust to whatever circumstances may develop, and that the real rewards of life are not to be found in, as the saying goes, accumulating piles to sit on, but in facing the zesty challenge of living without preconceptions and in playing each hand as it is dealt. What else is it all about! And if my adherence to this philosophy suggests that I am, as Jimmy phrases it, "a more of Indian than pretty many born-heres," I am proud of it. (And while we're on the subject: if a chap is to be branded with a "Hemingway complex" simply because he wants to get out and breathe some fresh air once in a while, I think it only fair that an equivalent label be attached to the pasty faces that never go anywhere—or create anything—because they are orally anchored to a cigarette or/and a bottle of hooch as though it were the nipple of some huge unseen breast which, if they should ever once let go, will be snatched irretrievably away. I would like to know what you call these guys, because it is to them that I will dedicate my first novel about a man who sells his soul for a guaranteed annual wage—or a guaranteed female in his sack.)

On the way to town I stopped, as promised, to pick up Maggie and Louis Bear Child, but they had already hitched a ride with someone else. I went on into Browning, killed a few rats,* and came right back to the ranch.

Nobody home yet, so I walked along the creek down to Paul's. Paul was not there—he is *always* going someplace—but I chatted briefly with the young chap who lives next door to him. This fellow is either a Many Hides or a Many Hides in-law—I never did learn which—and he is the one who made that silly remark about shaving lotion on the occasion of my wild midnight ride (The Midnight Ride of Paul Many Hides) to the home of Phillip Many Hides. At the time, I had considered this young man to be pretty much of an ass, but today I decided that he is not an ass at all—he is just scared. He has a wife and young child, and during our conversation he explained that an Indian who does not own his own land is pretty much a beggar. The Reservation was originally allotted to the Piegans as a group, but in 1912 fixed portions of the Reservation land were allocated to the Piegans as individuals. In 1918, the issuance of patents-in-fee permitted the individual Indian to sell or otherwise dispose of his personal land holdings, and when two succeeding years of drought were followed by a winter so severe that most Piegan livestock froze to death (sometimes it appears that even Mother Nature herself was against the Indian) many Piegans, out of the simple need to survive, were forced to sell their land for a fraction of its true value. And as if this weren't bad enough, unscrupulous Whites, with the connivance of equally unscrupulous officials of the Indian Service, flatly *stole* from the Piegans whatever choice properties they could not otherwise come into possession of: fee patents were issued to many Piegans without either their consent or their knowledge—in one famous case, a patent-in-fee was forced upon a poor soul who was not only partially paralyzed and suffering from tuberculosis but who had previously been by law adjudged an imbecile—and the lands were then foreclosed as payment for petty merchandise which the Indians had thought to be gifts from the local mercantile company. This land-grabbing deal was one of the most scandalous the West has ever known—within a decade, well over 200,000 acres of the very finest land on the Reservation became the property of Whites—and the true nature of the situation is pretty well made clear by the record of the administration of Blackfoot Indian affairs in the United States during that period. Between the years 1910 and 1921, seven different men acted the role of Superin-

---

* i.e., attended to some petty obligations.

tendent of the Blackfoot Reservation: three of these men were dismissed from the Indian Service completely; one was later sent to a federal penitentiary; and yet another fled from Browning in order to avoid indictment. I certainly do not hold with such utter nonsense as giving portions of the United States "back to the Indians" (the various American Indian nations took land from one another just as forcefully as the United States Government later took it away from the Indian, and it would be impossible to determine rightly to whom the land should be returned), and no person capable of rational thought would suggest a literal adherence to ancient treaties which were ridiculous in their inception (if certain West Coast Indians, equipped as they are with the White Man's modern implements, were to be allowed unrestrictedly to fish "wherever their ancestors fished," the Steelhead salmon would soon go the way of the buffalo). But I do believe that any American Indian who was in any way deprived of his private land holdings between the time of the issuance of the first patents-in-fee and the adoption of the Indian Reorganization Act of 1934—the Act provided against further defraudation—should be granted under law the prerogative of regaining ownership of the land upon payment to the present owner of the exact amount for which the land was sold, or for the specific amount of the obligations upon which the land was foreclosed. In the event that the original owner should now be deceased, said prerogative should accrue to the legal heirs, or, no heirs existing, to the Tribe. (P.S. It'll never happen.)

Although many Piegans bid farewell to their lands with a whiskey kiss, all this land-grabbing by Whites took place before it was legal for Indians to either purchase or consume liquor. It was equally illegal, of course, for anyone to sell or trade the stuff to an Indian, and Jimmy has revealed that the Chief threw one of the superintendents bodily across the Reservation line for peddling booze. And the Chief is just the man that could do it! Even today, at the age of 105, he has a 47" chest and a hand that could crush mine. The old fellow's strength is really fantastic, and he defeats both Jim and me in arm-wrestling without any apparent effort. God, when I think that the Chief was a full-grown warrior of nineteen when Custer got clobbered! No wonder I feel reverential in his presence.

Something I could not at first understand was why the Chief, with his magnificent personality, had for many years been an "Indian Police." The Tribal Police, as they are now called, constitute not so much a police *force* as a police *farce*, and the ones that I have met are either of the Keystone Kop variety or else, as a local resident described them, "A bunch of young drunks and wife-beaters." In Browning the cops do not have any police training and the magistrates do not have any legal or judicial training, and the whole law enforcement situation is really pretty sad. But Jim explained to me that this had not always been the case. He explained that the Chief's old warrior society, the Crazy Dogs—a very highly honored society to which one had to be elected—had not only been extremely fierce in battle but had functioned among their own people as camp police, attending to those various disciplines necessary to the maintenance of a neat and orderly encampment. The Chief's position of Captain of Indian Police was a logical extension of his authority as head of the Crazy Dogs, and Jim assures me that when his dad was in office the Indian Police were a functional and respected group. Jim says that the Chief was not afraid of any living man, Red, White, Black or Yellow, and that he slapped troublemakers in the pokey with complete disregard for their color, social standing or political influence. This, of course, did not sit very well with the Whites and "high-breeds" who, like the pigs in *Animal Farm*, considered themselves to be "more equal." And since the Chief was one of the original "untouchables"—you couldn't kill him, scare him, or buy him off—he was eventually forced from office.

Interestingly enough, though, the Crazy Dog Clan is still in existence, and it still functions. The Piegans are not often inclined to present their grievances before the local courts—and who can blame them!—but the Crazy Dogs have been known to call upon a thieving neighbor or an improvident husband and to employ their own persuasions toward reformation.

When Dad and Jim got home this evening, shortly after six, Jim informed me (with ill-concealed I-told-you-so) that one of the Tribal Council members is in jail "for drunk." ("He was pick up with drunk driving.") Jim had bought pork and beans, sweet rolls, white bread, Bull Durham and cigars. I have learned to anticipate Jim's contributions, and I had countered them by purchasing canned vegetables, blackberries, cherries, applesauce, fresh grapes, pipe tobacco and a new pipe for the Chief (on "Special" at Buttrey's).

At supper we gave the moose a rest and ate eggs, pork and beans, canned mixed vegetables, bread, and coffee tea or milk. Coffee is *Áh-siks-eh-kim-meh*, but tonight, while requesting a second cup, Jim used the term, *Óch-koh-tóke*, and this launched us into a noun vocabulary session which lasted all during the meal and for about an hour thereafter. The phrase, *óch-koh-tóke*, literally means, "like a rock," and Jim explained that the Canadian Blackfoots commonly employ it as a noun to refer to very strong coffee. After some effort I was able to establish that this metaphor, which has changed in both form and meaning, had its origin about one hundred years ago, when the Blackfoots first received treaty payments from the Federal Government. The treaty payments were made in the form of various implements, goods and foodstuffs; coffee, which was issued to the Indians in the form of unground beans (and which the Indians long considered a useless commodity) was referred to by the Blackfoots as "like little rocks."

While Jimmy and I discussed Blackfoot nouns, the Chief was occupied with other concerns, and after supper he sat in his chair with his eyes closed, gesturing oratorically with both hands—his way of talking to himself. My way is to come right out and talk to myself, which attracted some invidious comments from college roommates but which also assisted me in earning straight A's in language courses. Once a little Alpha Phi came trotting up to me after class and said, "What is your secret for learning languages so well? You *must* have a secret." I told her that there was no secret about it but that she could undoubtedly develop a better feeling for a language, and certainly improve her pronunciation, if she would spend a few odd minutes each day holding conversation with herself in the language in question. She said, "Oh, I couldn't do *that*—people would think I was *crazy* [a rollercoaster inflection on the *a*]." So I asked her whether she would rather be considered crazy and get an A or be considered rah-rah normal and flunk, and she said normal and flunk—and she did.

I fully believe that the Chief has the native intelligence to make *Phi Beta Kappa* at any university (although, since scholastic honors are awarded not for intelligence or achievement but for lucubration and conformity, the Chief would probably have ended up with a B average like the rest of us), and I was aware that in his mood of silent contemplation he was clarifying in his own mind some issue of importance. Many elderly persons are so bound up in the past that they cannot function in contemporary situations, but not so the Chief. He is a remarkably perspicacious (and perspicuous) individual, and he is fully and intelligently aware of the problems with which the Blackfoot Indian of today must deal—and he is aware that these problems must be resolved on a long-term basis.

The United States Government no longer recognizes the authority of any American Indian chief to represent his people in situations political or otherwise—ninety-nine percent of the present day Indians who call themselves "chief" have no more claim to chieftainship than

I have—but my Indian dad is a true chief from any point of view: he is Head Chief of the Piegans by virtue of both inheritance from and specific appointment by his father, old Onistáipokah (whose political authority *was* honored by the Government); he is a war chief by way of having actually led war parties against tribes hostile to his own nation; and he is a civil chief in that the Piegan full-bloods have allowed him to retain both the authority and the responsibility of representing them in matters relating to their welfare. The Chief is especially concerned about the future of the full-bloods (who now constitute a small minority on the Piegan Reservation), and he is currently preoccupied with the chore of appointing delegates to represent the full-bloods at some sort of intertribal conclave down at Billings. Here is a man who is not only living in the present, still fighting for the rights of his people, but who is so politically and socially far-sighted that he has already made plans to turn his chieftainship over to his son, Jim, so that Jim can carry on the good fight when the Old-timer is no longer able.

Jim and I concluded our linguistic discussion, and after a respectful while Jim went over and placed his hand on the old fellow's shoulder. Without opening his eyes, the Chief said, "*T'káh* [Who is that]," and when Jimmy reminded him that he had some letters to dictate, the Chief said that Jim was quite right and that he was grateful for having been reminded.

Jimmy said to me, "I did had some writing [paper] somewhere. Do you have, or not some?" So I provided some paper and the Chief dictated two letters to Jim. I shall type them up in the morning.

While the Chief dictated, I attacked my typewriter long enough to bring my journal up to the minute. Then, when the Chief was finished, he asked me to turn on my recorder. I did, and he told me the two stories that I have been most anxious to hear—the story behind the bullet wound in his left arm, and the story of his last and most famous war party.

The leaders of this war party were Tripod and Star Chief. We started from Belly River, in Canada, and since we were all mounted on good horses we made excellent time down to the Crow country. Our main rest stops were west of Great Falls and near Big Timber, west of Saw Mill [Billings]. Below Big Timber we stole a number of Crow horses and made a clean getaway.

We headed straight north and traveled without incident until we entered the Bear Paw Mountains. There we were attacked by a large party of Canadian Sioux—the ones that are now mixed in with the Gros Ventres over at Fort Belknap. [This would mean that the Chief's party was attacked by Assiniboines.]

At the time the battle began, I was functioning as rear scout for our party; it was my job to make certain that no enemy attacked us from the rear. The Bear Paw Mountains are very rugged country, presenting any number of opportunities for ambush, and that is exactly what happened to our party—an ambush.

When I heard the sound of gunfire I immediately galloped ahead and discovered that our party was pinned down at the base of a bluff. I was riding a brown horse, and by jumping the animal across a deep wash I was able to gain the top of a steep bluff on the enemy flank. I couldn't get a shot from up there —the terrain was venulous with coulees and washes and dry creekbeds—so I left my horse in the shelter of the bluff and made my way to the bottom. From there I was able to see the enemy, and I began to fire at them as rapidly as I could reload the old single-shot flintlock musket I was using. Unfortunately my weapon was not very accurate, and I do not believe that I killed any of the enemy; however, I did succeed in diverting the enemy fire away from the rest of our party, and during the first few minutes of my participation in the fight—during which time the enemy had not as yet determined that I was a single warrior and so were scrambling to find positions of greater safety—the rest of my party succeeded in making their escape. This meant that I was the only one still fighting, and when the enemy found this out they really let me have it. Almost immediately, then, I was shot clean through the left forearm.

By holding my musket under my left arm, I was able to load it and get off one more shot, but when I discovered that I was the only Blackfoot still fighting I pulled out and started back up to the top of the bluff where my horse was. The bone of my left arm was broken, my hand and wrist dangling as limp as a dead snake, and I moved on up the bluff with my rifle held in my right hand and the thumb of my left hand clamped between my teeth. I kept slipping and falling, and I could hear the bullets striking all around me, but the only way I could dodge was to move my head from side to side. But I made it safely up to where my horse was, and by leading my horse to the edge of a bank I was able to mount and still hold onto my gun.

All of our party had gotten safely away [the Chief did not say whether the party managed to hang onto the horses they had stolen from the Crows, or whether they were left behind], and when I caught up with them they doctored my wound. The bullet had passed entirely through my arm, so there was no problem there, and the fellows cleaned up my arm, applied a poultice made by chewing the roots of a beargrass plant, and fashioned some splints from pieces of wood.

It took us quite some time to get back to Belly River, and it was a long time before I finally regained full use of my arm. But regain full use of my arm I did, although, as you can see, my arm since that time has always been a little bit crooked. If I had gone to a White doctor, I probably would have lost my arm entirely. [Considering the penchant of surgeons of this period to amputate even the most superficially damaged limb, the Chief's final comment was not made without justification.]

The Chief's next story, a firsthand account of the final spilling of blood between the Blackfoot Nation and its traditional Indian ene-

mies to the south, represents not only the most authentically detailed narration of a Plains Indian war party ever recorded but an invaluable portrait of the desperate and somehow pathetic last days of a culture which had already heard the tolling of the knell. This verbal portrait is not entirely a pretty one—certainly not one to gratify the preconceptions of the romantic—for the Chief, as always, painted with a brush of complete and uncompromising honesty. The Old-timer spared neither himself nor anyone else in presenting the unvarnished facts, and the confident exactitude of his recall is a thing to be marveled at. The color of each horse, the clothing worn by his own party and by the enemy, the exact place a bullet from his gun struck an antelope: all this and much more he was able to tell me.

The war party here described is well known to history, and it bespeaks the uncommon modesty of the Chief that, until my first acquaintance with him in 1958, it had been believed that the last survivor of this adventure, a Blood Indian named Crazy Crow, had passed away twenty years before. The Chief's first mention of his participation in this historically important event was very casual, and it was not until now that I was able to induce him to relate the actualities of the Last Scalp Dance in any detail. But it has now been established beyond any possible doubt that the Chief himself is the final survivor of the affair, and listening to the old fellow recite the details of the last important Plains Indian war party, exactly as he had lived them, was to me every bit as thrilling as though Custer had suddenly popped from the shadows and asked me if I would like to know what really happened at the Battle of the Little Big Horn.

The famous war party itself, which occupied a time of nearly one month and involved a round trip by the participants of more than one thousand miles, took place in the spring of 1889, but the events which eventually prompted the raid began more than two years previous to that date.*

During the first few years following their shared tragedy of the near extinction of the buffalo, the Indian tribes of the Northern Plains lived in a situation of restless peace. Then one day in September of 1886, on the Blood Reserve just across the International Boundary in Canada, suddenly the peace was shattered. Ten horses

---

* For his gentlemanly assistance in verifying the historicity of the Chief's last war party, and for many other kind favors, I am very grateful to Hugh A. Dempsey, archivist of the Glenbow Foundation of Calgary, Alberta, Canada and editor of the *Alberta Historical Review*.

were stolen from a Blood named White Elk, and White Elk, who suspected (and correctly so) that the horses had been run off by a party of Gros Ventres from the United States, demanded of Blood Agent William Pocklington that he be allowed to lead a retaliatory raid across the "Medicine Line."

When White Elk persisted in his demand, Agent Pocklington at length issued passes to five Bloods and one North Blackfoot to travel to Fort Assiniboine, Montana Territory, in order to petition through proper authorities for the return of White Elk's stolen property. The delegation of Indians never completed their journey. A few weeks after their departure, in a hastily dug trench near the Sweetgrass Hills, a Blood named Big Wolf discovered the scalped and mutilated bodies of all six men.

At first the killers of the six Blackfoots were unknown: one rumor blamed the slaughter on White ranchers; another attributed it to American Cavalrymen who had caught the Indians killing cattle. But when word was received that Gros Ventres had performed a scalp dance within sight of the American soldiers at Ft. Assiniboine, all doubt was removed. Only an unseasonably early and very heavy snow prevented the Blackfoot war chiefs from leading a full-scale retaliatory raid across the Line against the offending tribe, and during the uneasy days which followed, Agent Pocklington presented the following report to his superintendent:

The younger Indians have decided among themselves to start for the Gros Ventre reserve as soon as the snow goes off the ground and revenge the deaths of their comrades. I am informed the party will muster four hundred strong.

All winter long the peaceful Head Chief of the Bloods, Red Crow, labored to dissuade his warriors from undertaking to slaughter the outnumbered Gros Ventres. But the following spring, just when it appeared that Red Crow's influence was making itself felt, Agent Pocklington had occasion to send the following urgent wire to the Commissioner of Indian Affairs:

Party of Indians stole eighty horses from Upper Agency Saturday night. Red Crow heaviest loser. Red Crow and large party pursuing them. Supposed to be Assiniboines and Gros Ventres.

The chiefs of the Blackfoot Nation have always been known for their high intelligence, and although Red Crow failed to overtake the raiders and recover his horses, it was he who suggested to the Indian Department that the only way to avoid wholesale slaughter would be to inaugurate a formal treaty among the tribes at conflict. Only about half of the Bloods were in favor of the treaty, and the Assiniboines were not much disposed to sign, but eventually the influence of Red Crow and of the head chief of the Gros Ventres, Lame Bull, prevailed and at Fort Belknap, Montana, on June 9, the Treaty of 1887 was successfully concluded.

Peace had been restored, but in the hearts of young Blood warriors still burned a fierce desire to avenge their murdered companions. The young Bloods had agreed to honor the treaty of their chief with the Gros Ventres and Assiniboines, but to the east were the Cree, and far to the south lay the camps of the ancient enemy of the Blackfoot, the Crow. The old ways were not yet dead. One more time the warriors of the Blackfoot Nation would strike their enemies and return to the camps on Belly River singing songs of triumph. One final time the Bloods and the Blackfoots and the Piegans would wear the black paint of victory. One last scalp dance, and there would be an end.

Calf Robe in Later Life   *Young Pine*

THE LAST SCALP DANCE

I had for quite some while been visiting the Blood camp on Belly River, over in Canada [the camp was located in the Belly River flats near the present site of Stand Off, Alberta]. I was the guest of my mother's brother, Running Wolf, a member of the Many Children Band of the Bloods.

One day in early spring my brother, Cross Guns, arrived at my uncle's lodge. Cross Guns had been living at the encampment of my father's band [the Skunk Band] on the South Piegan Reservation over in the States. Someone had stolen Cross Guns' horse, and he had trailed the thief over to Canada before losing the track. I helped my brother to search for his horse, but we never did find it. Finally Cross Guns said, "I have no horse, so I might as well go home again."

I said, "Brother, you do that. You go home, but when you get there you collect all the cartridges you can lay your hands on and pack them back over here. I think that your horse was stolen by one of those Crees from over around Medicine Hat, and you and I will just have ourselves a little war party against the Crees. You should be able to get back here in six days, so that is when we will start."

While I was waiting for my brother to return, a young man named Morning Howler came up from the camp of the Lone Fights [another Blood band] and told me that his brother, Young Pine, urgently wanted me to pay him a visit. Young Pine and I were close friends.

My uncle, Running Wolf, said, "I wonder why he wants to see you. Maybe he has a medicine bundle to give you."

I said, "I don't know, but I think I'll go right down to his camp and find out."

Young Pine's lodge was crowded to overflowing with young men, and among the young men were two older fellows, Calf Robe and Prairie Chicken Old Man. Young Pine beckoned for me to come sit beside him, and when I was seated he informed me that a war party was being planned. Young Pine and Calf Robe and Prairie Chicken Old Man were to be the leaders of the party, and they wished me to go with them.

I said, "That is agreeable to me. Cross Guns and I have been planning to go on a war party anyway, and I am waiting now for my brother to smuggle in some more rifle cartridges from the States."

Young Pine said, "Good. I am glad to hear that your brother is bringing more ammunition. If we get in a fight with the enemy, we will need it. As soon as your brother returns, we will leave."

Two days later, Young Pine sent Morning Howler up to ask

me whether my brother had returned with the ammunition. I said that he had not. I had expected that he would be back by that time, but he had not made it. So Morning Howler took the news back to Young Pine.

Later that same evening, another message from Young Pine advised me that I should go at once to the Lone Fights camp. I went immediately to Young Pine's lodge, and once again Young Pine beckoned for me to make my way through the thick crowd of young men to sit beside him. He said, "Are you still waiting for your brother?"

I said, "Yes."

Young Pine said, "Do you have a horse?"

I said, "No, I don't. I am not ready to leave yet."

There were even more young fellows present at this meeting than at the previous one. Young Pine spoke to them. He said, "All of you fellows who want to go on this war party had better cross the river tonight [the other side of the river was White Man territory] and steal all the horses you can and hide them in the brush. Tomorrow at noon we will have another meeting to complete our plans, and we will start on our war party tomorrow night."

All the young men started to leave then, but as I started to get up, Wolf Sitting, who was seated on the other side of me, grabbed my arm and pulled me back down. I knew that something must be up, so before speaking I waited until most of the other boys had left. "What is going on?" I said.

Young Pine said, "Well, we are going to leave tonight. There are too many fellows who wish to go on this raid, and the police are bound to catch some of them. The six of us will get the jump on them and sneak out tonight. We are going to raid against the Crows, and we will meet at the Pine Tree and begin our war party from there." [The Pine Tree is a large lone pine located near the St. Mary River between Stand Off and Magrath.]

The six of us were:

Young Pine
Crazy Crow (the youngest one—just a kid, really)
Prairie Chicken Old Man
Calf Robe
Wolf Sitting [Ma-kú-yaet-tòw-pi: properly, Wolf Sitting Alone. Wolf Sitting is referred to in Canadian Government docu-

ments as "The Scout," but the Chief informs me that Wolf Sitting was never known by that name. During his narration, the Chief sometimes referred to Young Pine by one of his other names, Sáh-pah-tàwa, which I translated as "Follows His Tracks" or "The Tracker," and it is possible that in official documents (which are not remarkable for their accuracy) this name was taken to refer to Wolf Sitting. The final member of the party, whom official records cite as "Hind Gun" or simply "the South Piegan," was of course the Chief himself.]

Late that night we all slipped past the camp police and met at the Pine Tree. We went east past the Pine Tree to a little creek where we rested a short while, then continued onward and by dawn were east of the place where Magrath is now located. Near a stream we killed a two-year-old heifer and went into the brush to make dry meat of it.

While the others were busy making the dry meat, Calf Robe and I kept watch from the top of a high hill. Eventually we saw a man coming. He looked like a Scout [an Indian scout for the Mounties or the Army, the Chief did not suggest which], so Calf Robe and I went down and directed him away from the rest of our party by telling him that we had been watching two antelope on the west side of the hill. Undoubtedly the man knew that we were lying, but he did not attempt to make any trouble. He said, "Well, I figure you boys are out on a warpath, but since you are from the Blood Reserve I don't have any authority over you. If you will excuse me for not eating with you, I think that I had better go over and see whether I can get one of those antelopes before they get away."

We broke camp immediately and traveled eastward the rest of that day and all of that night and at dawn took a break in a little coulee. Young Pine asked Crazy Crow to go bring some drinking water, but he refused. I don't know why Young Pine ever brought that kid, Crazy Crow, on the war party—he wasn't good for anything. I got up and said, "I'll go find some water. I think I hear some frogs up above."

I walked up the coulee until I came to a slough, and I brought back some water in a waterbag we had made by peeling the tripe from inside the stomach of the beef we had killed; the outside part of the stomach was our waterbag. It was not yet quite daylight, and when I got back with the water I told the boys that they had better strain it through their handkerchiefs because it might have some bugs or leaves in it. [An ancient Blackfoot belief held that for a man to drink from a vessel containing leaves or other sediment was to endanger his manhood. This superstition was later extended to include drinking from a cup which contains tea leaves or coffee grounds.]

From the coulee we went on to the place where Bad Head had been killed, and from there we traveled all night and reached Writing-on-Stone. [The Writing-on-Stone (*Aȟ-sin-náep:* It is Written), located in Canada in the Upper Sweetgrass Hills, is a cliff wall bearing pictographs and petroglyphs of ancient but otherwise uncertain origin.] As we approached Writing-on-Stone, Prairie Chicken Old Man scouted ahead to see whether there were any Mounties around. [This was a good place to be watchful for cops because it was common knowledge that Canadian Indian war parties would visit the Stone whenever possible before making a raid. The Indians believed that the fortunes of the war party could be read in the writing on the wall, and an unfavorable reading was often sufficient to send a war party skedaddling right back home.]

Prairie Chicken Old Man did not spot any police, so we made our camp near Writing-on-Stone. But no sooner had we gotten settled than we heard a noise. It was daylight now, but very foggy, and we did not have any field glasses. So when we heard

Crazy Crow

the noise we broke camp and moved southeast across the Medicine Line [the International Boundary] into the United States.

At Greasewood [a creek] we stopped to rest. We had killed a beef there, but upon butchering the beef we found that it was inedible. Every part of it, even the marrowbones, tasted as though of onion, so we abandoned the whole beef and in a steady drizzle of cold rain continued on toward the southeast.

We had started on this war party with only two horses among the six of us. Prairie Chicken Old Man had a roan, and Calf Robe had a bay. Young Pine and Crazy Crow were riding double with Prairie Chicken Old Man and Calf Robe respectively, while Wolf Sitting and I were running along on foot. It was decided that the mounted four would go ahead and scout around for more horses while Wolf Sitting and I went on by ourselves.

Wolf Sitting and I traveled until we came to a creek. [I feel quite certain that this was either lower Sage Creek or Big Sandy Creek.] Along the creek we found a woodcutter's tent. A beef quarter was hung up by the stream, so we helped ourselves to some beef and also took a slicker that was in the tent. Then we went on down the creek until we came to an old brush shelter, and there we started to dry the meat over a fire. Instead of making a small fire, the way we usually did, we built a large fire and threw on bunch grass and buckbrush in order to make a lot of smoke.

While we were drying the meat, the rest of our party showed up. They had not found any horses. Young Pine asked us why in the world we were making so much smoke, and I told him it was so that if any enemies came around they would think us White men getting wood and not attack us.

Just before dark of that same day we pulled out and went down the creek to look for horses among the several ranches in that area. After dark we came to a house with a large barn and corral, located above the place where old Joe Tatsey's brother-in-law lived. Leaving our equipment on the other side of the creek, we crossed over to scout around.

There were horses in the corral, and I went into the barn to see if I could locate a saddle. I was carrying some of those old-fashioned matches—the kind that sputter when you light them and burn with a blue flame. The first match I lighted would not burn, but by the light of the second match I saw that two White men were asleep in a stall. I guess they must have been dead drunk, because neither one of them moved a muscle.

I left the barn and went out to the corral and built a loop in my lariat with which to catch a horse, but just then a White man came out of the house dressed in a white nightgown and began to yell at me. I opened the corral gate and stampeded the horses and then jumped over the corral fence and ran back to where the other fellows were waiting. They asked me why I had stampeded the horses. I said, "I didn't do it. Maybe somebody else stampeded them."

We went back to the other side of the creek and picked up our equipment and then went down and crossed the Missouri River west of the ranch. Then we split up again, the same as before, planning to meet on a ridge the next day.

Early the next morning, Wolf Sitting and I killed a beef at a creek near the high ridge, and packed some of the meat up onto the ridge to wait for the others. The rest of the party showed up a short time later, but they still had not stolen any horses.

Young Pine said that we needed some water, so Crazy Crow and I took a water bag made from the beef paunch and went down to the creek. We scouted along the creek for a ways and came upon a small house with a lot of cordwood stacked by it. Crazy Crow wanted to raid the house, but I didn't think much of the idea. Crazy Crow persisted, though, and finally I agreed.

Under cover of a misty rain, we crept close to the house and lay down flat on the ground. Crazy Crow hit the house with a stone, and we waited a minute to see whether anybody would come out. Nothing stirred, and since there was no smoke coming from the chimney of the house we began to feel more confident. Crazy Crow threw another stone, and this time we charged and broke down the door of the house. Nobody was at home, and the house contained all manner of things: clothing, ammunition, tobacco, food—including a large number of canned goods —and the usual house furnishings. Rolled up on the floor was a canvas tent, and this we cut in half and used in packing away as much loot as we could carry. Considering that we also had to pack the water, each of us had a very heavy load. It was rather a torment having to move so slowly right out in the open, not knowing at what moment the owner of the house might return and shoot us down, and I said to Crazy Crow, "Well, if we can just make it over that first little ridge we will be all right." It was raining hard now, and I was glad that it was because it made the visibility very poor.

We made it back up to the high ridge where the other fellows were, and when the other boys saw Crazy Crow and me coming with all that loot they sang a victory song with our names in it. We immediately moved our camp farther down the ridge, and when we had made a shelter of the canvas, and had all eaten our fill, we had a good-luck ceremony.

Young Pine began the ceremony by singing a song. The words of the song were:

Married or single, it is a woman that sends us off on a war party and it is she about whom we think until we get back home again. She sends us away with a good-luck charm to wear and a good-luck song to sing.

Then each of us said a prayer and sang the song that our sweetheart had given us.

Wolf Sitting sang:

Whenever I see you, alone or in a crowd, no matter how great the distance, I never fail to recognize you.

Prairie Chicken Old Man sang:

As soon as I see you, I recognize you as my sweetheart.

My own song was:

Last Gun, If I never see you again,
I will do nothing but cry all day long.

Then, in order to have good luck on this war party, we all took new names.

Crazy Crow took the name, "Looks-Like-A-Coyote."

Calf Robe took the name, "Single Spot." [The name of his brother, a minor chief.]

Prairie Chicken Old Man took the name, "Many Mules."

Young Pine took the name, "Big, Fine Young Man."

Wolf Sitting took the name, "Front Wolf."

I took the name, "Everybody Talks About."

We started out again at dawn, and we had gone only a short

distance before spotting a lone antelope. Wolf Sitting and I went ahead to see if we could get a shot at the antelope. I knocked him down with a long shot, but upon our approach the animal leaped to its feet and began to run. We knew that it was wounded because it kept stumbling and falling down. Finally Calf Robe rode the animal down and roped it. We killed it then, but for a while we could not find where I had wounded it. Finally we discovered that my bullet had just barely clipped a tendon above its left front hoof.

We dressed out the antelope and took it up onto a pine hill for butchering. We were all yearning for a smoke. We had to-bacco [stolen from the cabin], but Young Pine's pipe, the only pipe we had brought with us, had been left on top of a hill up north of the Missouri. [Whether Young Pine left his pipe and tobacco on a hilltop for religious reasons or whether he simply forgot it, I was unable to learn. I suspect the former.] So we made a pipe by using a leg bone of the antelope for a stem and some clay moulded and baked in the fire for a bowl. It worked pretty well. [I suspect that the Blackfoots borrowed this leg-bone trick from the Cheyennes, who fashioned some rather nice pipes in this manner, usually employing a foot bone as a bowl.]

We avoided Fort Benton and all large settlements, but we spent quite a while scouting in the Missouri Valley for horses. Finally, at Wide-leafed Brush, I stole a sorrel horse, complete with bridle and saddle, from some White people who had killed my stepmother, Sharp Ears. [This happened near the present site of the town of Belt, Montana. The Whites to whom the Chief made reference were whiskey traders. Sharp Ears, who was not technically the Chief's stepmother but one of Onistái-pokah's earlier wives, had been killed some years before during an altercation between Onistáipokah and the whiskey peddlers. When one of the Whites pointed a rifle, Sharp Ears threw herself in front of her husband, thus receiving the bullet that had been intended for him. Onistáipokah, enraged, attempted to assault the Whites singlehanded but was dragged from the scene by several of his band.]

When Calf Robe found out that I had stolen the horse, he was angry. "Why did you steal from the Whites?" he said. "You better take that horse back before we have the soldiers after us."

I said, "That is easy for you to say because you already have a horse. Those White people owe me something for having killed my stepmother, so I will borrow a horse from them. I will return the horse on the way back, not before."

We had quite a few arguments about who was going to give the orders on this war party, and at Snake Nose Butte we split up into two separate parties. Prairie Chicken Old Man borrowed Calf Robe's knife, and in using it he accidentally nicked the blade. Prairie Chicken Old Man offered to replace the knife as soon as possible, but Calf Robe was so obnoxious about the whole affair that Prairie Chicken Old Man finally lost his temper and jumped on the knife and broke it in two. Calf Robe and Crazy Crow went off by themselves then, but eventually we all got back together and together we reached Elk River [the Yellowstone River] and crossed at the upper fork and went on to Beaver Head. [Beaver Head is a high butte, shaped like the head of a beaver, which is located near the confluence of Pryor Creek and the Yellowstone River.]

From up on Beaver Head we had a good view, and as dawn came up we could see two Crow camps nearby. One camp was small, but the other was pretty good-sized and had quite a few horses. A lot of the horses were pintos.

We waited on the Beaver Head until dark, then went down to raid the Crow camps. It was raining, and the night was as black as pitch. In order to reach the camp where the horses were it was necessary to ford a creek, and when the other fellows started to cross over, I held my horse back. Calf Robe turned his horse back, too. Prairie Chicken Old Man and Crazy Crow had been the first ones to spot the enemy horses, so the pick of the captured stock would go to them. Calf Robe and I wanted to count our own coups, so we turned south and went down to the other Crow camp, the small camp.

When we got to the other camp we sneaked up to a lodge that was set off by itself and looked inside. Inside was a woman and a small child. The woman was combing the child's hair. I said to Calf Robe, "There is nobody else around, so let us go in and kill them."

Calf Robe refused. He said, "We did not come here to kill. We came to steal horses." I did not know it at the time, but the woman in the lodge was a relative of mine. [Not a terribly unusual circumstance, this.]

By this time it was so dark and was raining so hard that we could not even find any horses, let alone steal them, so we went back down the creek and crossed over and met the rest of our party. Young Pine was rather put-out with us. He said, "Why did you guys sneak out on us? We had a heck of a time with those horses. We drove them into the river all right but we lost them. Whether they crossed over or came back downstream, we don't know. The river is running very fast, and it was too dark to see very much."

We moved on eastward through the dark night, and toward dawn we cut a railroad [the Northern Pacific] fence and went up on a pine hill. We stayed up on the hill all the next day.

On the following night we continued eastward toward Sheep Creek [the Bighorn River] and at dawn made our camp on top of a high hill. We stayed up on the hill the next day, and while we were watching for signs of more Crow camps we saw some wagons traveling east with wood.

After dark we went down to where the wagon camp was, thinking perhaps we could get away with the horses, but we discovered that most of teams were mules, with just a few draft horses among them. The horses were not worth stealing, and we figured that any outfit with so many mules probably belonged to White men anyway, so we split up into three groups of two men each and went on to the Big Horn to look for some Crow camps.

Crazy Crow and I located the first bunch of Crow horses. The horses were nothing to brag about—there were a lot of them, but they were not in very good condition—and Crazy Crow and I were debating whether to start driving the horses when Young Pine and Wolf Sitting showed up. Young Pine asked me to catch him a horse, so I caught him a brown horse that already had a rope halter on it. Then Young Pine caught a horse for Wolf Sitting, and the two of them moved off toward the northeast, toward the mouth of the Big Horn. That was the last we saw of them for several days.

I left Crazy Crow with the horses and went south and soon found an even larger bunch of horses. It had been so long since the Blackfoots had raided the Crows that the Crows were not guarding their horses very closely. This bunch was grazing unattended, as the first bunch had been. These horses were still in rather poor condition from the winter, but there were some fine animals among them, and I turned the whole bunch back and headed for the place where Calf Robe and Prairie Chicken Old Man were. It was now daylight.

310

Prairie Chicken Old Man started the animals moving west, and Calf Robe and I went further on down the Bighorn to a large Crow camp. I said to Calf Robe, "Can you speak Crow pretty well?"

He said, "Yes, I can."

I said, "Well, then, let's go straight on through the camp. If anybody stops us, you do the talking and I will do the killing."

As we were going through the camp, I saw a medicine bundle hanging by a lodge. I started for the bundle, to steal it, but Calf Robe stopped me. He said, "That is a good way to get us both in trouble."

We made it through the camp all right, without being stopped by anyone, and near the other side of the camp we located some really fine horses. We cut out seven of the very best animals and drove them due west, back behind the camp and out of sight. [This feat of going right through the middle of a Crow camp in broad daylight required a lot of guts but was not an achievement quite so remarkable as it might appear. Some Indian camps were very large, and the Indian penchant for visiting back and forth with their relatives in the various encampments made it quite possible for strangers to pass through a camp without attracting any special notice. White Quiver, the famous Piegan horse-stealer, made a regular thing of stealing choice horses from right in the very center of enemy camps. White Quiver was so accomplished in this undertaking that the Crows, who called White Quiver "Black Man," would frighten their children into obedience by threatening, "Black Man will get you."]

We turned the seven horses in with the bunch that Prairie Chicken Old Man was driving, and leaving Calf Robe to help drive the stock, I went back to the place I had left Crazy Crow with the first bunch of horses. For a while I could not find the horses, but eventually I discovered them in a swamp where Crazy Crow had allowed them to go. Crazy Crow had been unhorsed, and had lost one of his moccasins, and he was attempting to drive the horses on foot.

I said to Crazy Crow, "We had better leave these horses here. We already have as many as we can handle, and it is not worth the trouble of trying to get these horses out of this swamp."

Crazy Crow pointed to a large pinto and said, "That horse belongs to my father; it was stolen from him quite some time ago." [For many years the Crows and the Blackfoots stole horses back and forth from one another with such frequency that the action veritably constituted a game of horse ping-pong.]

I caught the pinto for Crazy Crow, but he was unable to mount the animal so I caught him a roan. He was unable to mount the roan either, so I caught him a palomino, and when he was unable to mount the palomino I became disgusted and left him there.

When I caught up with Calf Robe and Prairie Chicken Old Man they asked me where the boy was, and when I told them I had left him behind, Prairie Chicken Old Man said that I had better go back and get him. So I took a roan horse back and finally managed to get Crazy Crow aboard the animal, and then we started out to catch up with the other fellows. I thought that we could take a short cut by going up a canyon, but it turned out to be a box canyon and we had to back-track all the way down it.

Crazy Crow and I finally overtook Prairie Chicken Old Man and Calf Robe, and since Young Pine and Wolf Sitting had not showed up, the four of us drove the horses by riding one man at each corner of the herd.

When we got to the railroad, a train was going through. The people on the train must have thought that we were just out rounding up some horses because they waved at us. We waved back, and when the train was out of sight we cut the fence and crossed the railroad tracks and went on and crossed the Yellowstone River. Some of the poorer horses had played out even before we got to the river, so we had abandoned them.

We traveled steadily northwestward until reaching the Musselshell River. The water in the Musselshell was running bank to bank with the spring floods, and in crossing we lost three colts. We could see them going under, but there was nothing we could do about it.

Further on, several head of horses played out, so we left them there. A while later we ran into a sheep camp, and I signed to the sheepherder that there were several head of horses back down the trail that he could have.

At Wide-leafed Brush we stopped and slept all night. We were supposed to keep watch, but every one of us fell asleep. This was near the place that I had stolen the sorrel horse on the way down, and it was here that I turned the animal loose. I said to the horse, "I didn't steal you. I only borrowed you, and now I am returning you."

When we started out again, we saw some dust and thought it might be the enemy. But it was only a bunch of cattle. They were running around in a crazy sort of way, as though they had worms on their backs. [The cattle probably had heel flies.] One calf was running by itself, and we killed it and cooked it and rode along eating the meat off the cooking sticks.

At our next rest camp, a White man showed up. Calf Robe wanted to kill him, but I said, "We are not here to kill—you said so yourself. We have done enough damage by stealing all these horses." I signed for the White man to leave.

We figured we must be approaching a military or police encampment, so before continuing on north we swung back east for awhile. I went ahead to scout for soldiers, but I did not see any. When I got back I found that Crazy Crow had been unhorsed again and was tagging along behind the horses on foot. The other two fellows had gone on ahead. I caught him a mount and told him to get a move on, and after that we made better time.

We crossed the Missouri River at the upper crossing, near the place where we had broken into the house. We crossed on a raft we had built. Prairie Chicken Old Man attempted to cross in a small boat he had found, but the boat sank with him and we had to fish him out of the water.

North of the Missouri we all crawled into some tall sage and fell asleep. Early the next morning I awoke to find that all the horses except one roan were gone. We began to track them, and when Prairie Chicken Old Man found the mark of a picket rope dragging on the ground he became assured that the horses had strayed off by themselves. I was not convinced. I thought that somebody must have stolen them, and as we trailed them up a sandy creek I hung back at every blind corner, expecting an ambush. But, as it turned out, Prairie Chicken Old Man was right. The horses had strayed by themselves, and we finally overtook them.

When we reached the hill upon which Young Pine had left his pipe on the way down to the Crow country, Prairie Chicken Old Man asked Crazy Crow to go up and see if he could locate the pipe. Crazy Crow refused, but I volunteered to go. I was wearing a blue shirt, blue leggings, and a blue cap that I had stolen from the house on the Missouri. I had long braids, and before starting up the hill I stuffed them inside my cap so that if any enemy were on the hill they would think me a White man and not attempt to do me any harm. I left my rifle for Crazy Crow to hold, but when I was about half way up the hill I reconsidered this action and went back down and got my rifle. I had been carrying only my knife and a rope.

Upon reaching the top of the hill I found that the pipe had disappeared. The tobacco pouch was there, but it had been torn open and the tobacco scattered and soaked with rain.

I scouted further along the ridge and spotted a man whom I did not recognize. I held my rifle behind my back and began to back off toward the steep bluff where I could jump down in case I had walked into an ambush, which seemed likely. Then another man came out into the open and I recognized him as Young Pine. It was Young Pine and Wolf Sitting, whom we had not seen since leaving the Crow camps. I took off my hat and signalled that I was glad to see them. Young Pine and Wolf Sitting had captured three head of horses apiece, but the horses had the brands of White men on them. I told them they might get in trouble if they got caught with White horses. I said, "You better turn those horses loose. Most of the horses we are driving belong to me, and I will give you three head apiece.

I signalled for the boys down below to start moving the horses along, and Young Pine and Wolf Sitting and I went down the far side of the ridge to meet them. As soon as we got down below, Young Pine asked whether we had any meat. He said that he and Wolf Sitting had not eaten that day. I told him that we had a sirloin of beef [*sisk-tsi-ku-no-kuist:* more than one] and that we would eat as soon as Crazy Crow caught up to us with the horses.

Crazy Crow had been carrying our meat, but when he caught up he said that he had lost the meat somewhere back down the trail. We told him to go back and find it, but he refused, so I back-tracked and found the meat. We cooked the meat and ate it, and that was the last food we had for quite a while. While we were eating, the Ten Days Rain began.

Shortly we came upon the fresh trail of three riders, and we tracked them eastward along a sandy road. We thought that probably they were the members of another Blackfoot war party that had gone out at the same time as ours. This party was composed of Three Calf [also called Wipes-His-Eyes], Bee, and Many Bull. We trailed the riders for a long time, and at one point we were so close behind them that when I placed my hand in the ashes of their fire I got burned, but we never did catch up with them. By this time it was raining and snowing at the same time, and when we came upon an abandoned shack we rested for a while before turning north toward the Bear Paw Mountains. By the time we started out again, the trail of the three riders had been obliterated.

Not until reaching the foot of the Bear Paws, where there was plenty of dry wood, did we stop to build a shelter and make a fire. It was now two days since we had eaten the sirloin, but the weather was so bad, the rain and sleet so heavy, that we could do little but remain in our shelter and hope it cleared up. It was here that two of my horses, a mare and her young colt, both mouse-gray and both wearing bells, died. I figure that they must have frozen to death.

We remained in our shelter for four days, and although we took turns at going out hunting, nobody got anything. On the night of the fourth day, Young Pine and Wolf Sitting returned from the hunt empty-handed. It was now six days since any of us had eaten, and that night when everybody else was alseep I took a calf skin that I had been using for a saddle pad and began to cook it. I had allowed the hide to soak in the creek all day so that the hair would scrape out more easily, and now I singed off the rest of the hair in the fire, washed the hide once again in the creek, cut it into strips and pushed the strips beneath the ashes of the fire and raked hot coals over them. I allowed the hide to cook in this manner for quite a while, during which time Young Pine [here the Chief referred to Young Pine as, *Nit-sín-nai-mah:* My boss] awoke and began to take note of my actions. When finally I raked the rawhide from the ashes and began to chew on a piece, Young Pine said, "Let me try a piece of that." Then the other fellows began to wake up and ask for a piece, and among us we ate that whole hide. That is how hungry we were, and that is the only time I ever ate rawhide on a war party.

[The meaning behind the Chief's final comment is found in an ancient Blackfoot tradition. One of the favorite foods of the Blackfoot warrior on a war party was something called "Crow guts," the preparation of which necessitated that the intestine of some herbiverous animal be turned inside out and cleaned, stuffed with choice pieces of meat and cooked in hot ashes. The "Crow guts" was then cut into sections and distributed for consumption. However, if any member of the party had proved himself cowardly or unreliable, he was served last and his portion was stuffed not with meat but with pieces of rawhide. Receiving the "Rawhide guts," as this portion was called, was akin to being handed the white feather and was notice of ostracism.]

During the following night I had a dream, and upon wakening I told my dream to the other men. I said, "I dreamed of a log cabin that was caved in on one side. Near the cabin we killed two animals. I think they were antelopes. Two of us were butchering one of the animals on the west side of a hill and two of us were butchering the other one on the east side of the hill. I do not know where the other two of us were. As we were cooking the meat near the cabin, the enemy attacked us . . ."

At this point, Calf Robe interrupted me and said, "Don't tell any more of your dream."

I said, "No, it is all right. Later on in my dream we were sitting on top of a high hill cleaning a scalp. All of us were there, and none of us was even wounded. In my dream, Young Pine asked me if he could have first choice of the scalp. I told him that he could."

When I said that, Young Pine filled his pipe and handed it to me and said, "I accept your dream. When your dream comes true, I ask you for first choice on the scalp." I agreed to give Young Pine first choice. [When you offer a Blackfoot a pipe filled with tobacco, if he accepts the offering he cannot then refuse whatever request you present to him.]

The next day the weather was somewhat clearer, so we pulled out, and we had not gone very far before coming upon a log cabin with one side caved in—exactly like the cabin I had seen in my dream. Near the cabin we found the tracks of two beeves. We tracked the beeves across a small ridge and killed them both. Young Pine, Wolf Sitting and I were skinning out one beef on the east side of the ridge and the others were skinning out the other beef just across the top of the ridge on the other side.

A brown horse had played out on us and we had left it in a patch of brush about three hundred yards from where we were. As I glanced back I saw two horses there instead of one, and I said to Young Pine, "How many horses did we leave over there?"

Young Pine said, "Only one."

I said, "Well, there are two there now." So we all looked toward the horses, and then we spotted a man in a white

Hudson's Bay capote examining the brown horse. Then we spotted some other riders coming up, and that is when the shooting began.

Young Pine said, "We had better get out of here, but we will not leave the horses behind. You go tell the other fellows to get the horses going. Wolf Sitting and I will cover you from here."

We drove the horses until we came to a stream with heavy mixed timber. Here we dismounted and took cover to wait for the enemy. We did not know who the enemy were, but we thought it might be the Crows after us, so when the enemy showed up, Calf Robe stood up and called out in Crow, "Who are you? What are you up to?"

The only reply was a volley of rifle shots from the enemy. Calf Robe fell over backward, but he was not hit; he was just getting out of the way of those bullets. None of us was wounded, but some of the bullets came mighty close. One of them nearly hit me.

While we were exchanging fire with the enemy, Young Pine said to me, "I know this creek well. You take the point and have Calf Robe and Crazy Crow drive the horses on up the creek-bottom until you come to the place where the walls become steep. If these guys want a fight, that is where we will give it to them."

So I started on up the creekbottom. The snow was deep here, and there were a lot of flat rocks underfoot. The going was very slippery, and I was afraid that my horse might fall with me. Calf Robe and Crazy Crow were behind me, driving the horses.

Unbeknownst to me, the enemy had gone up a draw and headed us off, and as I rounded a sharp bend I ran smack into them. One of them was in the process of dismounting no further than the length of this house from me. I had my rifle held across the horse in front of me, and when I found that I was unable to turn my horse around—I was riding with just a hackamore— I turned him by hitting him on the side of the nose with my rifle barrel.

As soon as the fellow in front of me dismounted, he ran around to the other side of his horse for cover. By this time my horse was turning, so I pointed my rifle back with one hand and fired. Both the horse and the man went down, but I am certain that it was the horse I hit. Then, as I made it back around the bend, I could hear all hell breaking loose behind me. At first I thought that everybody was shooting at me, but when the rifle fire continued as I moved further back down the streambed, I realized that a battle was in progress.

I found Crazy Crow and Calf Robe down the stream a ways, guarding the horses. For a minute I joined them in forming a triangle perimeter, thinking that any second the enemy would show up. But soon it became apparent that the fighting was continuing up the creek. Some of the fire was coming from up on the bluff, and I knew that this must be our boys up there. I said, "Come on! The boys are having it out with those guys. Let's go up and help them." And I started to head up toward the top of the bluff.

Calf Robe said, "You better come back here," and I went back down. But when it became obvious that Calf Robe and Crazy Crow had no better plans than to wait out the battle down here in the timber, I started back up again. Calf Robe called again for me to come back, but this time I ignored him.

I crawled along the edge of the bluff until I located Wolf Sitting. He was in a perfect position for the battle, lying beneath a large wind-fallen pine, protected by both the trunk of the tree and the stump of a heavy limb. I crawled up beside him. "Where are they?" I said.

He said, "They are all right down there, hiding in that clump of willows."

I said, "How many are there?"

He said, "I'm not sure. I counted eight, but there could be more."

Young Pine had performed a masterful maneuver in anticipating the movements of the enemy and in bringing Prairie Chicken Old Man and Wolf Sitting around behind them. The enemy had been driven from their positions and were now flattened in the scant protection of a willow clump. Apparently the enemy had become convinced that they were fighting a force of only three men—during our first engagement they had seen only Young Pine, Wolf Sitting and me, and at the second meeting, where Calf Robe challenged them, they had not been able to see us because of the heavy timber. [Very possibly the enemy thought themselves in pursuit of the other Blackfoot war party, the one with only three members.] But now that a fourth rifle began to blaze at them, they began, one by one, to retreat from their position in the willows toward a patch of brush further back from us. We fired at them as they ran, but we could not hit any of them. Then, as the last man left the willows, I fired and I knew that I had hit him. I could *feel* that I had hit him.

This man we shot was an Indian, but he appeared to be dressed in a soldier's uniform. He had on a blue coat, blue pants, and a hat hanging behind his head on a cord. When we hit him he did not go down but staggered back into the willow clump he had just left. He stood there, shooting back at us, and we could see that his war party was moving away from us all the time, going from one clump of bushes to another, shooting back at us as they went.

At about this time, Wolf Sitting spied some horses hidden behind a hill. He figured they were the enemy's horses, so he went over to where they were and counted coup on them by striking each one with a stick. One of them was the prettiest thing I had ever seen; it was a buckskin with one glass [white] eye, and it was wearing a wide beaded bridle and a fully beaded Indian saddle.

The other three of us kept shooting at the enemy, and it was Young Pine who finally finished off the wounded man in the willows. Young Pine shot, and we could see the man turn slowly and fall face downward. Young Pine, Prairie Chicken Old Man and I all charged then, and it was I who reached the fallen man first. I threw myself on top of him, and while I was taking his belt and hat I looked around for his rifle, but Prairie Chicken Old Man beat me to it. I turned the fallen enemy over then, preparing to scalp him, but when I saw his face I jumped back. He was an awful sight. Blood was running from his nose and mouth, and his eyes looked as though they were frozen. The man had two braids. Young Pine scalped one, and then I scalped the other.

The enemy were still shooting at us, so we decided to pull out. Calf Robe and Crazy Crow came up to where we were, but they had abandoned all the horses except the two they were riding. The rest of the fellows started out, taking with them the captured enemy horses. Wolf Sitting was leading the buckskin with the pretty bridle and saddle, Young Pine was leading a roan with white mane and tail, and Prairie Chicken Old Man was leading a bay. Calf Robe and Crazy Crow weren't doing anything but riding the horses they were on. They were the only two who did not count coup in the battle.

I did not like the idea of leaving behind all those horses we had captured from the Crows, so while the other fellows went on ahead I went back and picked up three of the best horses that belonged to me and stampeded the rest. On the way, I found an enemy blanket.

As I began to catch up to the other boys, I observed that Wolf Sitting was sort of hanging back, waving and yelling something at me. I couldn't make out what he was saying until I got right up to him. What he was saying was that I should turn one of the horses loose so that I could move faster. I was riding a buckskin and leading a gray and a roan. I turned the gray loose, but the animal kept following close behind me so after a while I caught him up again.

I was the only fellow leading two horses, and when we got to a small hill with some chokecherry bushes on it I asked Calf Robe to cut me a whip from one of the branches. I said, "Hey, Dad, how about cutting me a whip?"

Calf Robe refused. He said, "You have two arms and two legs—cut your own whip!"

We went on to the top of a large hill. This was the hill I had seen in my dream. It was on top of this hill that Young Pine and I cleaned the blood out of the scalps we had taken. When the enemy had first attacked us, while we were butchering the beeves, I had put inside my coat a tripe, a tongue, and one kidney. Here on top of this hill we ate these things, raw. I had carried the fresh scalp under my coat along with the meat, and some of the blood from the scalp had gotten on the meat. That was the only time I ever ate human blood. You must remember that for an entire week the only food we had had was some rawhide, and we were much too hungry to be finicky. [It occurred to me that the Chief's party might at any time have eaten horse meat, but when I asked him about it he gave me a look as though he would not dignify such a question with an answer. Whether the eating of horse meat would have violated some religious or social taboo (as the eating of dog meat would have) or whether it would merely have been an admission of the warrior's inability to provide himself with proper meat, I do not know. At any rate, the only time the Chief mentioned his people's consuming horse meat was during the Starvation Year. Conversely, although most authorities claim that the old-time Blackfoots, with the exception of a few bands such as the Fish Eaters Band of the Bloods, would not eat fish, the Chief has made quite clear that he ate and enjoyed fish all his life.]

The hill we were on was not too far from an army post, and we hoped the Army did not locate us there because we knew that one shot from an army cannon could blow half of the hill off. But it was the best defensive position for many miles, with plenty of timber to hide us, and we settled down behind a wind-fallen tree to await the next show with the enemy.

While Young Pine and I were cleaning the scalps, Calf Robe said to me, "Well, I should have accepted your dream. This is the second time your dream came true. You dreamed that the enemy would attack us by the old cabin, and you dreamed that we would all be safe on top of a hill, cleaning a scalp." Now everybody except Calf Robe and I were asleep. We were on lookout, and when I glanced over at Calf Robe I saw that he did not look quite right—his face was sort of pale, and had a strange expression.

I said, "What's the matter, Dad? You don't look right. You must see something down there."

Calf Robe said, "Yes, I see something. I see some horses coming. I didn't even know about the battle you fellows had with the enemy back there where you took the scalps. But I will know something about this battle. I'll make those enemy drop their blankets."

I looked down where Calf Robe was looking, and far in the distance I could see some horsemen riding all scattered out. I woke up the other fellows, and we saw the riders gradually converge and stop in a group. Then they rode behind a hill, and that was the last we saw of them. We figured they were probably going to wait for dark to sneak up on us, so we prepared a defense and waited.

Toward evening I looked over at Calf Robe again, and he had that same strange expression on his face. I spoke to him, but instead of answering me he spoke to the sun. He said, "Sun, you know that I wasn't in the last battle with the enemy. But now I see some other enemies coming, and I swear to you that I will not stop fighting until every one of them has dropped his blanket."

Calf Robe was watching on the north side of the hill, and when the rest of us looked down there we saw [*Innakikoaks:* a bunch of police] some police dressed like soldiers. They were tracking us, and after they had tracked us up the hill as far as where the deep snow began, they turned around and started backtracking us toward the place we had killed the enemy.

We had no desire to tangle with Government troops, so when the troopers began to backtrack us we beat it down the south side of the ridge. The snow was deep and the going was rough. I was riding one horse and leading two, and on the way down my horse slipped and I fell off and cut my knee badly on a sharp rock. Just because my horse went down, do not think that I was a poor horseman; remember that I was handling three horses down a steep and slippery hill. My idea of poor horsemen were Calf Robe and Crazy Crow. Crazy Crow couldn't stay on a horse if you tied him on with baling wire. Calf Robe could stay on all right, but he did not know how to spare a horse and he played out every horse he rode. He had played out a brown horse just coming from the place we had had the battle, and now he played out the glass-eyed buckskin that Wolf Sitting had lent him.

When Calf Robe played out the buckskin, he asked me for one of my horses.

I said, "You have two arms and two legs."

Young Pine said to me, "Why are you acting that way? That is not like you at all."

I said, "Well, back down the trail I asked him to cut me a switch and he refused. He told me that I had two arms and two legs, and now I am getting even with him by giving him back his own words."

Young Pine lent Calf Robe a roan mare with a white mane and tail, and from there we went at a moderate pace until reaching Grassy Lake. At Grassy Lake we rested a while, and by the time we started out again my knee was very stiff and swollen.

We made our next camp at Big Rocky Coulee. I couldn't sleep anyway because of my knee, so I kept watch while the other fellows slept. As I sat on lookout I spotted an antelope coming toward us. I sat perfectly still, but every once in a while I would move my head from side to side. This motion intrigued the antelope and it kept coming closer and closer. I hesitated to shoot because of the situation we were in, but finally the antelope came so close that I could not resist knocking it over.

Quite understandably, my shot scared the breech clouts off of the other boys. They jumped up out of a sound sleep and scattered like quail without even grabbing their weapons. They sure chewed me out about shooting without warning them first, but of course I could not have warned them without spooking the antelope. When they chewed me out I said, "Well, I got him didn't I? Now we can eat."

By this time we were so hungry that we had to be careful how we went about eating. We ate the raw liver as we dressed out the antelope, but before even beginning to cook the muscle meat we all drank some blood soup. We took the paunch of the antelope and filled it with blood and tied it at both ends so that it would not leak. Then we dug a small pit, lined it with the skin of the antelope, and filled it with water. We made the water boil by dropping in stones heated in the fire, and into the boiling water we placed the paunch of blood to cook. After we had drunk the soup we began to cook the meat, and by the time the meat was cooked we all had good appetites and could eat as much as we pleased without getting sick.

Our next stop was at a lake on the flat south of Shelby. We killed a beef here, and using the beef hide and some sinew I was carrying, we made moccasins. By this time I was completely barefooted, and none of the other fellows was much better off. We didn't even remove the hair from the hide. We made our moccasins from the green hide just as it came off the cow.

We stopped only long enough to make moccasins and cook some meat, then turned north and finally camped at a small lake near the present site of the town of Sunburst. We considered that our war party was over now and that from here we would go on home, so it was here that we held our victory dance. We took turns at singing, and while one fellow sang the others danced. We blackened our faces with charcoal from our fire [black paint is Blackfoot victory paint], and those boys sure did look pretty with their faces all painted up that way.

We later learned that both the United States Army and the N.W.M.P. had been alerted to intercept our war party, but we managed to slip past them all. Upon leaving the site of our victory dance, we traveled until dawn and then hid out all the next day. On the following night we passed Magrath and arrived back at the Pine Tree. Here we had another small celebration, and after resting for a while in a patch of chokecherry bushes we moved on and arrived back at the Lone Fights camp just as it was breaking daylight.

At the Lone Fights camp we had a big victory celebration. All the men—even the old-timers—painted their faces black, and we sure did have a good time.

Until arriving at the Lone Fights camp we thought that the enemy we had killed was a Gros Ventre, but now we learned that in reality he was an *Asináiquon*.

I have here quoted the exact word employed by the Chief because there is some considerable disagreement (between myself and official records) about how the word should be translated. Historians generally agree that the Indian scalped by Young Pine and the Chief was an Assiniboine, but my information suggests that he was a Cree. Since the issue lies in a correct translation into modern English of the Blackfoot word *Asináiquon*, in attempting to shed additional light upon the matter I entered into correspondence with Hugh Dempsey, a noted historian and authority on the Canadian Indian who, as always, was very courteous and prompt in responding. The following paragraph is from a letter written to me by Mr. Dempsey:

"Also are you aware of a linguistic variation that has occurred within the past century? The present term for a Cree man is *asinákwan*, while some of the modern generation refer to the Assiniboine as *kiyh'spa*. Originally a Cree was called *siyéekwan* and an Assiniboine was *asinákwan*. As you may note, the latter is taken from the Cree root *assina* for stone, which has given us the modern term Assiniboine. However, during the latter part of the nineteenth century the Cree and Assiniboine were so frequently in mixed parties that the Blackfoot began to use the term Assiniboine collectively for the two tribes. Later, with the movement of the Assiniboine out of their region, they began to apply this term solely to the Cree and it is used as such today. Many of the Blackfoot are unaware of the origin of this word. In your interviews, I just wonder which term Jim White Calf was using or mentally translating when referring to the incident."

Mr. Dempsey's information suggests some measure of the difficulty encountered in working with the Blackfoot language, but, as any person so knowledgeable as Mr. Dempsey is well aware, his comments do not even begin to probe the linguistic complexities attaining to this matter. For instance, "Kiyh'spa" (properly [káiʔspa], a short form of the Blackfoot word [káiʔspàwa] which makes reference to persons who part their hair in the middle) is employed by the modern Blackfoot to describe not only certain Assiniboines but the Winnebago Indians, a group of Eastern Gros Ventres, and members of Plains Indian dancing societies variously called in English, "Grass Dancers," "Chicken Dancers," and "Fancy Dancers."

Of course, any reference to what a word in any language "originally" meant is linguistically unsound. *Sai-yí-quon* is definitely an old Blackfoot term, and although this term is today given only infrequent employment, it is universally recognized by the Blackfoot as referring to an individual Cree man.

But whether "asinákwan" was ever used by the Blackfoot as an exclusive reference to the Assiniboine is highly questionable. Blackfoot commonly provides numerous (and very flexible) references to various divisions—by way of cultural characteristics, geographical location, alliance with other tribes, etc.—of other Indian nations, and the root "assina," which may well derive from the Cree for stone [àsmí] but which is very close to the Cree phrase [aseàná] ("He is ready") is found in at least a dozen Blackfoot references both to the Crees and to other Indian groups. The most generalized reference to the Cree is, *Asináwa; Ah-páht-o-sey-sinawa* refers to the general group of Northern Crees; *Ist-tsís-sinawa* (Brush Crees) and *Kyái-yai-toh-moi-ist-tsis-sinawa* (Bear Hill Brush Crees) both refer to groups of Crees up around Edmonton and Hobbema; the Rocky Boy Crees are called *Oćh-koh-tok-ees-sinawa*. But while another word for the Rocky Boys (*Oćh-koh-tok-ees-koómahpi*), does not contain the root "assina," this Cree root does appear in Blackfoot words which mean Gros Ventres (*Aht-tśi-sinawa*), Assiniboines (*Ní-tsís-sinawa*), the Yankton Sioux (*Ó-mach-si-kai-sinawa:* Big Feet Indians), and a Canadian group of Ojibwa-Cree-White mixed-bloods (*Maht-su-áhpi-sinawa*).

All this is very interesting—at least to me—and I could go round and round the linguistic bush on this subject for quite a while, but the only relevant fact in this whole discussion is my knowledge of the Chief's idiolect—specifically, in this case, my knowledge of the terms which the Chief himself employs in referring to the various Indian tribes. In brief, although the Chief recognizes various references to the various groups of Assiniboines (including *Pináhpisin-awa,* which can refer to the Assiniboines or/and the Gros Ventres over around Wolf Point, Montana), the Chief in his story-telling employs only two terms: he calls an Assiniboine in close alliance with the Cree and Gros Ventres a *Ni-tsís-sinaiquon* (a "Real Indian" or "Genuine Indian"), and he refers to the Assiniboine-Sioux as *Ai-yak-kyok-sey* (The Paddlers). When the Chief employs the term *Asináiquon,* as he did in telling this story, he is definitely referring to a Cree and not to an Assiniboine.

I suspect that the whole confusion on this issue began when Young Pine told his story to the Blood Agent (I cannot help wondering what term Young Pine was using or mentally translating when he described the killing of the enemy). It is possible that Young Pine, for any number of reasons, might have lied about the identity of the man he killed, but it is even more likely that this part of his story, like most of the rest of it, was badly garbled in the translation. At any rate, until somebody proves the contrary I shall continue to accept the word of the Chief that the last scalp he ever took was that of a Cree. The Chief, after all, was there.°

It is problems such as this that make linguistics the fascinating (and frustrating) study it is. And it is situations such as this which cause me to stand in utter astonishment at the arrogance of those persons—totally untrained in linguistic science—who flit down to the nearest Indian reservation, hire a single and equally untrained Indian interpreter, and come away a few weeks later convinced that they have really penetrated deep into the soul of Indian culture. So they write a book.

At the Lone Fights camp I was given a present of a pair of blue pants, a white blanket coat, and some ammunition for my rifle. I asked where my uncle, Running Wolf, was camped, and was told that he was camped further down the river. Alone I moved on toward Running Wolf's lodge, and when I saw the tops of the lodgepoles I began to sing my victory song.

Running Wolf's wife ran and told him that somebody was coming down singing a victory song, and Running Wolf came out to greet me. I gave the scalp to my uncle, and he did a ceremony with his beaver bundle and placed the scalp inside the bundle. Later on the scalp disappeared from inside the bundle. I never did find out what happened to it. [I had thought this to be the same scalp that the Chief has tied to the

---

° The scalp was indeed that of a Cree. Eventually the Chief confided that final identification had been made by one of the victim's relations, a Cree Indian named Gropher.

handle of his briefcase, but I now discovered that I had been mistaken.]

A short while later, Red Crow [Head Chief of the Bloods] came down and told me that the Mounties were looking for me. He advised me to turn myself in to the Agent, so I did, whereupon the Mounties chained me in a Red River cart and took me to the stockade at Fort Macleod. One Mountie was driving the cart and another was riding alongside. Both the horses were sorrels. It was the spring of the year, and when we forded the Kootenai River I thought that the high water was going to be the end of me. The cart whipped around and started to turn over, but the driver threw his weight against it and we made it across all right.

On the other side of the river the Mounties unshackled me and went off into the woods for quite a while, leaving me alone. I figured they were giving me a chance to escape, but since I had promised Red Crow to turn myself in I stayed right there. Presently the Mounties returned and said, "Well, you had your chance. Now you are going to the Sandy [the guard house]."

[It is quite possible that Canadian officials had given orders that the Chief be allowed to escape. The Chief was a United States Indian, and this fact constituted rather a sticky wicket in Canadian-American relations. According to official Canadian Government records, the Chief, Young Pine and Wolf Sitting (called "The Scout") were in custody at Ft. Macleod from 18 May to 13 June, 1889, during which time American authorities made no response to communication on the subject from S. B. Steele, Superintendent of Macleod District. The Chief was smart enough to keep his mouth shut about having taken the scalp of an American Indian, so he was charged only with transporting stolen property into Canada. No formal complaint was ever filed by the owners of the stolen horses, so all three prisoners were released for want of evidence against them. Calf Robe, who turned himself in on 21 June, also was released.]

A couple of days after they locked me up, the Mounties brought in Wolf Sitting and Young Pine who also had turned themselves in to the Agent on the advice of Red Crow.

At this time there was a part-Indian scout and interpreter for the Mounties named Joe Potts. We Indians called him *Kyái-o-kos:* Bear Child. He was the grandfather of Francis and Aloysius Potts who now live in Browning. One day Potts came and took me to the office of the Superintendent of the Fort. My father was there, and for a while I couldn't understand why they wanted me there because nothing happened except that my father and the Superintendent, with Potts interpreting, swapped a bunch of stories back and forth.

Finally they had a little conference, after which Potts turned to me and said, "Well, I think we'll send you to the territorial prison." [*Mí-ku-tsís-sey-eet-tai:* Red River.]

I knew that he was trying to scare me, so I said, "O.K. I'd like to see what it looks like up there."

Potts said, "If you want to see that place, then you are a damned fool. You ought to have more sense than to go running off on war parties with that wild bunch."

At lunch time Potts started to take me back to the guard-house to eat, but the Superintendent stopped him. He said that we would all eat together in the officers' mess.

Later on the Superintendent gave my father a pass with which to cross on the ferry, and the two of them shook hands. My father thanked the Superintendent for taking good care of me in the jail, and the Superintendent said, "Well, I don't have any gifts to give you, but you can take your boy home with you. I am releasing him in your custody."

My father said, "Oh, no! I did not come here like a dog to drag his pup home by the scruff of the neck. My boy is a grown man, and you had better keep him right here until you feel disposed to release him as a man in his own custody."

I said, "Don't say that! I want to get out of here."

Potts said, "Don't complain to anybody! It is your own fault that you are in this jail."

The Superintendent said to my father, "You are an even wiser man than I thought you were. I will see to it that your son is well cared for and that he is not required to do any hard labor."

During my stay in the guardhouse, the only work I did was waiting on tables in the mess hall. Some of the other prisoners did the slave work—mopping floors and washing the dishes.

One day Young Pine, Wolf Sitting and I were taken to the courtroom where there was a meeting among the Indian Commissioner and the important chiefs. At length Red Crow said, "The Americans [the Gros Ventres and Assiniboines] put down the first blood by killing six of our people. Now we have killed one of them, and so the matter is finished."

Young Pine, Wolf Sitting and I were sitting in a row with myself in the middle. The Blood Agent [Pocklington] said that the Government wanted to hire fifty police from among the Bloods in order to help keep the peace. He asked Young Pine if he would serve, and after some hesitation Young Pine finally agreed. The officials said that they would make Young Pine head of the police, but later on Young Pine backed out of the deal.

When the whole affair was over and they gave us our release, the officials gave out tea and crackers and that kind of stuff. I told them I didn't want any, and I went immediately to the camp of my father's brother-in-law, Running Wolf.

The next day, Young Pine sent word for me to come to his camp. There was a big crowd in the lodge, but Young Pine said for me to step over everybody in order to sit by his side. That night we had the biggest victory dance of all. Everybody was there, and those of us who had been on the war party were honored. We told all about stealing the Crow horses, and about the battle. When we told about taking the scalps, everybody fired off their guns and made so much noise that several of the horses picketed nearby broke loose and stampeded. After that I was made a member of the Crazy Dogs.

Later on [in early July of the same year] we moved down to where we were going to have our Sun Dance. While my brother, Wolf Tail, and I were out cutting some willows in order to make a sweat lodge, my mother came down and told us that we had better get our horses and go back home.

I said, "Why should we go home? We are going to have a good time at the Sun Dance." My mother said that there had been a fight between the Bloods and the Mounties, and that there might even be a war starting.

Wolf Tail and I started back for the Sun Dance encampment, but when we got to the place where the bridge crosses the Belly River we met some people who told us that there was big trouble brewing and that all Americans were supposed to go home.

That was the last war party I went on, and that was the last scalp I [or anybody else] took. That is the end of the story.

The ruckus during the Sun Dance—the Indians referred to it as the "wrestling match"—which took place on the morning of July 4, 1889, was a very serious incident, and one which might well have precipitated full-scale battle between the Bloods and the Northwest Mounted Police. If such had been the outcome, the responsibility would have lain not with the Indians but with the N.W.M.P.

What happened was this: although both Calf Robe and Prairie Chicken Old Man had already been released from any charges stemming from their participation in the war party, Staff Sergeant Chris Hilliard, in charge of the Stand Off detachment of the N.W.M.P., led two constables and an interpreter, Henry Choquette, into the Medicine Lodge and attempted to arrest the two men. Not only had the Sergeant attempted to make the arrest without a legal warrant, but he had committed the incredible stupidity of violating the sanctity of the sacred Medicine Lodge, and in this act he came close not only to losing his life but to stirring up a rebellion among all the Canadian Blackfoots. As the Chief related in his story, Calf Robe had sworn to the Sun that in any future conflict with the enemy he would not stop fighting until the enemy had dropped their blankets, and when the Sergeant and his constables entered the sacred Òkáhn and laid hands on the two Indians, Calf Robe figuratively if not literally honored his oath. An angry group of Blood warriors deprived the police of their rifles and pistols, and ripped the uniforms from their backs. Only through the intervention of three prominent Blood chiefs—Red Crow, Blackfoot Old Woman, and Single Spot (himself a brother of Calf Robe)—did the police escape with their lives.

The incident stirred up a hornets' nest of controversy between the Indian Department and the N.W.M.P. A strong detachment of police was sent back to the encampment to arrest Calf Robe on a charge of using a deadly weapon to prevent an officer from making an arrest. Also arrested, on a charge of obstructing the police in the execution of their duty, were Young Pine, Sleeps-On-Top, Day Chief, Crop-eared Wolf, and Big Wolf (the man who, three years before, had discovered the bodies of the Bloods whose murder had started the whole business). The case of The Queen versus Crop-eared Wolf, Young Pine, Sleeps-On-Top, Day Chief [Tsis-tsi-koóm-i-nah: properly, Thunder Chief. Day Chief would be *Tsis-tsi-kúi-nah*] and Big Wolf was heard on August 6, 1889. With Police Superintendent Steele determined that the Bloods should be punished, and Agent Pocklington of the Blood Reserve equally determined in defense of the rights of his Indian charges, the trial was a tumultuous affair. Eventually the magistrate dismissed the charges against the Indians with the ruling that, since no warrants had been issued, the arrests had been illegal. The Crown Prosecutor was directed to withdraw all charges against Calf Robe, and there, at last, was an end to the matter.

Having already in hand the factual details of the Chief's last war party and scalp dance, it is interesting to view these events—and the events which they immediately precipitated—through official Canadian Government reports of the time. The following, dated November 30, 1889, is from the Annual Report of Superintendent S. B. Steele, Commanding Macleod District, Fort Macleod, to the Commissioner of the Northwest Mounted Police:

INDIANS

The Blood and Piegan Indians, whose reserves are located in this district, have given considerable trouble and annoyance during the past year, and unless some great change takes place it will not be lessened. The members of both tribes take every opportunity of procuring liquor of any description on every possible occasion—in fact, they even indulge in smuggling it across the line for their own use. This and horse stealing are the main causes of all our trouble with them; it seems impossible for them to resist indulging their apparent natural inclinations in this direction.

On the 2nd July the "Sun Dance" commenced on the Blood Reserve. On the 4th a constable from the Stand Off detachment then on duty at the Sun Dance reported to me at Macleod, that Sergeant Hilliard and two constables had tried to arrest an Indian, "Calf Robe," for pointing a gun at constable Zinkham, when trying to arrest him for horse stealing some time previous, and as the Sun Dance was then in progress some 200 or 300 of the Bucks assisted in rescuing "Calf Robe" from the police. On the following morning I ordered Inspector Wood, in command of a small party, to proceed to Stand Off and investigate the matter; he returned the following day, bringing with him several of the Indians who participated in obstructing the police in doing their duty. They were placed in the guard room.

On the 8th July, the five Indians that were placed in custody were brought before me and Inspector Wood, for their preliminary trial, Indian Agent Pocklington appearing for the defence, they were committed for trial at the next sitting of the Supreme Court, which was held on the 5th August, Indian Agent Pocklington and their chief, "Red Crow," going their bail pending the sitting of the court. The Crown prosecutor thought before the trial came off that there had been a good case made out, that the Indians had no cause or right to assault the police, even had there been no warrants issued; but the judge, on hearing the evidence, threw out the case, as I believe he decided it was not a legal arrest as no warrant had been issued, and the prisoners were released. In making this arrest, the non-commissioned officer was not in possession of a warrant, but I consider he acted perfectly right, there being so many bad Indians wanted at times that unless a man takes every chance offered he will likely lose his man altogether, as they give very few opportunities for arresting.

The impression has gone abroad that the Sun Dance is a religious festival; it may have been regarded as such at one time, but the experience of nearly all those whose dealings and occupations have brought them in close contact with the Indians, and who are well acquainted with their manners and customs, do not now consider it as such. It has degenerated into a gathering merely for the purpose of using up presents of tea, tobacco, &c., given them by their agents or begged from their white neighbors. It is a festival that should be discouraged; it has the effect of reviving too vividly old associations. Old warriors take this occasion of relating their experience of former days, counting their scalps and giving the numbers of horses they were successful in stealing. This has a pernicious effect on the young men; it makes them unsettled and anxious to emulate the deeds of their forefathers.

It was reported to me on the 30th of April that a party of fifteen Blood Indians had left for the Crow Reserve in the United States for the purpose of stealing horses. Sergeant Hilliard, in charge of Stand Off detachment, got the names of the Indians absent from the reserve in case they were needed. On the 22nd I received a telegram from R. S. Tingley, of Big Sandy, Montana, to the effect that some of our Indians were stealing horses in that vicinity, and requesting me to take action in the matter. I sent word to the outposts to keep a sharp look out for their return and also notified the agent at the reserve to warn me of their return, should they escape the notice of our men.

On the 4th of May I received another message from R. S. Tingley that they had stolen seventeen saddle horses from him. I immediately despatched Inspector Macpherson and all available non-commissioned officers and men to intercept, if possible this band of Indians, and also notified all outposts.

On the 7th of May I received a further despatch from R. B. Harrison, Helena, Montana, stating that the Bloods had run off forty horses belonging to the Crows. Scout Giveen was sent out at once to notify Inspector Macpherson in charge of the patrol then looking for these Indians, and to join his party. I also received a telegram from the Officer Commanding Fort Assiniboine, U.S., that nine Bloods had passed through the Bear Paw Mountains, having stolen stock belonging to the Crow Indians in their possession.

Several rumors came in from the reserve, brought in by Indians who claimed to have seen "Prairie Chicken Old Man's" party, and who reported that they were all killed by Gros Ventres in the Bear Paw Mountains.

On the 16th Inspector Macpherson's detachment captured the "Bee," who was one of the party, and sent him in here.

On the 18th he sent in "Hind Gun" together with "Young Pine" and the "Scout," who by the advice of the chiefs gave themselves up to the Indian Agent Pocklington, all of whom were placed in the guard room here.

"Young Pine" made a confession regarding the trip, and stated that the party comprised five Bloods and one South Piegan, and that on the Big Horn at the Crow Agency they drove off about 100 head of horses, the most of which were very poor and dropped along the trail. When returning on the second day they were surprised by a large party of Gros Ventres, who commenced shooting at them; they jumped on their horses and went further into the Bear Paw Mountains, the Gros Ventres continuing to fire on them, they firing in return, and saw some of the enemy drop; they continued to retreat, and noticing two Indians on the trail in front of them, they pursued them and killed one of them, an "Assiniboine." The "Scout" took his horse and "Prairie Chicken Old Man" his gun and scalp. At this moment a party of American Cavalry were seen coming to cut them off, so they continued their flight, leaving nearly all the stolen horses in the hands of the Gros Ventres, they however, arrived on the Blood Reserve with five of the stolen horses and one stray horse. These they handed over to their chiefs, who handed them over to us. Owners for these horses have not yet been found. I sent a description and brands to the Montana Stock Association, but they have not yet been claimed; they are at present running with our herd here.

On the 13th of June the Indian Commissioner, Mr. Hayter Reed, was here, and held a conference with these Indians in regard to their late conduct, and told them there had been no charge laid against them, as the parties from whom the horses had been stolen had lodged no complaint. They were dismissed with a good caution and an intimation that they were liable to be sent for at any time to answer to the charge.

On the 21st of June "Calf Robe," another of this marauding party, came to the post and gave himself up, but I released him, first giving him a good lecture as to his future conduct.

Two Indians during the year were tried and convicted of frequenting tepees kept by women and peddling same for the purpose of prostitution. They were both given six months hard labor. Severe sentences in these cases were given solely as an example to try and stamp out this pestilence.

Several minor cases of Indians being drunk were tried before me and other Justices of the Peace and punished accordingly, but in nearly all cases it was a matter of impossibility to convict the whites who furnished them with the hop beer, it being proven that the Indians themselves had doctored the beer by using tea and tobacco.

The North Piegans are the best behaved Indians I have anything to do with, very seldom having a case against any of them for misbehavior.

All Indians visiting the town of Macleod are required to have passes from their agents, failing which they are ordered at once back to their reserve.

The inaccuracy of Steele's report—among other things, he credits the Chief's war party with having gone from the Bighorn River to the Bear Paw Mountains, a crow's flight of about two hundred miles, in less than two days—can for the most part be excused. But Steele's obvious contempt for the Indian, and his attitude toward the Sun Dance, are beyond excuse.

It is all too characteristic of mankind that he tends to regard any religious celebration except his own as barbaric, depraved or, at the very least, uninformed. The following excerpt from the Annual Report of Superintendent R. Burton Deane, Commanding K Division, the N.W.M.P., Lethbridge, December 1, 1889, shows just how off-base a person can get with regard to a religious observance about which he has carefully avoided becoming educated. Superintendent Deane here proves that if you keep your actual knowledge on a subject down to an absolute minimum, your conversational possibilities with regard to that subject are unlimited.

INDIANS

. . . The Bloods think they are the cream of creation, and it is time for them to begin to imbibe some modification of the idea.

We have been unsuccessful in keeping them on the reserve. A firm and persistent pressure will in time have the desired effect.

I went to the sun dance on the reserve this year, and I came away with the impression that it serves no useful purpose whatever, and might be profitably replaced by some other form of entertainment. No more than half a dozen would-be braves underwent the ordeal, and some of them were only brought to the scratch by obtrusive and derisive encouragement. The Indians could not agree among themselves as to where it should be held, and Red Crow did not appear. It has the effect of bringing out all the bad qualities of the Indians, without any compensating advantage. It feeds the naturally cruel nature of the spectators, it panders to the lust of both sexes, and unsettles the marital relations of the Indians themselves; and last, though not least, it acts as an incentive to the triumphant participant to evince a courage to which he is far from feeling in the commission of some lawless act.

It was asinine reports such as this—Deane's comments could not be further from the truth—which induced the Canadian Government for many years to prohibit the Indians from holding their sacred Sun Dance observance. Just exactly what the nature of Superintendent Deane's character and attitude toward the Indian really were is made clear in another section of his report in which he expresses gratification that the Bloods, whom he was being paid to protect, had been robbed by a war party of "Belknaps" (Gros Ventres and Assiniboines) from across the International Boundary. Deane states:

On the 31st July I received a telegram from Col. Otis that the agent at Fort Belknap had reported that four of his Indians had left their agency on the 27th to raid the Bloods. I wired to Superintendent Steele at Macleod, and sent an Indian to warn the Indians on the reserve. I believe the Belknaps succeeded in getting away with two horses, and if so, I think it was a very salutary lesson for the Bloods, calculated to lessen their conceit and teach them not to provoke reprisals.

Of quite a different cut from Superintendents Steele and Deane was the Agent of the Blood Reserve, William Pocklington. Pocklington, a British gentleman of the old school and a close friend of the Prince of Wales (later King Edward the Seventh), went west with the "originals" of the Northwest Mounted Police in 1874. Having joined the Indian Department in 1881, Pocklington assumed the position of Agent of the Blood Reserve in 1884, just a year before the start of the Riel Rebellion. During the very dangerous period of the Rebellion, the Blood Agent camped right among his high-spirited Indians, and it was no small measure of his efforts which dissuaded the Canadian Blackfoots from joining the Metis-Cree in an insurrection which, if successful, would have rewritten the history of the Canadian Northwest.

Pocklington, respected by White and Indian alike, was a man of unimpeachable courage and probity, and although his account of the Chief's last war party (as related by Young Pine) suffers from translation into English by the interpreter—Indians have a very special way of telling a story, and unless you are an experienced linguist you can get all balled up in the translation—Pocklington's letters to the Indian Commissioner present both a comprehensive and reasonably accurate portrait of the events of the time and also make clear the steadfast and courageous efforts of the Agent in support of his Indian charges.

REPORT FOR APRIL   May 4, 1889.

A rumour is in the camp that some of the Bloods had recently been killed south of the Line, but whether there is any truth in the matter I have so far been unable to find out.

A party of six stole away in the night and have been away long enough to get into trouble.

I have been unable to trace the originators of the story, so possibly there is nothing in it.

Should anything definite turn up, will at once notify you. . . .

Pocklington

May 17, 1889.

Sir

I have the honor to inform you that on the 14th inst I sent you the following telegram in cypher which I would now confirm "War party Bloods returned Monday with horses—scalp dance last night am investigating Indians gave me four horses —Will report fully."

It would appear that some three weeks ago a party composed of the following Bloods viz "Young Pine" "The Scout" "Prairie Chicken old man", "Calf Robe" "Crazy Crow" & a South Piegan left here for the Crow Reserve to steal horses. Today "Young Pine" accompanied by "Red Crow" & others came to me at the Upper Agency & told me the whole story; he said "we arrived near the Crow Reserve without going near any white people or the Gros Ventres. we took lots of horses from the Crows and felt good. we did not have any trouble until we got to the Little Rockies & Bear Paw Mountain. we there had a bad storm and got lost. we stayed two days, the next day we made six miles and killed some antelope. it was not noon, we were eating when the Gros ventres charged on us. we ran off taking the horses. the Gros Ventres overtook us and started shooting at us and did their best to kill us. we thought they wanted to kill us as they killed six of us three winters ago. they ran us a long time & we got tired and angry. They fired a long time and we returned their fire.

"Calf Robe" who speaks Sioux and Gros Ventre shouted to them that we had been to the Crows and not near them. They fired at him while he was talking. We then tried our best to kill them. We fought as we ran and killed an Indian about 300 yds off and kept running away, the Gros Ventres after us. As we were running two Indians got off their horses ahead of us. We did not see them until they fired. We got hot (?), one of these two took after us. we charged on him and fired. he returned our fire. we ran him into some bushes got close to kim & killed him. He was an Assiniboine. We took his gun but did

337

not touch his clothes. The Gros Ventres were so close to us here that we had to leave the loose horses which we had stolen. After this we ran away up the Bear Paw Mountain, made rifle pits and stopped there a long time. we saw the Gros Ventres below us, they gathered together and climbed the mountain after us. it was now after noon. We saw what we thought were white men, got scared and ran away again down the mountain and crossed the Railroad, saw the Indians after us. it was near sundown our horses were done up and we rested a little time, the Gros Ventres being close up. at dark four of the horses gave out. the Gros Ventres got them. the horses we gave you were the only ones that did not give out. we travelled all night and did not have any further trouble.

The Gros Ventres killed six Bloods, who had a Pass, nothing was done to them. I though you would be glad that we had killed them. The Gros Ventres started the trouble. They stole "Red Crow's" horses and gave you lots of trouble to get them back. You know it is our custom to take revenge. the Indians are all glad at our killing the Indians for the six killed by them. I am ashamed to explain this to the Police Chief.

We killed them across the Line. The Americans paid no attention to our Indians who were killed. We depend upon you to get us out of the trouble.

If we get clear of this the Bloods will be glad and the trouble ended.

The time the Bloods were killed "Red Crow" made no trouble nor talked bad. it is three winters ago, we only killed two they killed six Bloods.

I was poor for horses and went to steal from the Crows not from the whites. We leave it to you and "Red Crow" to settle. I have told the truth."

On being closely questioned, I could elicite nothing further. They brought in five horses, four they have delivered to me, three of which are poneys the other a fairly sized branded horse. the fifth "Calf Robe" had, the Indians promised to get it.

After giving "Young Pine" a good talking to I advised him to get the rest of the party and give themselves up to the Police, to this he agreed and further that if the others did not go he and "The Scout" would go provided "Red Crow" and I would take them, to this we assented. I expect them here tomorrow.

It has been reported to the Police that some Bloods had been to the Big Sandy between Ft.Assiniboine & the Coal Bank

Missouri river, also to Grand Falls above Benton. I questioned the Indian closely on this subject, his reply was that they had not been there, but straight to the Crow Reserve.

The Bloods brought two scalps which must have been taken off the man killed in the brush, as they could not tell who the first Indian killed was.

There was more or less excitement when they first arrived but it has all cooled down since. "Prairie Chicken old man" was the leader of the party, he is a bad lot.

The general opinion around the Reserve is that the Bloods have now got even with the Gros Ventres.

I have the honor to be
Sir
Your obdt Servt.

(Wm.Pocklington)

The Indian Commissioner
Regina
Assa.

Blood Agency
22nd May, 1889.

Sir

I beg to acknowledge the receipt of your letter of the 13th inst re enclosing a communication from Col.Otis to the Comr. of the N.W.M.Police concerning some of the Bloods being on the war path and in reply would inform you that I fully reported the return of a war party on the 17th Inst with five horses. I have no doubt it is the same party that Col.Otis refers to as it is the only one I know having been in that district. as the same time, I believe the Indians did not steal from the Gros Ventres nor from the whites but from the Crows only. "Young Pine" who was one of the party is one of those Indians that cares for nothing and would be more likely to tell the truth than lies about it. "Young Pine" & "The Scout" are now in the Guard house at Macleod having gone in with me last Saturday afternoon.

As regards "Red Chicken" I know no Indian of that name on this Reserve, at the same time there may be such an one, as most of the Bloods have two or three names.

With respects to any blame being attached to anyone on the matter I am ready to shoulder the whole of it.

It is practically impossible to keep posted on all the movements of the Indians no matter how vigilant we are. Mills and I are constantly moving round and so soon as Indians are missed inquiries are instituted & the ticket taken in and before being re-issued the family has to show up.

Now regarding officers knowing by sight every male soul on the Reserve, owing to the fact that rations are issued twice a week (four times, twice above & twice here) it is the exception for the male adults to be present at the issue, the squaws in nearly every case draw rations and are seldom seen accompanied by the males. besides when parties leave it is invariably by twos & threes in the night and the usual reply to questions, is they have gone to cut logs, or tent poles, or hunting, etc. or they are camped on the St.Mary, the grass being better there. I quite understand the uitility of reporting war parties being absent to your office, but I cannot see the utility of reporting unless I am quite certain a party had gone & their destination. I heard this particular party was gone that it was the intention to hunt down by the St.Mary's Lakes where there was plenty of whiskey to be bought, another report was that they had gone to the Crow Reserve, but I did not credit it as our Indians have not been that far for a long time, and were led into this expedition by a South Piegan. I may here say the S.Piegan is in the Guard house at Macleod the other three of the party are still at large and I think left the Reserve.

Another small party (3) returned about the same time as the "Young Pine" party. the Police took one horse and have arrested "The Bean" [or "The Bear"] the balance of this party was composed of "Makes Complaints" & "Crane Bird". I cannot find where they went.

The Indians this year are much more scattered than in former years, a number of them wintered on the St.Marys side of the Reserve from above Whoop-Up on the Belly so far as the Rieklinger [?] Crossing on the St.Marys.

I will of course as in the past assist the Police in everyway.

Pocklington.

3rd June, 1889.

. . . Since the war party returned from the Crow country, the Indians have kept a very sharp look out for hostile Indians approaching. Scarcely a day passes that reports come in stating so many Indians afoot were seen in certain neighborhoods. One report was brought me to the effect that shots had been exchanged between Blood herders and strange Indians afoot but upon inquiry nothing could be confirmed

The fact is the Bloods are scared to death lest any war party of any size should come.

"Young Pine", "The Scout" & the S.Piegan are still in the guard-house awaiting prosecution from the U.S. side of the line. Major Steele informs me that he has wired several times but so far no one has come. I expect he will liberate the Bloods in the course of a few days.

Pocklington.

REPORT FOR JUNE   2nd July, 1889

The Indians having been occupied principally in getting ready for the Sun dance which bids fair to be of less importance than last year as there is a split among them, the Lower Indians will not join the Upper & the Upper say they will not join the Lower. it has looked for sometime past as if they would hold a sun dance in both camps, still I think in the end they will join and make one Medicine Lodge.

As directed by you I saw Supt.Steele about "Calf Robe" "Prairie chicken old man" & "Crazy Crow". he informed me there was no charge against them. I then saw "Red Crow" & told him to take the Indians in & that if they gave themselves up there would be nothing done to them. "Calf Robe" went in & was let go, the others at the time of writing have not done so, I will see them in a day or two & prevail upon them to do so.

Pocklington.

Bloods
9th July, 1889.

I have the honor to inform you that on the 4th inst the M.Police attempted to make an arrest of two Indians at the Sun Dance which might have resulted in serious trouble.

It appears that Sergt.Hilliard two constables & Interpreter Choquette while on their regular Patrol visited the Medicine Lodge & while there saw "Prairie Chicken Old man" & "Calf Robe" two of the Indians who were implicated with "Young Pine" & others in bringing horses over from the Crow Agency.

I may remind you that when you were here Supt.McDonnell informed us that he knew of no charge against these Indians. You requested me to see Supt.Steele on the matter which I did. he said he knew of no charge against them, and in my asking is there any charge against "Calf Robe" for drawing a rifle on the Police; he said No. After telling "Red Crow" this "Calf Robe" came in with the Chief gave himself up and was liberated. This was a few days after your visit. notwithstanding this, on the 4th July Sergt.Hilliard attempted to arrest him on this charge. of course the Indians were excited as the affair happened on the big day of the Sun-dance. "Red Crow" & other reliable men informed me that the Police drew their revolvers & flourished them around, that he and others endeaboured to prevent trouble, that the Police struck & kicked several Indians and I regret to state, said the Police must have been drinking as the Indians could smell liquor on them. The Police entirely deny that they were under the influence of liquor or even excited. The result of all this was that Insp.Wood with a party of Police came out to the Reserve on the 6th arrested "Calf Robe" "Big Wolf" "Crop eared Wolf" "Sleeps on top" "Young Pine" "Day Chief" for obstructing the Police in the execution of their duty.

Yesterday the 8th inst they were brought before. . . . Steele & Wood J.P.s I advised the Indians to be tried before Judge Macleod they elected to be so, during the preliminary hearing Sergt Hilliard under cross examination stated that he had no warrent for the arrest of "Calf Robe" & "Prairie chicken Old man" but was authorized by Supt.Steele to arrest them but not to take any *extra trouble* about it, that the Indians jostled he & his men so much that they lost their prisoners. of course the other Police present corroborated the Sergt's evidence.

I contended that as there was no charge against these men, the Police had no right to attempt their arrest and that it was a mad act to attempt it at the Medicine Lodge when the Indians are more or less excited. The Indians were committed for trial.

A separate charge was put in against "Calf Robe" for drawing his gun on a Policeman when endeavouring to arrest him. "Calf Robe" had already given himself up and liberated there being no charge against him. Yet the Police arrest this man for an offence committed on the 17th day of May last but strange to say the information is not laid until the 6th July, two days after the fuss at the Medicine Lodge the 4th inst. of course "Calf Robe" was also committed for trial. I have obtained Mr. Houltain to defend the prisoners.

The day after the trouble the 5th inst I visited the camp and talked with "Red Crow" & others. they were much excited. the best of their talk was that they could not understand how it was that after "Calf Robe" had given himself up, the Police should wish to arrest him. I talked to them a long time quieted them down & made them promise to do nothing without consulting me.

I started for town, saw Supt.Steele & in conversation with him on the matter concluded the whole thing was a mistake, particularly so as Steele told me that Sergt.Hilliard had no authority to make the arrest. Judge then my surprise when the Sergt. in his evidence before Supt.Steele stated he had Supt.Steele's authority to make the arrest. I consider the Police acted in a high handed manner & in such a say that if it is continued serious trouble is likely to result.

I may further state that Sergt.Hilliard in his evidence stated that his instructions from Supt.Steele to make the arrest were given three weeks ago & that he did not know "Calf Robe" had given himself up, and that it was the first time he had seen the Indians since receiving his orders.

I think some other form of arresting Indians should be taken but what that form should be I do not quite see. any change though would possibly be an improvement.

I succeeded in obtaining the Indians liberty until the Sitting of the Court. "Red Crow" being security for four of them & "Running Wolf" for "Big Wolf."

My reasons for retaining Mr.Haultain were because the case is an exceedingly complicated one and that I would have no chance against the Crown Prosecution.

Pocklington.

10th July 1889.

I beg to acknowledge the receipt of your letter of the 6th ult

343

re Indians scouts for the N.W.M.Police and would inform you that I had settled on "Young Pine" going himself & selecting three or four others, but since the fuss of the 4th inst with the Police, they do not seem much disposed to join.

Possibly after the affair is settled I may secure some.

Pocklington.

Bloods
8th August 1889.

I have the honor to inform you that on the 5th & 6th inst I attended the Sittings of the Supreme Court in the interests of the Indian prisoners in the following cases.

Regina vs "Crop eared Wolf" "Day Chief" "Young Pine" "Big Wolf" "Sleeps on top". This was a case in which the prisoners were charged with obstructing the Mounted Police in the execution of their duty. I am pleased to report that they were all acquitted, the Judge holding that the arrest was illegal.

Regina va "Calf Robe" the prisoner in this case was charged with standing a Policeman off with a rifle when attempting to arrest him for bringing in stolen property from Montana on or about the 17th May last. he was also acquitted the Judge holding that the attempted arrest was illegal. Mr.Haultain whom I had retained appeared for these prisoners . . .

Pocklington.

The Chief's last war party, the party composed of Young Pine, Wolf Sitting, Calf Robe, Crazy Crow, Prairie Chicken Old Man, and "Hind Gun" of the South Piegans, was not the last war party ever undertaken by members of the Northern Plains Tribes but it was the last one that really amounted to anything.

On the evening of August 8, 1889, the Gros Ventres and Assiniboines made a horse raid against the Bloods, but they were intercepted on the way home and the horses recovered. Morning Howler, brother of Young Pine, was the following year apprehended with three other Bloods attempting to steal horses from a White rancher in Montana. The four Bloods were sentenced to seven years in the Deer Lodge Penitentiary, and only Morning Howler survived the incarceration (Indians generally did not survive extended periods of imprisonment). During the 1890's a few other unfruitful raiding parties left the Blood Reserve, and in 1891 that incomparable Piegan horse-stealer, White Quiver, single-handedly stole some horses from the Crows and successfully took at least one of them all the way to Canada.

But the Chief's last war party was the last one to involve the spilling of blood in intertribal Plains Indian warfare, and the scalp dance held in the Lone Fights camp of the Bloods during the summer of 1889 was the last scalp dance ever held by any of the Plains Indian Tribes. The scalps that were the central item of the celebration were, of course, the scalps that had been taken by Young Pine and the Chief. And since the Chief allowed Young Pine to take his scalp first, the last scalp ever taken by a member of the Blackfoot Nation was taken by my Indian dad, Head Chief to this very day of the South Piegans.

After the stories had been told, we all enjoyed a hot bourbon drink while I taped the Chief's explanation of the Feather Game. The Feather Game is quite similar to the Stick Game (or Hand Game), and as is the case with all Indian gambling games, the Feather Game is very ritualistic and has strong religious overtones. Indian gambling games are conducted on the honor system and it would not be difficult for anyone to cheat if he really wanted to. But you never need worry about an Indian's cheating at one of these contests; such an act, he believes, would bring him much ill-fortune. Joe Morning Gun is the owner of a "Feather Bundle," and since I have now been accepted as a full-fledged Blackfoot, I have been invited to attend the Feather Game which will be played at Joe's house next Saturday night.

All the moose meat, with exception of a small amount which the Chief has allowed me to set aside for immediate use, is now on the drying racks, and this was one of the warmest and most congenial evenings I have ever experienced. It was twelve o'clock before the Chief finally said, "*Kén-yai-au-wah-nay-nàh-pi-quon*" [That's what the old White man says], and tumbled into the weary sack. Jimmy has retired, too, and now I shall do likewise.

A little colder this morning, another "hazy sun" day. No storm as yet, but Sweetgrass Hill has a hat on. Slept like the proverbial log until I heard Jim moving about building a fire in the good old Simmons S 161 stove. After several yawns and stretches, I rolled out to discover that it was 9:00—the latest any of us has slept. We were all very tired last night. The Chief was still in the sack, and this, I knew, meant that he was ill again.

When the Chief got up, I moccasined him, and for breakfast we ate the old rut of pancakes and eggs. I cooked the eggs, however, and insisted upon applesauce instead of syrup on the (ugh!) pancakes.

The Chief cannot find his spectacles. Jimmy has been splitting blocks all morning—a good indication of approaching cold weather, although Jim, himself, does not appear to be aware of the little actions and mannerisms which are his almost unconscious response to changes in the weather. Played back some recordings and was very disappointed with the quality. Darn recorder is just not doing the job.

12:00: Jimmy is boiling moose meat and potatoes in the same water—sort of a stew, I guess. Chief found his glasses in his coat pocket—where I had already looked a couple of times. I thought that probably we would find them on the kitchen table, where Jim had found the Dristan, because we have probably the only kitchen table in the State of Montana upon which you can lose things. Every bachelor household has its catch-all for things you don't need right now but which will surely come in handy later on—a letter you were supposed to answer, keys that might fit something but nobody knows what, half a cup of coffee from breakfast the other day when you were late to class, the reading notes you flunked a quiz for the want of, an apple you were going to bite into last month when the phone rang, a ½ gallon pickle jar with one pickle in it, etc.

In my own diggings these articles invariably gravitate mysteriously to the top of the refrigerator, of all places, but here on the ranch the general junk-magnet is the large—6 × 4—rectangular table, one long side of which is pushed against the kitchen wall beneath the window. Also pushed back against the wall is the world's most fantastic collection of lost treasure—anything, including my manuscripts, that happened to be on the table when Jim decided to set it for a meal, plus numerous things such as pliers, a file, a can of gun oil, etc., which have tottered from their rightful place on the window sill. Although this area undergoes frequent inquiry with regard to missing articles, when it comes to house-cleaning it is sacred ground and not to be defiled; you clean around it. I would most happily volunteer to clear off this portion (about ¼) of the table, but where in hell would I put all the stuff! As Jim says, "It's got to be someplace."

As I helped Jim to carry in the wood, he griped a bit about the Chief's inconsistencies, and I can't really blame him. Jim has a lot of work to do around the ranch, especially now that cold weather is approaching, and he is desperately trying to find a steady job before winter sets in. But the Chief is, after all, the Chief, and his concern is for the Blackfoots as a group, and Jimmy is required to spend a lot of time chauffeuring him around to meetings, etc. But this is the first time that I have heard Jim complain about the burden of his duties, and Jim never says a cross word to the old fellow himself. There is a great deal of genuine affection between those two, and Jimmy is certainly a loyal and dedicated son. Sometimes he even has to help the old-timer in the outhouse—and greater love hath no man. Come to think of it, the Chief must have been nearly seventy when Jim was gleamed up. Jim once mentioned that his mother died very suddenly, of some sort of internal hemorrhage. The Chief says that Jimmy's mother was the only woman he (the Chief) ever really loved, and that it took him a long, long time to find the right girl. I can certainly appreciate that.

The aspens are a really deep gold now, and the cottonwoods. I will surely miss this scenery.

Lunch was good—the meat tender and the potatoes excellent. The Chief drank of the broth. He has another cold, and this, of course, is the reason that Jim cooked the meat the way he did. I made a pot of tea and opened a can of figs. The Chief ate pretty well, but Jim's truck has another flat tire and he bolted his food and went outside to fix it ("If you fellas excuse me at the table, I got fix my tire"). Now that my time here is so short, I find myself taking especially careful note of such things as speech and mannerisms. Perhaps I am trying to store up memories, or perhaps I am attempting to establish a more objective attitude toward the necessity of leaving Montana and picking up a quite different life elsewhere—this might make it a bit less difficult to leave. Certainly I am being very analytical these days—pretty much the *náhpiquon,* really. The sky is becoming progressively overcast.

5:00: Went to town and discovered that one of my cheques has bounced. Oh well, back to reality! Or, as Chaucer phrased it:

> To you, my purse, and to non other wight
> Compleyne I, for ye be my lady dere!
> I am sory, now that ye be light.

On the way back from town the road was blocked by a gas station —a large, complete, concrete gas station, being transported on a flat platform behind some huge and powerful kind of truck. The thing was not moving more than about ten miles an hour, if that, and the gas station was so wide that it lapped over both edges of the road and completely blocked traffic in both directions. I crept along behind the monster for about a half-hour, finally getting past it by cutting through Starr School yard. Symbolism is fine, but this, I think, was laying it on a bit. I have often been stopped on the road by horses, sheep, cattle—once by a gigantic and immovable bull— but this is the first time that my return to the ranch was delayed by a perambulating gas station. Life is, indeed, "truer than fiction."

7:00: The Chief's cold is pretty severe, and he is coughing badly now. He is lying on the couch, praying. He played solitaire most of the afternoon. Jim and I went for water when I got back from town, and Jim is now preparing supper.

10:30: The Chief got up and ate supper, then went immediately to bed. I don't suppose that I ever will get the rest of those stories, but it doesn't really matter. At supper, the Chief said that he is looking forward to all the fun we will have when I come up next July for Indian Days. That is, he added, if we all get through the winter all right. He observed that there is, of course, the possibility that one or more of us might not make it through the cold weather. What a marvelous attitude! Here he is 105 years old, and suffering from a severe cold—but does he start feeling sorry for himself and whining that maybe *he* won't make it through the winter! No sir! The Chief believes that whether or not any one of us makes it is entirely in the omnipotent hands of the Great Spirit (although I have never heard him use precisely that term). People tell me that they don't see how I can be a Christian and still believe in the Indian faith. I don't see how I could be a Christian and *not* believe in it.

Phillip Many Hides stopped by after supper, ostensibly to borrow a Phillips screwdriver. Jim suggested that he came by hoping to get some meat. This had never occurred to me, but it is probably true. Phillip said that he passed by as we were working on the moose, but he didn't stop because he thought we were just digging a hole in the ground. (?)

Jimmy and I just finished drinking hot bourbons. We both have bum legs tonight. My leg held up fine while I skipped around the Pine Ridge like a mountain goat, danced like Fred Astaire at the Beaver Ceremony, and helped cart around moose quarters. But this evening I turned around from the stove—right on my face. Am overtired these days, and will go to bed now. Jim says that he is going to stay up and read a magazine. "I'm just well read a book, I think."

Buffalo Shield

Saturday, September 22

Our hero was wrenched from the fitful embrace of Morpheus (and morphemes) by his adoptive Indian brother and erstwhile buddy, James S. (for Sammy) White Calf, who, while attempting to introduce some warmth into the living-room, had persuaded the old Simmons stove to give out with a series of unearthly clanks à la Marley's ghost.

Joe Kicking-A-Woman came by and had breakfast coffee with us. We offered him food but he refused it, saying, "I already." Joe and Jim went off together after wood, and I did some typing. Later in the morning, with the Chief—who apparently didn't get much rest last night—asleep on the sofa, I put a few extra blocks in the stove and went to town to pick up the mail and to leave a change of address. The weather had cleared by now, and the day had decided to turn relatively clear and mild. On the way back, I stopped for a moment to say good-bye to Jim White Grass. I met practically everybody else in town, shopping. Am nearly broke now, but spent a precious $.97 on cough syrup for the Chief. The Chief's own cold remedy is sage tea, but he does not refuse the medications I offer him, and the syrup does seem to help.

After lunch, which consisted of some blissfully tender moose tenderloin which I had hidden away, I gave the Chief a large dose of cough syrup. It relieved his coughing long enough for him to get a good solid afternoon of much-needed sleep. The Chief ate well, as usual, but his cold is really pretty bad. During the late afternoon I attempted to grab a nap for myself, but once again a single fly was successful in keeping me bug-eyed awake.

Jim got back at six, and while I went down for water, Jim cooked supper. Apparently Jim has discovered some secret process of vulcanization, for he took some of the same tenderloin that I had cooked for lunch, the last of the fresh moose meat, and rendered it as tough as a saddle skirt. The dried moose meat is now hard and black, and I pray that it is more palatable than Jim's cooking because I will be living on it all the way back to Texas.

After supper, the Chief went right to bed. Jim went to the cupboard, came back holding up the booze bottle which contained about one good shot, and said, "Ask a now or you'll never get it some." I didn't want it, so Jim finished it off, and then we retired to the living-room to chat and work with the tape recorder until midnight.

Jim was anxious for me to play back the story about the magic shield, a story the Chief told me one day in Jim's absence. We have already been over the story a couple of times, but Jim says that it is his favorite ("It's a good story—it's the best I like"), and he wanted to go over it again, "Case if we might liable skipped out something." I am not terribly impressed by the story, and I think that Jim's fondness for it derives primarily from his passion always to champion the underdog. In this story, the underdog, a Blackfoot youth named Heavy-set Boy, wins out over all.

HEAVY-SET BOY AND THE MAGIC BUFFALO SHIELD

Once there was a young Blackfoot lad named Heavy-set Boy. Whenever his band made camp, Heavy-set Boy and his partner would go off by themselves to play. They would fashion small horses out of clay, and play at fighting the enemy and stealing horses from them.

One time a bunch of other boys went out from camp and began to tease Heavy-set Boy and his friend; they destroyed the clay horses that the two friends had made, and when Heavy-set Boy and his partner fought back, the other boys ganged up on them and made them cry.

Each day for four days the same bunch of bullies went out and picked on Heavy-set Boy and his friend. After the fourth time, as Heavy-set Boy lay in the grass, crying, he fell asleep and had a dream. In the dream there were seven buffalo: six bulls and one cow. The cow was wounded, and the bulls were doctoring her. As they doctored the cow, the bulls sang this song:

> Whenever I charge, nothing stops me.
> If anything gets in my way, I run right over it.

When the bulls had finished doctoring the cow, they spoke to Heavy-set Boy: "We feel sorry for you because you do not have the power to defend yourself against those who wish to harm you, and because we pity you, we are going to give you the power of our medicine. From now on, if you will sing the song you heard us singing, you will have the strength of six buffalo bulls to run down anything in your path."

Heavy-set Boy awoke then, and he told his partner that they never again need fear being picked on by any enemies, no matter how large or numerous.

The next time that the boys picked on Heavy-set Boy and his partner, Heavy-set Boy sang his buffalo medicine song, and charged the boys and knocked them all down and made them cry.

The gang of boys went back to camp and told that Heavy-set Boy had made them cry, so a gang of older boys went out to punish Heavy-set Boy and his friend. But just as the gang was about to grab him, Heavy-set Boy backed off, singing his medicine song, and then charged the big boys and sent them all flying.

The big boys went back crying to their fathers, then, and the fathers went out to punish the two young partners. But when Heavy-set Boy saw them coming, he backed off from them, singing his medicine song, and then charged harder than ever before. "When I charge, *nothing* stops me," he sang, and on his first charge he knocked several of the men unconscious. He backed off for another charge, and this time when the men heard him singing his medicine song they knew that he had great power, so they never bothered him again.

Later on, when Heavy-set Boy and his partner were a few

years older, they went out hunting and killed a bull buffalo. They brought the hide into camp and began to make a shield of it, and while they were working, an elderly gentleman named Wise Man came over and asked what they were doing. The two young men answered that they were attempting to fashion a shield from the hide of a bull buffalo but that they didn't know how properly to go about it. So Wise Man showed the boys how to make a shield. He heated the hide in a certain way so that it became smaller in size but much thicker, and then he placed it on a mould to give it shape, instructing the boys to call him when the shield became dry.

At last the shield was dry, and the boys called Wise Man, and Wise Man came and trimmed the shield to proper shape and fitted it with a handle and decorated it around the edge with eagle feathers. Then Wise Man asked Heavy-set Boy whether he wished any further decoration of the shield, and Heavy-set Boy replied, "Yes. I want you to draw on the shield six buffalo bulls, one buffalo cow, and one cottonwood tree. Then, when you have finished, go out and tell all the people in the camp that Heavy-set Boy is going to bring his shield out of his teepee and that they must all prepare their teepees for a strong wind."

When all that he asked of Wise Man had been done, Heavy-set Boy came out of his teepee carrying his shield. He moved toward the center of the camp, and then backward again toward his teepee. When he had repeated this motion four times, a high wind suddenly came up—a wind so powerful that even the dogs were blown off their feet. Those who had heeded the advice of Wise Man to prepare their teepees, were all right, but those who had laughed at him and had refused to prepare their teepees for a strong wind [the Blackfoots fortified their lodges against heavy weather by placing cottonwood logs around the lodge-bases] saw their homes blown away by the wind. These disbelievers were forced to seek shelter beneath the creekbank.

When finally the wind died down, Heavy-set Boy performed a ceremony involving his sister. He painted the girl's face, and told her that if ever any enemy attacked the camp she was to go immediately from the lodge and fetch him his shield from its place on the rack outside. He told her that she was not to enter the lodge with the shield but to throw it to him through the open doorway; she was then to stand aside, and she need not worry about the enemy because they could not do her any harm. Heavy-set Boy said to her, "You must fetch my shield when you hear me sing this song:

> Now, Lady, go out and bring me my shield.
> Do not worry. Nothing can harm you."

Then Heavy-set Boy asked his sister to bring a cottonwood log and place it in the doorway of the lodge. In the early days the Indians did not have any way of measuring things, but I would estimate that today the log would measure about four feet in length. Heavy-set Boy told his sister that if ever the camp were attacked by enemies, he would need the log as part of his buffalo ceremony.

Several days later, the Crees attacked the Blackfoot camp, and Heavy-set Boy sang the shield song, and his sister brought him his shield. According to instructions, his sister took the shield from its rack, walked once around the teepee, threw the shield to Heavy-set Boy through the open doorway, and then stepped aside.

Then Heavy-set Boy sang his buffalo medicine song:

> Whenever I charge, nothing stops me.
> If anything gets in my way, I run right over it.

Then he charged from the teepee and jumped on the log in the doorway and split it right in two. He was not carrying any weapon at all, but with the buffalo shield held before him he charged the Crees with the power of six buffalo bulls and sent them running for their lives.

Later on the Crees attacked the camp again. They tried to steal Heavy-set Boy's shield, but they could not budge it; it was as though they had tried to lift six bull buffaloes. Once again Heavy-set Boy made his ceremony, and when his sister threw him his shield he charged from his lodge in great anger and split the log in several pieces and killed every Cree in the raiding party. This time he sang:

> Nobody has the power to steal my shield.

From that time on, whenever the Crees found a Blackfoot camp they would look to see whether it was the encampment of Heavy-set Boy. If they saw the buffalo shield on its rack by his lodge, they knew that he was in the lodge, and they kept right on moving away from there as fast as they could go.

In my time, the shield became the property of Curly Bear, who went through a special ceremony in order to assume ownership of the shield and its power. Later on, Wades-In-The-Water went through the same ceremony, and then he was the owner of the shield. Wades-In-The-Water gave the magic shield to a Crow friend of his, and the Crow threw it onto the garbage heap.

After becoming satisfied that we had not "skipped out" anything from "Heavy-set Boy," brother Jim launched into an elusively anfractuous narration of an adventure which had befallen him while he was "in a armies," before he once again became a "civillain." It seems that, following completion of "basin training," Jim and his buddy found it a refreshing "chains" to put on a "carson hat [garrison hat]" and go "on a passes." The story continued for quite some time, and I suspect that I must have missed an installment or two because the first thing I knew some traumatic circumstance had induced Jim to "kill over in a knocked-out." I never did learn the nature of Jim's affliction, but he was "out under" for "ten-twenty minutes up maybe to hour" before he "final come to it." As I understood it, Jim was plucked from the depths of febrility by a good jolt from a pint of booze which his buddy happened to have "on handy." ("I asked him, I says, 'Hey, you better give me drink out of your whiskey.'") And our invalid was thus so effectively resuscitated that he dashed to the nearest restaurant, ate "some damn near everything," and proceeded to "date out" the best looking waitress imaginable.

Usually, Jim's autobiographical *chansons de geste* keep me in surreptitious stitches, but this night I was too weary to curl a lip. (By the time Jim and I concluded our bull session, I had just enough gas left to reach my sack before I "killed over in a knocked-out"; there was no opportunity at the time to record the events of the evening, and actually I am typing this early the next morning—Sunday morning—while Jim is outside cutting wood for the breakfast fire.) But even last night, in the very nadir of my energy and enthusiasm—when even the simple gesture of taking my writing pad out of my pocket made me wish for a bullet to bite on—I found myself sedulously jotting down the more meaty of Jim's catacreses, or neologies, or whatever they are. Whatever you wish to call them, Jim's original expressions pour forth so unexpectedly and in such profusion that if you don't write them down immediately, I guarantee that you won't be able to remember them an hour later.

I think that Jim is going to miss me as much as I shall miss him, and last night neither one of us was willing to suggest an adjournment in favor of the sleep which we both needed. But finally, when the witching hour had struck, and my head had long since turned into a pumpkin, and my chin had ricocheted off my clavicle for the umpteenth time, Jim said percipiently, "Hey, I bet you tire, ain't it!" ("Ain't it," is Browning, Montana's reply to the French, *n'est-ce pas,* and the phrase serves so well in the local idiom, and fills such an obvious gap in English, that I hereby nominate "ain't it" for formal adoption into the language.)

I was, indeed, "tire." But, being loath to confess my lack of endurance, I covered an insistent yawn and mumbled, *"L'ennui des riches."*

Jim, ever the agreeable companion, said, "Yah, an' you ain't only the one. You an' me, we're in it the same boot. I won't able kept my eye open."

So brother Jim and I toddled off to our slumbers—but not, of course, without first kicking off our "same boot."

The Feather Game which was scheduled to be held at Joe Morning Gun's house last night did not materialize because of the Chief's illness.

Jim just threw the moose tripe to the dogs. Finally!

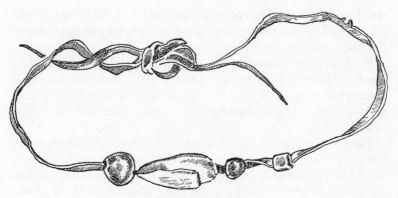

Medicine Necklace

There is no one but I here in this little campground, but this is aloneness, not loneliness. Perhaps if I could see cars going by on the highway I might feel a twinge of loneliness, but I have a private little world here—gratefully—and this morning, after having enjoyed a good honest night's sleep in the back of the station wagon, I heated some water on the faithful old Coleman camp stove and took a "possible" bath. Then a quick plunge into the clear, deep stream that runs obligingly nearby, a brisk rub with a towel—and now I feel great.

My entire diet for the past two days has consisted of dried moose meat and fresh fruit. The fruit is nearly all gone now, but there is plenty of moose left, and since I am almost flat broke ("Pretty damn bent," Jim would say), I will be chewing moose meat all the way back. Actually, I have never felt stronger; never before have I traveled with so little sensation of fatigue. I guess the old Chief knows what he is talking about (as usual) when he maintains that drying is the best method of preserving meat. Come to think of it, since the moose was dried without being cooked or even smoked, I have subsisted for two days on *raw* meat.

Today promises to be bright and clear—a pleasant change from the clouds and intermittent rain of the past forty-eight hours. On the first day, Sunday, I didn't even get out of Montana—thanks to a mysterious rash of flat tires (I don't think the car wanted to leave) and to the fact that I got a late start. Actually, I had not planned to leave until Monday, but on Sunday morning Sweetgrass Hill de-

357

cided to pull its hat down over its ears, and I was afraid that I might get snowed in. So, shortly after breakfast, I began to throw things into the station wagon.

Joe Kicking-A-Woman came around early, and Jimmy shook my hand and said, "I'll said good-bye case if I don't see you," and then he and Joe went off to haul in more toothpicks. This left the Chief and me alone together, and threw me alone upon such knowledge of Blackfoot as I possess.

The Chief was not at all offended by my abrupt decision to move camp, for precipitate comings and goings are very much a part of the Indian personality. Although the Old-timer was unhappy to see me leave, I think that he was secretly pleased that both my unannounced arrival and my hasty departure were so typically Indian. When I was packed and ready to leave, the Chief saw to it that my medicine necklace was properly fastened about my neck (so that I would be assured of a safe journey), and then he reached under the tablecloth and brought out an old photograph of himself in full Indian regalia. This was his farewell gift to me. I had, really, nothing to give him in return, so I just said, *"Tsi-tsíx-i-maht-tsi-tísp"* (Glad to have it). Actually, of course, I should have made at least a gesture of returning the Chief's generosity—even if I had just reached in my pocket and given him my dirty bandana. But the occasion was filled with emotion, and I was not equal to it. Offering my hand to the grand old fellow, and presuming upon the depth of our affection for one another, I spoke the most personal and meaningful of all Blackfoot phrases of farewell, *"Kits-ik-sím-aht-sím."* This phrase, which is also used as a greeting, loses nearly all of its meaning when given a purely literal translation into English: when used as a greeting, it states simply, "I shake your hand," and when used in farewell it means, "I have shaken your hand." But it implies so very much more than that; indeed, it implies such depth of affection that any attempt at translation serves only to limit unfairly the true depth of its connotations. It means, *Arrivederci, Auf Wiedersehen, Sayonara, Adieu, Vaya con Dios, Aloha,* and, Good-bye (in the sense that *good-bye* is a contracted form of "God be with you"). And yet, as does each of these terms of farewell, *Kits-ik-sím-aht-sím* possesses in addition a meaning which is inimitable to itself.

If I were required to effect a translation of the term I employed in saying good-bye to the Chief, I think that I would say that it means, "I take the warmth of your handshake with me," or perhaps, "Your friendship will warm me on my journey." At any rate, these are some of the feelings I attempted to convey when I said to my Indian dad, *"Kíts-ik-sim-aht-sîm, nín-nah"* (Farewell, my father).

And the Chief returned my affection full measure. Clasping my hand in both of his, he honored me by speaking two of the few words of English at his disposal—to make certain that I would understand: *"Kíts-ik-sim-aht-sîm,* my son."

I went to the car then, and as the last War Chief of the Blackfoot Nation stood in the doorway of the little ranch house that is his home, waving farewell, a faint, sad smile upon his marvelous face, I framed in the viewer of my movie camera the form of a man whose like this world will never see again, and let the film run out. I am confident that the pictures will come out just fine, but I really don't need them—not, that is, unless I find someone with whom I wish to share the wine.

I drove to the cattle gate, lowered it, drove through, and put the gate up behind me. Before getting back into the car, I turned and looked again toward the ranch house. The Chief was still standing in the doorway, still waving his hand. And although I knew that he could not possibly see me at this distance, I waved back.

It has been great—really great. But other things are calling now: scholarship, and the great and universal pursuit of scratching up enough loot to feed your face. So, until next summer—unless the Great Spirit should will that one of us not make it through the winter—I guess the time has come to say, *"Kén-yai-au-wah-nay-nàh-pi-quon."*